ENGLISH COSTUME

PLATE I

Two White Gowns of delicate fabric, showing high waist-line.
Décolletage finished by a soft fichu

From Heideloff "The Gallery of Fashion," c. 1795

ENGLISH COSTUME

From the Second Century B.C. to 1960

With Introductory Chapters on the Ancient Civilisations

Doreen Yarwood ✓

London
B. T. BATSFORD LTD

PRINTED IN GREAT BRITAIN BY JARROLD AND SONS LTD,
NORWICH, AND BOUND BY KEMP HALL BINDERY, OXFORD
FOR THE PUBLISHERS
B. T. BATSFORD LTD
4 FITZHARDINGE STREET, PORTMAN SQUARE, LONDON, W.1

To my husband
JOHN YARWOOD

PREFACE

THIS book is intended primarily for those embarking upon a general but comprehensive study of the history of English costume. At the same time it is hoped that it will serve as a useful work of reference, particularly in view of the large number of illustrations. During the course of several years' lecturing on the subject to art students, the author has appreciated that, while several competent books on English costume exist, yet their scope is generally confined to a short period in history, so that it becomes necessary to refer to a number of books in order to cover accurately the whole field of work. An endeavour has been made here, therefore, to place in one volume a fairly comprehensive survey of dress in England, from the earliest times to the present day. Five introductory chapters have been included on the ancient civilisations in order to trace the origins of our own costume.

To cover so large a scope in a book of this size, it is necessary, unfortunately, to curtail the expression of comparisons and opinions—in any case, a matter which may well be left to the personal taste of the reader—and limit the text to salient facts. The author regrets these omissions, but feels that their value is less to the student than an adequate number of illustrations, by which he or she can more clearly visualise the attire in question. Similarly, for reasons of space, no attempt has been made to describe and depict the dress of children or that of the less well-to-do sections of the population. The costumes shown herein are those of the average fashionable men and women of each period.

A bibliography is given both to act as a guide to those students who wish to obtain a more detailed knowledge, and to express the debt the author owes to the standard works on the subject. The excellent volumes, *Costume and Fashion*, by Herbert Norris, have been a particularly valuable source of information.

The author has been fortunate in receiving a great deal of valuable assistance and advice, and wishes to acknowledge, in particular, her grateful thanks to the Victoria and Albert Museum, the Bethnal Green Museum, the British Museum, London, and Miss Anne Buck, Keeper of the Gallery of English Costume, Platt Hall, Manchester, for helpful advice and permission to make sketches. Mr. E. A. MacColvin, of the Polytechnic Library, Regent Street, Mrs. Louie Bird and Mr. Hermon Cawthra have assisted greatly by providing interesting and varied material for illustrations, and an acknowledgement is due to Mr. John Yarwood, Mrs. Nelson Baker and Mrs. Gladys Allvey for help with the form and typing of the manuscript.

D. YARWOOD

London, 1951

CONTENTS

LIST OF PLATES

BIBLIOGRAPHY

BOOKS RECOMMENDED BY THE AUTHOR FOR FURTHER STUDY

ARETZ, G., *The Elegant Women from the Rococo Period to Modern Times*, Harrap, 1932.

BARTON, L., *Historic Costume for the Stage*, Black, London, 1937.

BOEHN, M. VON, *Modes and Manners*, Vols. 1–4, Harrap, London, 1932–5.

BOEHN, M. VON, and FISCHEL, O., *Modes and Manners of the Nineteenth Century*, 4 Vols., Dent, London, 1927.

BRADFIELD, N., *Historical Costumes of England*, Harrap, London, 1958 (new edition).

BROOKE, I., *A History of English Costume*, Methuen, London, 1936.

BROOKE, I., *English Costume of the Middle Ages, tenth to thirteenth centuries*, Black, 1936.

BROOKE, I., *English Costume of the Later Middle Ages, fourteenth and fifteenth centuries*, Black, London, 1935.

BROOKE, I., *English Costume in the Age of Elizabeth: the sixteenth century*, Black, 1933.

BROOKE, I., *English Costume of the Seventeenth Century*, Black, London, 1934.

BROOKE, I., *English Costume 1900–1950*, Methuen, London, 1951.

BROOKE, I., and LAVER, J., *English Costume of the Nineteenth Century*, Black, 1929.

BRUHN, WOLFGANG and MAX TILKE, *A Pictorial History of Costume*, Zwemmer, London, 1955.

CALTHROP, D. C., *English Costume from William I to George IV, 1066–1830*, Black, London, 1937.

CALTHROP, D. C., *English Dress from Victoria to George V*, Chapman and Hall, 1934.

CUNNINGTON, C. W., *Feminine Attitudes in the Nineteenth Century*, Heinemann, 1935.

DIEHL, C., *L'Art Chrétien Primitif et L'Art Byzantin*, Van Oest, Paris, 1928.

FISCHEL, O., *Chronisten der Mode*, Müller, Verlag/Potsdam, 1923.

HARVEY, J., *The Plantagenets 1154–1485*, Batsford, London, 1948.

HOLDEN, A., *Elegant Modes in the Nineteenth Century*, Allen and Unwin, London, 1935.

HOPE, T., *Costume of the Ancients*, Chatto, London, 1875.

HOTTENROTH, F., *Trachten der Völker*, Stuttgart, 1884.

HOUSTON, M. G., *Ancient Greek, Roman and Byzantine Costume*, Black, London.

HOUSTON, M. G., and HORNBLOWER, F. S., *Ancient Egyptian, Assyrian and Persian Costume*, Black, London, 1920.

HOUSTON, M. G., *Medieval Costume in England and France*, Black, London, 1939.

KEATINGE, M. W., *A First History of England*, Black, London, 1919.

KELLY, F. M., and SCHWABE, R., *Historic Costume 1490–1790*, Batsford, London, 1929.

KELLY, F. M., and SCHWABE, R., *A Short History of Costume and Armour 1066–1800*, Batsford, London, 1931.

KÖHLER, C., *A History of Costume*, Harrap, London.

KRETSCHMER, A., and ROHRBACH, C., *The Costumes of all Nations from Earliest Times*, Southeran, London, 1882.

LACROIX, P., *Manners, Customs and Dress during the Middle Ages*, Chapman and Hall.

LAVER, J., *Taste and Fashion—from the French Revolution until Today*, Harrap, 1937.

LAVER, J., *Dress, The Changing Shape of Things*, John Murray, London, 1950.

LAVER, J., *Children's Fashions in the Nineteenth Century*, Batsford, London, 1951.

LAVER, J., and MANSBRIDGE, J., *Costume* (*Junior Heritage Books*) Batsford, London, 1956.

LESTER, K. M., *Historic Costume*, Manual Arts Press, Illinois, 1925.

MOORE, D. LANGLEY, *The Woman in Fashion*, Batsford, London, 1949.

MOREY, C. R., *Medieval Art*, Norton, New York.

MORSE, H. K., *Elizabethan Pageantry—1560–1620*, The Studio, London, 1934.

NORRIS, H., *Costume and Fashion*, Vol. 1, *Evolution of European Dress through Earlier Ages*, Dent, London.

NORRIS, H., *Costume and Fashion*, Vol. 2, *Senlac to Bosworth 1066–1485*, Dent, 1927.

NORRIS, H., *Costume and Fashion*, Vol. 3, Book 1, *The Tudors 1485–1547*, Dent, 1938.

NORRIS, H., *Costume and Fashion*, Vol. 3, Book 2, *The Tudors 1547–1603*, Dent, 1938.

NORRIS, H., and CURTIS, O., *Costume and Fashion*, Vol. 6, *The Nineteenth Century*, Dent, London, 1933.

PICKEN, M. B., *The Fashion Dictionary*, Funk and Wagnalls, New York, 1957.

PLANCHÉ, J. R., *History of British Costume from the Earliest Period to the Close of the Eighteenth Century*, Bell, London, 1913.

SETTLE, A., *English Fashion*, Collins, London, 1948.

ŠROŇKOVÁ, O., *Fashions throughout the Centuries*, Spring Books, London.

TEMPEST, P., *Cryes of London*, London, *c.* 1711.

TRAILL, H. D., and MANN, J. S., *Social England*, 2 Vols., Cassell, 1903.

TREVELYAN, G. M., *History of England*, Longmans, London, 1948.

TRUMAN, N., *Historic Costuming*, Pitman, London, 1936.

TURBERVILLE, A. S., *Johnson's England*, Clarendon Press, Oxford, 1933.

WALKUP, F. P., *Dressing the Part*, Harrap, 1938.

WILCOX, R. T., *The Mode in Costume, Egypt 3000 B.C. to Present Men and Women*, Scribner, New York, 1947.

WILCOX, R. T., *The Mode in Furs*, Scribner, New York, 1951.

WILCOX, R. T., *The Mode in Footwear*, Scribner, New York, 1948.

WILCOX, R. T., *The Mode in Hats and Head-dresses*, Scribner, New York, 1945.

MAGAZINES AND JOURNALS

Ackermann's Repository.
Art, Goût, Beauté.
Art et la Mode, L'.
Belle Assemblée, La.
Burlington Magazine.
Costume Parisien, Le.
Court Magazine, The.
Femmes, Les.
Gallery of Fashion.
Gavarni.
Harper's (Bazaar)
Illustrated London News.
Journal des Dames.
Journal du Grande Monde.
Ladies' Cabinet of Fashion, The.
Ladies' Gazette.
Ladies' Museum.
Ladies' Treasury, The.
Lady's Magazine, The.

Lady's Pocket Magazine, The.
London Tailor and Record of Fashion.
Miroir Parisien.
Mode, La.
Mode Artistique, La.
Mode Illustrée, La.
Modes Parisiennes, Les.
Moniteur de la Mode, Le.
Nouveautés Parisiennes.
Nouvelle Mode, La.
Petit Courrier des Dames.
Punch.
Queen, The.
Salon de la Mode.
Studio, The.
Tailor and Cutter, The.
Townsend's Fashions.
Vogue.
Weldon's Ladies' Journal.

World of Fashion, The.

PRINCIPAL SOURCES OF ILLUSTRATIONS

ACTUAL COSTUMES AT   Platt Hall, Gallery of English Costume, Manchester.
                            Bethnal Green Museum, London.
                            Victoria and Albert Museum, London.
                            The London Museum (pre-1939).

THE BRITISH MUSEUM   Egyptian wall-paintings, Assyrian sculpture and reliefs, Greek vases, pottery, etc., Roman sculpture, etc., medallions, illuminated MSS., jewellery and arms.

VICTORIA AND ALBERT MUSEUM Actual costumes, fashion plates, miniatures, embroideries, jewellery, pottery, sculpture and reliefs.

The National Gallery. The Wallace Collection. The National Portrait Gallery. The Geoffrye Museum, London.

Sculpture, carving, monumental brasses, effigies, stained glass and mosaic work from Churches and Cathedrals in England and France. Fashion plates, drawings and magazines. Oil paintings, miniatures and drawings.

Students of costume will derive great benefit from visiting the London Museum collection now open at Kensington Palace, London, W.8, and the collection made by Doris Langley Moore at 32, Great Cumberland Place, London, W.1.

I
THE ANCIENT CIVILISATIONS

ANCIENT EGYPT

3000 B.C. TO 500 B.C.

THE earliest civilisation of which we have adequate records of costume is the Egyptian; its study, therefore, forms the most suitable beginning for a history of the subject. Fortunately for students of dress, these people spent a considerable amount of time, energy, and thought on the life which they presumed would follow after death. They believed that for a soul to make a successful and peaceful journey into the hereafter, the body must be kept in a preserved state, surrounded by the necessities and luxuries such as ornaments, jewels, etc., which it had had in life. So today there are yet extant wall-paintings, sculpture, painted sarcophagi, vases, and jewellery from the Egyptian tombs. These show clearly in scenes from everyday life the complete costumes worn at that time. The Egyptians had a distinctive style of drawing and painting, using mainly the elevation view, but as most of the work is in full colour and their sculpture also exists as a guide, their exact mode of dress is readily comprehended.

As with all ancient civilisations, the evolution of styles of dress was a gradual process occupying a long time; each mode was often worn for hundreds of years.

The earliest garment for men was a **loin-cloth** (see p. 3). It consisted of a long, rectangular piece of material, encircling the hips, tied in front, and some-times belted at the waist. In the early centuries everyone wore this garment, but later other types of dress were evolved; the loin-cloth remained the attire of slaves and the working classes, being worn only as an undergarment by wealthier men.

Loin-cloths were made originally of coarse linen, but gradually finer materials were produced, eventually even becoming almost transparent. These led to the development of new dress styles, the first of which was similar to the loin-cloth in shape, but larger, forming an ankle-length **skirt** (see p. 3). It was often superimposed on the loin-cloth, but being partly transparent did not obscure it. The skirt was not tied like the loin-cloth, it was fastened by a girdle which encircled the waist twice and hung down in front to the ankles. A **cape**, or **mantle**, of similar material often accompanied the skirt. Several variations of this existed, mostly rectangular in shape, in divers sizes. Placed across the back, the two top corners were then brought together and tied on the chest, with the rest of the fabric hanging over the shoulders and upper arms, reaching waist-length at the back, or—if a larger version—ankle-length. Sometimes one end of the mantle was tucked in the girdle on the left side, forming a sleeve (see p. 2). Alternative styles were circular in shape with a hole cut in the centre for the head, and, being gathered a little at the back and front, fell in graceful folds all round the body to waist-length.

1

EGYPTIAN

QUEEN
1125 B.C.
WHITE CAPE AND
SKIRT.
BLUE AND RED
GIRDLE
YELLOW AND
RED HEADDRESS

RAMESES III
XXND DYNASTY
WHITE LOIN CLOTH
TRANSPARENT
SKIRT AND CAPE

RAMESES II
IN BATTLE ATTIRE
1270 B.C.
DARK BLUE CROWN
GREEN AND BROWN
CHEST DECORATION
WHITE SKIRT
APRON - BROWN, BLUE
AND YELLOW
NATURAL
LEATHER
SANDALS,
BLUE AND
YELLOW
QUIVER

GIRL IN SIMPLE
FITTING TUNIC
EMBROIDERED
BORDERS
SASH AROUND
WAIST

2

EGYPTIAN

PRIEST IN FUNERAL
PROCESSION
LEOPARD SKIN
WHITE LINEN
SKIRT
SANDALS

AMENHETEP I
1125 B.C.
WHITE TRANSPARENT
SKIRT OVER
WHITE LOIN
CLOTH
TRIANGULAR
APRON IN
DARK BLUE,
RED AND
YELLOW.
RED AND
YELLOW
GIRDLE

WHITE
TRANSPARENT
GOWN.
RIBBON BANDS
AND LOTUS FLOWER
IN HAIR

WHITE LOIN CLOTH
BEADED COLLAR
ARMLETS

Another garment also worn later in the period, by upper classes, was a form of **gown** or **shirt.** A large, rectangular piece of material, about eleven feet by four, was folded in half and sewn part-way up the sides with a hole cut for the head. It was ankle-length when worn. Some versions were loose and flowing, others girdled and draped. At first, the shirt was open on the right side with the shoulder bare and a loose sleeve on the left arm, but later both shoulders were covered. Yet another version had the sides of the garment unfastened, with a long, very wide sash, tied at the hip, with a long end hanging down in front. Middle-class people also wore this shirt, but in coarser material, and usually only knee-length.

The earliest feminine garment was a close-fitting **tunic** covering the body from under the breasts to the ankles. Embroidered borders ornamented the top and bottom edges, and the garment was supported by wide shoulder-straps, also coloured and embroidered. A girdle often encircled the waist twice, with the ends hanging down the side or front, nearly the full length of the tunic. Even in later centuries, when women wore other varieties of dress—similar to those of the men—this tunic was still adopted by the poorer women though originally it had been worn by all classes, whatever their station (see p. 2).

In later times, the ankle-length **skirt, cape,** and **gown** were also worn by women. The gown material was knotted under the left breast, causing folds to radiate from there to the ground. Alternatively, a high girdle was worn under the breasts (see p. 5).

Under later dynasties, all costumes contained more material and, by using pleats or gathers, beautiful lines of drapery were achieved.

Soldiers, and kings in battle attire, wore cross-over painted leather bands on the chest. Designs were brightly coloured, often representing birds' wing feathers.

High officials arranged their loin-cloths or skirts to finish with a triangular portion in front, hanging from the waist. Later, the King wore a separate, triangular apron. Attached to the belt, the apron was decorated by pleats radiating from a bottom corner. A highly coloured decorative emblem was superimposed (see p. 5).

The ornamental, coloured **collar,** attached to, or superimposed on, the costume of both sexes, was no doubt the most typical feature of Egyptian costume and formed an integral part of it. It was embroidered, painted, or made of beads.

Linen, cotton, and wool were the **materials** in use. Wool was chiefly for poorer people, or embroidery. Linen was at first, as already stated, coarse, but later much finer textures were produced, and became the principal fabric.

Bright **colours** were much admired during the earlier dynasties; later, the upper classes usually wore white, reserving colour for ornament and decoration. These included yellow ochre, soft blue, bright green, red, dull purple, and black.

Decoration was generally confined to the collar, borders, girdle, triangular apron, and head-dress. Typical motifs were geometrical shapes, the lotus flower, or feathers. Wool embroidery, painted fabric, beads, and jewels were employed. In later dynasties ornamentation was more extravagant, including gold in the colours.

Jewellery was exquisitely fashioned, and in later times varied and intricate. Turquoise, lapis lazuli, and other precious stones were delicately set in gold.

EGYPTIAN

SENUSRET III
STRIPED, LINEN
HEAD-DRESS

FEATHER AND JEWEL
HEAD-DRESS

PHARAOH'S RED
CROWN WITH
FEATHERS

FELT, WOOL AND
FEATHER HEAD-DRESS

FEATHER FAN
WITH LONG
HANDLE

RADIATING PLEATS OF
TRIANGULAR APRON
SENUSRET III 2000
B.C.

SANDALS

SMALL
SHORT-HANDLED
FAN

COMBINED CROWN
OF LOWER AND
UPPER EGYPT

Men and women adorned themselves with armlets, bracelets, and collars, but only women wore anklets and ear-rings.

Many poorer people went barefooted, undismayed in the warm climate enjoyed in Egypt. Upper and middle classes, however, wore **sandals** made of leather, papyrus, or plaited palm fibre. Those of the nobility were turned up at the toe, embroidered, bejewelled, and made of bright coloured leather (see p. 5).

The Egyptians indulged in a distinctive manner of dressing the coiffure. Most men shaved their heads, and women had their hair cut very short, then nearly everybody wore **wigs.** The poorest people resorted to cheap wool caps, whilst others had wigs made of hair or sheep's wool attached to a net foundation, so that the head was kept cool and yet protected from the sun. Wig styles were various: the nobility assumed a long style, the women especially often had tresses reaching to the waist at the back. Commoners wore a shorter, bob-style version. Wigs are almost invariably depicted as black.

In consequence of their inherent desire for cleanliness the Egyptians were usually clean-shaven, but kings, priests, and other high officials wore a **false beard** made of plaited hair. This was held under the chin by a strap, which fastened over ears, under the head-dress.

A variety of head-dresses existed for the nobleman. Crowns of divers styles were worn, made of felt, wool, and metal, often embroidered, painted, and be-feathered, with long, dependent lappets or ribbons to the shoulder (see p. 5). Alternatively, a striped linen or cotton head-dress was seen. Fastened tightly round the forehead, it fell in folds of drapery at the back and sides to shoulder-level. The head was also decorated with such features as feathers, jewels, and ribbon bands, particularly by women, who, except for queens, rarely covered the wig with an actual head-dress. Typical of the queen's head-dress was a cap, shaped in the form of a bird's wing and tail, culminating in a vulture's head on the forehead.

Combs made of ivory, metal, or wood were in use late in the period. **Hair-pins** of the same materials have also been found. **Mirrors** of bronze or ivory were important feminine toilet requisites. They were circular or oval and polished on one side.

The Egyptians used **cosmetics** of many kinds: red for the lips and cheeks; green eye-shadow; black for the eyebrows. Oils, creams, and perfumes were lavishly employed.

The **umbrella** and **fan** originated in Ancient Egypt. Both had long handles, and were carried by slaves or bearers for ladies of rank and position. Later, a small, short-handled fan was designed, to be carried by individual ladies.

ASIA MINOR AND MESOPOTAMIA
2000 B.C. TO THE FIRST CENTURY A.D.

In Asia Minor and Mesopotamia, several civilisations rose and fell during the forty centuries before the birth of Christ. Each succeeding peoples made their contribution, large or small, to the evolution of costume. There is little information of the costume of the first of these civilisations: that of the Sumerians.

BABYLONIAN AND ASSYRIAN

KING OF BABYLON
1100. B.C.

ASHUR-BANI-PAL
KING OF ASSYRIA
668-626. B.C.

ASHUR-NASIR-PAL II
KING OF ASSYRIA
883-859. B.C.

PRIEST
870. B.C.

7

Some years before 2000 B.C., the Babylonian or Chaldean civilisation began. Then, about 1600 B.C., the Assyrian peoples came to these lands and gradually became powerful. For many years the two empires existed together, but eventually the Assyrians became the sole masters: the two empires merging into one great civilisation which prospered until the fall of Nineveh in 612 B.C. It is, therefore, proposed to commence our present study with the costumes of the Babylonians and Assyrians.

These peoples were great builders and sculptors. In consequence, there is a wealth of information available about the dress of various sections of the population. However, there are considerable gaps in our knowledge, especially of feminine attire, because women were rarely portrayed. Some sculpture was in the round, but the greater part was relief work, often painted, though unfortunately much of the colour has faded with time.

Babylonian and Assyrian costumes were very similar, especially in the later period when the two cultures merged together. **Materials** used were heavier than those of the Egyptians. Wool was chiefly worn, also linen was seen mainly in royal and upper-class costume. Peasants sometimes wore fur skins. A distinctive feature of all garments was trimming with fringes or tassels of various lengths. A liking for bright, strong **colours** was evinced, particularly by the upper classes. Purple was usually reserved for royalty, but plum colour, royal blue, rich dark greens, brick red, and yellow ochre were much in vogue among the nobility. White garments with coloured all-over patterns were also popular. The clothes of poorer people were confined to duller hues: grey, brown, dull greens, or natural colour. Combined with this love of strong colours was an equal appreciation of lavish **ornamentation** and decoration of clothes and accessories. This was achieved by embroidery in coloured wools, with gold and silver thread, and jewels or printed patterns. Designs were all-over patterns, or borders. The typical motif was the rosette, and others based on circles, squares, foliage, and fruit.

Two types of garment existed. The **tunic**—a basic item of dress—was simply cut with round neck, short sleeves, and reaching to the knees. A broad, decorated band encircled the waist, and tassels or fringes ornamented the hem. The amount of decoration varied with the rank of the wearer, the king's tunic being almost entirely covered with gold embroidery and jewels (see pp. 7 and 10). An ankle-length tunic was reserved for upper-class wear (see p. 7), and the shorter tunic comprised the sole outer garment for slaves and poorer classes. The second item of clothing was a **shawl**, or shawls. This or these were worn in various ways. Edges were always fringed or tasselled, such fringes forming a decorative feature showing distinctly the lines of draping. Rectangular in shape, the size and proportions varied according to the manner of wearing. For instance, a small, square or rectangular variety was worn like an apron at the back, attached at the waist by long cords under the belt; it varied in length from about sixteen inches to ankle-length (see p. 10). In addition, or alternatively, another shawl encircled the chest with one end tucked in the belt and the other thrown over the left shoulder. Sometimes a large shawl was wrapped several times round the body at knee-, hip-, and waist-level, with the end thrown over the left shoulder (see p. 7). Two belts, one on top of the other, were often worn to hold these garments in position: one very broad made of leather or linen; the other a narrow, bright-coloured leather one. Another type of shawl, predominantly fringe, forming a sort of scarf, was also draped many times round the body.

Underwear consisted of a loin-cloth of light-coloured linen or wool for men, and a short tunic for women.

Different uniforms existed for **soldiers,** according to whether they were foot-soldiers, archers, light archers, etc. A short tunic, square back shawl, and a leather waist-belt sometimes on top of a broad band, comprised the dress of the foot-soldier. Heavy archers were attired in an ankle-length tunic covered with scales, or plates, like a coat of mail. Helmets were of leather or metal, either simple and round-shaped, or ornamented with metal crescent shapes or a spike. Wooden shields, reinforced with leather or metal, were circular or rectangular. Arms included a bow, a quiver and arrows, and an axe or dagger (see p. 10).

The scanty information available on **feminine costume** leads to the supposition that women wore similar garments to men; an ankle-length tunic with three-quarter-length sleeves, and a large shawl wrapped round the body (see p. 10). There does not seem to be any instance of a woman wearing the shawl tucked in the waist at the back, apron-fashion.

Like the Egyptians, the Babylonians and Assyrians wore **sandals.** These were made of bright-coloured leather, and, unlike the Egyptian version, had a leather back-piece covering the heel. Straps attached the front part to the foot (see p. 14). A knee-length leather **boot,** open up the front and laced across with leather thongs, was worn by soldiers. Shorter, calf or ankle boots were also used by civilians.

These people took great pride in their **hair** and **beards.** Both were long, curled, and waved into tight ringlets. In most cases, natural hair was thus treated, but false hair was added if nature did not achieve the desired length and thickness. Curly moustaches were also cultivated. Black hair was greatly favoured, and again when nature failed, artifice triumphed. Perfumes and oils were used copiously. The feminine styles of coiffure were identical with the masculine. Both men and women wore a fillet or ribbon band round the forehead.

The most typical head-covering was tall, with curved sides to a small, circular top, surmounted by a truncated cone. It was generally known as a *mitre,* and was made of felt, or wool, embroidered in bright-coloured and gold bands with rosettes or squares. The royal head-dress had long ribbon bands hanging at the back (see p. 7). A variation of the mitre was basin-shaped, of white felt and decorated on each side by curved horn shapes (see p. 14). Another typical head-dress of Babylonian origin was a circular metal, leather, or felt **crown,** also embroidered, and with long, dependent ribbon bands. For royal use the top was ornamented by a row of feathers. A narrower crown was used by the nobility or priests, becoming like a fillet or jewelled head-band (see p. 14). Women also wore a fillet, sometimes with an attached veil. An alternative style was a combination of the mitre worn underneath the jewelled fillet (see p. 7). Peasants wore fitting caps of felt or wool.

Cosmetics were in use, but not to the same extent as by the Egyptians. Black dye was applied to eyebrows, and rouge to the lips. Perfumes and oils were profusely added.

ASSYRIAN

Assyrian hunter
in the reign of Sargon II
720. B.C.

Assyrian
Queen

Assyrian soldier
690. B.C.

Assyrian
attendant
in the reign of
Sennacherib
700. B.C.

Jewellery designs were massive, and as in embroideries, the rosette and circle motifs were prominent. Chief metals were gold and bronze, heavily encrusted with jewels and stones. Men and women wore armlets, bracelets, necklaces, ear-rings, jewelled belts, and fillets (see p. 14).

As in Egypt, the long-handled **umbrella** and **fan** were carried by slaves and attendants. Many designs of the umbrella existed, but all based on one main pattern with spokes, which curved downwards oppositely to the arc of the top of the umbrella, from the outer rim to the centre stem (see p. 14). The fan was of feathers, usually four or five coloured plumes, with a curved metal or wooden handle (see p. 10).

An almost direct continuation of modes is found in the subsequent civilisation of the Medes and Persians, giving similarity of dress except for an omission of fringing and rather less ornamentation. Wool was still the chief **material**, though linen and leather were more often employed than formerly. The Persians were experts at the art of **embroidery**, especially appliqué work, though the designs were similar in many respects to those of the Assyrians. They fashioned brightly-coloured, ornamented borders in wool and, to some extent, all-over patterns.

Colours were similar to, but, especially later, subtler than, those used by the Assyrians. In the fifth century B.C., a dull red was the predominant colour with purple for royal wear. Lower classes wore dull, sombre hues.

Persian garments were, however, more numerous and varied than the Assyrian. A long-sleeved **tunic** was worn by the middle and lower classes. Very simple in cut, with round neck and a leather belt at the waist, it was usually knee-length, though sometimes a longer version was worn (see p. 12). Underneath the tunic appeared either drawers and woollen stockings, or **trousers**. This was the first time that trousers were introduced as an item of costume, and though primitive in cut they bore a certain resemblance to masculine styles of the present day. They were cut wide at the top but narrow at the ankle, and were fastened round the waist with a belt or cord. Sometimes they were made of leather, or alternatively, wool (see p. 12).

An alternative to the tunic was a robe, often called the **candys** (kandys), worn chiefly by kings and nobility. Similar in cut to the Egyptian robe, it was worn first by the Medes and later by the Persians. It had a round neck and was very full and long so that, when belted at the waist with the material pulled up a little at each side or in the centre front, graceful folds were formed as the drapery fell to the ground, forming an uneven hem-line. Another characteristic feature of this garment was the sleeve which, though fitting on the shoulder, fell in many folds as the material widened towards the wrist (see p. 12).

Outer garments comprised a **coat,** or a **cloak.** The former was made in several simple styles, about three-quarter or full length, open down the front and with long sleeves. Cords fastened the coat in front at neck- or waist-level. Sometimes a collar was added to the garment. Front edges were often embroidered. Two types of cloak were used: a rectangular piece of material which was simply draped round the back and shoulders, or a circular shape which had a hole cut in the middle for the head, and the fabric fell round the body nearly to the knees, back and front (see p. 12).

Yet scantier knowledge is available of the **feminine costume** of the Persians

PERSIAN

PERSIAN KING

PERSIAN SOLDIER

PERSIAN MAN –
COAT – TUNIC
AND
TROUSERS

PERSIAN MAN –
CLOAK – ROBE
AND
CHIN CLOTH.

12

than of that of the Assyrian. The existing records seem to indicate, however, that the women's garments were similar to those of the men, even to the wearing of trousers. The robe and coat were apparently fuller and looser in cut, generally reaching ankle-level.

Persian **soldiers** wore a simple uniform of tunic and trousers. Outside this, encircling the waist, was a leather belt with an attached dagger or sword in a leather sheath. This was further secured by leather thongs passed round the upper leg and hips. The head was covered by a felt or woollen cap, or a metal helmet, sometimes crested and ornamented by plumes or horse-hair. Arms included a long pike or long-bow and arrows, and a shield.

Unlike the Assyrians and the Egyptians, the Persians usually wore **shoes** or **boots** in preference to sandals. The natural coloured leather or felt shoe was cut simply, fitting the foot, fastened on top by button or laces, though for the wealthy, richly embroidered and dyed in various colours. The boot, worn by soldiers or for travelling, was similar to that of the Assyrians.

Like their forerunners, the Persians were fastidious in their care of the coiffure. They adopted the same manner of curling and waving the **hair** and **beards** into frizzed ringlets.

Head-dresses also closely resembled the Assyrian styles. The shorter **crown** was similar, made entirely of metal with painted or jewelled decorations, or of feathers of various colours. The royal crown was usually blue and white with ribbon bands hanging at the back (see p. 14). Alternatively, a white linen or wool **chin-cloth** was worn, so named because it covered the head and chin and fell in folds of drapery round the neck and shoulders. Two main styles of this head-covering existed: one was shaped round the head, the other draped in a cone-shape on top (see p. 14). The most typical middle- and lower-class wear was a felt or leather **cap** of Phrygian shape (see p. 12).

Cosmetics were used by men and women. Perfumes and oils were applied to excess.

Similar again to Assyrian design was the Persian **jewellery.** The same patterns of armlets, bracelets, necklaces, etc., were made, with various precious stones to enhance the heavy metal-work.

The **umbrella** was rather more conical in silhouette than the Assyrian model, and was generally attached to the main stem by only six spokes. **Fans** of plumes and feathers were used. A long **cane,** decorated with a knob at the top, was often affected by noblemen.

ANCIENT GREECE

600 B.C. TO 100 B.C.

Sources of information on the costume of Ancient Greece are chiefly: wall-paintings, vases, literature, sculpture, and relief friezes. The Greeks were masters of the art of draping material—as is clearly seen in examples of Greek sculpture—and their style of dress depended upon this art. Garments were generally not sewn but draped around the figure in various ways, then pinned at specific points. Their manner of dress has had a strong influence on that

MESOPOTAMIAN

ASSYRIAN HEAD·DRESS OF WHITE FELT MITRE STYLE

ASSYRIAN FILLET OR MITRE – METAL – JEWELLED DECORATION· LONG RIBBON BANDS

ASSYRIAN OR BABYLONIAN UMBRELLA

PERSIAN SHOE

ASSYRIAN AND BABYLONIAN SANDALS

BRACELETS AND ARMLETS

PERSIAN CONE SHAPED CHIN CLOTH

PERSIAN FEATHERED CROWN OR MITRE

of later civilisations, notably that of Ancient Rome, and subsequently Western European, including that of the British Isles.

At first, the upper classes employed principally wool and linen as **materials**, the latter fabric often being so thin as to be almost transparent. Later, cotton, muslin, and silk were imported from the East. Peasants usually dressed in coarsely woven woollen garments. The Greeks had gained an expert knowledge of **weaving** from the Egyptians. **Decoration** was achieved by printing, painting, or embroidering the material, the woven design being unknown to the early Greeks. **Motifs** and **designs** included all-over patterns of flowers, leaves or animals, or historical or mythological scenes. Also typical were geometrical patterns—for example, the "key" design—especially for border decoration at hem- and neck-line. The Greeks were also adept at making felt, a material greatly used for cloaks, hats, and shoes.

Upper-class garments usually were white, especially in early times, ornamented by coloured, gold, or silver borders. Other colours in use by the average man or woman were dark or bright red, orange, yellow, stone colour, greenish yellow, and bright yellow-greens. Purple was usually reserved for the aristocracy. Peasants wore sombre hues of dull green, grey, or brown.

The basic masculine garment was a *chiton*, of which there were two distinct styles, the *Doric* and the *Ionic*, each of these being subject to sundry variations. Both styles formed a "tunic", ending just above the knee for normal wear, and ground-length for the older men, or for ceremonial occasions. The **Ionic chiton** was rectangular and made of linen or cotton. Early in the period, it was not sewn at all, but folded to enclose the torso, without fastenings at one side, the top edges being pinned on each side by a fibula (a Greek type of safety-pin), and drawn to the waist by an encircling girdle. Later, after 400 B.C., the garment was wider, and the two top edges were held together at several places by fibulae or clasps, leaving a hole for the neck. The sides were sewn up part-way, and the arms passed through the side spaces left, thus forming a sleeve which was pinned in several places from neck to elbow. A single or double girdle was worn, at waist, or waist and hips, forming a bloused portion in between. The **Doric chiton** was also rectangular and generally made of wool. The top was folded over about six to eight inches before placing round the body, when the two folded top edges were clasped by a single fibula on each shoulder. The garment thus had no sleeves. It was girded similarly to the Ionic, and side-seams were open, sewn part-way, or fastened by fibulae in the same way. An alternative style was achieved by first making a very deep overfold, and wearing the girdle on top of it, so forming a short, full overskirt. In both Doric and Ionic styles, the rectangle of material was placed with the shorter dimension parallel to the height of the wearer (see p. 16).

A *himation* was draped over the chiton for outdoor wear. It formed a rectangle some six feet by twenty of wool or linen, with coloured border, and was wrapped round the body to form a sort of cloak. No fastenings of any kind were used, the draping of this garment being considered an art of importance. The usual method was to drape one end of the material over the left arm, take the rest over the left shoulder, round the back, and over the left shoulder again. The right arm was thus left free for action. The himation was sometimes worn without a chiton underneath, especially by philosophers.

GREEK

DOUBLE-GIRDED
WOOLLEN CHITON —
CHLAMYS OF
HEAVIER MATERIAL
SANDALS

PHILOSOPHER —
HIMATION —
LONG IONIC
CHITON

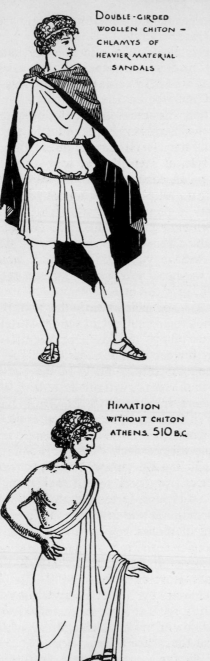

HIMATION
WITHOUT CHITON
ATHENS. 510 B.C

WARRIOR —
4TH C. B.C.

16

Many figures are portrayed in this way in Greek sculpture, but often more for artistic design rather than strict accuracy (see p. 16).

An alternative style of cloak, the *chlamys*, was in use after the fifth century B.C. It was of wool and smaller than the himation, being a rectangle of about six feet by three. The method of draping was simple, being merely arranged round the shoulders from the back, and fastened on the right shoulder by a brooch, leaving the right arm free. The four corners were usually weighted as a precaution against the wind. This cloak was used for riding, military service, or in bad weather; it also served as a blanket when sleeping in the open (see p. 16).

A well-known Greek masculine **hair-style,** as seen in their sculpture, is the short curly head encircled by a fillet or metal band. In actual fact, although the wearing of a fillet was common during the whole period, on the whole, hair was worn long until about 450 B.C., either in plaits coiled round the head, or in long ringlets hanging loose, with curled ends on the forehead. Beards and moustaches often adorned the faces of older men, with these hair-styles. Later, in the fourth century B.C., the hair was cut shorter and frequently worn in curls. The face was then usually clean-shaven, though a number of men favoured side-whiskers similar to those of the Victorian era (see pp. 16 and 20).

Hats were seldom worn, though two main varieties existed: the *petasos* and the *pilos.* The former was a broad-brimmed felt hat, mainly used for travelling, and when not in use hung round the back of the neck by a cord attached to each side of the brim. The pilos was a peasant hat, also made of felt, but without a brim. Warriors wore magnificent helmets of shining metal—usually brass—ornamented by coloured plumes and locks of hair from a horse's tail or mane. The Corinthian was the chief of these (see pp. 16 and 20).

Grecian men were usually barefooted in the early years of the civilisation, and even later on footwear was rarely worn indoors. There were, however, many designs of **sandal,** made of leather, with leather, cork, or wood soles. Natural coloured leather was dyed, preferably gold, yellow, or red, for use by the aristocracy. **Shoes** were also worn. Cut appropriately for each foot, they were fitting, and fastened at the ankle. A type of leather **boot,** known as a *buskin,* was in use for riding and military wear. It was laced up the front from the toe to just below the knee. The upper part was often lined with fur, with the paws or head of a small animal hanging over the top (see pp. 16 and 20).

The principal feminine garment was also the **chiton,** Doric and Ionic, as worn by men, except that the garment always reached the ground. The **Ionic chiton** was often held in place by a band worn on top of it, and fastened in various ways. The most usual methods were either: a cross-over band on the chest and back, then tied at the waist; or a band round each shoulder, looped over, then crossing horizontally across the back, also to be tied in front at the waist. The double-girded chiton was also worn. In all these methods the fullness of the material was kept loose between the bands, drooping over them in places. Late in the period, an alternative type of Ionic chiton was seen; it was unbelted and had a deep overfold hanging loose. The **Doric chiton** was ground-length and had a deeper overfold of about twenty inches, often with the girdle worn over it, but was otherwise identical to the masculine version. For outdoor wear the overfold could be drawn over the head as a covering (see p. 18).

GREEK

Ionic chiton —
cross-over band
on chest and
back —
embroidered
edge —
ribbons in
hair

Peplos worn
over doric
chiton —
stephane and
gold net on hair

Woollen doric
chiton with long
overfold — girdle
worn on top

Plain white linen
ionic chiton —
coloured wool
himation

18

Often worn on top of the Doric chiton was a tubular-shaped garment known as the *peplos*. It fell in graceful folds over the chest and back, from a clasp on each shoulder. The sides were weighted at the bottom edges, which were patterned and, combined with the shape of the figure, resulted in the back and front edges being higher than those at the sides (see p. 18).

Grecian women often wore a fitting, broad band of linen or wool next to the skin, from below the breasts to hip-level, as a support to the figure. It was held in place by straps over the shoulders.

The feminine **himation** was usually only worn over the Ionic chiton (the Doric chiton, being of wool and having an overfold, did not necessitate the wearing of a cloak to the same degree). It was slightly smaller than the men's and was draped in various ways: sometimes it served as a cloak and head-covering combined; sometimes as a cloak only, worn round the shoulders with the ends hanging down each side. Alternatively, one end was thrown over the left shoulder, the rest of the material was passed round the back, under the right arm, and the other end draped over the left arm, or perhaps the latter end might be tucked in the chiton girdle or flung over the left shoulder again. Other ways of wearing this garment also existed, usually variations of those already described. The himation was made of coloured, woven material, with a border, but about 450 B.C. embroidered all-over patterns of birds or animals were popular (see p. 18).

Early in the period, the feminine **coiffure** was arranged in curls on the fore-head, with waves on the crown, which terminated in ringlets standing stiffly out at the sides and back. A metal or ribbon fillet encircled the head. From the fourth century B.C. onwards, the hair, always worn long, was dressed in a *chignon* at the back, with curls on the forehead and round the ears. A coloured scarf, ribbon bands, or a gold net were some of the decorations which orna-mented the chignon. Typical of the period was the *stephane*, a curved metal band, worn high on the forehead, from which it projected upwards and slightly forwards. Made in many and varied designs, costly and jewelled versions were worn by the aristocracy. Most women had naturally fair hair, but some dyed their hair darker shades or wore a wig. Hair-pins were about four or five inches long and made of bone, metal, or ivory. Combs were of wood or ivory, ornamental types being seen as a hair decoration in place of the stephane (see pp. 18 and 20).

Outdoor head-covering was adequately furnished by either a **veil**, made of linen or muslin, or by the folds of the himation.

Grecian women went barefooted or wore **sandals** of masculine styles.

Inspired by Egyptian and Assyrian designs, the Greeks adopted the feather **fan** for general use after 550 B.C. Later, fans were also made of silk or cotton stretched over a frame. Small fans were carried by the women themselves, but larger, long-handled versions were plied by bearers for ladies of importance (see p. 20).

Similarly, the Greeks copied the idea and designs of the **umbrella.** These were made of thin gaily-coloured material on metal or wooden frames. Again, a larger, long-handled type was carried by a bearer for the noble lady (see p. 20).

Jewellery was simple and strictly utilitarian in the early centuries, the predominant examples being fibulae and the stephane. As time passed more

3

GREEK

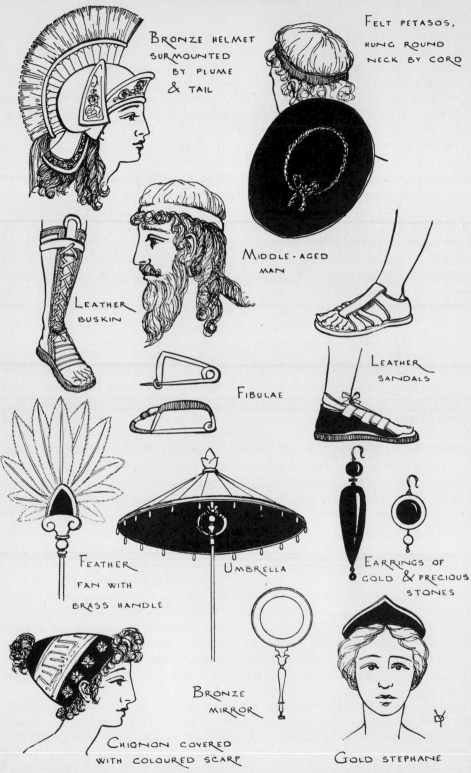

Bronze helmet surmounted by plume & tail

Felt petasos, hung round neck by cord

Middle-aged man

Leather buskin

Fibulae

Leather sandals

Feather fan with brass handle

Umbrella

Earrings of gold & precious stones

Bronze mirror

Chignon covered with coloured scarf

Gold stephane

jewellery was made and designs became more ornate. Gold, silver, and bronze were in use and, in later centuries, were studded with jewels such as sapphires, rubies, lapis lazuli, and emeralds. Ear-rings, bracelets, rings, necklaces, and hair ornaments were among the items of adornment worn by Grecian ladies (see p. 20).

ANCIENT ROME
SEVENTH CENTURY B.C. TO THE FIFTH CENTURY A.D.

Broadly speaking, Roman costume was an adaptation and elaboration of the Greek, especially during the Republican era. Again, as in the case of the Greeks, our knowledge is from the study of their arts: sculpture, wall-paintings, mosaics, literature, jewellery, and arms.

The best-known and perhaps most important of their garments, the *toga*, was, however, a notable exception to this emulation of Grecian styles: it was of Roman origin. During the first two centuries of the period it was often the only garment worn by the men, except for a loin-cloth. Later, the wearing of a toga became an official indication of a Roman citizen. As with the Greek himation, the material was wrapped round the body; no pins or fastenings were used. Being considerably larger than the himation, and the draping more complicated, to wear it effectively demanded even more artistry than in the case of the Greek garment. In shape, the material formed a segment of a circle of which the chord was approximately eighteen feet in length, and which was five and a half feet at the greatest width. Various methods of draping prevailed, but the commonest is described here. Some five feet of the straight edge of the material was placed against the centre vertical line of the body at the front, with the extreme end at the feet, and the curved edge to the left outer side. The remainder of the material, some thirteen feet, was then thrown over the left shoulder, passed loosely round the back, under the right arm, and once again partly over the left shoulder, and partly over the left arm, the second end thus hanging loose there. The portion of cloth on the chest from the first layer was then pulled out a little to form folds of curved drapery over the second layer. When required, the material encircling the shoulders at the back could be pulled up over the head to form a covering for outdoor wear. The toga acted, to a certain extent, as a denoter of rank; it appeared in various colours and with different insignia. For example, a plain toga in natural colour was the wear for an ordinary citizen; senators, knights, and other noblemen had white togas with purple bands of various widths; emperors, generals, governors, and other exalted personages affected purple embroidered all over in gold designs. Wool was the usual material, but later the more elaborate toga was also made of silk. From the first century A.D., under Imperial rule, it gradually came about that the toga was increasingly reserved for important persons, and for ceremonial wear. As its general use declined, so richer materials were employed in its making, with more ornate designs and ornamentation, and more complicated methods of draping (see p. 22).

As the use of the toga declined, other cloaks and mantles appeared. Chief among these were the *paludamentum, sagum, abolla, laena, paenula, lacerna,*

ROMAN

HADRIAN
WHITE TUNICA
LORICA
GILDED & TASSELLED
LEATHER EPAULETTES
AND SKIRT
DARK
PALUDAMENTUM
EMBROIDERED &
FURRED,
LEATHER BOOTS

PAENULA AND
HOOD - SHORT
TUNICA - SANDALS

SHORT TUNICA -
TOGA - CALCEI

TUNICA TALARIS -
PURPLE PALUDAMENTUM
GOLD EMBROIDERED
BORDER - RED
CALCEI

22

and *pallium*. Of these, the first two were military cloaks, the former for generals and officers, the latter for the ordinary soldier. Both cloaks were similarly shaped and fastened like the Greek chlamys. The paludamentum was the larger of the two, and made of a dark-coloured wool, purple, dark green, or brown (see p. 22). The sagum was of coarser red material. The abolla, lacerna, and laena were also similarly shaped to the chlamys. The first was worn mainly by the upper classes. It was usually red and made of wool, linen, or silk. Of similar application was the lacerna which sometimes had an attached hood, and was made of a thin material in gay colours. The thick woollen or felt laena was the cloak for the peasant classes. A heavy cloth cloak with an attached hood, the paenula was worn by everyone. Open down the front, it reached to calf-level. The various colours included brown, grey, purple, and black (see p. 22). The pallium was originally identical with and, at first, worn in the same manner as, the Greek himation, but later it was used only by important persons, and the manner of wearing changed, the material being folded lengthwise till it resembled a long scarf. This was draped in various ways round the shoulders with loose hanging ends, and usually on top of another cloak. Worn in this way, the evolution of the garment can be traced through the later civilisations to become eventually a church vestment.

The basic masculine garment was the *tunica*, made of wool or linen, almost identical with the Greek chiton, and, similarly, in two styles, one knee-length, the other ankle-length. The former, at first left open on the left side, later sewn up, was cut with or without sleeves. Such sleeves were not set-in, but cut in one piece with the garment (see p. 22). Upper classes wore white, also purple later, while natural colour or brown sufficed for poorer men. Purple stripes, known as *clavi*, decorated the white tunica from shoulder to hem, and, at first, indicated rank. Later, however, they came to have a purely decorative function. All-over designs and border patterns became fashionable in the last two centuries of the period. Executed in wool embroidery, they were reserved for noblemen. The ankle-length tunica, known as the tunica *talaris*, was worn only by the nobility on ceremonial occasions, and by older men (see p. 22). When made of purple material covered in gold embroidery it was called the tunica *palmata*, and generally used by the emperor, or generals. The tunica *manicata*, with long, fitting sleeves, appeared in the last two centuries of the period. Out of doors, an important citizen always wore a toga, or other mantle, on top of his tunica. The lack of such covering denoted the working man or peasant. In the late second century A.D., another style of tunic was introduced, known as the *dalmatica*, as the idea was adopted from Dalmatia. A loose garment, usually unbelted, it reached calf- or ankle-level. It was furnished with loose, flowing sleeves; the edges of these, together with the front of the garment, were decorated with two clavi, often embroidered in colours on the purple background. The dalmatica was made of wool or linen in white or natural colour. The tunica was then worn underneath.

The chief item of **underwear** was the loin-cloth. After the first century B.C., the upper and middle classes wore on top of this one or more under-tunics, similar in style to the ordinary short tunic, but usually sleeveless.

The attire of the Roman **soldier** was also copied largely from the Greeks, though adaptations were made later. The Roman general or officer wore a

ROMAN

TUNICA INTERIOR - STOLA - PALLA AND VEIL

PALLA AND STOLA

DALMATICA OVER STOLA - VEIL

PALLA - STOLA - TUNICA INTERIOR

24

leather tunic with a skirt cut into strips, usually gilded and fringed. Similar strips on the shoulders formed epaulettes. A white tunica was worn under this tunic. The skirt of the former was somewhat longer than that of the latter. A bronze or brass cuirass, the *lorica*, covered the breast and back. It was hinged on the right side, and buckled with leather straps on the left. Moulded to fit the body, on top of the tunic, it covered the torso to the hips. Depending on the rank of the wearer, it was embossed with designs of mythological scenes or geometrical patterns. Brass plates on the shoulders assisted in keeping the lorica in position. The paludamentum was worn on top of the uniform, or carried (see p. 22). **Helmets** of brass, iron, or bronze were similar to those of the Greeks, but not quite so spectacular. Plumes or horse-hair, dyed red or blue, ornamented the top (see p. 27). Leather boots, fur-lined, with the animal's head and paws protruding over the tops, were the usual footwear (see p. 27). Alternatively, sandals, strapped on at the ankle, were worn. The ordinary soldier had a plain leather jacket over his tunica, with a superimposed armour made of strips of bronze or iron horizontally encircling the chest and waist and attached to vertical strips over the shoulders. His helmet was a simple metal affair, basin-shaped, with cheek-plates. Footwear consisted of strong-soled sandals, or heavy, rough leather boots (see p. 27).

The feminine Roman costume was closely modelled on that of the Greek. The Roman *stola* was practically identical with the Greek Ionic chiton. During the Imperial period, this garment—for noble ladies—was often made of silk, and with more material in the width than the Greek prototype, but was otherwise unchanged. Ladies of rank wore the stola very long, forming a train at the back, and with the fullness of material drawn up at the waist to form folds over a bejewelled, gold girdle (see p. 24). The garment was usually richly decorated with embroidery. Under the stola was worn another gown, made of fine wool or linen, similar in style but simpler in cut and less full, having long, short, or no sleeves. It was known as the tunica *interior* (see p. 24). In the third century A.D. the fashion for the **dalmatica** affected women's as well as men's costume. It gradually superseded the stola as the gown for modish ladies, the stola becoming a long-sleeved type worn underneath as a tunica interior. The feminine dalmatica was like the masculine, except it was full-length. During the succeeding century a girdle was adopted, also heavier ornamentation. Sometimes the material had an all-over pattern (see p. 24).

The *palla*, the feminine mantle, was a direct copy of the Greek himation, similarly draped. When the dalmatica became popular, other cloaks appeared as they were easier to wear over this voluminous garment. The **paenula** was chief of these. It was often worn without its hood, and a **veil** became a fashionable head-covering in place of the palla folds, as previously. As in Greece, this veil was rectangular, made of fine linen or silk in various colours, and varied in size according to rank (see p. 24). At the end of the period the palla reappeared as the masculine pallium.

Women's **underwear** consisted of a simple tunic or loin-cloth and a band to support the breasts.

Wool was a principal **material** for clothes, though linen, and later cotton and silk, were also worn. Silk was expensive and used only by the wealthy. **Decoration** was largely by embroidery; an art at which Roman ladies excelled.

Coloured wool, and gold and silver thread were used for this. Painted and printed designs were also seen. Motifs were similar to those of the Greeks, though circles, squares, and crescent shapes predominated. Simple, soft **colours,** usually on a white background, were preferred until the later decadent period, when vivid purples, reds, blues, and greens became the vogue.

Many types of **footwear** prevailed among the Romans, but generally men preferred to wear shoes or boots rather than sandals. The commonest style was the *calceus*, made of leather, ankle-length, being tied at the top in front. Natural-coloured leather was used for the average person, though it was dyed in various colours, particularly red, for noblemen (see p. 22). A felt, sock-like version was worn by poorer men. The *crepida*, alternative footwear, was part sandal, part shoe, being open on top and laced across, then tied at the ankle. **Sandals,** made of leather, in various styles, were generally worn indoors (see p. 27). The military boot, already described, is illustrated on the same page. Women wore chiefly sandals or brightly-coloured calcei.

In the early centuries masculine **hair-styles** copied those of the contemporary Greek. Long beards and moustaches were also worn. Later, from the second century B.C., hair was cut short and brushed over the forehead, and men were usually clean-shaven. This vogue remained for many years until an emperor, in the second century A.D., once more set the fashion for beards, but this time trimmed short and curly. A tendency to shaving then reappeared towards the end of the period. Poorer classes, slaves and peasants generally had long, flowing hair and beards during the whole era. The styles of feminine coiffure varied considerably: Greek modes were emulated; alternatively, a vogue for coiled plaits on top, or at the back of the head, achieved great popularity; curls and ringlets were also worn (see p. 27). False hair was sometimes added to the coiffure; and Roman ladies often dyed their hair, red being a favourite colour during the Gallic campaigns, in imitation of the Gauls. Pearl ropes were popular in the late period of excessive ornamentation.

Like the Greeks, Roman men wore little **head-covering,** apart from the military helmets already discussed. The Greek petasos was worn, also a version of their pilos, called a *pileus* (pilleus) by the Romans. The hood, used either separately, tied with strings under the chin, or attached to a cloak, was known as the *cucullus*. A fillet was the usual decoration for the brow. Various crowns were typical of the Roman costume, of which the best known is perhaps the crown of gold laurel leaves worn by a victorious general, or emperor. Crowns made of other types of leaves, in gold, were indicative of lesser triumphs. The veil and the palla sufficed for feminine head-covering, though a fillet, or **stephane,** initially like the Greek, later much more ornate, was worn by noble ladies for decorative purposes. Also later, nets made of gold and jewels were used to cover the hair.

Extensive use was made of all **cosmetics,** especially eye-shadow, rouge, carmine for the lips, powders, gold-dust for the hair, and perfumes. Exquisitely carved or painted toilet-boxes were possessed by most of the well-to-do women. The Romans, particularly those of rank, valued cleanliness, and often bathed more than once a day.

Jewellery, again, was greatly emulative of Grecian designs, though later in the period it became heavier and more extravagant in pattern, being much

ROMAN

ROMAN HELMETS –
BRONZE OR BRASS – RED HORSE HAIR
TRIMMING

110 A.D.

200 A.D.

220 A.D.

LEATHER
BOOT –
FUR LINING

1st C. A.D.

ORDINARY SOLDIER –
TUNICA – LEATHER JACKET –
METAL ARMOUR

BONE PIN
4TH C. A.D

METAL
HAND·MIRROR

SANDALS

GOLD RING
AND ONYX
2ND C. A.D

SILVER
RING
5TH C. A.D.

EARRING –
GOLD, RUBY
AND PEARLS

encrusted with precious stones, and lacked the elegance and charm of the earlier Greek craftsmanship. Men wore little jewellery, except for a ring, made of one of various metals, with gold reserved for the aristocrats (see p. 27). Women, on the other hand, adorned themselves with bracelets, necklaces, ear-rings, jewelled girdles, fibulae, rings, and hair-pins. Cameo brooches and rings, as well as pearls, emeralds, rubies, and amber, were popular. Other feminine requisites included boxwood or ivory **combs,** polished metal **mirrors,** small handkerchiefs, and tiny hand **fans** (see p. 27). As in the earlier civilisations, long-handled fans, and **umbrellas,** of similar patterns to the Greek, were carried by slaves.

BYZANTINE
FIFTH CENTURY A.D. TO THE TWELFTH CENTURY A.D.

Byzantine art, culture, and costume resulted from the three combined influences: Roman, Christian, and Oriental. The heritage from the Romans was direct and of great consequence. In the fourth century A.D., more than a hundred years before the fall of its capital city, the Roman Empire was administered in two parts, Eastern and Western. The Roman Emperor Constantine made his headquarters for the eastern portion at Byzantium. Subsequently, in A.D. 330, he renamed the city Constantinople, after himself. Even after the fall of Rome, in A.D. 476, the eastern dominions of the Empire continued to flourish, indeed to such purpose that it was considered to be the centre of culture, commerce, and fashion until the Middle Ages. The Christian influence—the effects of this religion were becoming widespread—with its abhorrence of immodest behaviour, brought about the custom of covering the limbs: outer garments had long sleeves, and hose was worn on the legs, thus contrasting greatly with the freedom of the dress of the earlier civilisations. In church vestments, garments and styles were evolved of which traces could still be seen until comparatively recent times. The Oriental contribution to Byzantine costume—the result of geographical proximity—was in the form of rich colourings and materials, patterned fabrics, and the abundant use of jewels, especially pearls, to add to the splendour of embroideries. It is generally considered that the peak of Byzantine culture and power was reached in the sixth century A.D., under the Emperor Justinian. In costume, and in commerce, one of his most notable contributions was to set up the manufacture of silk, using silkworms obtained from China, via Persia. The Empire then monopolised this industry in Europe, and remained the centre of the trade in the commodity until the Middle Ages. Consequently, silk, in its various forms, was more readily available for the manufacture and enrichment of garments than it had been in any of the civilisations previously discussed.

Accurate evidence of the Byzantine dress remains in the decoration of churches by sculpture, reliefs, ivory carvings, fresco paintings, and numerous mosaic mural adornments.

Despite the rich embellishment of costume—seen at its height in the dress of the nobility—the cut of individual garments was simple, mainly following Roman lines, so that the effect of the ensemble was dignified and impressive.

BYZANTINE

6TH CENTURY
NOBLEMAN -
MANTLE AND PALLIUM
EMBROIDERED
LONG TUNICA

7TH CENTURY OFFICER
DARK
PALUDAMENTUM
METAL LORICA -
LEATHER SKIRT
AND EPAULETTES
WHITE TUNICA
HOSE
LEATHER BOOTS

12TH CENTURY
CHURCH DIGNITARY
PALLIUM -
TUNICA - MANTLE

6TH CENTURY
EMPEROR JUSTINIAN
PURPLE PALUDAMENTUM
GOLD EMBROIDERED
TABLION
WHITE TUNICA
GOLD EMBROIDERY
PURPLE HOSE
RED SHOES

The principal garment, the **tunica,** modelled on Roman lines, had long, fitting sleeves. It was worn all the period, varying only in colour and ornamentation. As with the Romans and Greeks, the shorter version was the usual wear for the proletariat, the ankle-length tunica being reserved for noblemen, and older men, for ceremonial occasions. White silk, with gold or coloured embroidery, was popular with the upper classes. A gold, jewelled girdle encircled the body just below the waist-line. Decoration, sometimes by appliqué work, was normally confined to the edges of the hem and cuffs, and a square or circular motif on the shoulders and hips (see p. 29). The **dalmatica,** also of Roman origin, was either used as an alternative to the tunica, or as an extra garment on top of it. Its wide, flowing sleeves were usually three-quarter length, revealing the long tunica sleeves. One or more under-tunics, with long or short sleeves, were worn.

The **paludamentum,** late Roman style, was in general use for upper-class wear. Rich, vivid colours were the vogue; purple was reserved for the emperor. The garment was abundantly ornamented, often all over the silk material. Jewellery, especially pearls, encrusted the embroidery. A typical feature of the emperor's cloak was a rectangular design on the front edges, called the *tablion*; this received even more sumptuous and ornate decoration (see p. 29). A shorter rectangular cloak, of linen or wool, like the Greek chlamys, was worn by the ordinary man. The **pallium** had now evolved into a band of material, worn by noblemen or church dignitaries, on top of other garments; it was embroidered with motifs of a circular, or square design, or—when worn as a church vestment —by crosses (see p. 29).

Hose covered the legs, made of silk or wool in bright colours for the nobility. Poorer men wore cloth hose, or loose breeches, sometimes cross-gartered with strips of linen on top.

Footwear was decorated without stint. The noblemen wore an embroidered, jewelled, fitting **shoe,** fastened by buttons or strings on the instep. Alternatively, he might wear a tall leather **boot,** dyed in a bright colour, with red preferred, and ornamented with pearls. Brightly-coloured leather **sandals** were also seen. Footwear for other classes was similar but plainer, in natural coloured leather. The soldier's boot was of the Roman type, though simpler, and sometimes the uppers were toe-less (see p. 33).

At first, military armour was like the Roman: officers wore the **lorica** on top of a leather tunic, with the same strip-form skirt, and a short tunica underneath (see p. 29). **Helmets** were a combination of Greek and Roman styles (see p. 33). Later, however, the lorica was gradually replaced by small scales, or plates of armour on the torso, an early prototype of chain-mail.

The masculine **hair-style** was short and simple, the hair usually being turned under all round the head (see p. 33). Noblemen were mostly clean-shaven or grew moustaches. Beards became fashionable again in the later centuries.

Head-covering for the nobleman was provided by a round **hat** with upturned brim, by a **crown,** or by a **fillet.** The hat was of silk or linen, in rich colours, lavishly bejewelled. The crown, of metal, usually gold, appeared in various styles, all equally profusely studded with jewels and filigree work. Ropes of pearls hung from the emperor's crown or fillet (see p. 33). Other men wore simple, round woollen or cloth **caps.**

BYZANTINE

10TH CENTURY
PALLA — EMBROIDERED
BORDER
STOLA —
PEARL EARRINGS AND
PEARL ROPES IN HAIR

6TH CENTURY
LADY OF RANK —
GOLD AND JEWELLED
CROWN & COLLAR
UNDERTUNIC —
STOLA — EMBROIDERED
BORDERS —
JEWELLED BELT

6TH CENTURY —
EMPRESS THEODORA
PURPLE PALUDAMENTUM
JEWELLED COLLAR
AND CROWN —
WHITE STOLA —
EMBROIDERED
BORDER

11TH CENTURY
EMPRESS EUDACIE
EMBROIDERED
PALUDAMENTUM WITH
TABLION
EMBROIDERED STOLA
JEWELLED GOLD COLLAR
AND CROWN.

31

For feminine attire, the Roman **stola** had returned to favour at the beginning of the period. It was, this time, slightly shorter, so did not trail on the ground; also it had the same long, fitting sleeves as the masculine tunica. The hem and sleeves were exquisitely embroidered in rich colours, and the neck-line finished by a jewelled collar, worn on top of the gown. This collar—rather reminiscent of the Egyptian version—was often made of gold or silver, encrusted with jewels, usually culminating at the edge with a row of drop pearls (see p. 31). The alternative **dalmatica** was also still worn, with sleeves like the masculine version. Embroidered bands or clavi still ornamented the garment, in addition to the other decoration on the hem, sleeves, and neck-line. Both stola and dalmatica were girdled by a leather or metal jewelled belt at a high waist-line. One or more undergowns or under-tunics were usual.

Though the empress wore a **paludamentum** similar to that of the emperor (see p. 31), the usual feminine wrap was still the **palla,** draped as in Roman times, its folds serving as a head-covering (see p. 31).

The Oriental influence was markedly evident in the feminine **coiffure** and **head-dress.** Though the hair was long, yet after plaiting and coiling, it was barely visible under the Eastern **turban** which was almost always worn. This turban consisted of a circular, padded roll of silk material in red, black, or purple for royal and noble wear, and in various other colours or white for other women. Pearl ropes and jewelled, embroidered bands encircled the roll at intervals, with ropes of pearls dependent from the sides. Covering the top of the head, attached within the turban, was a fitting cap of similar material. A veil sometimes hung from the back of the head-dress. For the empress, and noble ladies, a crown surmounted the turban (see p. 33).

Excessive **decoration** of all Byzantine garments was typical, achieved by embroidery in coloured silks and wools, with an indiscriminate use of gold and silver thread and jewels of all kinds, but especially pearls. The tablion was the prime recipient with, perhaps, the entire paludamentum as second. The tunica and stola received their share, especially on hems, sleeve edges, neck-lines, and shoulder and hip designs. **Motifs** tended towards geometrical shapes: squares, circles, etc.; however, animals, plant life, and the human figure were also much used themes. **Colours** for the nobility were always rich: royal purple, then red, bright green or blue, gold and black as favourites, with the tunica usually white.

Jewellery was in keeping with the costume, and afforded an extravagant finish. In addition to the jewelled collar, there were bracelets, rings, jewelled girdles, brooches, fibulae, and pendant crosses (see p. 33). Gold was the basic metal in use; it was fashioned into exquisite filigree work, also used for the setting of jewels and mosaics. Pearls were ever predominant, but other precious stones, emeralds, rubies, sapphires, etc., were present in great quantity. Noblemen affected almost as much jewellery as the ladies, particularly in the form of ear-rings and brooches.

BYZANTINE

Masculine hair style

Gold and jewelled crown and collar – pearls and emeralds 6th century

Gold earring 6th C.

Gold and jewelled fibula

Gold earring with emeralds 6th C.

Folds of palla forming head-dress over padded turban. 11th century

Gold filigree pendant cross 6th. C.

Soft shoe – bright colours jewelled decoration 6th. C.

Soldier's leather boot. 6th. C.

Red leather boot pearl decoration

Leather sandal 6th. C.

Metal helmet – coloured plumes 6th C.

Gold and jewelled crown and collar 12th Century

33

II

EARLY BRITISH AND NORMAN

EARLY BRITONS

SECOND CENTURY B.C. TO THE SEVENTH CENTURY A.D.

INFORMATION about the dress of the inhabitants of the British Isles prior to the first Roman invasion in 55 B.C. is scanty. Intact remains of jewellery and arms have been discovered in many parts of the country, but to obtain a knowledge of the complete attire we have to depend on the written accounts of the traders to, and conquerors of, our land, particularly the Romans. A fairly accurate picture of the costume worn at the time of the original Roman invasion can be constructed from these records. The fallacious idea that the sole covering of our ancestors consisted of designs in woad, possesses some justification in that warriors, preparing for battle, stripped the torso, which was tattooed blue with woad (a plant from which the blue dye was extracted), so presenting a, doubtless, terrifying aspect to the enemy, especially when the ensemble was completed by arms and fierce-looking helmets. The tattooing appears to have been connected with nobility of rank. However, the whole body was usually clothed, and the tattooing not visible.

These early peoples had some knowledge of weaving, spinning, and dyeing, gained presumably from visiting traders from eastern Europe. Their cloth was thick and coarse, and dyed in bright primary or secondary colours with red as the favourite, and blue, black, green, yellow, and natural colour. The wool or coarse linen fabric was plain, striped, or woven in a check pattern, the last being presumed an early prototype of the plaid. Skins of animals, with or without the fur, were also used as clothing for warmth.

Masculine costume comprised three main garments: a **tunic, cloak,** and **breeches** or **trousers.** Though primitive in design and cut, these garments fulfilled their chief function adequately: to provide warmth in a climate more inclement than that enjoyed by the Eastern civilisations. Thus arms and legs were covered in winter not for religious reasons, as with the Byzantine peoples, but of necessity. The tunic, essentially simple in style, had long or short sleeves, a round hole for the head, and was knee-length, or shorter for the younger men. A leather belt, often decorated by bronze or iron brooches, encircled the waist. The cloak was a rectangle or circle of about four feet by four or five, fastened by a brooch on the chest or right shoulder. This garment was fur-lined or entirely of fur-skin. The cloth was dark and unpatterned, commonly blue or black. The trousers, known as *braccae*, were primitive indeed, being merely fastened at the waist and ankles by a thong threaded through the material, then tied. They were made out of woollen cloth or skins (see p. 35).

Men of rank usually wore an **undergarment,** a fact which seems to have surprised and impressed the Roman invaders not a little. Made of a coarse,

EARLY BRITONS

Pre-Roman period

Pre-Roman
Warrior -
Cloak - Fur inside -
Cloth outside -
Check Tunic -
Leather Belt -
Sword -
Braccae -
Shoes -
Metal Helmet

British Chieftainess
Pre-Roman period
Dark Cloak -
Check Gown -
Red, Yellow
and Blue
Leather Belt
Shoes

Pre-Roman
Male Costume
Striped Tunic -
Fur Skin on Top -
Braccae -
Shoes

light-coloured linen, it resembled a short-sleeved shirt. Sometimes a loin-cloth or short breeches were also worn.

The most vivid description of women's costume is contained in the account by Dion Cassius of that worn by Boadicea, the renowned British chieftainess. From this, and other records, we gather that feminine costume consisted of an ankle-length **tunic**—in the same check, striped, or plain material as those used by men—and a **cloak**. The former had short or long sleeves with a round hole for the head. Sometimes it was left ungirdled, but normally a leather belt encircled a high waist-line (see p. 35). Hip-belts, in the form of metal circular brooches, with a dagger and purse, were also seen. Another garment known as the *gwn*, or gown, was often worn on top of the tunic by women of rank. This was usually three-quarter length, had short or no sleeves, and was of a check or striped pattern (see p. 35). The cloak was identical with the masculine garment. **Underwear** consisted of a simple, short linen tunic. More than one such tunic was worn in very cold weather.

Both sexes, but particularly the women, were inordinately proud of their long, flowing **hair.** Men often wore it to shoulder-length, and had long, drooping moustaches, with side-whiskers surrounding a clean-shaven chin. Women's hair was grown to waist-length at the back. A metal fillet often encircled the feminine forehead.

These people generally went bareheaded, except for the warriors' helmet and an occasional use of a fur or woollen **cap** by the men.

Footwear was in the form of a shoe of elementary design in rawhide. One piece of leather comprising side and upper had a thong threaded through holes in the top edges and tied at the instep (see p. 39).

Poorer men and women or those of less civilised tribes were clad only in the skin of a large animal, pinned on the shoulders with a crude brooch, or even a thorn. Sometimes they wore a short tunic of very coarse, dull-coloured cloth underneath the fur-skin. A leather belt might be worn round the waist. They were usually barefooted and bareheaded.

The early British **warrior** wore the usual tunic and was clad as other men, except for arms consisting of a sword or dagger in a sheath attached to a leather waist-belt; a long spear or an axe; and a round, oval, or oblong shield, embossed, and of sizes ranging from two feet six inches to five feet in height (see p. 35). The metal helmet—a distinctive feature of the ensemble—was of bronze or iron, often embossed, and later enamelled also (see p. 39).

The **jewellery** of these early peoples was distinctive. Made of iron, bronze, and occasionally gold, it was massive in design, but attractive in its simplicity. The *torque*, the most valued and typical feature, was a necklace of twisted gold, bronze, or iron wire. The metal used, and the elaboration of the design, served to denote the wearer's rank. In addition, metal bracelets, armlets, brooches, and pins were in constant use. They were incised or embossed, and occasionally decorated with coral or other stones. Bead necklaces were also a feature. Bronze hand-mirrors, incised on the back, of a later date, have been found (see p. 39).

From A.D. 78, England became an occupied territory under Roman rule, which lasted until the fifth century A.D., when, some years before the fall of Rome, the last occupying forces were withdrawn. The early Britons learned

EARLY BRITONS

Pre-Roman period
Woman of the people
simple gown of
coarse material
fur skin pinned
on right
shoulder

Common man-
Pre Roman
period

Male costume
during later
Roman occupation
period -
plain tunic and
mantle of Roman
style - sandal

Lady of rank
Roman occupation
period.

a great deal from their conquerors; in particular, the influence of Roman costume styles was considerable. The original British costume, already described, changed and developed slowly to an almost completely Romanised style, which, by the second century A.D., was worn by many members of both sexes of the upper classes. Some stalwarts at first adhered rigidly to the original modes, but eventually the newer fashions became generally accepted. However, long sleeves were usually retained in the **tunic**; **braccae** were only discarded, to leave bare legs, in warm weather, and by the upper classes; also, many women still retained the fashion for wearing a shorter **gown** over the long Romanised one. Finer **materials** were imported, but middle and peasant classes still used the old, coarse, home-woven cloth. **Sandals,** of Roman design, became an alternative to shoes, though many people still went barefooted indoors.

Warriors also gradually assumed Roman military dress, a modification of that of the ordinary soldier. **Helmets,** however, retained much of their original character.

Men's **hair** was worn shorter, usually only nape-length. Women, although still wearing long hair, braided it, and coiled the plaits, after Roman styles, except poorer women, who still had loose and flowing locks.

Jewellery shows the influence of Roman craftsmanship, but did not lose its individuality. Pleasing and interesting designs resulted from the combination of the old and the new conceptions.

Examples of dress, arms, and jewellery during this period are depicted on pp. 37 and 39.

The epoch through which the inhabitants of the British Isles passed between the departure of the Romans and the establishment of Anglo-Saxon rule in the seventh to eighth centuries A.D., is commonly referred to as "the Dark Ages". It is an apt title, since we know little of the history of that time except that continual tribal and racial warfare for supremacy existed. Not only was building, culture, indeed civilisation itself retrogressive, but much that had been built up in previous eras was destroyed. Consequently, there is little knowledge of the costume of this time beyond what has been gained from the excavation of graves, chiefly jewellery, arms, and pottery. It is presumed, however, to be a combination of Roman, ancient British, and Saxon modes, indicating a retrogression from the Romanised costume back to the earlier types of garment: indeed, a reflection of the general life of the community.

THE ANGLO-SAXON PERIOD IN BRITAIN
SEVENTH CENTURY A.D. TO A.D. 1066

Prominent among the races striving for supremacy in the continual wars during the Dark Ages were the Angles, Saxons, and Jutes. These peoples, all of German origin, had successively invaded Britain in the fifth century A.D., after the departure of the Roman legions. Although fighting continued until the ninth century, the country was, to some extent, unified under a combination of these invaders some time earlier. The Anglo-Saxon rule then lasted till 1066,

EARLY BRITONS

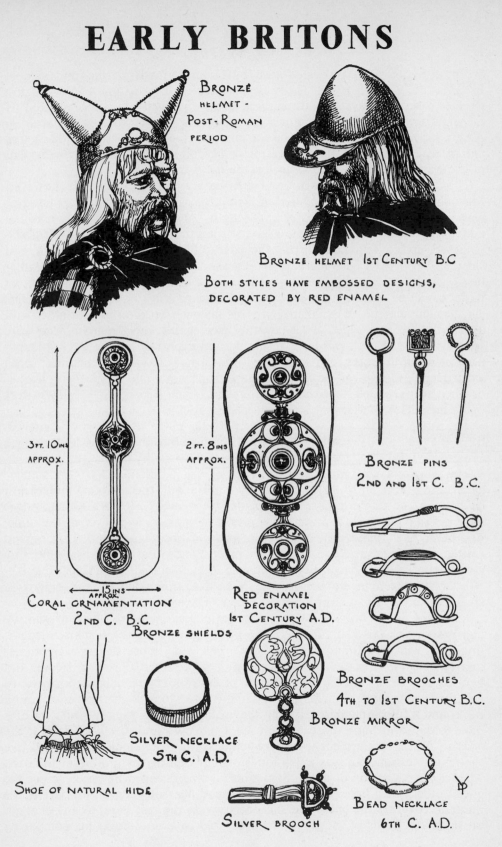

BRONZE HELMET - POST-ROMAN PERIOD

BRONZE HELMET 1ST CENTURY B.C.

BOTH STYLES HAVE EMBOSSED DESIGNS, DECORATED BY RED ENAMEL

3 FT. 10 INS APPROX.

2 FT. 8 INS APPROX.

15 INS APPROX.

CORAL ORNAMENTATION 2ND C. B.C.
BRONZE SHIELDS

RED ENAMEL DECORATION 1ST CENTURY A.D.

BRONZE PINS 2ND AND 1ST C. B.C.

BRONZE BROOCHES 4TH TO 1ST CENTURY B.C.

BRONZE MIRROR

SHOE OF NATURAL HIDE

SILVER NECKLACE 5TH C. A.D.

SILVER BROOCH

BEAD NECKLACE 6TH C. A.D.

39

except for their temporary conquest by Danish invaders, who remained in Britain from 1013 to 1042. These events affected the costume of the English people in several ways: the Romanised dress style was almost eliminated by the eighth century; Roman names for garments were gradually replaced by Anglo-Saxon ones; the modes were a mixture of early British, Anglo-Saxon, and later, but evanescently, Danish; and masculine attire became chiefly that of the warrior, owing to the almost perpetual wars.

The number of garments worn and their basic types, changed little, however. Masculine civil dress still consisted of **tunic, cloak** or **mantle,** and **bracco** and/or **hose.** The simple tunic was still knee-length, long-sleeved, and with a round neck. The centre front of the neck-line was slit to facilitate donning. Brightly-coloured embroidery embellished the edges of the neck-line, slit, hem, and sleeves. The skirt was sometimes slit up the sides to hip-level, and a leather belt encircled the waist. The king's tunic was fuller and longer. One or more under-tunics of similar style, but usually sleeveless and unadorned, were worn. The semicircular or rectangular cloak was fastened on the right shoulder with a brooch. Various types of leg-covering were used: knee-length bracco were seen, with a long sock (*socca*) covering the lower part of the leg; or full-length hose of wool, linen, or leather fastened round the waist and, sometimes, socca worn on top, to mid-calf-level. Cross-gartering from ankle to knee with leather or linen strips, gilded for royalty, was typical. Only poorer working men were bare-legged (see p. 41).

The Anglo-Saxon **shoe** was commonly black, made of leather or material, fitted the foot, and was fastened on the instep by a button or laces. Gilt designs ornamented the nobleman's shoe.

The **warrior's** costume resembled that of the Roman occupation soldier, consisting of a linen tunic (as previously described in this chapter) underneath a leather tunic to the hips with elbow-length sleeves. Sleeve and hem edges were cut in points. On top was either a coat of mail, almost covering the tunic, or a metal breastplate. The cloak, cross-gartered hose, black leather shoes, and leather or wool conical cap covered by metal bands, and often surmounted by a metal cockscomb decoration, completed the ensemble. Short, black ankle-boots were sometimes worn instead of shoes. Arms included a round, embossed shield, a long spear, a sword, and a dagger or axe (see p. 41).

Feminine dress comprised three main garments: the **gown** (gwn, or gunna), **undergown,** and **cloak** or mantle. The fitting gown was three-quarter length, ungirded, with the round slit neck-line. The wide, loose sleeves were three-quarter length. Brightly-coloured embroidery bordered the neck, sleeve, and hem edges. Later, a front centre panel of embroidery reaching from neck to hem became typical. The simple undergown had long, tight sleeves, a round neck, and a full, long skirt reaching the ground. It was usually white, or of a pale colour, and undecorated except for a narrow band of embroidery at the wrists. A shorter garment was worn underneath. The cloak was shaped like the man's version, but was much longer, often trailing the ground at the back when worn by a lady of rank. Sometimes it was fastened by cords across the chest; otherwise a hole was made for the head near one edge, with part of the material covering the chest and shoulders whilst the rest hung to ankle-length at the back. Folds of the cloak could be used as a head-covering, comparing

ANGLO-SAXON

10TH CENTURY
NOBLEMAN
BLUE TUNIC - WHITE
AND GREEN BORDER
BRIGHT RED HOSE
DARK RED CLOAK
BLACK SHOES

WARRIOR
TUNIC - LEATHER
TUNIC ON TOP -
ALSO COAT OF MAIL
DARK CLOAK
HOSE - CROSS -
- GARTERED
LEATHER SHOES
BRONZE
HELMET

LADY OF RANK
PALE GREEN HEAD-RAIL
DARK BLUE MANTLE
BRIGHT GREEN GOWN
COLOURED BORDER
WHITE UNDER-GOWN

QUEEN
DARK RED MANTLE - GOLD CORD
FASTENING - EMBROIDERED
BORDER
PALE BLUE GOWN -
EMBROIDERED HEM AND
FRONT PANEL
WHITE UNDER-GOWN AND
VEIL

with the Roman palla. The outer edges were frequently ornamented with an embroidered border (see p. 41).

The men still wore their **hair** loose and uncurled, reaching the nape of the neck or shoulder-level. Beards and moustaches were sometimes grown, especially by the middle and lower classes. Women's long hair was braided, then coiled at the nape. The hair is never seen in illuminated manuscripts: it is hidden by the head-dress.

In general, civilian men were bareheaded, except for the **Phrygian,** or conical cap, which was occasionally used. These were of leather or wool, sometimes embroidered with a border (see p. 43). Royal crowns were square or round in shape, gold, and studded with jewels (see p. 43). The feminine head-covering was a **veil** or *head-rail.* There were two main styles of veil: in one, a hole was made for the face, and a fillet or crown held the material in place on the head; the other was of rectangular shape, draped over the head, also held in place by a metal band. In both cases, the thin, white or light-coloured fabric was draped elegantly down the back. The head-rail was smaller and more strongly coloured, and similar in shape to the second veil style. One end was generally draped under the chin, with the other over the left shoulder.

Better woven and finer quality **materials** were available by this time, though wool and linen still provided the usual wear. Silk was known in Britain from the eighth century, but, being very costly, was rarely employed, except for the dress of the nobility in later centuries. Knowledge of the art of **embroidery** was developing: brightly-coloured wools, and gold and silver thread traced border designs on the edges of the majority of garments; the most popular **motifs** were circles, squares, dots and, less commonly, floral patterns.

The Anglo-Saxons, especially those of the upper classes, preferred brilliant **colours:** red was still predominant, but green, purple, and blue were in vogue. White also appeared during this period, especially for the tunics of the nobility, which were decorated with gold embroidery in imitation of the Byzantine fashion. Much more sombre hues were found in the dress of the lower-class people.

Jewellery still retained some of its former individuality, but was by this time more refined in taste, expert in craftsmanship, and varied in design. Although bronze was still used for plain and utilitarian ornaments, gold, and to a lesser degree silver, had now become the chief metals for work of high quality. These noble metals were used in making crowns, chain necklaces, ear-rings, brooches, rings, and pendant crosses. Enamel-work on the metal was still seen. Stones and jewels were set in larger items of adornment. Bead necklaces, particularly of amber, were still worn. Waist-belts were often enriched by metal brooches, or jewels.

ENGLISH NORMAN KINGS 1066-1154

WILLIAM I	1066–1087	HENRY I	1100–1135
WILLIAM II	1087–1100	STEPHEN	1135–1154

The beginning of Norman rule in England, marked, as is well known, by the defeat of the Anglo-Saxons under King Harold, by William, Duke of Normandy and his Norman followers in A.D. 1066, brought about considerable changes

ANGLO-SAXON

KING - SQUARE GOLD CROWN

IRON HELMET WITH BRONZE PLATES 7TH CENTURY A.D.

SOLDIER - LEATHER CAP - SURMOUNTED BY METAL BANDS

33 INS.

BRONZE SHIELD - GILT COVERED STUDS

SILVER PENDANT CROSS - JEWELLED CENTRE 814 A.D.

SILVER TREFOIL BROOCH 796 A.D

BONE COMB 9TH CENTURY A.D.

INSCRIBED AGATE RING

SILVER BRACELET

METAL PIN

KING - JEWELLED GOLD CROWN

PHRYGIAN STYLE OF CAP — EMBROIDERED BORDER

in English life; order and legislation, unity, and, important for the student of history and costume, fuller records, in diverse forms, of the life of the period. These records increased in numbers, and in types and quality throughout the Middle Ages, until the Renaissance, when the general appearance of oil-painting, especially portraits, produced material which can be readily understood and interpreted by the modern student without leaving doubt as to the exact mode of dress. In the period covered by this chapter, the chief sources of information on costume are the written and illuminated manuscripts, the Bayeux Tapestry, religious sculpture, and remains of actual jewellery and arms still extant. Fortunately for us the artistic illuminators of the Middle Ages, in general, depicted their figures in the dress worn at their own time, and not at the period of the illustrated scene, presumably owing to lack of knowledge of earlier costume. Styles changed slowly still, one fashion lasting for several generations. The Bayeux Tapestry, commonly presumed to be the work of Queen Matilda (the wife of William I) and her noble ladies, in commemoration of the invasion and conquest of England, is valuable in that it shows a variety of the costumes worn by various members of the community, though they are predominantly military.

Dress for men and women throughout Norman times was comparatively loose, showing similar lines of drapery to the Anglo-Saxon period. The Norman conquerors brought little in the way of new styles, except their peculiar method of hairdressing, in which the head was shaved at the back to just above the ears; noblemen in the reign of William I adhered to this style. Both sexes still covered the arms and legs; indeed, this clothing of the limbs persisted all through the Middle Ages, and till after the Tudor period. The reigns of William II and Henry I were marked by fantastic, long, trailing garments for men and women; knots were often tied in the material to make progression possible. The early Crusades affected styles at the end of the reign of Henry I and during that of Stephen. Returning noblemen brought Eastern—particularly Byzantine —ideas into dress, colours, and jewellery, together with new materials, finer and richer than those to which English people had been accustomed. At this same time were also seen the early, modest beginnings of tight-lacing for women. To some extent this was only a temporary innovation, coinciding with the more waisted gowns which accompanied the long, trailing draperies of Henry I's time, vanishing after this, and then reappearing to provide a suitably slender figure for the Edward III cotehardie.

The masculine **tunic,** at the time of William I, was little changed from the Anglo-Saxon version. There were still two lengths: knee-length in common use for all in everyday life, and ankle-length for the best dress of a nobleman. Apart from this the two styles were similar: decoration was mainly confined to border patterns of squares, circles, and other geometrical motifs, embroidered at the hem, sleeve edges, neck edge, and opening; sleeves were long, fitting or loose, three-quarter or full-length, and usually fuller at the shoulder; the neck was round, and slit in front to permit donning over the head; the whole garment was loose-fitting and confined at the waist by a leather belt (see p. 45). Some-times the skirt was slit up the sides, often showing the under-tunic at the bottom. Frequently several tight-sleeved under-tunics were worn, according to the rank of the wearer, and the weather conditions. The king, on State occasions, wore

NORMAN

NOBLEMAN
TEMP. WILLIAM. I
TUNIC - EMBROID-
-ERED BORDERS -
UNDERTUNIC SHOWS
AT WRISTS -
MANTLE -
CONTRASTING
COLOURED
LINING -
BRAIES -
HOSE ON
TOP -
LEATHER
SHOES

NOBLE LADY TEMP
WILLIAM I -
DARK BLUE MANTLE -
GOLD CORDS - WHITE GOWN
BLACK, RED, GREY BORDER
DESIGN - WHITE UNDER-
GOWN - CREAM
COUVRECHEF - GOLD
CORD GIRDLE

LADY OF QUALITY
c. 1130

NOBLEMAN c.1105
ELONGATED TUNIC,
UNDERTUNIC AND MANTLE -
LONG HAIR AND BEARD

45

an ankle-length super-tunic of richer material and decoration. This was known as a dalmatic, a survival of the Eastern garment of similar name. Its belt was usually studded with jewels. During the reign of William II, the short tunic became longer and fuller, and the ankle-length style evolved into a long, trailing garment, held up in front or tucked in the belt to enable the wearer to walk. Sleeves also lengthened and eventually completely enveloped the hand (see p. 45). These modes continued into the reign of Henry I, becoming more ludicrous and unwieldy until, towards the end of his reign, Eastern styles, introduced by returning Crusaders, influenced the mode. The long tunic reverted to ankle-length, though the skirt remained very full, and an uneven hem-line with radiating folds was produced by the material being tucked into the belt at the sides. The garment became tighter-fitting on the upper part of the body, and was enhanced by a decorative coloured collar, in emulation of this distinctive and typical feature of Byzantine dress (see p. 47). The regal dalmatic was less subject to these changes of style. Richer materials became the vogue for the nobleman's wear in the reign of William II—a tendency increased by the introduction of new silk fabrics into the country by the returning Crusaders.

Out of doors, a semicircular or rectangular **mantle** or **cloak** was normally worn on top of the tunic. For the upper classes this cloak was ankle-length at the back; for other men it reached the calf. As in Anglo-Saxon days, the fastening consisted of a brooch worn on the right shoulder, or in front (see p. 45). By about A.D. 1090, the mantle became subject to the extravagant influences of the time: richer fabrics were employed, and often fur linings; the garment became longer and more voluminous till, in Henry I's reign, one end was, of necessity, held over the arm, and the material often trailed on the ground at the back (see p. 45). With the return of a shorter tunic, smaller mantles also came back. Heavier and richer materials, also the use of fur and contrasting coloured linings, remained, however.

A *sherte*—similar to our shirt—constituted the chief male **underwear.** One or more of these were worn, made of white linen. On top, loose trouser-like garments known as *braies* or *chaussés* were put on. These reached the ankles, were made of linen, silk, or wool, and were tied by a draw-string at the waist.

Leg-covering was provided by **hose,** worn on top of the braies, and reaching the knee, where they were held up by a garter or rolled over. Hose sometimes had a portion under the arch of the foot, sometimes were only ankle-length. An alternative leg-covering was simply to cross-garter bands of linen on top of the braies—a method particularly used by the peasants and soldiers. As the result of a gradual process during the Middle Ages, the braies became shorter and the hose longer. Some progress in this direction can be discerned by the time of Henry I's reign, when the hose often reached to mid-thigh level, on top of the braies. On the whole, hose were ill-fitting in Norman times—a great contrast to the immaculately cut "tights" of the later medieval period.

Shoes at the time of William I were simple in style and fitting to the foot. Made of leather in bright, rich colours, they generally reached the ankle, fitting there with a coloured band fastened by a button, or buckle at the side or in front (see p. 49). Noblemen wore embroidered and jewelled shoes. In keeping with the lengthy garments of Henry I's time, shoes also embodied idiosyncrasies.

NORMAN

NOBLEMAN TEMP. STEPHEN COSTUME SHOWS EASTERN INFLUENCE - DECORATIVE COLLAR - SHORTER GARMENTS

LADY TEMP HENRY 1 - VERY LONG GOWN, MANTLE AND VEIL - PENDULOUS GOWN SLEEVES KNOTTED

NOBLE LADY TEMP STEPHEN - GATHERED BODICE - SINGLE GIRDLE - LONG PLAITS WITH METAL CYLINDER ENDS - MANTLE - VEIL

NOBLE LADY TEMP. STEPHEN - DOUBLE - GIRDED GOWN.

47

These took the form of long toes to the shoe, often stuffed, and cut into bizarre shapes, such as the horns of a ram, or a fish-tail (see p. 49). Apart from such extremes of fashion, only affected by the nobility, little change occurred in styles.

The strange Norman **hair-style** has already been mentioned. This idea, of brushing the short hair forward on to the crown and forehead and shaving the back of the head to the ears, or even higher, was originally Norman. The custom persisted during the reign of William I, but by 1090 most Normans had adopted the English coiffure of long, flowing hair. In 1066, the average Norman was clean-shaven, but as the popularity of long hair grew, so did the desire for beards and moustaches, especially among older men. Later, in the reign of William II, indeed, during the whole period of the vogue for extremely long garments, the coiffure appeared to follow suit: hair was long and flowing, beards also were long, and worn in one or more points (see p. 49). Efforts were made to check these unhygienic hirsute growths, but apart from a tendency towards more curled and formal styles, they remained relatively long till after 1154. A fillet was often worn round the brow.

Most men in Norman England went bareheaded. For inclement weather, however, or for older men, the **Phrygian cap** was still the commonest head-covering (see p. 49). Alternatively, a felt or woollen flat **cap** was worn (see p. 49) or a **hood** attached to the shorter cloak. The latter style was used mainly for travelling.

The feminine **gown** at the time of William I was also loose; its cut was similar to the male tunic, with the round neck, slit in front, full or tight sleeves, long or three-quarter length, with bands of decoration at the neck, sleeve, and hem edges. Women wore a girdle, an object of great pride, and composed, according to rank, of gold or silver cord, or coloured wool, in long strands, knotted at intervals, and ending in tassels. The girdle was tied low on the waist, with the ends hanging nearly to the ground. Though the gown was now often ground-length, the old Anglo-Saxon fashion for three-quarter length still survived, with the undergown showing from knees to feet, and at the wrists. Ordinary gowns were made from linen or wool, though the nobility used finer, imported materials, popularly silk (see p. 45). By 1090, women also were attracted by the fancy for long, trailing garments. The early signs of this were seen in the sleeves, which became long and pendulous at the wrists, though often quite narrow and fitting as far as the elbow (see p. 45). By 1100, women carried the idea of long and voluminous garments to even greater excess than the men had done. The full skirt trailed on the ground to form a long train at the back, though the gown was fairly fitting to the hips, achieved by being laced at the centre back and front. Long girdles were still worn, though the gown was sometimes now ungirded. The sleeves reached incredible widths at the wrists, and often had to be tied in knots to keep them off the ground (see p. 47). As already mentioned, a modest corset or stays of leather or material were considered necessary to show off these more waisted gowns. Returning Crusaders brought new, finer materials in silks and muslins which gave rise to new styles. By about 1130, the trailing, unwieldy garments were abandoned, with a return to ground-length gowns. The thin fabrics lent themselves to gathering and pleating so, until 1154, the gown was full-skirted, wide-sleeved, and yet clinging to the line of the breasts, waist, and hips by dint of lines of gathers or tucks

NORMAN

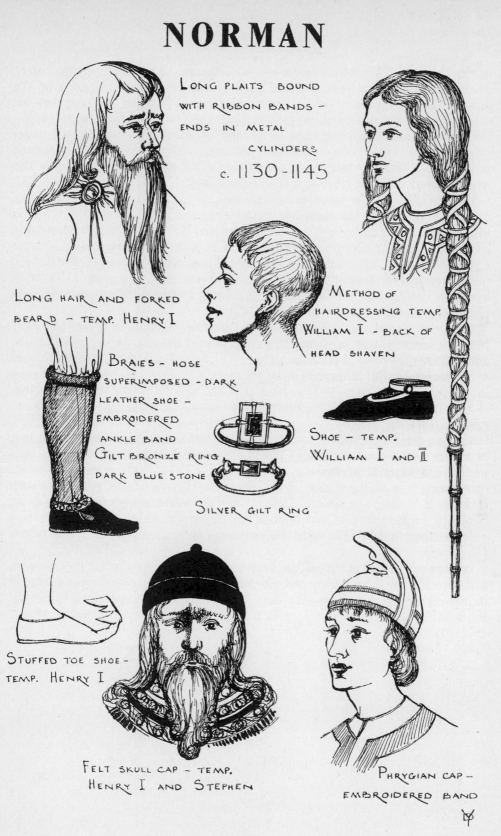

Long plaits bound with ribbon bands — ends in metal cylinders

c. 1130 - 1145

Long hair and forked beard — temp. Henry I

Method of hairdressing temp. William I — back of head shaven

Braies — hose superimposed — dark leather shoe — embroidered ankle band Gilt bronze ring dark blue stone

Silver gilt ring

Shoe — temp. William I and II

Stuffed toe shoe — temp. Henry I

Felt skull cap — temp. Henry I and Stephen

Phrygian cap — embroidered band

49

in these places. The double girdle is also a feature of this time, being passed round the waist from front to back, then to the front again to fasten on the hips. It was flat, made of leather, embroidered and jewelled, with long, silken tasselled threads hanging to the ground from the front fastening (see p. 47).

Feminine **underwear** comprised an undergown, usually sleeveless, and under this a shorter, white linen or silk long-sleeved undergarment called a *camise*, or *chemise*, which was worn next to the skin. It is presumed that women also wore drawers of some kind, and hose on the legs.

The feminine **mantle** in 1066 was semicircular, and normally held in place by cords tied across the chest. A metal, ornamental boss fixed the cords at each side of the mantle and, in the case of the nobility, both ornament and cords were gold or silver, sometimes jewelled. The mantle was ground-length at the back, often enhanced by a border with, usually, a contrasting coloured lining (see p. 45). Like the gown, the mantle increased in size by 1100, often sweeping the floor for several feet at the back, but normal proportions were resumed in the reign of Stephen (see p. 47).

As in the case of Anglo-Saxon women, the **hair** was always covered in early Norman times. It was, presumably, parted in the centre, as before, then plaited and coiled at the nape of the neck. The **veil** and head-rail (the latter was termed a *couvrechef* by the Normans) were worn in a similar manner to the Saxon mode (see p. 45). From 1090 to about 1130 the veil, in common with the other clothes of the time, was long, often being tied in knots at back and front to raise it from the ground (see p. 47). A welcome change came about 1130, lasting till after 1154, when noblewomen led the fashion of divesting the hair of all its voluminous draperies. Having once accepted this idea, ladies then went to the opposite extreme and endeavoured to show as much hair as possible by growing it to an inordinate length; then, where nature failed to achieve such excesses, false hair was added. Two plaits were worn, either bound by ribbon bands or encased in silk, and later metal cylindrical cases, where possible of gold or silver, finished the ends. Plaits often reached knee- or even ankle-level (see p. 49).

In the early medieval period **jewellery** was limited to brooches, rings, crowns, and coronets for the nobility, and jewelled girdles. Craftsmanship was steadily improving. Gold and silver were the chief metals, set with precious stones for the wealthy. Enamel work and gold filigree were still practised (see p. 49).

III

THE PLANTAGENETS

HENRY II	1154–1189
RICHARD I	1189–1199
JOHN	1199–1216

FROM the time when such motives as vanity, interest, imitation, and the desire for variety first began to supersede mere necessity in costume design, it has generally been possible to trace the effect of the main factors in the life of the English people, in each successive age, on the fashionable wear. At times the influence is difficult to discern, at others it is manifest; but, on the average, economics, wars, politics, royalty—indeed, the whole historical background of the period—has had some relation to the fashion in costume. A preliminary study, however, of the dress in England, in the reigns of these first three Angevin[1] kings, appears to belie these assertions. Thus there is no major change in the world of fashion during this time, though the reign of Henry II, for instance, is considered by the historian to be a notable one for England. Out of the anarchy left by Stephen, Henry II created order, legislation, and a good administration, which was the early, yet enduring, foundation for the subsequent English society. Richard I spent the greater part of his reign fighting in the Third Crusade. King John was, as is popularly known, a bad king: extravagant, selfish, cruel—a tyrant. On preliminary consideration, the student might well expect abrupt changes in fashion, reflecting the conditions in these different reigns. Not finding such immediate evidence, he could be excused for regarding sceptically the thesis of a relation between historic events and costume. Nevertheless, if a closer, more careful study of this period is made, though there are no major changes in dress styles, yet the costume in the reigns of the first three Plantagenets is truly, if not obviously, influenced by the conditions of the times. During the reign of the first Angevin king, costume acquired again the dignity and simplicity of the early Norman period; the trailing monstrosities of the reign of Henry I, and the crimped, gathered full-nesses of the gowns at the time of Stephen, gave place to simple draperies once more. Materials and decoration, at least for the nobility, were still richer than in 1066, but style and cut were unpretentious and dignified. So dress was a reflection, in its lack of assumption and peculiarity, of the reintroduction of order into English life. Again, the continual absence of Richard I from England, and the concentration of the energies of the royalty and nobility on the Third Crusade, resulted in a lack of concern about costume; little alteration in styles took place. Lastly, the extravagances and love of fine clothes, jewels, and materials of King John brought in a more ornate, decorated form of dress, yet without greatly altering the actual style. The king's wardrobe was immense, and his noblemen vied with one another to possess garments more richly furred, jewelled, coloured, and ornamented.

[1] The Plantagenets were also known as the Angevins, since they were of the house of Anjou.

PLANTAGENET, 1154-1216

HENRY II IN STATE DRESS -
REDDISH-BROWN MANTLE -
CRIMSON DALMATIC, GOLD
DESIGN AND BORDER -
TWO UNDERTUNICS SHOW
AT HEM -
GREEN FOOTWEAR,
GOLD DESIGN -
WHITE, JEWELLED
GLOVES.

ELEANOR OF AQUITAINE,
QUEEN OF HENRY II
PATTERNED GOWN, LONG
GIRDLE - MANTLE -
BARBETTE, VEIL & CROWN

RICHARD I IN STATE DRESS -
BLUE MANTLE WITH
GOLD BORDER -
RED DALMATIC -
GREEN & WHITE
UNDERTUNICS -
RED FOOTWEAR
WITH GOLD
DECORATION

KING JOHN IN STATE DRESS
GOLD MANTLE, GREEN
LINING - CRIMSON
DALMATIC, GOLD BORDER
GOLD, JEWELLED GIRDLE -
GOLD CLOTH UNDERTUNIC
RED HOSE -
BLACK SHOES

There are still extant life-size, often coloured, marble and stone effigies of the English sovereigns and their queens from the time of Henry II. Those of the first two Plantagenets and their queens are in France, but that of King John —the first example in England—is in Worcester Cathedral. The effigies provide an important addition to our knowledge of costume from this time onwards.

The principal masculine garment, the **tunic,** had by 1154 returned to its original early Norman length—either knee-length for average wear, or ankle-length for the nobility on formal occasions. Bands of embroidery at the hem, neck, and sleeve edges were still usual, though a new factor in decoration had now appeared—jagged, cut edges to the hem, or edge of the shoulder cape, known as a *"dagged"* edge. This was the modest beginning of those cut and lacerated edges which became an obsession with the well-dressed man of the late fourteenth century. The leather **belt** now evolved into a definite style; it was gilded and jewelled for noblemen, buckled in front, and with a long end hanging to the ankles. By about 1190, the upper sleeve was cut much wider and deeper, so producing a considerable fullness of material which formed attractive folds when the belt was tightened at the waist. Though rather shorter by 1200, the tunic received much more decoration in the form of jewelled embroideries and appliqué work, in rich colours, particularly at the neck, sleeves, and hem. Costly imported materials were the vogue for noblemen, especially gold or silver cloth, or richly-coloured silks (see pp. 52 and 54).

The costly, heavy **mantle** lined with fur or contrasting coloured silk, and edged with a jewelled, decorative border, was worn on formal occasions. It was long and voluminous, fastened as previously and draped over the left arm, or tucked in the girdle (see p. 52). The shorter style—about calf-length—with or without a hood attached, was used, as in Norman days, by the average man for outdoor wear in cold weather. A more abbreviated **cloak** was introduced by Henry II, and consequently known as the cloak of Anjou, whilst Henry himself was called "Curt-Manteau", because of his partiality towards this style.

Masculine **underwear** still comprised a sherte, or shertes, braies supported by a draw-string at the waist, but now only knee-length, and one or more under-tunics.

Hose increased in length as the braies became shorter, now reaching high up the thigh. They were attached to the waist-band of the braies by strings at back and front and, by the end of the twelfth century, had a complete foot portion. Red was the popular colour for noblemen, sometimes decorated by gilt leather cross-gartering. The hose were better fitting now.

Shoes were still simple and shaped to the foot. They were of fabric, silk, or leather, dyed in rich colours, or gilded for the nobility, jewelled and embroidered (see p. 52). Buttons or buckles were still the principal fastenings. Loose leather **boots** were worn by many men, with a better-fitting, short, roll-top style for noblemen (see pp. 54 and 56).

Varieties of the **Phrygian cap** still continued to be worn by many men throughout this period (see p. 56), but its popularity was waning in favour of the **hood.** Until the time of Henry II, hoods attached to the cloak, or worn separately, had served the common man as a head-covering in bad weather, and for travelling, but from about 1160 the hood, attached to a shoulder cape, became fashionable for all. In fact this vogue, in many and various forms, was destined to continue in the highest fashion and popularity for a further three

PLANTAGENET, 1154-1216

BERENGARIA OF NAVARRE
QUEEN OF RICHARD I

MAN IN SHORT
TUNIC - BRAIES -
HOSE - SHORT
BOOTS - PHRYGIAN
CAP
c. 1160-1200

c. 1190-1210 -
VEIL AND WIMPLE-
GOWN -
MANTLE

ISABELLA OF ANGOULÊME
QUEEN OF KING JOHN.

hundred years with all classes. By 1160, the hood was still similar to that of the Normans, with a small point on top. The head-portion was, however, attached to a shoulder cape which was buttoned or brooched in the centre front. The cape edges were popularly dagged (see p. 56). As alternative head-covering were worn hard felt **hats**, round and fitting to the head, usually decorated by a patterned border (see p. 56). Although the head was more often covered during the reigns of Henry II and Richard I than in Norman and Anglo-Saxon times, a reversion to bareheadedness took place after 1190. Many noblemen wore only a fillet round the brow, to display their long locks.

Hairdressing also became more dignified in 1154; the hair was short, whilst the shaving of beards and moustaches was general, in contrast to the flowing locks and long beards worn during the three preceding reigns (see p. 56). Small, trim beards and moustaches became fashionable in Richard's time, but by 1200 hair and beards were longer once more, though more moderate than those of a century previously.

The feminine **gown** became subject to the same sobering influences as the male costume. It was simple, flowing in graceful lines, and not tightly fitting to the figure at any point. The full skirt reached ground-level, also formed adequate folds at the waist where it was confined by a belt—after the masculine design. The neck-line was unchanged whilst sleeves loose at the upper arm, but fitting at the wrist, completed the mode. Materials for the noble lady's gown were richer than previously, including gold and silver cloth, plain or patterned silks, with coloured, embroidered borders at the neck and sleeve edges. At the end of the twelfth century, a reticule, or purse, made of silk or leather, often hung from the girdle on the left side. After 1190, women's gown styles also tended to utilise more sumptuous materials, with richer colours and decoration. Jewelled, patterned girdles ornamented the fuller gowns (see pp. 52 and 54).

The feminine **mantle** had altered little; it was, however, in common with other garments of the time, fashioned from richer materials than previously, and lined with fur or silk of a contrasting hue. A vogue existed for wearing the mantle almost off the shoulders in front in order to display the gown to advantage (see pp. 52 and 54).

Underwear had not changed except that, because of the slightly lower neck-line to the gown, the camise sometimes showed above at the throat.

The **coiffure** appears to have been dressed in plaits, coiled at the nape of the neck, as in early Norman times, but two innovations in **head-covering** are introduced at this time. Eleanor, the queen of Henry II, is reputed to have taken the lead in popularising the first of these—the *barbette*. This was a strip of white linen passed under the chin and pinned on top of the head. It could be worn alone, or with a **veil** or **couvrechef** on top (see pp. 52 and 56). These latter head-coverings were considerably reduced in size compared with those previously worn. The vogue for the barbette, with or without the veil, continued throughout this period. The second innovation, the *wimple*, first appeared at the end of the twelfth century, and remained fashionable for about two hundred years. It consisted of a piece of linen or silk, usually white, pinned to the hair on either side of the face and draped in graceful folds round the neck and throat. A veil was then worn on top, held in place by a fillet encircling the forehead (see pp. 54 and 56).

PLANTAGENET, 1154-1216

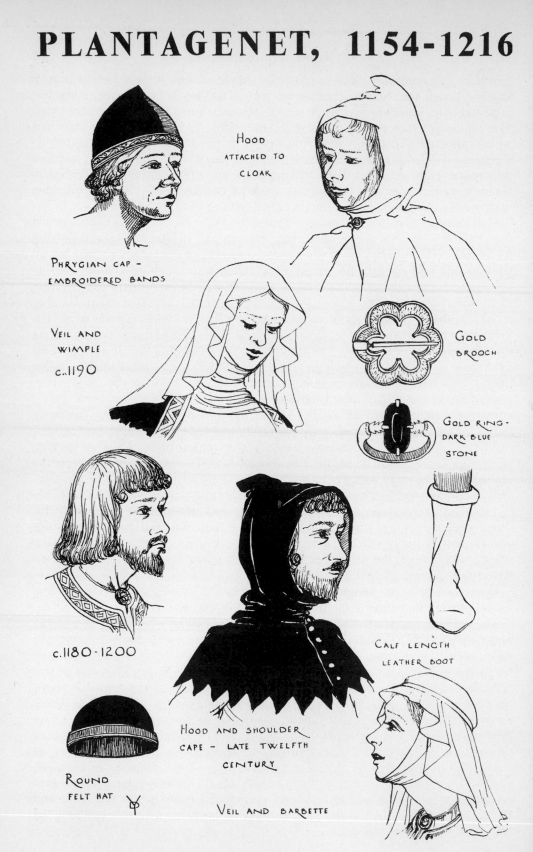

HOOD
ATTACHED TO
CLOAK

PHRYGIAN CAP -
EMBROIDERED BANDS

VEIL AND
WIMPLE
c. 1190

GOLD
BROOCH

GOLD RING -
DARK BLUE
STONE

c. 1180 - 1200

CALF LENGTH
LEATHER BOOT

ROUND
FELT HAT

HOOD AND SHOULDER
CAPE - LATE TWELFTH
CENTURY

VEIL AND BARBETTE

The feminine style of **shoe** was, as far as is known, very similar to that worn by men.

Designs in **jewellery** and types in use were similar to those of Norman times (see p. 56). Jewelled fillets, worn chiefly by men, were a popular feature of King John's reign.

Home-woven **cloth** was improving in quality, though the rich materials of the late twelfth and early thirteenth centuries worn by the nobility were, as yet, still imported from farther east. In especial demand were cloth of gold and silver, and costly silks of varied quality.

HENRY III   1216–1272

The reign of Henry III, indeed the whole of the thirteenth century, after 1216, is noted for its simplicity in dress; the extravagant ornamentation and full, flowing garments of the King John period had gone, and in their place came plain, almost unadorned, simple yet dignified clothes. Materials were still rich and heavy, but their very weight effected and enhanced the simple line and cut of the garments. New ideas in dress appear: the surcote, a plain, sleeveless super-tunic, worn by both sexes, adapted from the tabard of the crusading knights, and which evolved into a sleeved, more complicated garment; the masculine coif, which almost covered the hair and was often worn under a hat; the continued progress of the hood into more varied modes; the numerous styles of feminine hair-covering typified by the pillbox-shaped coif; the barbette, and the gold and jewelled nets covering the hair, which were known by so many different names, crispine, crespinette, etc., and, lastly, the introduction of a new material, velvet, which was imported from Italy.

Sources of knowledge in costume were increasing in numbers and improving in quality. The thirteenth century was a great age for sculpture and Gothic architecture in Europe: in England, Westminster Abbey was erected under the auspices of Henry III—an enthusiastic patron of the arts—as well as great cathedrals in the Gothic style, notably Lincoln with its magnificent front displaying hundreds of figures carved in stone, and later Wells. As well as exterior sculpture, the cathedrals and churches of this time contain numerous wall-paintings, stained-glass windows, memorial brasses, carved figures in wood and stone, and bronze or marble effigies of sovereigns and their consorts. Moreover, the quality of draughtsmanship and colour of the work of the artistic illuminator was steadily improving throughout the Middle Ages.

The principal top garment for men was now the *surcote* (surcoat). It evolved from an adaptation of the tabard worn over his armour by the crusading knight, and had gradually assumed popularity for civilians. At first it was sleeveless with a very deep armhole, since it was only sewn up the sides from the hem to hip-level. A leather belt, buckled in front with a long end hanging down, was sometimes worn at the waist, but the surcote was alternatively worn loose and ungirded (see p. 58). It was also known as the *cyclas*, being originally made from rich material of a similar name. Later in the reign, when various styles of sleeves were added, the term *gardcorp* (gardecors) was also adopted to describe this garment. The most usual form of sleeve was full and long, slit above the elbow in front, through which the arm could pass; the remaining

PLANTAGENET, HENRY III

DARK GREEN SURCOTE
WITH GOLD BORDERS
AND DESIGN OVER
BLUE-GREY TUNIC
GREY HOSE
BLACK SHOES
WHITE COIF

NOBLEMAN -
ORANGE MANTLE -
FUR EDGED & LINED
DARK GREEN SURCOTE
BROWN TUNIC
GREY HOSE
BLACK SHOES

SIMPLE
UN-GIRDED GOWN
MANTLE -
COIF OR FILLET-
BARBETTE

LADY OF RANK -
BLUE-GREY MANTLE
WITH FUR LINING -
PINK GOWN -
JEWELLED BELT -
CROWN ON TOP OF
COIF - BARBETTE -
GOLD CRISPINE

tubular-shaped material then hung down behind the arm to hip-level or knee-level (see p. 60). Other more ordinary sleeves were fashionable as well. Various lengths of surcote prevailed, reaching either to calf, ankle, or ground. The skirt portion was commonly slit up the centre front and back, and/or sides, as far as the knees (see p. 60). Vertical slits were often made in the garment at hip-level, in front, so that the hand could be slipped through to the belt on the tunic underneath, where a purse was often attached. These slits were called *fitchets*.

The ordinary **tunic** was little changed and though occasionally worn as an outer garment, yet more frequently served as an under-tunic to the surcote. Here too a girdle was optional. The neck was still round, though now sometimes fastened by a row of buttons; sleeves were long, fitting at the wrist and fairly full at the armhole, and the hem-line varied according to that of the surcote, though sometimes the tunic hem was visible for several inches below the surcote (see p. 60). Fashionable men wore a leather purse hung from the girdle when the latter was worn. Fur linings achieved a certain popularity.

With the advent of the surcote, **cloaks** or **mantles** were generally reserved for State, formal occasions, and for travelling. The long mantle was retained for formal wear. It was made of rich material, with fur edges and linings usual. A mantle of circular design was gradually replacing the semicircular one, though the same fastenings—either a brooch on the right shoulder or cords across the chest—remained (see p. 60). The shorter cloak, of plainer material, was retained for travelling.

Underwear was unaltered, though hose were better fitting, especially when worn by noblemen.

Shoes still followed the shape of the foot, culminating in a small point at the toe, and were fastened at the ankle by a button. Leather and rich fabrics, embroidered in geometrical designs, usually in gold, were the average materials (see p. 62). Black leather **boots** were more popular with the commoner.

Masculine **hair-styles** had reverted to shorter modes. The hair was worn flowing in loose waves at the sides, ending in curls or a curled roll at the back, just below ear-level. Another long curl was worn across the brow. This distinct style stayed in vogue as typical of the remainder of the thirteenth century (see pp. 60 and 62). Many men were clean-shaven, though some grew short curly beards and moustaches (see pp. 60 and 62).

Equally typical of this period was the unusual head-covering known as the *coif*. Made of white linen or silk, it took the form of a cap which covered the hair except for the curl on the forehead and at the back, and was tied under the chin with strings. The coif was worn both indoors and out, but when worn outdoors it was often surmounted by a hat. These **hats** were still very simple in style, round, with or without a turned-up brim, and with a small point on top. The hood attached to the shoulder cape still retained its popularity, and remained unaltered in shape throughout this reign. Sometimes the coif was worn underneath it (see pp. 58, 60, and 62).

For the first three decades of the reign of Henry III the **gown** worn by the women was almost unchanged from that described in the Henry II period (see p. 58). The purse or reticule hanging from the girdle was still in vogue. Towards 1250 the wearing of a girdle decreased in popularity, and the same style of gown

PLANTAGENET, HENRY III

HENRY III IN STATE DRESS - UN-DECORATED MANTLE AND TUNIC ORNAMENTED FOOTWEAR

CYCLAS OVER ANOTHER GOWN VEIL AND WIMPLE c. 1260

SURCOTE WITH HANGING SLEEVES - TUNIC - COIF AND HAT.

CITIZEN - GREY TUNIC - GREEN HOSE - BLACK SHOES.

then hung in full, graceful, vertical folds from the breasts to the ground (see p. 58).

In the year 1251 is the first mention by a chronicler of the **surcote,** or **cyclas,** as the feminine version was more commonly called. Although women adopted this type of garment later than men, yet as a feminine vogue it lasted for considerably longer; indeed, after its gradual development into what was known as the "sideless gown", it remained the official State feminine dress until the early fifteenth century. After 1251 the cyclas, like the male version, had a low, round neck, no sleeves, and a very wide, deep armhole reaching nearly to the hips. It was made rather more fitting at the waist and hips than when worn by men, and the fuller skirt reached to the ground and formed a small train at the back. No girdle was worn on the cyclas, though the undergown—which remained similar to the gown styles prior to 1251—sometimes had a simple belt from which the purse depended when carried. Though normally lacking in embroidery or elaborate decoration, the cyclas was fashioned from costly materials. Women were frequently depicted holding up the cyclas at one side to accentuate the graceful folds and to show the contrasting material of the undergown (see p. 60).

After the adoption of the cyclas or surcote, the feminine **mantle** also fell into disuse except for formal and State wear. It was still long and voluminous, sweeping the floor at the back, and was made from heavy silk or velvet lined with fur or contrasting coloured silk (see p. 58).

Women's **hair** was dressed as before, except that towards the end of the period the coiled plaits were dressed nearer the sides of the neck.

Two more new styles of feminine head-covering were introduced in the reign of Henry III, and worn in addition to, or as an alternative to, the **barbette** and the **wimple.** These were the *crispine* and *coif.* The crispine was a net encasing the hair, attached to a metal fillet or band worn round the brow. The net, which varied in material and style according to the wealth and position of the wearer, was preferred to be of gold or silver thread, studded with jewels at the points of intersection in the mesh. These network bags or cauls were known at this time by different names: *crispine, crespin, crespinette,* and were destined, in many and various forms, and called by new names, to remain an integral part of feminine head adornment until the rise of the hennin in the fifteenth century (see p. 62). The coif, also known as the **fillet,** was a pillbox-shaped hat made of white silk or linen. It was two or three inches deep and had a flat top. Later the sides were pleated or pressed into vertical ridges (see p. 62). In some cases the hat had no top, only the sides, so that the top of the head could be seen from above (see p. 62). The crown, when worn by noblewomen, was placed on the outside or top of the coif (see p. 58). The barbette was generally depicted as being worn under the coif, and over the crispine, though sometimes, particularly for indoor wear, only the crispine, or crispine and barbette, were worn. A small **veil** surmounted the coif in many cases. The ensemble, veil, coif, and barbette was normally white (see p. 62). As already mentioned, the wimple was also still fashionable during this reign. As in the previous period, it was worn in conjunction with the veil, which was held in place by a fillet round the brow. The wimple, which was often tucked in the neck of the gown, would be probably worn on top of a crispine (see p. 60).

PLANTAGENET, HENRY III

HENRY III

GOLD AND JEWELLED NET - CALLED A CRISPINE OR CRESPINETTE

COIF OR FILLET - SURMOUNTED BY A VEIL - BARBETTE - ALL IN WHITE

WHITE FLUTED FILLET OR COIF, AND BARBETTE - ON TOP OF CRISPINE

GOLD BROOCH

GOLD AND SAPPHIRE RING.

GOLD RING.- LARGE SAPPHIRE CENTRE STONE - 4 SMALL AMETHYSTS

GOLD EMBROIDERED SHOE

HOOD

WHITE COIF AND BARBETTE OVER CRISPINE.

FELT HAT ON TOP OF COIF.

The range of **materials,** particularly imported ones, was increasing at this time. The first reference to velvet—imported from Italy—is found in Henry III's reign. English and foreign furs of many kinds were used for linings and edges to mantles and surcotes. Ermine was the royal preference, but other furs, particularly sable, squirrel, and fox, were in great demand. Silks of several varieties, wools, linen, and cotton were in common use.

In keeping with the extreme simplicity of the period, **decoration** was used sparingly, being confined to borders when used at all. Designs were unpretentious and dignified, usually in geometrical or plant forms.

Fine craftsmanship in **jewellery** was evident by the thirteenth century, although ornamentation was still—as in the previous two centuries—utilitarian in purpose, being confined to brooches, rings, girdles (when worn), crowns, and the added innovation, the crispine (see p. 62).

EDWARD I   1272–1307
EDWARD II   1307–1327

During the last three decades of the thirteenth century costume was noteworthy for simplicity of line, lack of decoration, and paucity of accessories, perhaps more so than for any other period in England after the Norman Conquest. Undoubtedly, Edward I was in no small measure responsible for this state of affairs, since, by personal example, he encouraged unpretentious modes for the nobility—a lead which was naturally emulated by other classes of the community. No important new ideas were introduced to the world of fashion: these years merely evinced a gradual development of the clothes worn in Henry III's reign.

The first quarter of the fourteenth century was, in a sense, a time of transition. The early years saw little change in styles, yet in the period 1310–1320 it is possible to discern, by small indications such as the tightening of garments at the waist, the laying of the foundations of the typical fourteenth-century dress of the Edward III and Richard II era. The last seven years of the reign of Edward II appear to witness the prelude to these later designs, visible in the growing popularity for parti-coloured clothes, the shorter tunic with elbow-length sleeves and short hanging streamers or tippets, buttons on the sleeves of the under-tunic, the new method of wearing the hood with the facial opening placed on the head, and the waisted gowns with full gored skirts worn by the women. These developments were merely embryonic in Edward II's reign, and only reached maturity in the time of Edward III.

In masculine apparel, the **surcote** or **gardcorp**, with sleeves, acted as the outer tunic. That typical hanging sleeve of the latter part of the reign of Henry III (as described previously) was still in vogue until the dawn of the fourteenth century, especially among the middle and professional classes (see p. 66). A more normal sleeve style, however, gradually replaced the hanging type; it reached to just below the elbow, and was fairly wide, showing the long, tight sleeve of the under-tunic to the wrist. In the early fourteenth century it became fashionable to wear a row of small buttons on the outer side of the under-tunic sleeves from elbow to wrist; these buttons facilitated donning the garment, and allowed a closer fitting sleeve to be achieved (see p. 66). In the time of Edward I, the surcote was almost unchanged in cut from that worn in the previous reign

PLANTAGENET, 1272-1327

EDWARD II IN STATE DRESS -
TUNIC, SLIT IN FRONT
OF SKIRT — NARROW
DECORATIVE BORDER -
JEWELLED GIRDLE -
FUR-LINED MANTLE.
DECORATED EDGE -
EMBROIDERED
GLOVES

ELEANOR OF CASTILE
1st QUEEN OF
EDWARD I -
SIMPLE UNGIRDED
GOWN WITH LOOSE
THREE-QUARTER
SLEEVES -UNDER-
GOWN - LONG,
PLAIN MANTLE.
CORDS HELD
ON CHEST

MAN-TEMP. EDWARD I
SURCOTE DECORATED
BY WHITE LINED
DESIGN ON
ALTERNATING
BANDS OF
ORANGE & GREY-
UNDER-TUNIC
GREY
HOSE - BLACK
ANKLE BOOTS

LADY — TEMP. EDWARD I
c. 1300. SURCOTE OR
CYCLAS WITH TRAIN, ON TOP
OF UNDERGOWN. -
GORGET.

(see p. 64). In the early fourteenth century, although the surcote was still ungirded, it became more waisted, and the shorter, calf-length style was more popular. The vogue for counter-change designs on garments, which reached a peak in the late fourteenth century, then first took a hold on the styles of the day. This method of decoration was applied to the tunic, hood, hose, and shoes, and later also to women's gowns. The dividing-line was usually vertical, though "quarterly" parti-colouring was later very modish, wherein two or four colours were used, divided in quarters by a horizontal and a vertical line. In the latter part of Edward II's time, this vogue was normally confined to two colours, on the hood and surcote. A common feature was a fur lining to the surcote, and/or under-tunic. Rich, heavy materials were employed for these garments during the whole period concerned in this chapter, though embroidered decoration was rarely used.

The **mantle** was still reserved for formal wear or for travelling; for other occasions the surcote sufficed. The mantle was circular or semicircular in shape; for travelling, a hood was attached to the everyday version. The formal mantle for full-dress wear was fashioned from rich cloth, velvet, or silk; fur linings were still popular, though a contrasting coloured silk one might also be used. This garment was very long and full. Cord or brooch fastenings were still used (see p. 64).

Masculine **hair-styles** were very similar to those of Henry III's reign. Small curly beards and moustaches were grown by some men, especially the older ones; others were clean-shaven (see p. 68).

The **hood** was, at this time, the most typical head-covering. As yet the actual style was unaltered, but the beginnings of all the peculiar variations in this article of apparel which were to be made during the fourteenth and fifteenth centuries were now to be seen. In the reign of Edward I the *liripipe* appeared. This was actually an elongation of the small point which had been part of the top of the hood since before Henry II's day, so forming a long tubular piece of material, often stuffed, which hung down the back. During the reign of Edward I this appendage reached a length of some two or three feet, but by 1327 it was often five or six feet long when worn by fashionable gentlemen; it was then usual to hold the end in the hand, or allow it to fall over the left arm (see p. 66). The **coif** was still worn, either alone or under a hat or cap. **Hats** were in several styles, either with or without a brim, with round crowns, and usually made from felt, velvet, cloth, or wool. Fur trimmings were popular.

Masculine **underwear** was still virtually the same as it had been in the reign of the first Plantagenet king. **Hose,** reaching mid-thigh-level, and attached there by strings to the waist-belt of the braies, was now fitting to the leg, particularly when worn by the upper classes.

Shoes were still fitted to the natural shape of the foot, but pointed toes were becoming fashionable. Fur edges and fur linings were in vogue; embroidery often decorated the nobleman's shoe. Laces or buttons were used as fastenings. In the reign of Edward II the shoe normally reached the ankle, where it was buttoned; an opening showed on the instep (see p. 68). Short boots, from ankle to mid-calf height, were seen all through the period. These also had pointed toes, and were buttoned or buckled round the leg with an opening on the instep (see p. 64).

PLANTAGENET, 1272-1327

C. 1310
HOOD WITH
LIRIPIPE -
SURCOTE - SLIT IN
SKIRT - BUTTONS
ON SLEEVE OF
UNDER-
TUNIC

LADY - TEMP. EDWARD II
SURCOTE WITH ELBOW LENGTH
SLEEVES - UNDERGOWN
HAS BUTTONS ON SLEEVES
FROM ELBOW TO WRIST -
CRISPINE AND
FILLET

MAN - TEMP.
EDWARD I -
WOOLLEN CAP -
SURCOTE WITH LONG
HANGING SLEEVES

LADY - TEMP. EDWARD II
WIMPLE AND VEIL -
SURCOTE WITH THREE -
QUARTER SLEEVES -
UNDERGOWN -
MANTLE

PLATE II

An early style of Cotehardie, and heavy plaque Hip-girdle can
be seen under the mantle on the right-hand figure

*Edward III and David II of Scotland, 1357.
From an Illuminated MS. in the British Museum*

By the time of Edward I, the feminine version of the **surcote** or **cyclas** had developed, in many cases, into an overgown with wide three-quarter-length sleeves. No **girdle** was worn. The material clung to the figure down to the breast-line, then hung in many attractive folds to the ground. Indeed, the gown was so long that it swept the floor at the back and ladies formed the habit of holding up the fabric on one side, thus producing additional lines of drapery. The gown had a plain round neck, and was often completely un-decorated. The undergown was visible on the lower arm and at the hem, from where the gown was lifted (see p. 64). The sleeveless surcote or cyclas, with the wide, deep armhole, was still worn. The same styles continued through the reign of Edward II with minor alterations: namely, the neck-line was lower and became very wide to the edges of the shoulders; the gown now fitted closely to the hips; sleeves were narrower and elbow-length, the undergown sleeves were buttoned from elbow to wrist in the same way as the masculine under-tunic, and a row of buttons sometimes ornamented the top of the centre front of the gown (see p. 66).

The feminine style of **mantle** underwent virtually no change in the reigns of Edward I and Edward II (see pp. 64 and 66).

The distinctive method of dressing the **hair** of this period was to coil the plaits in a circular fashion on each ear, forming what we would term, in the twentieth century, "ear-phones". This style was evolved early in Edward I's time and remained in vogue until after the death of Edward II (see pp. 66 and 68). However, members of the royal family were often depicted—especially in sculpture—with loose, flowing tresses under a crown (see pp. 64 and 68).

A **crispine**, made of gold, silver, or coloured silk cord, frequently studded with jewels, was still in the height of fashion. It was attached to a metal fillet, as in the Henry III period, and either covered the whole coiffure, or was worn in two parts which only encased the coiled plaits on the ears (see pp. 66 and 68). The **wimple** was, undoubtedly, the most popular head-covering during this period; it was often worn alone, so leaving the hair above the coiled plaits uncovered. When worn in this manner, it was referred to as a *gorget*. The lower edge of the material was then commonly tucked into the neck-line of the gown (see pp. 64 and 68). Out-of-doors, a veil would usually be worn on top, as previously (see p. 66). In the reign of Edward II, the coiled plaits on the ears were often padded in order to make them stand out farther from the head, consequently the gorget or wimple which covered them also projected from the sides of the face (see p. 68). A narrow edition of the **barbette** and **coif** was worn as an alternative to the wimple; it was usually superimposed on a crispine.

After freedom from tight lacing since the middle of the twelfth century, the early beginnings of that striving after a slender waist—seen at its height in the Tudor and Georgian eras—are found in the reign of Edward II. Once again the gown styles were more fitting on the waist and hips and, in consequence, ladies wished to display their figures to advantage. At this time, however, the tight lacing was still in a mild form.

Fabrics in use, **decoration,** and styles of **jewellery** had altered little since the time of Henry III, except that there was perhaps even less ornamentation on garments than before. Borders to tunics, gowns, and mantles were sometimes seen but, on the whole, most garments appeared to be undecorated, except

6

PLANTAGENET, 1272-1327

Edward I

Edward II

Margaret of France
2nd queen of Edward I

Temp. Edward II -
crispine and narrow
barbette and coif

Gold brooch -
set with rubies
and sapphires

Gold signet
ring - sapphire
centre

White gorget

Inscribed gold brooch

Gold brooch

Wimple,
veil and
crispine

Shoe - temp. Edward II

Feminine coiffure -
temp. Edward II - plaits
coiled on the ears -
crispine

Woman's shoe

for those worn on formal State occasions. Illustrations of jewellery can be seen on p. 68.

EDWARD III   1327–1377
RICHARD II   1377–1399

After the first twenty-five years, the fourteenth century was one of striking changes in costume. Revolutionary ideas were introduced; indeed, in the reign of Edward III the whole silhouette was transformed. For centuries previously dress, though subjected to many variations, had always been fundamentally in the form of loose, flowing draperies never held to the body by more than a girdle, then suddenly—so it appears to the casual observer—in 1327 the garment was made to fit the figure closely and well: tailoring had begun. Actually the transformation was not so rapid as it seems to one who merely compares the fashions of Edward III's time to those of his predecessors. As already mentioned, the latter part of Edward II's reign saw the prototypes of the new styles, and even in the time of Henry III inklings of the change to come were discernible. Nevertheless, what had been merely a minor movement was so greatly accelerated with the advent of Edward III that a modicum of surprise is felt. Many of these innovations came from France, Spain, and Bohemia. England had close connections with the Continent, by royal marriages, wars, and commerce.

The new fashions which became speedily adopted as the accepted custom of the fourteenth century soon after the accession of Edward III were colourful and lively. Counterchange patterns were all the vogue for hoods, mantles, tunics, and hose, either in undecorated bright colours worn parti-coloured, half or quarterly, or in actual designs, counterchanged on the other half of the garment. Heraldic motifs enjoyed an immense popularity: sometimes a mantle or a tunic would be emblazoned on one half with an enormous heraldic lion whilst the other half might have smaller heraldic insignia in different colours, or, alternatively, the same design would be counterchanged. Monograms and initials were also the mode, particularly in the last quarter of the century. Many varieties of geometrical and floral designs patterned all over the material were used; these also were often counterchanged, or occupied only one half or quarter of the garment. Brilliant colours, costly materials, fur, fur linings and edgings and jewelled embroideries were all the rage, culminating in the extravagant displays under the fashionable, but foppish, King Richard II. The simplicity and unpretentiousness of the time of Henry III and Edward I had vanished completely.

Once the new styles had become customary wear by 1330–1340, they remained fairly static during Edward III's reign, merely becoming a little more extreme in their brevity, colours, and designs, but the last quarter of the century under Richard II, with the adaptation of yet newer ideas brought by his wife, Queen Anne, from Bohemia, witnessed excesses in all styles. The brevity and close fit of garments became accentuated, whilst contemporarily there was introduced the voluminous houppelande, fashioned from expensive material which swept the ground at hem and sleeve.

The fourteenth century was an era of dagged edges. This strange method of decorating a garment by cutting its edges into various jagged shapes began—as already noted—in the time of Henry II. As a means of ornamentation it was used intermittently until the reign of Edward III, when it became, by 1360, not just a decorative edge, but one of the major features of masculine attire. Except for the hose, no external garment escaped the dagges. The shoulder cape, the hood, the tunic hem, the tippets, and the mantle edge all received attention with dagges varying from simple V-shaped cuts to complicated leaf shapes, or imitation torn leather designs. This peculiar feature was not, however, found to any extent in women's garments during the fourteenth century, partly owing to the different design of their dress, and the vogue for fur edges. With the rise of the houppelande in the last decade of the century, dagges became, nevertheless, a feminine mode also.

The fitted gowns of the period added to the dictates of feminine vanity inevitably brought about the use of the corset. Perhaps it was as well that the ladies of 1330 did not realise that their modest corseting would become more and more acute, resulting finally in the extremities of the Elizabethan, Hanoverian, and Victorian ages, with but short relaxation between times with Cromwellian and Empire dress. It was a subjugation that only ended finally in the twentieth century, and who can say what will be in store in the twenty-first? Yet, fortunately, it is unlikely that in these days of the emancipation of women a return of such metal cages is probable; after all, who would care to enter a rush-hour tube train in a farthingale?

The surcote for masculine wear had, in 1327, become a thing of the past. The outer tunic was now a brief-fitting garment known as the *cotehardie*, distinguished from any previous style of tunic by several distinctive features. It had a round neck and was fastened by a row of buttons from neck to hem down the centre front; the sleeves were very tight-fitting, and also had a row of buttons fastening them on the underside of the arm, from elbow to wrist; the **belt** was worn at hip-level, and was a distinctive feature in itself, being composed either of leather with attached jewelled, metal plaques, or of the metal plaques only, round-, square-, or diamond-shaped, linked together, the central one often being larger than the others. The cotehardie was much shorter than any previous tunic style, being worn, in 1327, with the hem half-way up the thighs (see p. 75). It remained the fashionable tunic for men throughout the century, with its characteristics becoming more notable and extreme as time passed. By 1360 it left almost all the thigh exposed, and by 1380 the hem-line was on the hips (see pp. 73 and 75). The jewelled metal hip-belt was in vogue during the whole century, but in Richard II's reign the cotehardie was so short that men often reverted to a jewelled metal waist-belt as an alternative. The hip-belt was deeper and heavier than the waist-belt, reaching its maximum size and extravagance about 1370 (see pp. 71, 75, and 77). Sleeves also altered during the period: by 1345–1350 the cotehardie sleeve only reached to the elbow, where it was finished by a cuff or band which then fell for three or four feet in a streamer about two or three inches wide. These streamers were known as *tippets*. At first they were plain and white; later, especially from 1360 to 1380, they were longer, coloured like the garment, lined with a different colour, and often dagged into leaf shapes, or to imitate torn leather (see pp. 71 and 73). The mode declined rapidly after 1380, and new varieties of sleeve appeared: a fitting, long sleeve was worn, without tippets or buttons, or a wide, long sleeve, very broad at the wrist, with a turned-back cuff, often of fur. A further

PLANTAGENET, 1327-1399

EDWARD III
IN STATE DRESS -
COLOURED MANTLE
AND TUNIC -
GOLD EMBROIDERED
EDGES.

PHILIPPA - QUEEN OF EDWARD III
COTEHARDIE - JEWELLED
GIRDLE - EMBROIDERED &
JEWELLED. NECK-BAND &
WRIST-BANDS - ERMINE
LINED MANTLE - LONG CORDS
AND TASSELS - JEWELLED,
GOLD, CYLINDRICAL CAULS
AND CROWN.

c. 1335 - 1345.
COTEHARDIE -
TIPPETS - FITCHETS -
NO GIRDLE -
FILLET ON BROW.

GENTLEMAN OF
FASHION - TEMP,
EDWARD III c.1365.
HOOD AND LIRIPIPE -
PARTICOLOURED SHOULDER
CAPE, COTEHARDIE & HOSE -
JEWELLED GIRDLE - PURSE -
DAGGER - DAGGED EDGES
TO CAPE, COTEHARDIE
AND TIPPETS

71

alternative was known as a *bagpipe* sleeve which was tight at the wrist, and fairly fitting at the armhole, but formed a full loop in between. The two fuller modes attained great popularity (see pp. 77 and 79). The demand for **dagged** hem edges, parti-coloured or counterchange patterns, heraldic, geometrical, or floral designs increased during the century, the vogue for all these being at its height from 1360 to 1400 (see pp. 73, 75, 77, and 79). Gold or silver cloth, velvet, brocade, silks, and jewelled embroidered fabrics were used for the cotehardie, as for other garments, and fur edges and linings were in great demand. Some attempt was made in Edward III's reign to curtail this lavish expenditure on the wardrobes of noblemen, the upper classes, and merchants, but it had little effect. Indeed, there is no doubt that in the fourteenth and fifteenth centuries, as in Tudor and Stuart times, the male—as in nature—was the more gorgeously apparelled of the sexes, in contrast to the position in the nineteenth and twentieth centuries.

The **shoulder cape** was a typical feature of Edward III's time. In earlier times, as already described, the shoulder cape was attached to the hood. This mode continued in vogue in the early part of Edward's reign, but as the method of wearing the hood changed (see the section on headgear) a shoulder cape was still worn on top of the cotehardie independently of a hood. Consequently the actual neck-line of the cotehardie was rarely, if ever, shown in Edward's time. Dagges were again the usual means of decorating the bottom edge, and if the cotehardie was patterned or parti-coloured, the cape would probably receive the same attention (see pp. 71 and 75). In the reign of Richard II the shoulder cape disappeared, and a new style was seen: the cotehardie neck-line was finished by a very high, stand-up collar which terminated under the ears and chin with a circular frill or fur edge, reminiscent of a miniature ruff (see pp. 77 and 79).

The **under-tunic** to the cotehardie copied the latter's accentuated waist and brevity. In 1327 it was not visible under the cotehardie, but later, when the sleeves of the upper garment only reached the elbow, the under-tunic sleeves were seen from the elbow to the first row of knuckles of the hand. This partial covering of the hand was a characteristic feature of this long sleeve throughout the century. These sleeves were buttoned on the forearm in order to achieve a perfect fit (see pp. 73 and 75). The under-tunic was known by various names during the fourteenth and fifteenth centuries. In 1327 it was most often referred to as a *gipon* or *jupon*, whilst later, towards the end of Edward III's reign, it was known as a *paltock*. The character of the garment also changed during the period. In 1327 it was merely an under-tunic, very similar to the cotehardie in style: buttons or laces fastened it down the centre front, the length was always just a little less than that of the cotehardie, and the neck low and round. Like the cotehardie it became shorter, so that by Richard II's reign it was barely hip-length. At this time the under-tunic was also padded at the chest to accentuate the small waist, and acquired, like the cotehardie, a high collar. By about 1350–1360 the gipon was first used to support the hose, in place of the braies which had performed this function since early Plantagenet times. A row of eyelet-holes was made in the bottom edge of the gipon, and similarly along the top edges of the hose, then the two were laced together on the hips. In Richard's reign, when the paltock was very brief, the hose had developed into tights,

TEMP. EDWARD III –
MANTLE FASTENED BY
BUTTONS ON SHOULDER –
DAGGED HEM –
COTEHARDIE – JEWELLED
GIRDLE – DAGGED HEM

TEMP. EDWARD III –
VELVET SIDELESS SURCOTE –
TRIMMED WITH FUR –
SILK COTEHARDIE –
WITH JEWELLED HIP
-GIRDLE – GOLD,
CYLINDRICAL
JEWELLED CAULS

LADY - TEMP –
EDWARD III –
PARTICOLOURED
COTEHARDIE –
TIPPETS - HIP-GIRDLE

COTEHARDIE WITH HERALDIC
COUNTERCHANGE DESIGN
TEMP. EDWARD III –
TIPPETS – JEWELLED METAL
GIRDLE – UNDERTUNIC –
BUTTONS ON SLEEVE –
HOOD AND LIRIPIPE –
HOSE POINTED TOES

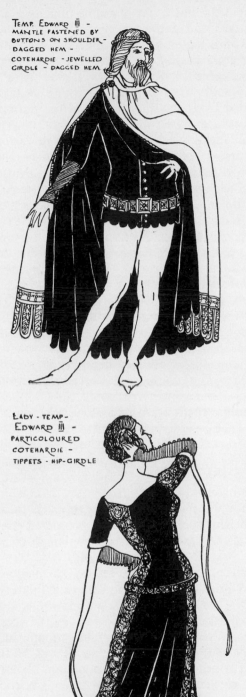

and were laced to the paltock all round the body. At the same time also, this lacing method was often used to attach the sleeves of the paltock to their armholes. The eyelet-holes and laces with tag-ends were known as *points*.

The second major development in dress during the fourteenth century was the advent of the *houppelande* in the reign of Richard II. It was worn in Germany and Spain prior to its introduction into England. Striking contrasts in fashionable masculine dress resulted from the appearance of the houppelande: the extremely brief-waisted cotehardie vied with the long, voluminous houppelande, both styles enjoying an equal popularity. There were various types of houppelande, but several features were common to all the modes: they were all very full; a jewelled metal or leather belt encircled the waist, creating there many folds of material; the same high collar as that of the cotehardie was worn; sleeves were normal in width at the armhole but terminated in very wide edges at the wrists, the ends often sweeping the ground; costly, rich materials were employed, chiefly velvet or silk, with a leaning towards the same heraldic, monogrammatic, floral, or geometric designs as the cotehardie, but on a larger scale. The designs were sometimes printed on in gold or silver. Fur linings were highly popular. The length of the garment varied: it reached either mid-calf- or ground-level; in the latter case, the fabric often swept the floor at the back. The houppelande was, in many cases, buttoned from collar to hem down the centre front, but if one of the unbuttoned styles was worn, the skirt would probably be slit up one or both sides from hem- to hip-level. Complicated designs in dagges were immensely popular; they ornamented the sleeve edges, the hem, and the side-slits. The houppelande served as an outer garment for both indoor and outdoor wear, with the cotehardie normally underneath (see pp. 75 and 79). Specific types of ornament were connected with the wearing of the houppelande: the most typical of these was a gold or silver **chain** worn round the neck, to set off the high collar. Attached to the chain, which was frequently set with jewels, would probably be an ornamental small **dagger,** also jewelled. Again, a further means of ornamentation was the *baldric,* a circular band of ribbon or material about three inches wide which hung round the body on top of the houppelande from the left shoulder to the right hip. The baldric was generally brightly coloured, with embroidered edges and small gold or silver bells frequently hung from the complete length of the outer edge (see p. 75).

Two fine examples of the **houppelande** can be seen in Plate III, which is a reproduction of a portion of the Wilton Diptych. The kneeling figure of Richard II is clad in a scarlet houppelande embroidered all over with a gold design, and having a fur lining, the edges of which can be seen at the collar and wrists. The left-hand standing figure is wearing a blue houppelande embroidered in gold with an all-over pattern; the long blue sleeves of the cotehardie can be seen at the wrists. The other coloured reproduction, Plate II, shows Edward III clad in a fairly long **cotehardie** of the earlier style. A portion of the jewelled plaque girdle can be seen on the hips. The shoes of that period are clearly represented here, too, with the instep straps, low fronts, and pointed toes.

The cloak or **mantle** was fastened on the shoulder by three or four buttons in the fourteenth century. It was ankle-length, the hem often being dagged,

PLANTAGENET, 1327-1399

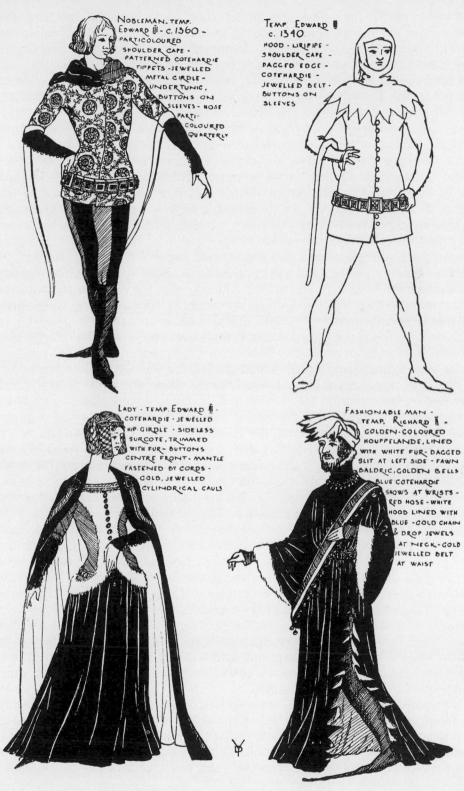

NOBLEMAN. TEMP. EDWARD III - c.1360 - PARTICOLOURED SHOULDER CAPE - PATTERNED COTEHARDIE TIPPETS - JEWELLED METAL GIRDLE - UNDER TUNIC, BUTTONS ON SLEEVES - HOSE PARTI- COLOURED QUARTERLY

TEMP. EDWARD III c. 1340 HOOD - LIRIPIPE - SHOULDER CAPE - DAGGED EDGE - COTEHARDIE - JEWELLED BELT - BUTTONS ON SLEEVES

LADY - TEMP. EDWARD III - COTEHARDIE - JEWELLED HIP-GIRDLE - SIDELESS SURCOTE, TRIMMED WITH FUR - BUTTONS CENTRE FRONT - MANTLE FASTENED BY CORDS - GOLD, JEWELLED CYLINDRICAL CAULS

FASHIONABLE MAN - TEMP. RICHARD II - GOLDEN-COLOURED HOUPPELANDE, LINED WITH WHITE FUR - DAGGED SLIT AT LEFT SIDE - FAWN BALDRIC, GOLDEN BELLS BLUE COTEHARDIE SHOWS AT WRISTS - RED HOSE - WHITE HOOD LINED WITH BLUE - GOLD CHAIN & DROP JEWELS AT NECK - GOLD JEWELLED BELT AT WAIST

75

and was popularly flung back over the left shoulder to leave the right arm free
and expose the mantle lining of costly material or fur. A hood might be
attached (see p. 73). The wearing of a mantle, except on State occasions, became
superfluous with the advent of the houppelande in Richard II's time.

Masculine underwear still consisted of a **shirt** and **braies,** but the style of
the latter, like the gipon, was altering slowly during the fourteenth century.
As the hose had lengthened, the braies had correspondingly shortened, thus
when the gipon began to be used to support the hose in the mid-fourteenth
century, the braies became abbreviated to mere trunks.

The construction of the **hose** also changed considerably in this period, from
about mid-century: the legs of the hose were still separate, but they reached
the hips and fitted closely into the fork, being laced at several points to the
gipon, as already described. In Richard II's reign the two legs finally united
at the top to become "tights", reaching hip-level where points attached them
all round the body to the lower edge of the paltock. It was at this time that
the *cod-piece* was introduced; this was a small bag which covered the front of
the fork between the legs, and was attached to the hose by points. Throughout
the century the hose were immaculately fitting, with the foot and leg portions
in one piece. In common with other garments the hose were frequently parti-
coloured throughout the fourteenth century, either in halves or quarters, or
perhaps with the two legs in different colours (see pp. 71 and 75). Partly as a
result of this fashion, and partly because of the long toes to the foot portion,
shoes were seldom worn in the second half of the century. Soles were added
to the hose under the foot, and wooden clog soles, known as *pattens*, were
attached by leather straps for outdoor wear. The hose were made from velvet,
silk, wool, or cloth, and in the second half of the century a jewelled garter
encircled the leg below the knee, in a purely ornamental capacity. The length
of the footwear varied considerably during the century. A small point beyond
the toe was normal in 1327, but a few years before the mid-century the point
began to lengthen. This material beyond the end of the toe tapered to its point,
and was stuffed with tow or hair. By 1360 the nobleman's footwear had reached
six inches or more beyond the toe (see p. 71); a diminution in length then took
place for a few years, but a final peak of the fashion was reached when noblemen
in Richard II's reign wore footwear twelve to sixteen inches beyond the toe
(see pp. 75 and 79). These points became so unwieldy that one reads of the
use of gold chains to attach them to the garter below the knee to enable the
wearer to walk; however, there is no evidence of this style in the illuminations
to the manuscripts of British costume. The fashion is reputed to have been
introduced by Queen Anne and her people from Bohemia: consequently the
styles were known as *crackowes*, after the Polish city of Cracow (see p. 81).
Shoes, when worn, were of equivalent length and shape to the hose foot portion.
They were made of velvet, cloth, or leather, and normally had an instep strap
and were cut low in front (see p. 81).

Masculine **hair-styles** in 1327 were still fairly short. The hair was usually
parted in the centre, and was waved to just below the ears, where it terminated
in a long curl. Apart from a tendency towards looser, more natural waves and
curls, this style remained in vogue till Richard's time. Then greater attention
was paid to the coiffure, as indeed to the whole toilet, and the hair was carefully

PLANTAGENET, 1327-1399

RICHARD II IN STATE DRESS·
RED VELVET MANTLE
LINED WITH ERMINE -
ERMINE SHOULDER CAPE·
GOLD, JEWELLED NECKLACE
AND PENDANT — RICH BLUE
DALMATIC WITH GOLD DESIGN
AND BORDER - GOLD
SHOES - RED HOSE -
GOLD, JEWELLED
CROWN.

ANNE OF BOHEMIA -
1ST QUEEN OF RICHARD II
COTEHARDIE ·GIRDLE
ON HIPS - BUTTONS
CENTRE FRONT -
MANTLE.

GENTLEMAN-TEMP.
RICHARD II - COUNTER-
CHANGE, TRELLIS-PATTERNED
COTEHARDIE IN LIGHT &
DARK BLUE -GOLD DAGGER·
JEWELLED GIRDLE -
PEARL GREY HOSE

FEMININE HOUPPELANDE-
c.1398-
FUR COLLAR-
JEWELLED GIRDLE -
LEATHER PURSE -
TURBAN STYLE
HEAD-DRESS

waved, then curled so that it stood out at the sides in a group of curls and was rather shorter than previously. During Edward's reign beards and moustaches had been optional, but in the last two decades of the century they became modish. The moustache was generally in two parts, and the beard small, pointed, and sometimes forked (see p. 81).

The **hood** was still the headgear of the century, but its manner of wearing began to change about 1340. Early in the reign the hood was worn as before 1327 (see pp. 73 and 75). Then this vogue which had lasted for so long gave way to a new style. The opening which had previously been left for the face was now placed on the crown of the head; the rest of the material, including the shoulder cape, was carefully arranged in folds at the front, side, or back of the head, the dagged edges giving it a cockscomb appearance; the **liripipe** then hung as before, or was bound round the head-dress. This new method of wearing the hood remained the height of fashion for the rest of the century (see pp. 71, 75, and 81). Rich materials were used, and contrasting coloured linings which showed in the folds of the material, now on top of the head. Towards the end of Edward's reign, **hats** began to make their appearance once more, though they never superseded the hood as a fashionable head-covering in this century. Sometimes they were worn on top of the hood, sometimes alone. Various shapes were seen, all fairly small and fitting, usually with turned-up or roll brims. Beaver, felt, or velvet was used, with fur, feather, or brooch decoration (see p. 81).

During this period the feminine gown was also known as the **cotehardie,** and had several of the characteristics of the masculine garment. It was waisted and fitting as far as the hips, where the same type of jewelled metal **hip-girdle** was worn; the sleeves were identical with those of the men, having buttons and **tippets,** and showing the under-sleeve on the forearm. Parti-colouring, counter-change designs, heraldic, geometric, and floral motifs were equally popular with women as with men. The neck-line was low and wide, almost off the shoulders. The bodice was buttoned centre front to below the waist, and **fitchets** were placed for the hands in front on the hips (see pp. 71 and 73). The skirt was long, very full and gored from the hips (see pp. 71 and 73). In Richard II's reign tippets declined in fashion, as they did on the masculine cotehardie (see p. 77).

The undergown, worn beneath the cotehardie, was sometimes known as a *kirtle*; it had no girdle and was visible only on the forearm.

About 1330–1340 the old-fashioned cyclas or surcote blossomed forth as the new "*sideless gown*" or "*surcote*", to become the typical feminine mode of the fourteenth century, and early fifteenth century. It was worn on top of the cotehardie, though alternatively the latter was often uncovered during the whole century. The new sideless surcote had altered to some extent from the old cyclas, so that all that remained of the bodice front was a narrow central band of fur which broadened at the neck into two fur shoulder-bands worn, like the cotehardie, nearly off the shoulder. At the lower end, the central band again divided into two strips of fur which edged the "armholes", now reaching to below hip-level. A row of buttons, or a jewelled metal band, ornamented the centre front of the fur bodice. The skirt fell from its edge at the hips in numerous vertical folds to the ground, and was very full and long, generally forming a

PLANTAGENET, 1327-1399

YOUNG MAN - TEMP.
RICHARD II -
SHORT, DARK BLUE
COTEHARDIE, WITH
JEWELLED WAIST-BELT -
BAG-PIPE SLEEVES -
DARK BLUE HOSE

NOBLEMAN - TEMP. RICHARD II -
RED COTEHARDIE WITH GOLD AND
BROWN DESIGN - JEWELLED
WAIST-BELT - ERMINE CUFFS -
PARTICOLOURED HOSE - ONE
LEG BLUE - ONE WHITE -
GOLD, JEWELLED
GARTER - FUR -
TRIMMED HAT.

MAN - TEMP.
RICHARD II -
FUR-LINED
HOUPPELANDE -
JEWELLED WAIST-BELT -
PURSE AND DAGGER -
HOOD WITH DAGGED
EDGE

LADY - TEMP. RICHARD II -
SIDELESS SURCOTE - FUR
FRONT AND EDGES - JEWELLED
BUTTONS - COTEHARDIE -
JEWELLED HIP-GIRDLE - GOLD
FILLET ON BROW

79

train at the back. Side-slits to the hips were sometimes seen. Fur bands were often used to ornament these slits, and the hem. When the sideless gown was worn, the cotehardie was visible on the arms and sides of the bodice as far as the hips, where a portion of the jewelled hip-girdle could be seen. Rich, costly materials were employed for both garments, chiefly velvet, silk, and fur linings (see pp. 73 and 75). In Richard's time, the central fur bodice strip became even narrower, the "armhole" lower, and the skirt even longer (see p. 79). It is amusing to note that whereas it was considered immodest for the ladies of the fourteenth and fifteenth centuries to uncover the arms, yet the gown was extremely *décolleté* judged by modern standards of day dress.

Towards the end of Richard's reign the **houppelande** was worn by women as well as men. At this time the feminine garment was almost the same as the masculine, although some of the similar features were dispensed with in the next century (see p. 77).

The feminine **mantle** had altered little since the thirteenth century, except that it was now worn almost off the shoulders in line with the cotehardie and sideless gown. It was fastened across the chest by long tasselled cords attached to jewelled, embossed, circular brooches on each side of the mantle. The garment was very long, forming a train at the back when worn on formal occasions. Costly materials were used, popularly velvet, with a fur lining, and a jewelled embroidered border (see pp. 71 and 77). A shorter mantle with hood attached was worn for travelling.

In the early years of the reign of Edward III, the feminine **coiffure** was almost unaltered from the early fourteenth-century style. After about 1340, however, it developed somewhat in order to accommodate the head-dress of the time. The plaits were then arranged in vertical, cylindrical shapes on either side of the face, false hair being added to supplement the plaits if the lady's own hair was not sufficiently thick or long. The metal **fillet,** which still encircled the forehead, was then often passed over one set of plaits and under the other to hold them in position against the sides of the head (see pp. 71 and 79). This fillet was usually made of precious metal, and jewelled.

The two main types of head-dress in the fourteenth century still comprised the **wimple** and the **crispine,** sometimes worn with a small transparent **veil.** The wimple—known as the **gorget** when worn alone—was *à la mode* during the whole century, but in the closing years it was more frequently worn by older or less fashionable women. In this century, though, it was commonly pinned under the hair at the sides, not on top as hitherto, and the lower edge was tucked into the gown neck-line (see p. 81). The gold, silver, or coloured net, known previously as the crispine or crespinette, was also in vogue for this century, but its character altered by about 1340–1345. Instead of covering the whole head, or being shaped in two round side-cauls as before, it was fashioned into two vertical cylinders worn on either side of the face. These cylinders were attached to the metal fillet—or crown, if worn—and open at the top so that the coiled plaits could be inserted; the bottom was also often open. These cylindrical cauls, which were made of gold, silver, or other metal mesh, had a solid band at the top and bottom. Expensive patterns had both mesh and bands studded with jewels (see pp. 71, 73, and 75). A small transparent veil was often attached to the back of the head-dress (see p. 81). This type of

PLANTAGENET, 1327-1399

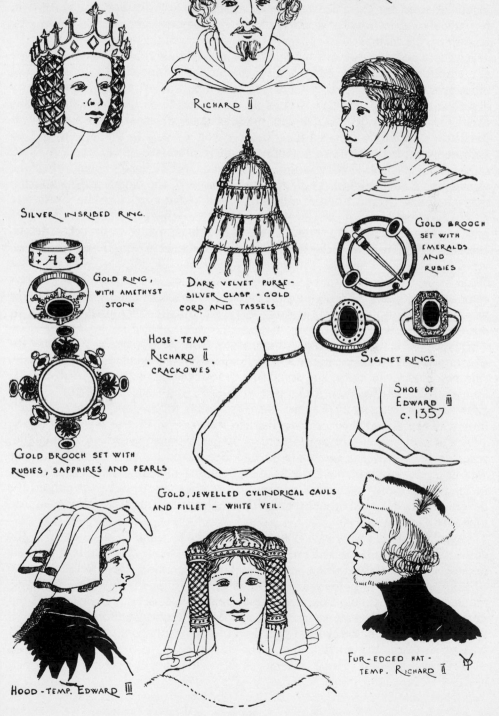

QUEEN PHILIPPA -
GOLD CROWN AND
CYLINDRICAL SIDE CAULS

RICHARD II

LADY. c.1340
JEWELLED, GOLD FILLET ON BROW &
WHITE GORGET.

SILVER INSRIBED RING.

GOLD RING,
WITH AMETHYST
STONE

DARK VELVET PURSE -
SILVER CLASP - GOLD
CORD AND TASSELS

GOLD BROOCH
SET WITH
EMERALDS
AND
RUBIES

SIGNET RINGS

HOSE - TEMP
RICHARD II
. CRACKOWES'

SHOE OF
EDWARD III
c. 1357

GOLD BROOCH SET WITH
RUBIES, SAPPHIRES AND PEARLS

GOLD, JEWELLED CYLINDRICAL CAULS
AND FILLET - WHITE VEIL.

HOOD - TEMP. EDWARD III

FUR - EDGED HAT -
TEMP. RICHARD II

81

head-dress was known by various names: as a **reticulated** head-dress, as jewelled **side-cylinders,** as cylindrical side-**cauls.** A hood was also worn by women for outdoor wear, especially during the later part of the century.

Feminine **footwear** resembled the masculine styles, although the extremes of length affected by the men were never attained. Soft leather shoes, dyed in bright colours, jewelled and embroidered for noblewomen, were fastened by a strap on the instep.

Jewellery and accessories for both sexes had become more numerous in type and elaborate in craftsmanship and design during the fourteenth century. The most typical item of jewellery was the massive hip- or waist-**girdle** (already described) worn by men and women alike. Attached to the masculine girdle, usually on the left side, was a **dagger** made of gold, silver, or other metal, often jewelled. Commonly inserted in a leather **purse** or pouch, the dagger was an accepted part of the attire of a gentleman of fashion (see pp. 77 and 79). This purse might also be jewelled and embroidered. In Richard's reign, when the wearing of a chain round the neck became modish, the dagger might alternatively be hung from it. Ladies also wore a purse hanging from the girdle (see p. 77). Other items of jewellery, in addition to the cylindrical cauls, were massive **rings** set with precious stones, **signet rings,** exquisite **brooches, fillets, coronets,** and **crowns,** and the forementioned **chain necklaces.** These necklaces, worn by both sexes on the houppelande, were usually made of gold or silver chain with drop jewels, or hanging pendants, or crosses (see p. 75). **Garters** were also set with precious stones. Sapphires, rubies, emeralds, pearls, filigree work, enamelling, and carved ivory were all employed in various jewellery designs (see p. 81).

Expensive, rich **fabrics** were still imported during the fourteenth century for Court wear, and for the upper classes. Such materials included velvet, brocade, silk, gold and silver cloth, and some furs. However, in the reign of Edward III an important development took place in the weaving trade in England. Under Edward's auspices many Flemish weavers came to England to set up their looms. They taught their craft to English weavers, so that as a result of their skill and experience, fabrics, particularly wool, were soon woven in England, whereas previously the raw material had been exported to Flanders, and the woven fabric reimported. Indeed, this beginning of really fine cloth-weaving in England not only reduced the importation of materials, but soon caused the development of a new export trade. The majority of furs were also produced at home.

Decorative motifs were varied but, on the whole, small in scale early in the century, becoming large and even enormous by 1360–1370. Heraldic insignia and designs made from initials were typical of this period. These were patterned on a large scale all over the garment—cotehardie, houppelande, sideless surcote, or mantle—in parti-coloured and counterchange forms. Equally popular, but perhaps less known, were geometrical and floral designs, similarly executed. It was a century of patterned and parti-coloured fabrics, contrasting markedly with styles of the thirteenth (see pp. 73, 75, and 77).

PLATE III

Two excellent examples of the Houppelande in red and blue,
patterned in gold

From the Wilton Diptych, c. 1396, *in the National Gallery*

IV

LANCASTER AND YORK

THE HOUSE OF LANCASTER

HENRY IV   1399–1413
HENRY V   1413–1422
HENRY VI   1422–1461

BLOODSHED and upheaval were rife in England during the fifteenth century: the Hundred Years War had much of its disastrous course to run when the century opened, whilst the second half of the century witnessed the civil strife of the Wars of the Roses. The wars, violent changes in monarchy, and unsettled life of the people brought about frequent changes in costume: there was an ever-growing desire to try new styles, which were carried to extremes only to give place to others of a sharply contrasting nature. The French Court had a considerable effect on English fashions, an influence which, to some degree, was reciprocated. Indeed, there was a close connection between the two countries which produced much interchange of ideas despite the fact that the strongest link was warfare. The lead given in dress by the Burgundians during the second half of the century was particularly predominant.

Oil paintings, although still small in number at this time, are yet extant to add to the other sources of information on costume. These assist considerably in enabling us to acquire accurate knowledge when taken in conjunction with the sculpture, tapestries, illuminated manuscripts, etc., on which it was necessary to rely entirely to obtain information of earlier times.

Fabrics in use continued to be rich and costly during the fifteenth century: fur linings and trimmings were still very popular; motifs were essentially large, often one repeat only being possible on the front of a garment; parti-coloured clothes and dagged edges were in great demand in the first quarter of the century, but the fashion for them declined, particularly in masculine wear, after that. Efforts were made once more to stem the rising tide of extravagance in dress by reviving the earlier edict of Edward III against costly furs, jewels, embroideries, and fabrics, but only a temporary effect was achieved.

Masculine dress in the first sixty years of the fifteenth century was divided into two distinct foundational types: the **houppelande,** and the short **tunic.** Both these were equally fashionable, though perhaps older men tended to prefer the former, particularly in its more formal version of mid-fifteenth century. In the time of Henry IV, the houppelande was very similar to that seen in the latter part of the fourteenth century. The gold neck-chain, with a jewelled centre and/or a hip-chain were still in great demand, as also was the silk or leather baldric, with bells attached. Gold and silver bells were indeed even more popular in the early fifteenth century than in the late fourteenth, and they were frequently attached to the waist-belt on gold chains, all round the body. The houppelande was made of velvets, silks, or other rich materials, generally covered with a large pattern, and lined or edged with fur (see p. 85). In the reign of Henry V only small alterations in cut were seen: the high collar gave place to a lower, round neck-line, above which showed the retained high collar of the under-tunic; epaulettes were frequently worn; dagged edges were not so common; bells, suspended on chains to the waist-belt, reached a peak of popularity; bag-sleeves were worn as an alternative to the other sleeves; three-quarter-length and ground-length houppelandes were equally favoured. Apart from these changes in small detail, the garment retained its original form (see p. 87). In Henry VI's reign, a distinct change in the silhouette of this garment evolved gradually, the new style becoming fully established as the accepted mode by mid-fifteenth century. The principal innovations were the pleated, vertical lines of the centre front and back running from neck to hem, and the padded shoulders; these alterations lent a more formal, less voluminous appearance to the houppelande. The lower, round neck-line with the high collar of the under-tunic showing above was still retained, and the belt still at the normal waist-line. The hem was ankle-level, or just cleared the ground. Side-slits were again popular in the skirt. The sleeves were indeed of new design, being cut wide at the top and narrow at the wrist; the upper part was pleated or gathered into the armhole, and was padded there on the outside upper arm. This was the first time shoulder padding had been introduced in costume. The neck, wrist, and hem were popularly trimmed with fur. Large designs were embroidered, woven, or printed all over the garment (see p. 89). From about 1450 to 1460 an alternative method of wearing the girdle was in vogue: it encircled the hips instead of the waist, but both styles are shown in illuminated manuscripts of the time. The short tunic—or cotehardie as it had been termed in the fourteenth century—underwent similar alterations to the houppelande. In Henry IV's reign it also still retained its former characteristics, although the hem-line was much lower than in Richard's time, in fact knee-length was the average wear. As with the houppelande, gold neck-chains, and daggers and purses fastened on the girdle were still in vogue. In the next reign, also in common with the long garment, the neck-line of the tunic was lowered to the pit of the neck, and the under-tunic, with its high collar, showed above. The tunic neck was either round or V-shaped, and usually fur-edged. During the reign of Henry VI there were several styles of tunic. Bagpipe sleeves were still popular early in the reign, the hem-line was still low, either knee- or calf-length, girdles were seen at hip or waist, fur edges to wrists, neck, and hem were increasingly in demand (see pp. 85 and 87). About 1335–1350, the *bag-sleeve* was all the rage: it formed a large bag or pouch which had an opening in front through which the arm was passed. The rest of the bag portion hung down behind the arm, and the tighter, long sleeves of the under-tunic were then visible on the forearm (see p. 89). The wearing of these sleeves by servants was deprecated by their masters, as they provided excellent receptacles for unlawfully acquired household valuables. By 1450–1460, the tunic had reached a similar stage of development to the houppelande. It was pleated centre front and back from neck to hem, sleeves, which were full at the top and narrower at the wrists, were padded at the upper end, and pleated or gathered into the armhole, and the round neck-line predominated, with the under-tunic high collar prominent above. At the same time the tunic had become very brief once more, and by 1460 the skirt portion

HOUSE OF LANCASTER
1399-1461

GENTLEMAN c. 1400-1415 -
GOLDEN VELVET HOUPPELANDE,
LINED WITH WHITE SILK -
GREEN COTEHARDIE SLEEVES -
BLUE BALDRIC - GOLD BELLS -
GOLD NECK-CHAIN & BROOCH
SET WITH RUBIES - GOLD HIP
CHAIN & DAGGER - JEWELLED
GIRDLE

LADY. c. 1435-1440 -
GOLD HORNED, JEWELLED
HEAD-DRESS, (RUBIES) -
WHITE, TRANSPARENT VEIL -
RED HOUPPELANDE WITH
WHITE LACE-EDGED COLLAR
AND GOLD, JEWELLED
BELT.

LADY. TEMP. HENRY IV. -
BLUE COTEHARDIE WITH WHITE
BORDER - APPLE GREEN
UNDERGOWN AND TURBAN -
DARK GREEN MANTLE - RED
LINING - GOLD CORDS AND
TASSELS - WHITE VEIL.

GENTLEMAN OF FASHION
c. 1425 -
BLACK CHAPERON -
DEEP BLUE TUNIC
TRIMMED WITH LIGHT
BROWN FUR - BLACK
AND GOLD WAIST-BELT -
LIGHT BROWN HOSE.

85

was merely a pleated frill on the hips, with the girdle encircling the waist. As with the houppelande, large designs and fur trimmings and linings were the fashion all through Henry VI's reign (see p. 87).

The **paltock**—still the common name for the under-tunic—resembled that of the fourteenth century. From about 1415, when the neck-line of the outer tunic was lowered, the high collar of the paltock was clearly visible above for some two or three inches in depth. The paltock itself was now only waist-length, still attached to the hose by "points", but at waist- instead of hip-level as previously. The sleeves reached to the first row of knuckles early in the century, but were wrist-length after 1420. A shirt and braies, as described in the Edward III period, completed the masculine **underwear**. These were not visible.

By the fifteenth century **hose** had become genuine "tights". Fastened at waist-level by "points" to the paltock, they completely covered the body from there downwards. The **cod-piece,** as described in the previous chapter, was still used. The length of the foot portion of the hose varied considerably in the fifteenth century. It will be remembered that the peak of the fashion of long-pointed toes to the footwear and hose was reached at the end of the fourteenth century. After this, this fashion declined rapidly, footwear being almost normal in length during the latter part of Henry IV's reign, and during that of Henry V. Early in Henry VI's time greater lengths again came in, reaching a climax of fashion between about mid-century and the end of the reign. Often **shoes** were still not worn, soled hose sufficing for indoors, with **pattens** or wooden or cork clogs attached by leather straps, and known as *poulaines*, for outdoors (see p. 91). Shoes, when worn, were of a similar length to the hose foot portion. The chief styles were cut high on the instep and at the back, and were without fastening; leather, velvet, and cloth were used for manufacture, with embroidery and/or fur linings and edges (see p. 91).

Mantles and **cloaks** were styled as in the fourteenth century, but were seldom worn in the fifteenth century, except for State and formal occasions; the houppelande obviated the need for them.

The outstanding feature of the masculine **hair-styles** of this period was brevity. Early in the fifteenth century the hair was cut simply, fairly short, loosely curled at the sides and back, and usually parted in the centre. This mode gradually gave place to the typical Henry VI cut, a most unattractive style: the hair was curled under all round the head, with no parting, and was very short, being above ear-level. The back and side hair was then shaved up to the hair-line (see pp. 89 and 91). Most men were clean-shaven during the whole period.

The **hood** remained the chief head-covering for men during this time. In the reigns of Henry IV and Henry V it was worn in the same manner as that popular during the fourteenth century (see pp. 87 and 91). Indeed, by 1422, it had been worn in that manner for nearly a hundred years. At the time of the accession of Henry VI, however, the hood entered upon its final phase and use as the most fashionable head-covering of the day. The new version was more formalised and static. During the previous century the hood had to be rearranged in its appropriate folds every time it was donned, an operation requiring time and patience. At last, in the 1420s, the idea was conceived to make the hood

HOUSE OF LANCASTER
1399-1461

GENTLEMAN TEMP. HENRY VI.
CRIMSON VELVET TUNIC WITH
GOLD CIRCLE DESIGN -
BLACK AND GOLD HIP-
-GIRDLE - PALE GREY FUR
TRIMMING - BROWN UNDER
-TUNIC SHOWS AT NECK -
BROWN HAT - GREY FUR
TRIMMING OVER
SKULL CAP - RED
HOSE - BLACK
SHOES.

LADY OF RANK - TEMP. HENRY V.
CRIMSON VELVET SIDELESS
SURCOTE, TRIMMED WITH WHITE
FUR - JEWELLED BUTTONS -
VERMILION COTEHARDIE -
JEWELLED HIP-GIRDLE -
RETICULATED HEAD DRESS
AND VEIL.

NOBLEMAN TEMP. HENRY V.
HOUPPELANDE IN DULL RED
VELVET - DULL PINK HOOD -
GREEN PALTOCK SHOWS AT
NECK - JEWELLED GIRDLE
WITH GOLD BELLS AND CHAINS.

GENTLEMAN. c. 1455.
BLUE CHAPERON - BROOCH
DECORATION - TUNIC, GREY
AND RED DESIGN - PALE
BLUE PALTOCK - BLUE HOSE -
BLACK SHOES.

portion into a padded tyre which was placed squarely on the head; this was known as the *roundlet*. The material which had previously formed the shoulder cape was attached to the inside of the roundlet, and was draped over it in becoming folds; the **liripipe** was then attached to the opposite side. The liripipe also had changed in form; it was no longer stuffed, but consisted of a double thickness of material, two or three inches wide and five or six feet in length, which hung down to be held in the hand, tucked in the girdle, or twisted round the roundlet or the neck. The whole hood was often referred to as a *chaperon* (see pp. 85 and 87). During the reign of Henry VI the chaperon, when not in use, was typically slung over the shoulder, where it hung down the back suspended by the liripipe, the other end being held in the hand or tucked in the belt (see p. 89).

Various styles of **hats** began to appear about 1430, and were worn as alternatives to the chaperon. Fur brims and feather decorations were popular (see pp. 87 and 91).

Although the chief style of feminine gown in this period was based on the houppelande, the **cotehardie**, with or without a sideless gown on top, was still worn by many women in the reigns of Henry IV and Henry V, whilst for formal or State occasions, it lasted till about 1450. The cotehardie was similar to that worn in the previous century; ladies often held up the skirt material at one side to accentuate its beauty of line. Sleeves were still long, reaching to the first row of knuckles at first, later to the wrist only, and were tight-fitting (see pp. 85 and 87).

Worn in conjunction with the cotehardie, the **sideless gown** or **surcote** remained in fashion for the same period. Apart from the fact that the front strip of fur was even narrower than before, it was identical in style to that of the end of the fourteenth century (see p. 87).

The most popular gown of the period was based on the houppelande; in fact, for the first half of the century it was known as a **houppelande.** As described earlier, the feminine houppelande worn about 1390 had a high collar like the masculine pattern. In the fifteenth century the neck-line was the chief distinction between the masculine and feminine styles. The ladies' garment, at first, had a small V-shaped neck, finished by a large square collar, otherwise it closely resembled the men's wear. The extremely wide sleeves with dagged edges, the voluminous long skirt, and the large all-over patterns on rich materials, were all the same, except that the jewelled girdle was worn high, almost under the breasts (see p. 89). As the century proceeded, the feminine neck-line became lower and lower; by about 1335–1340 it was still V-shaped with a large collar, often lace-edged, but the point of the V was quite *décolleté*. At this time the sleeves also were changing from the very wide type to a rather less full style, whilst dagged edges had gone out of fashion (see p. 85). This evolution continued until, by 1450–1460, the garment had altered considerably, and was then referred to as a gown: the low V-neck reached the high waist-line at centre front and back, it was tight-fitting at the bodice and sleeves, though the skirt was still full and very long, especially at the back, but more fitting on the hips, and so did not cause the numerous folds where the girdle was drawn tight. Fur trimmings were usual at the neck-line, wrists, and hem; all-over designs with large repeats were the vogue; and either the undergown

HOUSE OF LANCASTER
1399-1461

MAN WEARING MID-C15 STYLE OF PATTERNED HOUPPELANDE - FUR-TRIMMED AT NECK, HEM, WRISTS & SIDE-SLIT - LEATHER WAIST-BELT AND PURSE - UNDER-TUNIC SHOWS AT NECK - CHAPERON, AND LIRIPIPE.

LADY. c. 1455-1460.
GOLD STEEPLE HENNIN COVERED WITH WHITE, TRANSPARENT VEIL - GOLDEN BROWN GOWN WITH GREEN DESIGN - GREEN BELT - WHITE FUR TRIMMINGS - WHITE UNDERGOWN SHOWS AT NECK.

LADY. c. 1440-1445
PATTERNED HOUPPELANDE - PLAIN COLLAR - JEWELLED GIRDLE - DAGGED EDGES TO SLEEVES - HEART-SHAPED HEAD-DRESS WITH LIRIPIPE AND JEWELLED CAUL - BROOCH CENTRE FRONT.

MAN TEMP. HENRY VI
DARK GREEN TUNIC WITH BAG SLEEVES - CRIMSON UNDER-TUNIC SHOWING AT SLEEVES AND NECK - CRIMSON HOSE - GREEN CHAPERON

or a piece of material acted as a "modesty bit" at the low neck in front (see p. 89).

Like the men, ladies did not often wear a **mantle** or **cloak** in this period—the houppelande sufficed. However, a mantle was worn over the sideless gown or cotehardie for outdoors, travelling, and on formal occasions. Like the cotehardie, it was worn partly off the shoulders, but otherwise was unaltered from the styles worn in the fourteenth century (see p. 85).

The varied selection of incredible head-dresses worn by the ladies of the fifteenth century have been the target for the wit, sarcasm, and reprobation of writers both of the time and of today. Nevertheless, many of these creations, though absurd and impractical, were artistically attractive and interesting. Variety, extremity, originality, and the complete envelopment of all the hair, were the keynotes of these designs, of which there were, broadly speaking, four main types: the *reticulated*, the **turban,** the **heart-shaped,** and the *hennin*. Some of these styles were more particularly favoured in certain periods in the century, others were fashionable almost all the time, and acted as alternative wear. All the styles were seen in many and varied guises. The reticulated head-dress, where all or part of the hair was encased in a metal mesh, had been in constant use since the days of Henry III, with many variations of shape, wearing, and appellation (see earlier references). In the first half of the fifteenth century the latest way of wearing these nets was introduced. The nets were still in two parts, worn over the ears and attached to a metal fillet or crown which encircled the brow, but with the coming of the fifteenth century the shape of these two side-cauls changed from their previous cylindrical form to squarer, more box-like creations. These became larger and wider during the reigns of Henry IV and Henry V, reaching an incredible climax of width about 1430–1440. To add to the impracticability and absurdity of this erection, a wired veil, commonly forming a horned or pointed shape on each side of the head, was superimposed (see pp. 87 and 91). The main trend at this time (about 1435) was to achieve great width in the design; it was later in the century that height was the aim instead. After mid-century, this type of reticulated head-dress was gradually superseded by other modes, though a rounder caul with a horned veil, or a horned caul with veil superimposed, were in vogue about 1450 (see pp. 85 and 91). The turban enjoyed some popularity in the first years of the century, but its greatest vogue was immediately following the fall of Constantinople in 1453, when the Eastern influence was strong. The turban, of various sizes, was a padded roll of velvet, silk, or cloth, usually decorated by pearl ropes, brooches, or plumes, and, in common with all other head-dresses of the day, was surmounted by, or superimposed upon, a veil. Alternatively, this veil was sometimes wound under the chin, in a similar manner to the earlier barbette (see p. 85). The third type of head-dress, the heart-shaped pattern, though popular for a long time, was more specifically the style of Henry VI's reign, ousting, to some extent, the reticulated head-dress. In this newer mode, the jewelled metal cauls were still worn underneath, but they were now more pliable nets of a rounded shape covering a larger part of the hair, and not protruding at the sides. On top of these was worn a padded roll of material, velvet, silk, or other rich fabric, which was shaped to dip in the centre front and back, but rise at the sides. A jewelled brooch usually ornamented the

HOUSE OF LANCASTER
1399-1461

RETICULATED HEAD-DRESS WITH WIRED VEIL — TEMP. HENRY V

PALE BUFF HAT WITH BLUE BRIM — TEMP. HENRY V OR VI

STEEPLE HENNIN AND WIRED VEIL — c. 1455-1460

MASCULINE HAIR-STYLE — TEMP. HENRY VI

WOODEN PATTEN — LEATHER STRAPS

SHOE — EMBROIDERED IN GOLD.

SAPPHIRE AND PEARL, GOLD BROOCH.

HORNED, WIRED VEIL OVER GOLD, JEWELLED CAUL — MID-FIFTEENTH CENTURY.

GOLD, PECTORAL CROSS SET WITH PEARLS

VELVET PURSE WITH TASSELS.

GOLD RING, SET WITH DIAMOND & RUBIES

GOLD RING WITH AMETHYST

HEART-SHAPED HEAD-DRESS — BROOCH AND JEWELS, OVER GOLD AND JEWELLED CAUL — VEIL ON TOP.

SILVER GILT RING.

HOOD — TEMP. HENRY IV

centre front of the roll, whilst other jewels and ropes of pearls encircled it.
A veil was normally superimposed on the head-dress, and, about mid-century,
ladies often appropriated the liripipe style of the men, wearing it attached to
the back of their head-dresses (see pp. 89 and 91). The last of the chief types of
head-covering worn until 1461—the hennin—is perhaps the best known. This
mode, which never achieved quite the popularity in England that it did on the
Continent, was in several designs, the most typical being the steeple or dunce's
cap silhouette. It was introduced into England about mid-century, though its
real vogue was from roughly 1460 onwards. The cap was made of brocade,
velvet, gold, or silver cloth stiffened into a conical shape and attached to a
black velvet frontlet just visible as a loop on the forehead, and was worn at
an angle of about forty degrees from the vertical. A transparent veil was always
worn on top of the hennin, and generally supported on a wire framework to
achieve a picturesque silhouette. A double-wired veil was commonly used;
alternatively, clouds of soft transparent material flowing from the point of
the cap were equally fashionable, especially later (see pp. 89 and 91). Finally,
the original shaped **hood** was worn by women when travelling, or for poorer
women.

Accessories carried or worn by men and women were still chiefly confined
to the dagger in the man's belt in the first quarter of the century, a purse hung
from the girdle of men or women during most of the period (see pp. 85 and 89),
and the baldric, as mentioned before in this chapter.

Jewellery was rapidly becoming more intricate and varied in design. Gold
or silver neck- and hip-**chains** remained in vogue for men and women so long
as the high collar was worn, but declined in popularity as the neck-line of the
tunic and houppelande were lowered. Jewelled **necklaces,** set in gold or silver
with a central piece, came into fashion about mid-century when the feminine
neck-line became *décolleté*; pearls, enamelled and filigree work, and gold chains
were especially favoured (see p. 85). **Brooches** of many designs were in great
demand for hats, head-dresses, and the corsage (see p. 91). Gold or silver,
enamelled, engraved, or jewelled **pectoral crosses** and **reliquaries** attached to
a gold chain were frequently seen (see p. 91). **Rings** of all kinds: signet, jewelled,
enamelled, or engraved were worn by men and women, often in considerable
numbers on each hand (see p. 91). **Crowns, coronets, fillets,** and **cauls** were
more heavily jewelled, and of finer, more intricate workmanship than hitherto.

As previously mentioned, the fifteenth century was an age for gorgeous, costly
fabrics, large **designs,** and rich, brilliant **colours.** Velvet, brocade, silk, gold,
and silver cloth all retained their fourteenth-century popularity; linen, gauze,
and muslin were used for head-dresses, veils, and trimmings; many varieties of
furs were used indiscriminately for edgings and linings in all masculine and
feminine outer wear. Designs, generally forming an all-over pattern, were
predominantly floral, with large repeats, in vivid colour. Parti-colouring and
counterchange designs were mainly found during the first quarter of the
century.

THE HOUSE OF YORK

EDWARD IV   1461–1483
EDWARD V   1483
RICHARD III 1483–1485

The short period of Yorkist monarchy was one of bloodshed, anarchy, and transition: a prelude to the more orderly government under the Tudors. This unrest affected the costume of the time, which was subject to constant change and ludicrous extremity of styles. English costume, like that of the rest of the Continent, was also largely influenced by the Burgundians, who for a short while reigned supreme in the world of fashion.

At first acquaintance, it is difficult to trace the principal trends in the dress of this time, there are so many and varied themes in both men's and women's attire evident in the wealth of illuminated manuscripts and in the oil paintings, sculpture, stained glass, etc., of the period. Men's clothing was chiefly note-worthy for the brevity of the tunic, contrasting strongly with the long gown worn contemporaneously. Both garments were formally pleated vertically at centre back and front, were fur-trimmed, and had large, padded or hanging sleeves. Hats, which seemed to have at last replaced the hood and chaperon in popular favour, were of an infinite variety of styles: tall, round, peaked, or padded. In feminine wear, all the ingenuity and imagination of the designer appears to have been devoted to the head-dress: like men's hats, these were many and varied, ranging over the tall steeple hennin, the padded turban, the jewelled horned head-dress, and the butterfly style. Gowns were attractive but not new, having merely evolved from those of Henry VI's reign, the main features being a low furred neck-line, a small high waist, long, fitting sleeves, and a deep fur hem.

The extremely brief **tunic** had altered considerably in cut compared with its prototype—the cotehardie of Edward III's reign. The waist was small and accentuated by a padded chest and shoulders, whilst the frilled or pleated skirt was very short, barely covering the hips. Contemporary writers were scathing in their condemnation of this tunic because it exposed the buttocks. The round neck-line at the pit of the neck showed the high paltock collar above. The waist-belt was now no longer the glorious affair of formerly, but merely a narrow leather belt, perhaps jewelled or embroidered. Many styles of sleeve were worn: one typical fashion was a long sleeve, slit in front at elbow-level to allow the arm to pass through, and with the long tubular portion hanging down behind the arm; alternatively, the slit extended along the whole length of the sleeve from the shoulder, and hung down behind the arm as an open cylinder of material; the ends of these sleeves were often tied together at the back (see p. 96). A heavily padded sleeve was equally popular; this was very wide at the top, padded, then gathered or pleated into the armhole and culminated in a narrow wrist-band (see p. 94). Again, there were plain, fairly full sleeves to the wrist, or some styles were full to the elbow then very tight on the forearm (see p. 94). The tunic almost invariably had pleats in the centre panels, front and back, which radiated symmetrically from the waist both upwards and

HOUSE OF YORK, 1461-1485

LADY WEARING PALE PINK
GOWN — TRIMMED WITH
BROWN FUR, AND GIRDED
WITH COBALT BLUE VELVET BELT —
GOLD CLOTH UNDERGOWN
WITH BLACK LINE DESIGN
SHOWS AT HEM & NECK —
GOLD HENNIN WITH BLACK
VELVET BAND — WHITE
TRANSPARENT VEIL

GOLD AND BLACK
BROCADE LONG TUNIC —
FUR TRIMMINGS — GREEN
FELT HAT — BLACK
CHAPERON & LIRIPIPE —
DARK GREEN VELVET
UNDERTUNIC SHOWS AT
NECK AND SLEEVES —
BLACK SHOES.

VERY SHORT GREY CAPE —
-TUNIC — FUR TRIMMING —
GOLD UNDERTUNIC
SHOWS AT WRISTS &
NECK — LEMON YELLOW
HOSE — RED FELT HAT
WITH PALE YELLOW
PADDED EDGE.

MAN WEARING SHORT, BROWN
AND GOLD, PATTERNED TUNIC —
TRIMMED WITH FUR — PLEATED
CENTRE FRONT AND BACK —
PADDED SLEEVES — DARK
GREY UNDERGOWN SHOWS
AT NECK — GREY FELT HAT —
PALE GREY HOSE —
BLACK SHOES.

94

downwards (see pp. 94 and 96). The neck, wrist, and hem edges were usually trimmed in fur (see p. 94).

Despite the superficial contrast, the long **gown** and short tunic had many features in common: the same round neck with protruding high paltock collar; the same sleeve styles as those just described; the formal, symmetrical pleats back and front; the fur edges to neck, wrist, sleeve-slits, and hem were usual. The chief difference between the garments was their lengths; the long gown reached to the ankles or the ground, and the skirt was often slit to the knees at the sides, or back and front. The garment was either belted or hung loose from neck to hem. Large all-over designs were a feature of all tunics, long or short (see pp. 94 and 96).

A new garment, especially typical of the Yorkist period, was the loose, short **cape** or **tunic.** The cape style was circular, fastened on one shoulder by a button or brooch, and reached to just below the waist. The tunic style was very similar in cut, flowing out loosely to the same length as the cape, but had various types of sleeves, as described earlier in the chapter. Fur edges usually finished the neck, sleeves and, perhaps, the hem (see p. 94). These garments were also the subject of much disapproval by the writers of the day.

The **paltock,** or under-tunic, was sometimes referred to in this period as the *doublet*—a prelude to Tudor dress. It had not altered greatly since Henry VI's time, its main aspects had merely been accentuated. The long, fitting sleeves were usually attached to the armholes by points. A common feature was a sleeve slit at the back of the elbow, laced across, but showing the white shirt through the lacings.

Gentlemen's **hose** still fitted immaculately from waist to toe, and the manly figure was indubitably shown to advantage—or otherwise, depending on its proportions—by the fashion for brief tunics and capes. The **cod-piece** was still used. The foot portion of the hose still varied in length until 1480 when footwear returned to normal shape, and long toes finally went out of fashion. In 1461, very long toes were in vogue, but a gradual decline in length was seen until 1480. With this decline, the wearing of **shoes** became normal once more. There were several styles of shoes of which the most typical was unfastened, cut high on the instep and low at the heel (see p. 98). **Clogs** and **pattens** were worn under the soled hose for outdoors until about 1480. Towards the end of Yorkist rule, **boots** returned to fashion once more. These had been impracticable during the long era of the extended toes. They were thigh-, knee-, or calf-length, and generally had turned-down tops and laced-up sides. Soft leather was the chief material for footwear, though velvet, silk, and brocade were still in use for shoes.

Men began to wear their **hair** rather longer and in various styles from 1461 onwards. The short bowl crop of Henry VI's time was still worn in the reign of Edward IV, but was then much longer, having a fringe on the forehead and a "page-boy" style at the sides and back. This cut remained fashionable until the end of the period, but gradually lengthened as the century progressed, and by 1485 the hair reached the shoulders. Other men wore their hair in curls at the sides and back, sometimes it was quite bushy at the sides; these styles also lengthened towards 1485 (see p. 98). Most men were clean-shaven.

As already mentioned, **hats** began at last to supersede the hood as fashionable

HOUSE OF YORK, 1461-1485

MAN WEARING A BLUE
AND SILVER PATTERNED,
LONG, UN-BELTED TUNIC -
FUR-TRIMMED UNDER-
-TUNIC SHOWS AT NECK -
LEMON FELT HAT & PLUME -
DARK BLUE HOSE

DARK BLUE, VELVET GOWN -
WHITE FUR TRIMMINGS -
PALE GREY UNDERGOWN -
RED GIRDLE - GOLD
CHAIN NECKLACE -
GOLD HENNIN -
BUTTERFLY VEIL.

MAN WEARING SHORT
TUNIC - WAIST-BELT - SLIT
SLEEVES , TIED AT SIDE -
UNDERTUNIC SHOWS AT
SLEEVES AND NECK -
CHAPERON - HOSE -
SHOES

LADY WEARING GOLD CLOTH
GOWN WITH CRIMSON
EMBROIDERED DESIGN -
GOLD CHAIN GIRDLE -
ERMINE TRIMMING -
BLACK UNDERGOWN SHOWS
AT CORSAGE, LACED ACROSS
WITH GOLD LACING -
DARK BLUE HENNIN-
BLACK VELVET BAND &
FRONTLET - WHITE
TRANSPARENT VEIL

headgear for men after 1461. The **chaperon** was still seen until about 1480, but often only hanging down the back of the wearer by its liripipe, while a hat was worn on the head (see pp. 94 and 96). These hats were of many styles, too numerous to consider fully here, but the chief varieties were the tall sugar-loaf shape, the inverted flower-pot style, the tall hat with turban edge, the round hat, the full crown style tucked into a deep band, and the new style of velvet bonet. Felt, beaver, and velvet were the commonest materials; fur trimmings and feather and jewelled brooch decorations were usual. Tall ostrich plumes came into use for the first time as ornamentation for headgear to remain popular almost until the twentieth century. Small spray feathers were also in great demand. The liripipe, despite the decline of the chaperon, remained popular, and was transferred to any of the hat styles. Illustrations of ten of these various hats appear on pp. 94 and 98.

The feminine **gown** of the Yorkist period was designed to show to advantage the tall, slim figure. The houppelande cut had now been abandoned, the new gowns evolving from those worn about 1450–1460. The neck-line was very wide and low, reaching nearly to the girdle in the centre front and back, and was almost off the shoulders. It was generally V-shaped or round and almost invariably fur-trimmed. The **undergown,** which usually had a low, wide, square neck, showed at the centre front and back with the gown often laced across it (see p. 96). The **belt** or **girdle** of about three or four inches deep, was drawn tightly around a high waist-line just below the breasts. Sleeves were long, tight-fitting, and finished with a fur cuff. The skirt was ground-length in front and often had a train at the back; when held up, it displayed the undergown, which was of almost equal richness, in contrasting colour and design (see pp. 94 and 96). A fur band, between three inches and two feet in depth, finished the hem (see pp. 94 and 96). As with the masculine tunics, large all-over patterns in floral or geometrical motifs decorated these gowns (see p. 96).

The head-dress indubitably provided the *pièce de résistance* in feminine attire. The **hennin** retained its popularity until the end of the period. The steeple variety was more fashionable in the earlier part; it was still very tall, being from eighteen inches to two or three feet in height, but now rather narrower near the top. Towards 1470 a wide black band of double material was worn over the top of the hennin where it encircled the head, and the two lappets hung down behind to the level of the shoulder-blades. The black velvet frontlet was still present underneath. These same lappets were later to be seen on the Tudor gable head-dress. A large transparent veil still enveloped the hennin, though usually it was not now wired, but hung in flowing drapery at the back almost to the ground. Gold and silver cloth, brocade, and velvet were the principal materials used for the actual hennin which was clearly visible through the transparent veil (see pp. 94 and 96). The truncated hennin rose to popularity later in Edward IV's reign, and remained in the height of fashion till after 1485. There was normally no black band on this style, but the frontlet was still to be seen on the forehead. Embroidered and printed designs were placed on the hennin itself, with a jewel set in the centre front of the head-dress. Veils were worn in many different ways on this hennin; the best-known style was, perhaps, the wired **"butterfly"** one, in which the veil was generally "wired" in three wings which radiated from the central point on the forehead (see pp. 96 and 98).

HOUSE OF YORK, 1461-1485

GOLD, JEWELLED AND VELVET HEAD-DRESS

VELVET HAT WITH LIRIPIPE

FELT HAT AND PLUME

BUTTERFLY STYLE OF HENNIN. GOLD NECKLACE WITH PEARLS.

VELVET HAT AND PLUME

INSCRIBED GOLD RING

SILVER GILT RING

ENAMELLED, GOLD RELIQUARY.

GOLD RING AND PEARLS

SILK, JEWELLED, PADDED TURBAN — VEIL

BLACK FELT HAT AND BROOCH

ELIZABETH, QUEEN OF EDWARD IV

MAN - TEMP. RICHARD III

GOLD, ENAMELLED RING.

SAPPHIRE, GOLD RING.

FELT HAT WITH BROOCH AND PLUME.

PLATE IV

The Truncated Hennin and Butterfly Veil; note the wearing
of necklace and a pendant

*Elizabeth Woodville, c. 1463, from the
portrait at Queen's College, Cambridge*

Concealment of all hair was still complete, and this was carried out to such an extent that ladies plucked out any hair which grew, in defiance of the dictates of fashion, on the temples or nape of the neck. However, towards the end of Edward IV's reign, the head-dress was worn tilted farther back on the head, and a modicum of hair was allowed to be shown on the forehead and temples (see pp. 96 and 98). As well as the hennin, new versions of the **heart-shaped** head-dress and the **turban** were equally in favour (see p. 98). The former had now developed into a more pointed or horned creation, with the top padded roll usually taking the form of a metal band surmounted by gold and jewelled work. The side-cauls were often velvet pads, jewelled and banded with metal edges (see p. 98).

A reproduction of the painting of Elizabeth Woodville on Plate IV shows clearly the truncated **hennin** with a **butterfly** veil. The low, round neck-line of gold-embroidered material to match the cuffs and hennin with the undergown visible above is also evident. The two types of necklace, so popular in the fifteenth and sixteenth centuries, should also be noted, the smaller one encircling the neck and, on top of it, the jewelled pendant on a thin black cord.

Although the use of a **corset** to give a slender figure was less necessary in the first half of the century when the fashion for the voluminous houppelande was at its height, it became essential again in the second half with the return of more tightly fitting gowns, although it had not changed in type.

Jewellery was similar in design, workmanship, and type of ornament to that of the earlier part of the century. The trend was towards more ornate, intricate work, and for even more jewellery to be worn on the person, especially rings, necklaces, and hat-brooches (see p. 98).

Expensive **fabrics** were worn: velvet, brocade, cloth of gold and silver, all kinds of silk. Fur edges, trimmings, and linings appeared on all garments. **Designs** were large, floral, or geometrical; they were utilised in all-over patterns on gowns and tunics indiscriminately.

V

THE TUDORS

HENRY VII   1485–1509

THE reign of Henry VII is often described by authorities on costume as one of transition: a time which sees the completion of the change-over from medieval to the more typical Tudor dress—as seen in the time of Henry VIII—and which compares with the more overwhelming changes from medieval life and learning to the Renaissance with its new birth of vigour and culture. This impression of the years 1485–1509 is undoubtedly true, but it should be borne in mind that the garments of the time have distinct characteristics and qualities, and should not be regarded as merely the result of transition. For example, the loose, open, voluminous masculine gown, closely resembling a modern dressing-gown, is particularly typical of these years; again, there are such developments as the shortened version of the gown, the petticotte with its long, hanging sleeves, the large beaver hats with numerous ostrich plumes of bright variegated colours, the waist-length paltock or doublet, showing the white shirt in the gap between it and the "points" attachment to the hose, and, in feminine attire, the gowns, pinned up at the back to the waist, the laced-across bodices, and the long, hanging sleeves. The features which show most clearly the transition from the old medieval life to the new Renaissance ways are the early gable hoods—forerunners of the well-known later Tudor style—the square neck-line, the early and modest slashing and puffing on clothes, the broader toe, and the exposure of the exquisitely embroidered white shirts—including their feminine counterparts—at the neck, wrists, and through the slashings and lacings. All these were innovations in the Henry VII period and were to acquire noticeable, definite, and familiar characteristics in the later Tudor reigns when they were popularised by those admirers of rich and beautiful clothes—Henry VIII and his daughter, Elizabeth. When the first Tudor, Henry VII, came to the throne a new era opened for England, costume was affected no less than other aspects of our national life. The example set by the king and his queen, Elizabeth of York, was for a dignified, yet rich mode of dress. This example was followed by many, although, as in most generations, the dandies and coxcombs of the day dressed more extravagantly and effeminately in their short brocaded stomachers, petti-cottes, and long locks with gigantic hats and plumes.

The old sources of information on dress are still useful to gain a knowledge of this period—sculpture, illuminated manuscripts, tapestries, memorial brasses, etc.—but oil painting now began to take its place as the chief source of information about contemporary art and modes. The portrait painters of the day were rarely English, but Flemish and German artists came to England to paint persons of rank and importance, thus leaving to us accurate pictures of English costume.

The chief masculine body garment in this period was now the **paltock** or,

TUDOR, HENRY VII
1485-1509

GENTLEMAN OF FASHION -
EARLY 16TH CENTURY -
PATTERNED GOLD AND
BLUE BROCADE GOWN
WITH GREY FUR
TRIMMINGS - DARK BLUE
SILK LINING - CRIMSON SILK
SASH - PALE GREY DOUBLET -
BLACK VELVET NECK-LINE -
WHITE SHIRT AT NECK - GOLD
JEWELLED COLLAR & PENDANT
CRIMSON HOSE - BLACK
LEATHER SHOES - BLUE CAP
SURMOUNTED BY FAWN
BEAVER HAT WITH BLACK
FAWN AND RED PLUMES.

ULTRA FASHIONABLE YOUNG MAN -
GREY SHORT GOWN OR
PETTI-COTTE LINED WITH PINK
TURNED BACK EDGES - LONG
HANGING SLEEVES - DARK
RED VELVET DOUBLET LACED
ACROSS BROCADE
STOMACHER - WHITE SHIRT -
EMBROIDERED BAND AT WAIST -
PINK HOSE - BLACK SHOES -
FAWN BEAVER HAT OVER
GOLD NET - PLUMES IN
BRIGHT COLOURS

NOBLEMAN WEARING GOLD
CLOTH GOWN LINED & TURNED
BACK WITH GREY FUR - SLEEVES SLIT
ON TOP OF ARM SHOWING DOUBLET
SLEEVE - PINK SASH AT WAIST -
BLACK DOUBLET OPEN TO
WAIST AND LACED ACROSS
WHITE SHIRT - GOLD,
JEWELLED COLLAR -
BLACK VELVET BONET -
GOLD ORNAMENT

GENTLEMAN WEARING GOLD CLOTH
GOWN, TURNED BACK TO SHOW
BLUE SILK LINING - LONG
HANGING SLEEVES, SLIT IN FRONT -
BLACK VELVET DOUBLET, SLASHED
ON CHEST & SLEEVES IN TWO
PARTS SHOWING WHITE SHIRT -
LACED TO PURPLE HOSE AT
WAIST - FAWN STOCKINGS
TO KNEE - BLACK LEATHER
SHOES - BLACK VELVET
BONET IN HAND

as it was frequently termed in Tudor times, the **doublet.** It was more often worn without another tunic on top in the time of Henry VII, in contrast to the earlier fifteenth century and later Tudor times. The doublet closely resembled the paltock of the previous period, but a greater part of it was now visible. The white shirt worn underneath showed in between the lacings of the points at the waist. The neck-line varied considerably at this time: sometimes it was a deep square—the forerunner of styles in the next reign—sometimes it had turned-back revers, but the most usual style was a low V reaching to the waist at the centre front. This V would then be laced across a brocade *stomacher*, which formed an ornamental insertion over the shirt. As an alternative to the waist-length doublet, a short skirt was sometimes attached, just covering the hips. An ornamental belt was occasionally worn at the waist. The sleeves were frequently separate articles—as indeed were the majority of sleeves in Tudor times—and were attached to the armholes by points. In many cases the sleeve itself was in two parts, upper and lower, attached to each other at the elbow by points. The fashion for connecting two edges of material by points was employed to excess in the whole Tudor period: indeed this form of attachment was often used when no fastening was necessary, being purely ornamental. The metal tags to the laces were called *aiglets* or *aiguillettes*. The vogue for slashes or cuts in garments began in this reign, and the doublet was often slashed on the chest and sleeves. The white shirt was then puffed through the openings. Aiguillettes were sometimes employed to connect sleeve slashes (see p. 101).

The **over-tunic,** on the rare occasions when it was worn, was of similar style to the doublet, but it usually had a skirt either attached to the bodice or worn as a separate article, like a kilt. It was longer than the doublet skirt, reaching about half-way down the thigh.

The typical outer garment of this period was the **gown,** which closely resembled a modern dressing-gown. It opened centre front and either hung loose to the ground or was tied at the waist by a silk sash or scarf. The broad lapels on the chest were turned back to show the rich lining of fur or contrasting coloured silk, and sometimes remained turned back to three or four inches in width as far down as the feet. The garment was very long and full, forming numerous folds all round the body. Sleeves varied considerably in style: the chief of these were the very wide type with turned-back cuff, and the extremely long, hanging style with a slit in front at the top to allow the arm to pass through. As with the doublet, costly materials were in use for the gown, velvet, brocade, gold or silver cloth, or silk being the most popular, with fur or silk linings (see p. 101).

The short coat or *petti-cotte* was identical in every respect to the gown, except that it only reached to the hips or knees. Long, hanging sleeves were usual on this garment which was much favoured by fashionable young men (see p. 101).

A circular **cloak** which reached to the knees, and was made from warm materials in bright colours, was worn for travelling and riding.

The **shirt** became of considerable importance in Tudor costume, as it was now visible in several places and not totally covered as in the Middle Ages. It was invariably white, made from fine materials—silk or lawn—cut very full and gathered or pleated into a neck-band and wrist-bands. Embroidery, preferably in black silk thread, adorned the neck-line and wrists of the most expensive shirts. The neck-line, at first, was round and fairly high, but was gradually lowered till the square neck became predominant by 1500. The shirt was usually visible at the neck above the doublet, at the wrists, between the hose and doublet lacings, and through slashes in the doublet (see p. 101).

Hose, made from velvet, silk, or cloth, were almost unaltered in cut from the Yorkist styles. The **cod-piece** was worn as before. Thick woollen or leather **stockings** were sometimes worn on top of the hose to the knees, turned down at the top to form a cuff (see p. 101).

Shoes were now generally worn; the pointed toe had at last completely vanished and a broad, round toe had taken its place. The most fashionable styles had an instep strap, or were cut very low at the back, without any fastening. Leather was the commonest material, but velvet, silk, or cloth were used for the nobility. **Boots,** calf- or knee-length, were worn for riding, travelling, hunting, and for military wear. They were often laced up one side (see pp. 101 and 106).

The typical masculine **hair-style** was shoulder-length, worn loose and flowing, and with a fringe on the forehead. Men were usually clean-shaven (see pp. 101 and 106).

The numerous and varied selection of hats of the Yorkist period had, by the reign of Henry VII, resolved into two main styles of **headgear**: the velvet bonet and the beaver hat. The former—nearly always seen in black, but occasionally in coloured velvet—was the standard early Tudor style of masculine head-covering. It was round or square shape at this time, with a turned-up brim all round, which was often slit in one or more places, or even had a portion cut away, the edges being held together by ornamental gold, silver, or coloured laces with aiguillettes. Medallions, brooches, or other jewelled metal ornaments decorated the upturned brim (see pp. 101 and 106). The beaver hat—popularised by the youth of the day—was round with a large upturned brim, usually worn on the head at a rakish angle, on top of a coloured skull-cap or net, which was visible at one side. Fawn, white, or black were popular shades for this hat, which was decorated by ostrich plumes of variegated colours. A silk scarf was sometimes tied round the hat and fastened under the chin (see pp. 101 and 106).

For the first few years of Henry VII's reign, feminine **gowns** retained the same characteristics as those worn in the reign of Edward IV, but as the sixteenth century approached certain new features of style were apparent: a square neck-line at the front replaced the low V or U shape; the gown became more voluminous and folds were seen at the waist where the girdle held the material to the body; sleeves became more varied in type, closely following the masculine modes—the long, hanging sleeve, slit in front to allow the arm to pass through, the full, wide type with turned-back cuff and the fitting style with small pointed or square cuff were all in vogue; the back of the bodice was frequently open in a V to the waist then laced across showing the undergown, and the rear portion of the skirt was often pinned, buttoned, or brooched up to the waist to show the rich lining of the gown and equally costly undergown fabric. Deep or narrow fur hems, linings, and trimmings remained fashionable throughout the reign. Girdles were corded and tasselled with long hanging ends, or took the form of jewelled, embroidered belts. Materials were still rich and heavy, satin, velvet, and brocade being particularly favoured, but designs, though still large in

TUDOR, HENRY VII
1485-1509

LADY c. 1495 - DARK VELVET
GOWN LINED WITH FUR - SKIRT
BUTTONED UP TO WAIST AT BACK
BACK OF BODICE LACED ACROSS-
SILK UNDERGOWN - BLACK
VELVET HOOD, LINED WITH PALE
SILK & EDGED BY GOLD
EMBROIDERY, OVER WHITE
COIF - GOLD, EMBROIDERED
BELT

LADY - LATE 15TH CENTURY -
BROCADE GOWN WITH
DEEP FUR HEM - HANGING
SLEEVES - SILK UNDERGOWN
SHOWS AT NECK, FORE-ARM
AND HEM - GOLD CORD
GIRDLE - BLACK VELVET
HOOD - GOLD EDGE -
SILK LINING - GOLD
JEWELLED NECKLACE

ELIZABETH OF YORK
QUEEN OF HENRY VII -
PATTERNED GOWN WITH
ERMINE TRIMMING -
UNDERGOWN SHOWS AT
NECK & HEM - BLACK
VELVET GABLE HOOD -
METAL FRONT - GOLD,
JEWELLED LAPPETS. GOLD
JEWELLED NECKLACE

GOLD GOWN PATTERNED IN
SELF-COLOUR- TURNED BACK AT
CENTRE FRONT, WRISTS, & PINNED
UP AT BACK TO SHOW WHITE SILK
LINING - PURPLE VELVET UNDER-
-GOWN - BLACK VELVET HOOD
LINED WITH SILK

motif, had greater dignity, and unpatterned fabrics were increasingly in demand. The gown was nearly always held up in some way to show the undergown skirt, and this garment was usually also visible above the gown at the neck (see p. 104).

The white **chemise** (camise) was the undergarment which corresponded to the men's shirt, though presumably rather longer. The gathered frills at the neck and wrists with the embroidered motif were generally visible, and the former often followed the square neck-line of the gown (see p. 104).

The **mantle** was still used by noblewomen for outdoors, while a cloak with hood attached was the usual wear for others.

There was still little of the feminine **coiffure** showing when the head-dress was in place, though from the small amount which could be seen, it was apparently still parted in the centre, straight or waved on the temples, and commonly braided in coiled plaits at the nape of the neck. At the beginning of the sixteenth century the plaits were often encased in striped silk and bound round the head, only showing on the forehead where the head-dress did not obscure them. No hair was then visible. This style of hairdressing was obviously designed to fill in the gap left on top of the head by the gable-shaped framework.

The well-known and typical early Tudor head-dress was the *gable hood*, a peculiarly British mode. It was known by various names descriptive of its hard, framed shape—*kennel*, *pyramidal*, or *diamond*—but gable is doubtless the best known of these titles. Although the hennin and other distinctive fifteenth-century head-dresses had vanished from the world of fashion by the early years of Henry VII's reign, and the hood had replaced them in feminine favour, it was not until the dawn of the sixteenth century that the true gable hood appeared. The early hood styles had no framework inside to hold their shape; they were made of velvet, usually black, and the front edge was folded back for some three or four inches to form lappets on the shoulders and show the contrasting silk lining. The hood was normally slit part-way up behind these lappets, the remainder of the fabric then hung in folds down the back to shoulder-blade-level. A cap or **coif** was worn under the hood, to which it was often pinned. A black velvet **frontlet** was still sometimes seen on the forehead. The edges of the hood were often embroidered in gold or colours (see p. 104). From these early styles the actual gable hood developed, and remained the English head-dress until nearly the end of Henry VIII's reign. The white linen or silk coif was still worn as a foundation, though it was rarely visible after the hood had been put on. A metal framework acted as a base to the hood, to form the gable shape; the front part of this framework—the new **"frontlet"**—was usually made of gold, studded with jewels; it was narrow, and reached to the shoulders on either side of the face. The black velvet lappets, of double material, were then pinned to the coif on top of and behind the frontlet; they were about four to five inches wide and long enough to lay upon the shoulders in front, and were often decorated by gold and jewelled embroidery. The remainder of the black velvet, semicircular hood was then pinned to the coif behind the double band, and hung, as before, in numerous folds down the back of the wearer (see pp. 104 and 106).

Masculine **accessories** comprised a leather purse or pouch attached to the waist-belt, wherein a dagger was still often inserted. **Gloves** were carried, or

TUDOR, HENRY VII
1485-1509

HENRY VII
RED GOWN - WHITE FUR LAPELS
AND SLEEVE LININGS - GOLD
DOUBLET SHOWS AT NECK AND ON
SLEEVES — (CONTD. OTHER SIDE
OF PAGE).

HENRY VII - PROFILE VIEW -
BLACK UNDERTUNIC -
BLACK HAT - CREAM TURNED
UP BRIM.

QUEEN ELIZABETH OF YORK
BLACK VELVET GABLE HOOD WITH
GOLD, JEWELLED LAPPETS AND
FRONTLET - RED VELVET GOWN -
GOLD AND PEARL EMBROIDERED EDGE

VELVET BONET STYLES, DECORATED BY GOLD LACING & MEDALLIONS

SILVER BROOCH

BLACK LEATHER BOOT -
TURNED BACK WITH BUFF
LEATHER

HENRY VII
BLACK BONET -
JEWELLED COLLAR

SILVER GILT POMANDER

SILVER ENGRAVED RING.

WHITE BEAVER HAT WORN
OVER BLUE CAP - PINK
SCARF TIED UNDER CHIN -
BLACK AND WHITE
OSTRICH PLUME

tucked in the belt, by both sexes. The gloves were of a gauntleted style and made of leather or fabric.

A considerable amount of **jewellery** was worn by both men and women. The heavy gold or silver, jewelled **collars** were still very fashionable, particularly with men, while **neck-chains** of lighter weight, wound two or three times round the neck and having a pendant or cross hanging in front, were equally popular, and worn by men and women alike. **Brooches, medallions** or **jewelled pins** ornamented all headgear. Many **rings** of all types, jewelled or signet, were worn on each hand. The *pomander*—usually pendent on the hanging girdle end—came into vogue late in this reign. Made of gold or silver, often jewelled, it was about one and a half to two inches in diameter and contained perfume; it opened on a hinge when desired (see p. 106).

HENRY VIII   1509–1547

Henry VIII seems a familiar character to us, through the medium of portraits by Holbein and his followers, numerous word pictures from history books and, in recent times, the films. That corpulent, swaggering, pompous figure, magnificently attired in silks, velvets, furs, jewels, and embroideries, romanticised by his amours, cruelties, and appetite seems a living reality. This impression is, however, as the historian is aware, only a part of the truth. Henry VIII accomplished a great deal of good for England; he was, particularly earlier in his life, conscientious and untiring in his work for our country; again he was shrewd and wise, though, being human, he made his mistakes, some of them serious. Among his human weaknesses was an inherent love of finery, clothes, rich fabrics, jewels, and furs. He had a handsome figure when a young man and knew how to show it to advantage. With advancing years, he became, particularly later in life, extremely fat; with increasing age his absorption in his wardrobe increased likewise. Enormous sums of money were spent on his clothes, so that in the familiar portraits which are still extant, almost every square inch of his clothes are seen to be covered with embroideries, furs, and jewels. The court naturally emulated such a king, as indeed did all who had the wealth to do so; the upper and merchant classes in England at this time were lavishly dressed. Men particularly sought after rich materials, furs and jewels —vanity in dress was then no feminine prerogative. The contrast between the apparel of rich and poor was, as can be imagined, very marked under these Tudors. Actual styles of dress were similar; the difference was in ornamentation and quality of material.

England was not, however, by any means the only country to embark upon a period of extravagance in dress. On the Continent, France, under Francis I, vied with England in this respect. The parade of fashion, known so aptly as "The Field of the Cloth of Gold", held near Ardres in Normandy in 1520, where the two kings met with their retinues and set up their respective courts resplendent in gold and silver apparel, is depicted in paintings which give us visual evidence of their splendour. But the actual cut and design of the dress of this period came chiefly from Germany, Switzerland, and Spain. The typical puffed and padded doublets, sleeves and hose, the costume slashed in all conceivable places from top to toe, to show the finery of the undergarments

TUDOR, HENRY VIII
1509-1547

NOBLEMAN: c. 1510-20 -
LIGHT SILK DOUBLET SHOWS AT
SLEEVES, SLASHED TO SHOW
WHITE SHIRT WHICH IS ALSO VISIBLE
AT NECK & WRISTS - DARK RED
VELVET JERKIN OR OVER-TUNIC
WITH GOLD ORNAMENTAL BANDS
AT NECK & HEM - SLEEVES TURNED
BACK TO SHOW GOLD CLOTH
LINING - GOLD, JEWELLED COLLAR
GOLD NECK CHAIN & MEDALLION
JEWELLED FRONT TO JERKIN -
GLOVES - BLACK BONET -
JEWELLED - WHITE PLUME -
WHITE HOSE & SLASHED
SHOES

LADY. c. 1530 -
BLACK VELVET GOWN -
GOLD EMBROIDERED NECK-
-LINE & GOLD CHAIN GIRDLE-
PURPLE VELVET TURNED
BACK SLEEVES - GOLD
CLOTH FALSE SLEEVES,
SLASHED TO SHOW WHITE
UNDERGARMENT, ALSO
SEEN AT WRISTS & NECK-
RED VELVET CENTRE
BODICE PANEL - GOLD
CHAIN NECKLACE -
BLACK GABLE HOOD -
GOLD CROSS-BARRED
EMBROIDERY &
GOLD, JEWELLED
FRONTLET - SILK
STRIPED HAIR
-COVERING

PRINCESS - 1544 -
DULL RED GOWN -
EMBROIDERED ALL-OVER
DESIGN IN GOLD - RED
VELVET TURNED BACK SLEEVES
FALSE SLEEVES & UNDERSKIRT
IN WHITE SATIN - BLACK EDGING TO
SLASHES & AIGLETTES - WHITE
FRILLS AT WRISTS & NECK-
PEARL NECK-EDGE &
NECKLACE WITH
PENDANT - BLACK
VELVET FRENCH HOOD
WITH PEARL BANDS
& RED CENTRE
BAND - JEWELLED
GIRDLE

LADY OF RANK . c. 1515-20 -
GREEN VELVET GOWN LINED
WITH WHITE SATIN WHICH SHOWS
AT TURNED BACK CUFFS -
BLACK VELVET NECK-BAND-
PINK UNDERGOWN &
WHITE UNDERGARMENT SEEN
AT NECK & WRISTS -
JEWELLED NECK-LINE -
BLACK GABLE HOOD -
GOLD FRONTLET - GOLD
EMBROIDERED LAPPETS -
PEARL NECKLACE - GOLD,
JEWELLED GIRDLE

which were pulled through the slashes, the separate sleeves, the fastening of all parts of the costume with ornamental, jewelled aiguillettes, and the later masculine "square silhouette" were products of Germany and Switzerland. The vogue for puffs and slashes was never carried to such excesses in England as on the Continent. Nevertheless, it was the prevailing keynote in dress of the time. Shorter gowns and skirted doublets became the vogue so that men showed their legs below the knees once more. As the reign proceeded, the silhouette became wider and wider, reaching, by 1540, the typical "square cut" seen in portraits of Henry, where the width of the shoulders is literally equal to the length of the gown.

The Spanish influence was seen mainly in feminine dress, with the introduction of the canvas petticoat—forerunner of the farthingale—which resulted in the absence of folds in the skirt, so showing to advantage its gorgeous fabrics and large floral designs. The gable head-dress in its various guises held its own till the end of the reign, though the alternative hood introduced from France in the middle of the period provided competition, being sponsored by several of Henry's later queens. Feminine dress was rather less flamboyantly splendid than the masculine—man was the more royally plumed in Tudor times—though slashes, puffs, jewels, furs, and embroideries were present in fair profusion on most gowns and hoods.

Oil paintings of the period provide the chief source of information on costume. The principal portrait painters of the day in England were still not of English extraction, but Flemish, French, and German. Hans Holbein the Younger is the best known of these; he was Court Painter to Henry VIII later in the reign and his portraits of Henry himself and his later queens are famous. Holbein had several followers and imitators, all of whom practised a style which, fortunately for students of costume, was noted for great clarity, colour, and detailed draughtsmanship.

The **doublet** was established by 1509 as the chief masculine body garment. It was worn with or without another tunic on top; in the former case it is often difficult to tell from a portrait which garment is which as they both follow so closely the same cut and design. The doublet was a close-fitting garment on the torso, with a low, square neck, trimmed with bands of velvet or fur, or alternatively a band of jewelled embroidery, but the neck-line tended to rise after 1540 to a higher, round or square shape; the chest portion was padded to enhance the manly figure; sleeves were often detachable, and were worn in various styles, usually wide to a full turned-back cuff early in the period, and later either slashed in two or three puffs, or worn fairly full at the top, padded and tapering to a more fitting wrist-band. Slashes on the chest and sleeves, in rows, were common, showing the white shirt material pulled through the gaps. Jewels or jewelled aiguillettes were often set at the corners of the slashes. The skirt of the doublet was commonly a separate item and known as a *base*. This was formed in tubular pleats held in place by bands stitched horizontally on the inside of the garment; the skirt was tied with strings at the waist-line and reached to just above the knees; it was sometimes open in the centre front. A band or bands of velvet or embroidery, known as guards, commonly ornamented the hem. A sash or belt might be worn at the waist, on top of the doublet (see pp. 108, 110, 112, and 114).

TUDOR, HENRY VIII
1509-1547

LADY. c. 1530 -
BLACK VELVET GOWN -
PURPLE VELVET TURNED BACK
SLEEVES - GOLD NECKBAND
& TASSELLED GIRDLE -
GOLD CHAIN NECKLACE-
RED VELVET FALSE
SLEEVES, SLASHED TO
SHOW WHITE UNDER-
-GOWN, VISIBLE AT
WRISTS & NECK, ALSO-
BLACK VELVET GABLE
HOOD - GOLD, JEWELLED
FRONTLET - STRIPED
SILK HAIR-COVERING

HENRY VIII. c.1538 -
CRIMSON VELVET GOWN, BROWN FUR
TRIMMING & GOLD EMBROIDERY- PALE
GREY SILK DOUBLET, JERKIN & BASE-
BLACK EMBROIDERY- SLASHED IN
ROWS ON CHEST & SLEEVES OF
DOUBLET, SHOWING WHITE SHIRT, ALSO SEEN
AT FRILLS AT WRISTS & COLLAR-
JEWELLED FRONT TO
DOUBLET- GOLD &
JEWELLED COLLAR-
GOLD CHAIN &
MEDALLION-
WHITE DOUBLE SASH
WITH GOLD CHAIN &
DAGGER- WHITE HOSE
& SLASHED SHOES-
GLOVES - BLACK CAP-
JEWELLED EDGE-
WHITE PLUME

YOUNG LADY. c. 1543. -
DARK VELVET GOWN WITH
RAISED, SELF-COLOUR DESIGN-
TURNED BACK SLEEVES IN
PATTERNED DAMASK - WHITE
SATIN FALSE SLEEVES &
UNDERSKIRT - WHITE FRILLS
AT WRISTS & NECK - SLASHES
IN SLEEVES - PEARL NECKLACE
& CROSS - BLACK, GOLD
& WHITE FRENCH
HOOD

JANE SEYMOUR. 1536-.
DARK RED VELVET GOWN -
EDGES & TURNED BACK
SLEEVES COVERED BY GOLD
NET EMBROIDERY- JEWELLED
GIRDLE - UNDERGOWN & FALSE
SLEEVES OF BLUE-GREY SELF-
-COLOURED PATTERNED FABRIC-
BLACK GABLE HOOD- JEWELLED
FRONTLET- GOLD EMBROIDERY-
GOLD, JEWELLED NECKLACE,
& PENDANTS - WHITE
WRIST FRILLS & PUFFS

110

The **over-tunic,** sometimes worn, was often called a *jerkin.* As just mentioned, it was so similar in style to the doublet that it is difficult to discern one garment from the other. The jerkin was often sleeveless and open on the chest to the waist in a deep U or V shape, thus disclosing much of the doublet to view. A skirt or base would probably be worn on top, in the same material and colour as the jerkin (see pp. 108, 110, 112, and 114).

The long and voluminous **gown** described in the Henry VII period was, in Henry VIII's reign, generally much shorter and wider. The average, well-dressed man wore it knee-length, hanging loose, open in front, displaying his doublet and base, and lined with fur which, turned back, formed collar and revers reaching to the hem. Sleeves were enormous padded puffs to the elbow, where they were slit to allow the arm to pass through, whilst the remainder of the material hung in full and numerous folds to the hem. Velvet was the usual material, embroidered in bands on the sleeve and hem, sometimes jewelled. The width of the garment was identical with the length (see pp. 108, 110, 112, and 114). Older and more serious men wore a calf- or ankle-length gown, less full and wide and with less pretentious, normal-shaped sleeves (see p. 114).

The beautifully embroidered white **shirt** had now assumed even greater importance. It was the same as that described earlier, but because of the deep, square neck-line of the doublet a greater part of it was now visible, thus showing it to advantage. It also appeared through the numerous slashes on chest and sleeve and in the frills at the wrists. The finest of white fabrics were used. A small turned-down embroidered collar was sometimes substituted for the gathered frill, a style particularly popularised by Henry VIII (see pp. 108, 110, 112, and 114).

During the reign of Henry VIII masculine **hose** underwent a fundamental change once more. Until about 1520 the hose remained as they had been worn in the fifteenth century. After this time, however, the hose were made in two parts, upper and lower. The top part, reaching from waist to mid-thigh, was fairly full, sometimes slashed and made of velvet, silk, or cloth. Its top edge was attached by points to the doublet waist, as before. It was called by various names—breeches, hose, upper hose, etc. The lower portion, still sewn to the upper part, took the form of a tight-fitting stocking, with foot portion attached, as before. These stockings or hose, as they were called, were still cut to the shape of the leg and made from velvet, silk or cloth as hitherto. The two parts of the hose were sometimes made in two different colours. The top, full portion, however, was rarely seen since it was hidden under the doublet skirt. The **codpiece** was still worn, as in the fifteenth century, but was padded in this period, to become obtrusive.

The typical feature of the **footwear** of this time was its breadth. In contrast to the elongated styles of the fourteenth and fifteenth centuries, the designs of the first half of the sixteenth century were extremely broad at the toe. Shoes were either cut high on the instep and low at the back with no fastening, or cut very low at the back and front with probably a strap fastening on the instep; in the latter style the toe-front was only about two inches long. Slashes, embroidery, and jewels were the invariable decoration. Leather was the usual material, in black or colour; velvet, silk, or brocade were also in use for the wealthy (see pp. 108, 110, 112, 114, and 117). Boots were worn by soldiers and

TUDOR, HENRY VIII
1509-1547

MAN. c 1532. -
BLACK VELVET GOWN WITH LIGHT FUR
TRIMMING - BLACK VELVET JERKIN &
BASE - BLACK HOSE & SLASHED SHOES-
CRIMSON SILK DOUBLET, SLASHED
ON CHEST & SLEEVES TO SHOW WHITE
SHIRT, WHICH IS ALSO VISIBLE AT
NECK & WRISTS - GREY
SASH - BLACK CAP -
GOLD CHAIN &
MEDALLION -
DAGGER & TASSEL

YOUNG MAN WEARING LIGHT
GREEN CLOTH DOUBLET WITH
BLACK VELVET TRIMMING -
SLASHES ON CHEST & SLEEVES-
UPPER SLEEVES IN SLASHED
PUFFS - WHITE SHIRT SHOWS
AT NECK, THROUGH SLASHES &
AT WRISTS - GREY HOSE-
BLACK SLASHED SHOES

ANNE OF CLEVES. 1539-
DEEP PINK GOWN WITH
GOLD BAND TRIMMING -
UNDERGOWN IS SEEN
WITH LOW, SQUARE NECK -
WHITE EMBROIDERED
UNDERGARMENT REACHES
HIGH NECKLINE - GOLD
WAIST-BELT -
FLEMISH
HEAD DRESS

CATHERINE HOWARD
c. 1539 - BLACK GOWN
YOKE, HALF-SLEEVES &
UNDERSKIRT IN VELVET-
REST IN SILK OR SATIN-
WHITE COLLAR - GOLD
SLEEVE ORNAMENTS &
AIGLETTES - BLACK
EMBROIDERED WHITE
FRILLS AT WRISTS-
GOLD CHAIN
GIRDLE,
PENDANTS
& NECKLACE -
BLACK VELVET
FRENCH
HOOD - GOLD
BANDS - WHITE
CENTRE - BAND

for riding and travelling. They were made of leather, mid-thigh length, broad at the toe and slashed in rows on the leg.

Various lengths were seen in masculine **hair-styles** in the time of Henry VIII. For the first few years of the reign, long, flowing hair, like that fashionable in his father's time, was the mode, then Henry himself led the vogue for short, curly hair once more. After 1520, he wore it very short in imitation of the French, and men followed suit. **Beards** and **moustaches** were optional but they had returned to fashion with the majority of men by 1530. Various styles were seen, all short and fairly full, with the chin sometimes shaved in emulation of Henry VIII (see pp. 108, 112, 114, and 117).

The distinctive hat or cap of the first ten to fifteen years of Henry's reign was the black velvet **bonet** which had been so popular since the late fifteenth century. As time passed the bonet became more heavily decorated with jewels, brooches, and plumes. Gold cords and aiguillettes were still employed as fastenings to hold together the cut edges (see pp. 108 and 114). About 1520, another type of black velvet cap appeared. This had a flat crown and brim, the latter partly turned up, and it was often worn on one side of the head. The soft material of the crown was pleated or gathered into the brim, which was stiffened. The brim was turned up at a greater angle later in the reign. Jewels and ornaments were then attached to the under edge and a large ostrich plume was laid along the top. This flat type of cap was worn by all classes of men till Elizabethan times; it was made of velvet, jewelled and plumed, for the wealthy, and of plain wool or cloth for poorer men (see pp. 110, 112, 114, and 117).

The silhouette of the feminine gown during the remainder of the Tudor period from the accession of Henry VIII was largely dependent upon the *farthingale* and the **corset**: the era of the imprisonment of the female form had begun. Before the actual farthingale was introduced, ladies wore a canvas petticoat underneath their other petticoats. The canvas type was fastened by tapes at the waist and was stiffened, so descending with increasing circumference to the ground. The farthingale (verdingale) introduced by Henry's first wife from Spanish styles, was modelled on this petticoat, later in the reign whalebone hoops being inserted horizontally at equal intervals down the garment, increasing steadily in diameter from waist to ground, so that a cone-shaped silhouette resulted. Several ordinary petticoats were worn on top of the farthingale to hide the whalebone bands. The corset was equally important in producing the correct figure to show the gown to advantage. A modest laced type was worn until the 1530s, similar to that worn in the fifteenth century, but after this a corset made from metal bands, padded and covered with leather and velvet or silk, encased the body from just below the breast-line to the hips, accentuating the slender waist. The corset was hinged on one side to open. The farthingale was then tied by its tapes on top of the corset, at the waist.

The early **gowns**, from 1509 to about 1530, showed little trace of the farthingale shape, however. They had a low, square neck-line with a jewelled, embroidered neck-band, a fitting bodice, and a very long, full skirt with a train at the back. The **girdle**, encircling the waist and hanging in one or two long ends almost to the ground, was rich and ornamental, being made of gold chain or cord, with tasselled ends and jewelled at intervals on the cord. Alternatively, heavy jewelled ornaments hung on the end of the girdle—cameos, pomanders,

TUDOR, HENRY VIII
1509-1547

HENRY VIII. c. 1536 -
GOLD CLOTH GOWN WITH DARK FUR -
SILVER BLUE DOUBLET, JERKIN & BASE -
DOUBLET & SLEEVES SLASHED IN
ROWS, EMBROIDERED AND
JEWELLED - WHITE SHIRT SHOWS
THROUGH SLASHES & AT NECK
AND WRISTS - GOLD CHAIN &
MEDALLION - GOLD EMBROIDERY
ON COLLAR - WHITE SASH -
BROWN GLOVES -
WHITE HOSE &
SLASHED SHOES -
BLACK HAT -
JEWELLED -
WHITE PLUME

MAN. c. 1520-30 -
DARK GREEN CLOTH GOWN -
GREY FUR COLLAR & LINING -
BLACK VELVET BONET -
MEDALLION - WHITE PLUME -
GREY HOSE - BLACK SHOES -
WHITE SHIRT SHOWS AT
NECK AND WRISTS

LADY MARY TUDOR -
DARK VELVET GOWN -
ERMINE EDGED TURNED
BACK SLEEVES - GOLD
NECK-EDGE - SLASHES IN
FALSE SLEEVES SHOW WHITE
UNDERGARMENT - FRILLS AT
WRISTS - JEWELLED GIRDLE,
NECKLACE & PENDANT -
FRENCH HOOD -
JEWELLED EDGES

PRINCESS. c. 1546.
PATTERNED BROCADE GOWN -
JEWELLED NECK-LINE &
GIRDLE - UNDERGOWN
& FALSE SLEEVES OF
RAISED VELVET - SLASHED
SLEEVES - WHITE SHOWS
THROUGH SLASHES & AT
IN FRILLS AT WRISTS -
FRENCH HOOD -
JEWELLED NECK-LACE
& PENDANT

114

PLATE V

The "square silhouette", provided by a gown with
puff sleeves. Note exquisitely embroidered shirt

*From a portrait, "A Gentleman in Red",
c. 1548, at Hampton Court Palace, reproduced
by Gracious Permission of H.M. The Queen*

or pendants. Sleeves were in various styles, similar to those of the masculine doublet; at first, the long, wide, loose sleeve with turned-back cuff of the Henry VII period was worn, later, by about 1525, slashed, puffed sleeves appeared. After about 1530 several innovations were apparent in the gown: the neck-line became lower and wider, so that it was partially off the shoulders, and slightly arched in the centre front; the neck-band was more heavily jewelled; the bodice, on top of the corset, became tighter fitting, with a slenderer waist; the skirt was frequently open in the centre front in an inverted V-shape from the waist showing the rich fabric and pattern of the **undergown,** while the over-skirt, following the farthingale silhouette, fell without folds to the ground, except at the back, where the fullness of material was concentrated in drapery and a train. Sleeves were very tight on the upper arm and opened out into a large bell-shape which was then folded and pinned back on to the material on the upper arm, showing the fur or embroidered silk lining and falling in rich folds to below knee-level. Under or **false sleeves,** usually of matching fabric to the undergown, were attached under the inside of the upper sleeves. These false sleeves were padded, later to enormous dimensions, in a flat, wide shape, decreasing in width towards the wrists. They were ornamented by slashes which were jewelled and fastened by aiguillettes. The girdle was more costly than ever, heavily encrusted with jewels and terminating in a jewelled pendant or pomander. This style of gown is seen clearly in the drawing on p. 110 from the portrait of Jane Seymour, Henry's third queen, in 1536. The Flemish style of continental gown, without a train, is seen in the drawing from the portrait of Anne of Cleves, Henry's fourth queen, in 1539, on p. 112. The extra widening and flattening of the false sleeves and narrowing of the upper arm sleeves which took place after 1540, can be seen in the drawing dated 1546 on p. 114. An alternative neck-line which became fashionable after 1538 is seen in the drawing from the portrait of Catherine Howard, Henry's fifth queen, c. 1539, on p. 112, which also shows a square yoke of different material from the rest of the bodice and a stand-up collar, lined with white, fastened in front by a brooch. Drawings of the earlier gown styles can be seen on pp. 108 and 110. Materials in use for the gown and undergown were very costly and usually imported. Large patterns in raised velvet pile or brocade were in vogue and seen to advantage in the farthingale skirts, unbroken by folds of drapery.

The white **undergarment,** comparable to the masculine shirt, was equally exquisitely embroidered and edged with cut-work. It was visible at the neck, in a narrow band above the similar shape of the gown neck-line; it also appeared through the false sleeve slashes and in frills at the wrists. Gold, silver, or black silk thread was favoured for the embroidery.

The **gable hood,** that peculiarly English head-dress, was worn in its varying styles throughout the reign. Until about 1525 it was unaltered in shape and ornamentation from that worn in the latter part of Henry VII's reign, as described previously (see p. 108). After this time, the fashion for pinning up one or both decoratively embroidered and jewelled lappets on to the top of the hood was introduced, and sometimes all, or a portion, of the black velvet hood itself was pinned up. Various alternative ways of performing this were evolved, as can be seen in the drawings on pp. 108, 110, and 117. By about 1530,

9

the metal jewelled frontlet was shortened, the ends being only level with the mouth, and the sides curved inwards towards the cheeks at a greater angle than hitherto. The striped silk hair-covering, used to fill the gable front shape, was also in vogue all through the reign.

The **French** style of **hood** was introduced into England about the middle of the reign. It was constructed in a similar manner to the gable style, on a metal framework attached to a white coif underneath, but the shape was a curved horseshoe or crescent silhouette instead of the angular one. It was also set back farther on the head and showed considerably more hair on the forehead, which was not encased in a silk covering, but worn parted in the centre and straight or waved on the temples. The jewelled band or frontlet was sometimes formed into two jewelled bands, one in the front of the head-dress and the other some inches farther back. The white coif, or a coloured band, was then often visible between the jewelled ones. The black velvet hood fell in vertical folds down the back. This head-dress was popularised by Anne Boleyn and Catherine Howard, and later was worn by Henry's daughters, Mary and Elizabeth. Towards the end of the reign, the hood began to supplant the gable style in popularity, its curved edge was kinder to the face than the angular shape (see pp. 108, 110, 112, 114, and 117).

Masculine accessories still included the **dagger** in an ornate jewelled sheath, and now attached to the waist-sash by cords forming a sling, with tassel appended also a **pouch** or purse slung from the sash (see pp. 110 and 112). **Sticks** or canes were sometimes carried. **Gloves** were increasingly favoured by both sexes, carried or worn, gauntleted in style and made of leather or kid. Embroidery and jewels were used for ornamentation. Perfumed gloves were introduced at the end of the reign (see pp. 108, 110, and 117). **Handkerchiefs** were also becoming more fashionable for the upper and middle classes: white linen with gold or coloured embroidery was usual.

Jewellery worn by both sexes in this reign was exquisite in workmanship and lavish in its splendour and quantity. Heavy, jewelled, gold **collars** were still worn by men of rank, and gold **chains** with a hanging pendant or medallion were worn by both sexes. **Necklaces** fashioned from various jewels, encircled the feminine neck several times, terminating in a jewelled **pendant.** Another pendant often hung on the corsage of the gown. Pearls were used in great profusion in jewellery and jewelled embroideries, for both sexes. **Brooches** and **medallions** ornamented caps, doublets, and gowns. **Girdles** were jewelled and costly, with hanging pendants or jewelled **pomanders.** Many **rings** were worn on each hand, on thumbs and fingers indiscriminately (see pp. 108, 110, 112, 114, and 117). The use of precious metals and the finest jewels in such profusion was reminiscent of the Roman and Byzantine Empire dress. In England it was the beginning of Tudor grandeur and lavishness, reaching its crescendo at the end of the century.

Fabrics were varied and costly. Velvets, brocades, satins, silks, and damask were imported. Fine linens and wool were also used a great deal. **Colours** were rich and vivid, especially for the well-to-do, though Henry VIII passed a law forbidding the wearing of purple to everyone but royalty. Gold and silver cloth and embroideries studded with jewels were in great demand. **Furs** were used excessively for linings and trimmings. **Motifs**, which were large, were

TUDOR, HENRY VIII
1509-1547

ANNE BOLEYN
2ND QUEEN OF HENRY VIII -
BLACK VELVET FRENCH HOOD WITH GOLD &
PEARL EDGES - BLACK GOWN - PEARL &
BLACK LINE EDGING - BROWN FUR SLEEVES

CATHERINE PARR
6TH QUEEN OF HENRY VIII -
GABLE HOOD - JEWELLED FRONTLET - STRIPED
HAIRCOVERING - DARK GOWN - PEARL
JEWELLED   NECKLACE
PENDANT

HENRY VIII c 1538
BLACK VELVET CAP - JEWELLED - WHITE
PLUME - JEWELLED, GOLD COLLAR -
BROWN FUR - PALE GREY DOUBLET WITH
BLACK EMBROIDERY - JEWELS -
WHITE COLLAR

BLACK
VELVET CAP
c. 1543

BLACK VELVET CAP

c. 1538

GOLD, JEWELLED
RING

GOLD RING WITH
TURQUOISE & GARNETS

CATHERINE OF ARAGON
1ST QUEEN OF HENRY VIII
BLACK GOWN - BROWN FUR TURNED BACK SLEEVES -
GOLD FALSE SLEEVES, BROWN EMBROIDERY - BLACK
VELVET GABLE HOOD - GOLD & JEWELLED EDGES -
JEWELLED PENDANTS

LEATHER GLOVES -
EMBROIDERED

BLACK VELVET FRENCH
HOOD - JEWELLED, GOLD
EDGE - WHITE CENTRE
BAND

GOLD, ENAMELLED RING
WITH DIAMOND

GOLD POMANDER CASE
WITH PEARLS

SLASHED SHOE
STYLES

BLACK VELVET FRENCH
HOOD - JEWELLED,
GOLD EDGE

predominantly floral, chiefly representing the vine, the pomegranate, and the rose, though designs of birds and animals also were utilised.

EDWARD VI   1547–1553
QUEEN MARY   1553–1558

The reigns of Edward VI and Queen Mary are uneventful in the history of costume, in sharp contrast to the preceding and succeeding ones of their father and younger stepsister respectively. This was partly because it was only a short period—eleven years; partly because Edward VI, a young, delicate boy, had little energy or natural interest for indulging in a love of finery as his father had done; and partly because Queen Mary was much more concerned with her fervent desire to re-establish the Catholic religion in England than with popu- larising the latest whim of fashion. As a result there were no innovations in dress during this time, only small adaptations of the existing styles, with a tendency towards emulation of the Spanish modes in the reign of Queen Mary, consequent upon her marriage to Philip II of Spain in 1554.

In masculine attire, the "square silhouette" became less marked, and by the end of Mary's reign the Spanish trend towards a narrower outline, a shorter, more padded doublet, the lower waist-line, visible breeches, and short capes was apparent. There was, however, little or no abatement in the vogue for puffs and slashes. In feminine dress, the Spanish farthingale and metal corset reigned supreme: the female form was moulded by them to the requisite fashion- able shape. The French hood had supplanted the gable style, and this head-dress with its near relation the jewelled, heart-shaped cap, were worn by all. The costumes of both sexes were still profusely decorated by jewelled embroideries, fur trimmings, gorgeous patterned velvets and damasks, and a wealth of jewellery. Footwear slowly returned to a more normal width during this period, from the wide, square toes of Henry VIII's reign towards the natural-shaped shoes of Elizabethan times.

The **doublet** altered slowly from that worn at the end of Henry VIII's reign, towards the more Spanish version seen in England in 1558. The neck-line was raised from the low, square style to a fairly high collar; the waist-line was lowered, first to the natural position, then to a dip in front below the normal line; the skirt (or base, as it had been called in Henry's time) became shorter till it was only a few inches deep in 1558; the doublet, often slashed on the chest as before, was open in the centre front from neck to hem; buttons, aiguillettes, or hooks acted as fastenings; slight padding, in front, was introduced after 1554—a prelude to the bombast of the next reign—and a new type of decoration, known as *picadils* (*pickadils*), in the form of slashed rolls or tabs, was seen at collar and shoulder edge. Sleeves were still fairly fitting, though fuller at the top, and usually slashed, then ornamented by aiguillettes. A belt or sash was still worn at the waist with a second belt attached to it, to hold the dagger and/or sword-hanger (see pp. 119 and 121).

The **jerkin** was frequently worn on top of the doublet (though the latter was still sometimes seen without a jerkin), and the two garments were almost indistinguishable, so similar were they in cut. The chief difference, and therefore the easiest means of identification, was in the sleeves: those of the jerkin were

TUDOR, 1547-1558

EDWARD VI. c. 1550 -
CRIMSON VELVET GOWN · GOLD
BANDS - LINED WITH ERMINE-
SILK DOUBLET - EMBROIDERED-
SLASHED SLEEVES & BREECHES-
BLACK VELVET CAP - JEWELLED -
PLUME — DAGGER & TASSEL —
WHITE HOSE - SLASHED
SHOES

PRINCESS MARY TUDOR. c. 1549
BLACK VELVET & SATIN GOWN -
YOKE - WHITE SATIN LACE EDGED
COLLAR - WHITE SATIN FALSE SLEEVES-
GOLD AIGUILLETTES - WHITE SATIN
UNDERSKIRT - BLACK & GOLD
EMBROIDERED WHITE COLLAR,
RUFF & WRIST RUFFLES -
BLACK VELVET HOOD - WHITE
BAND - GOLD, JEWELLED
BANDS - GOLD CHAIN
GIRDLE & PENDANT
BOOKCASE - JEWELLED-
PENDANT CROSS &
MEDALLION

GENTLEMAN. c. 1550 -
BLACK JERKIN SLASHED ON
CHEST - LEATHER, JEWELLED
BELT - LIGHT SILK DOUBLET
SHOWS AT SLEEVES & ON
CHEST - BLACK CAPE — SILVER EDGE
BLACK BREECHES - HOSE -
SLASHED SHOES - WHITE
FRILL AT NECK &
WRISTS - BLACK
VELVET CAP-
JEWELLED —
PLUME - GLOVES

PRINCESS MARY. c. 1552-
BLACK VELVET GOWN - FUR
TRIMMING - GOLD EMBROIDERED
GAUZE PARTLET - SMALL WHITE
RUFF AT NECK & WRISTS - GOLD
JEWELLED COLLAR &
GIRDLE — WHITE SATIN
UNDERSKIRT &
UNDERSLEEVES WITH
LINED EMBROIDERERY-
GOLD, JEWELLED HEAD-
DRESS - WIRED FRAME-
WORK FRONT - PEARL
EDGE

either very short and in a large puff, or merely epaulettes or wings, thus exposing the full-length doublet sleeve, usually of a different colour and material. Vertical slashes were also common on the chest part of the jerkin, rendering the doublet visible through them, or, if the latter was slashed also, the shirt was seen. Velvet, silk, brocade, or satin were popular fabrics for both garments, with coloured, gold, or silver embroidery, frequently encrusted with jewels (see p. 119).

Little change was seen in **gown** styles during this period, except for a slight narrowing of the "square silhouette" of 1547. The wide fur, or contrasting coloured silk, revers, the large puff and hanging sleeve, the open front and voluminous short folds at the sides and back were still the characteristic features of the gown. Bands or guards of velvet, fur, or jewelled embroidery still adorned the sleeve, hem, and collar (see pp. 119 and 121).

A clear example of masculine attire as worn at the end of Henry VIII's reign and the early part of that of Edward VI can be seen in Plate V, "A Gentleman in Red". This portrait, with its distinctive red colour scheme in silk and velvet, shows a red silk **doublet** with gold line embroidery. The garment is open centre front and has a fairly deep basque skirt. The double **waist-belt,** with gold fittings, supports a gold **dagger** and **tassel** on the right side. The red velvet **gown** is lined with red silk, visible on the wide revers; doublet sleeves are visible on the forearm. The white **shirt,** embroidered in black silk thread, can be seen on the chest and in the neck and wrist ruffles. **Breeches, cod-piece, hose,** and **cap** are also in red velvet, the last of these being ornamented by a jewel and a white plume. Red **shoes** have jewelled, gold lines of embroidery.

The **cloak,** slowly returning to fashion in the latter part of Edward's reign, was so popularised by the adherents to the Spanish styles of dress that by 1558 it had almost superseded the gown in public favour. The length varied considerably, reaching hip, knee, calf, or ankle; collars were optional; fur linings and edges of embroidered band trimmings were a usual form of decoration, and an ornamental hood was often attached (see p. 119).

With the abbreviation of the doublet and jerkin skirt, the upper parts of the hose, referred to in the previous chapter as **breeches** or **trunk hose,** were now partially visible. Early in the period they were short and, with the fairly long doublet skirt, little of them could be seen, but as the hem of the skirt was raised the trunk hose became longer, so that by 1558 they reached well down the thigh. The trunk hose, still sewn to the stockings, were slashed in *panes* or strips of material, embroidered and jewelled, and secured at the waist and on each leg by a fitting band. The lining, often of a different colour and fabric, showed through the slashes (see pp. 119 and 121). The **cod-piece** was still padded, but was now more visible owing to the shorter doublet skirt.

Long, fitting **stockings** of velvet, silk, or cloth, sewn to the trunk hose, covered the foot and remainder of the leg.

Owing to the higher doublet neck-line, the **shirt** was visible through the slashes on chest and sleeves only, and in the wrist and neck ruffles. These ruffles were, by the reign of Queen Mary, really miniature **ruffs,** and were tied in front of the neck by strings or tapes. Black, gold, or silver embroidered edges and motifs were still common on the shirt and ruffles.

TUDOR, 1547-1558

EDWARD VI -
BLACK VELVET DOUBLET &
GOWN - GOLD & JEWELLED
EMBROIDERY - SILK LINING
TO GOWN - PUFF & HANGING
SLEEVES - BREECHES OF SAME
MATERIAL SHOW BELOW DOUBLET
SKIRT - BLACK HOSE &
SHOES - SWORD -
DAGGER - GLOVES -
BLACK VELVET HAT-
JEWELLED -
PLUME - WHITE
FRILLS AT NECK
& WRISTS

LADY, c. 1551 -
DARK VELVET GOWN &
TURNED BACK SLEEVES -
JEWELLED GIRDLE & PENDANTS-
EMBROIDERED COLLAR & LACE-
EDGED OUTER COLLAR -
FALSE SLEEVES & UNDER-
-SKIRT OF PATTERNED
VELVET AIGUILLETTES ON
SLEEVES - GLOVES - BOOK-
BLACK VELVET HOOD -
JEWELLED BANDS

QUEEN MARY, c 1553 - 4 -
DARK BLUE VELVET GOWN WITH
SIMILAR LINING - UNDERGOWN
& FALSE SLEEVES OF BROCADE-
JEWELLED GIRDLE, COLLAR &
WRISTBANDS - HANGING
CHAIN & POMANDER -
JEWELLED PENDANT &
AIGUILLETTES - BLACK
VELVET HOOD - JEWELLED
BAND - WHITE WRIST
FRILLS - COLLAR LINING
& PARTLET

PHILIP OF SPAIN, c. 1553-
LIGHT SILK PADDED & SLASHED
DOUBLET & BREECHES -
WHITE COLLAR · & WRIST FRILLS-
DARK GOWN EMBROIDERED
IN GOLD - DARK FUR REVERS -
GOLD NECKCHAIN - LIGHT
HOSE - SLASHED SHOES -
DAGGER - SWORD -
BELT - GLOVES

121

Masculine **hair, moustache,** and **beard** styles remained more or less unchanged during this period from those worn at the end of Henry VIII's reign.

The soft velvet, flat **cap** with stiffened velvet, upturned brim, so fashionable with all classes of men since about 1530, held undisputed place as the typical masculine head-covering throughout these two reigns. Black was the usual colour, though others were occasionally seen. There were several types of ornamentation, but invariably included was an ostrich plume, usually white, jewels, brooches, or aiguillettes on the other side of the brim, and a jewelled cap band (see pp. 119 and 121).

The extremely broad, short toe-caps of 1547 slowly gave place to a more natural-shaped **shoe** in Queen Mary's reign; it was cut high on the instep, once more, with no fastening and a low-cut back. Slashes were an integral part of the design, either in rows or a definite pattern. All colours were seen, in leather, velvet, or silk (see pp. 119, 121, and 124). **Boots,** when worn, were also shaped to the foot, and were thigh-, knee-, or calf-length, made in leather.

As in masculine attire, only small changes were made in feminine **gown** styles in this period: the basic design remained unaltered. The **farthingale** was now universally worn—except by the poorer and peasant classes—and this, in conjunction with the metal **corset,** formed the typical small-waisted and cone-shaped skirt silhouette, so familiarly associated with the Tudors. Small differences can, however, be perceived distinguishing the fashionable 1547 gown and the one of 1558: the actual waist-line became lower, with a dip in the centre front, as in men's costume, and this was accentuated by the line of the girdle; the corset was narrower, giving an even slenderer waist than previously; three different styles of neck-line were seen, the most popular of which was the higher version with a yoke and stand-up collar, lined with white fabric, edged with embroidery or lace, and fastened by a brooch at the corsage, but the high neck-line surmounted by a small ruff or frill, like the masculine doublet style, and the low, square, arched *décolletage* were also often seen. The neck and shoulders were, however, no longer uncovered when the last-named of these styles was worn; the intervening area was covered by a *partlet* worn under the gown, made of transparent gauze or muslin, embroidered in gold, silver, or colour, and ending in a high neck-line finished by a small ruff or frill. These feminine **ruffs** were generally open in the centre front, to dip in a V-shape where they were tied. A similar partlet and ruff were also worn inside the open, stand-up collar neck-line. The turned-back, bell-shaped outer sleeve displaying the padded and slashed under or false sleeve was still fashionable and was worn throughout the period. Ruffles could be seen at the wrists, and the white undergarment showed through the slashes, which were decorated by the ever-popular, ornate aiguillettes. Another type of sleeve was worn alternatively after 1550—a fitting style, slashed or embroidered for ornament, with a large puff at the shoulder, terminating in a tight band on the upper arm; sometimes the puffed part belonged to the gown and the tighter portion to the undergown. The skirt over the farthingale was still creaseless except at the back, showing the costly fabrics and large, intricate patterns to advantage. It was still open in front in an inverted V, displaying the rich material of the undergown. Trains were now smaller or not worn at all. Velvet was still the most popular gown material, either plain or patterned, with brocade, satin, silk, and damask as alternatives. The **girdle** was as costly as ever, being made of precious metal, encrusted with jewels, and ending in the inevitable pendant jewel or pomander. Gold chain girdles were in great demand. Fur trimmings, gold and silver embroidery, also coloured work, were employed lavishly on the gowns (see pp. 119 and 121).

A loose, open garment, of Spanish origin, resembling a cross between a **gown** and a **coat,** appeared in Queen Mary's reign. It had a high, standing collar and was brooched in front at the neck. The garment was open in the front and, having no other fastening, hung to the ground, widening steadily towards the hem in the same shape as a farthingale, except that it began from the neck instead of the waist. The gown or undergown was then visible in front. Sleeves were either short puffs or had a hanging sleeve attached to the back of the puff.

Although the pinned-up version of the **gable hood** continued to be worn by older and less fashionable ladies, the **French hood** finally supplanted it in public favour in this period. The shape of the hood altered slightly between 1547 and 1558: the front edge of black velvet or jewelled metal band was curved more to terminate at the ear; a white satin or silk band was worn behind this, and the rear jewelled band was then placed higher and farther back on the head. The black velvet hood then fell vertically down the back, as before. In Queen Mary's reign, the shape of the hood was flatter on top and more curved at the sides (see pp. 119, 121, and 124). Another similar head-dress, one popularly associated with Mary, Queen of Scots, was the heart-shaped, jewelled, white gauze or silk **cap.** This had a frontal framework to effect the heart-shape which framed the face, and the head-dress was worn fairly far back on the head. Gold network and jewels lavishly adorned this cap (see p. 119).

Rather more **hair** was visible with these two head-dresses than with the gable hood: it could be seen on the forehead and temples. It was now usually waved and fluffed out on the temples instead of being drawn back tightly, as before.

Feminine **shoes** were similar to those described for the men.

A tremendous amount of **jewellery** was still in use, and it was of the same high quality, workmanship, and richness as in Henry VIII's time. Collars, necklaces, pendants, rings, pomanders, aiguillettes, girdles, and reliquaries were all worn in abundance, made of precious metal and set with most beautiful jewels (see p. 124).

Materials, designs, and **decorative trimmings** were almost identical to those worn in the previous reign. **Embroidery** was still exquisite, worked in silk and gold or silver thread; **lace** edging, though still rare and expensive, was used more and more to trim these embroideries.

Accessories carried and worn by both sexes were the same as those described for the last reign.

QUEEN ELIZABETH 1558–1603

Many and varied indeed are the historical, romantic, and theatrical accounts written of the age of Elizabeth; this variation appears to be due largely to the opinion of the writer on the social and economic characteristics of that age. For instance, some depict it as the greatest and most glorious epoch in our history, others pay less attention to the glory and more to the lack of sanitation and hygiene; some stress that it was a time of great activity in commerce,

TUDOR, 1547-1558

RED VELVET CAP & WHITE PLUME, AS IN COLOUR PLATE - 'GENTLEMAN IN RED'

LADY - 1553 - BLACK VELVET FRENCH HOOD - JEWELLED BAND - SMALL RUFF - WHITE COLLAR

EDWARD VI - BLACK VELVET CAP - JEWELLED - DARK PLUME - WHITE EMBROIDERED NECK FRILL - BLACK, GOLD EMBROIDERED, JEWELLED DOUBLET - DARK SILK LINED GOWN

EMERALD & GOLD RING - ENAMEL DECORATION

SAPPHIRE & GOLD RING

DIAMOND & GOLD RING - ENAMEL DECORATION

EDWARD VI - BLACK VELVET CAP - JEWELLED - WHITE PLUME - ERMINE REVERS TO GOWN - WHITE COLLAR

DETAIL OF FULL-LENGTH DRAWING OF PRINCESS MARY TUDOR c.1549

DIAMOND PENDANT CROSS - GOLD SETTING WITH PEARLS

INSCRIBED SILVER RING

LEATHER SHOE - EMBROIDERED GOLD & PEARL DECORATION

SILVER LOVE RING

SLASHED BUFF LEATHER SHOE

GREEN LEATHER SLASHED SHOE

BLACK VELVET GOWN & HOOD - WHITE SATIN COLLAR LINING & UNDER YOKE - JEWELLED BAND ON HOOD - GAUZE EMBROIDERED PARTLET - RUFFLE

literature, and art; others condemn it for its false glitter and pageantry. But whatever the personal opinion, there can be no doubt that in the realm of costume this period was supreme in its lavish display, by both sexes, of jewels, gold, silver, and jewelled embroidered fabrics, false hair, and padded and wired under-structures to distort and accentuate to an incredible degree the human form, particularly the feminine one. Indeed, no other court in the history of the Western world has matched its splendour, except perhaps the later French courts of Louis XIV or Louis XVI and Marie Antoinette. It is questionable, of course, whether this ostentatious presentation was desirable, or, indeed, beyond a certain point, attractive, but in this book it is endeavoured to state the historical facts dispassionately, without undue personal comment, so while some costume writers revile, condemn, or applaud the extremity of style and glamour of this age, an effort will be made here merely to describe as simply as possible.

Queen Elizabeth herself undoubtedly led and encouraged the tendency towards even greater displays of finery than were fashionable in her father's, brother's, and sister's reigns; it is true that she issued several edicts against this lavish apparel, as her relatives had done before her, but they had only a very limited effect, particularly in view of the fact that in her own dress she ignored these edicts. She inherited from her father, Henry VIII, an abiding love of fine clothes and jewels, and perhaps owing to the fact that these things were largely denied to her in her youth, she carried these desires to excess when the power was accorded to her. Portraits of Elizabeth early in her reign are fairly modest in display and similar in style to those of the two preceding reigns, but as she grew older, towards the middle and end of her long reign, her dresses became more and more heavily ornamented with gold and silver, jewelled embroideries, flowers, lace frills, and jewellery, particularly long ropes of pearls. She was fairly slim and encouraged the wearing of the narrow, long metal corset and farthingale, and the later development of this—the wheel or hoop farthingale. She also greatly favoured the wearing of the ruff—that typically Elizabethan article of dress, although it was also worn in the earlier and later reigns. She delighted in various styles of coiffure, resorting in later years—so popularising the fashion—to wigs of different hues. It is said that at her death her wardrobe numbered dresses in thousands and wigs in hundreds.

The apparel of Elizabethan men was almost as gorgeous as that of the women, although it was slightly more natural in form. The male had, by this time, conceded first place to the female in the pageant of colour and finery, but he did not lag far behind. The equivalent masculine extremities of style of the eighties were seen in the cartwheel ruffs, large padded trunk hose, or the extremely brief variety, the peasecod-bellied doublet and the tall plumed hat.

The Spanish influence on dress, which had begun in Queen Mary's time, continued throughout the reign of Elizabeth: it could be seen in the men's short capes, trunk hose, padded doublets, and tall hats, and in the feminine farthingale, ruffs, and jewels. Towards the end of the century, however, the French influence became competitive, especially in women's dresses, as could be seen in the French wheel farthingale.

The **doublet** developed steadily in this reign towards an extreme style about 1580–1590, and then commenced to return to a more normal silhouette with the dawn of the seventeenth century. Until about 1570 it remained a fitting

TUDOR, ELIZABETH
1558-1603

GENTLEMAN. c. 1567.
EMBROIDERED, SILK JERKIN -
DOUBLET OF VELVET SHOWS AT
SLEEVES - RUFFS AT NECK & WRISTS -
JEWELLED COLLAR & PENDANT -
EMBROIDERED PANES ON
TRUNK HOSE - CLOTH CAPE - SILK
LINING - HOSE - GARTERS -
SHOES - BLACK VELVET
HAT - OSTRICH PLUMES
JEWELLED BAND

· c. 1560 ·
DARK VELVET GOWN WITH
GREY FUR TRIMMING - VELVET
PATTERNED UNDERSKIRT -
JEWELLED, EMBROIDERED
PARTLET &
UNDERSLEEVES -
GAUZE RUFFS AT
NECK & WRISTS -
JEWELLED, GOLD
GIRDLE & POMANDER -
PEARL NECKLACE -
JEWELLED, GOLD
WRISTBANDS & CAP

LADY. c. 1560-70 -
DARK GREEN VELVET SURCOTE
OR OVERGOWN - JEWELLED, GOLD
EMBROIDERED EDGE - PADDED
ROLL WINGS - WHITE SATIN
GOWN - SLASHED SLEEVES -
JEWELLED FRONT &
GIRDLE - POMANDER -
LACE - EDGED RUFFS AT
NECK & WRISTS -
GLOVES - JEWELLED
CAP

EARL OF LEICESTER.
c. 1560-70 - CRIMSON
JERKIN & TRUNK HOSE -
GOLD EMBROIDERY &
BUTTONS - GOLD, JEWELLED
NECKLACE - BLACK VELVET
HAT - JEWELLED BAND -
WHITE, EMBROIDERED
EDGED RUFFS AT NECK &
WRISTS - BELT -
HOSE - SHOES

body garment, buttoned, hooked, or laced up the centre front, with long, fitting sleeves, a short skirt, and a high neck. As time passed the waist-line became lower, especially in front where it dropped to a low point; the neck-line rose higher until it was almost under the ears; the skirt became shorter, formed in small tabs at the waist-line, and the front of the doublet was padded. Stuffed, slashed rolls or wings, called **picadils,** decorated the shoulders. From 1570 to about 1595, the more extreme modes developed, reaching a climax 1580–1590: the front of the doublet became heavily padded with stuffing known as *bombast,* consisting of rags, bran, hair, etc., to droop forward over the low-pointed waist-line which reached almost to the fork by 1580–1590—a style known as a *peasecod-belly* or *peasecod doublet*—whalebone or metal strips were inserted in the seams of the doublet to maintain the correct shape; the skirt consisted only of very small tabs; sleeves became fuller and more padded to a leg-of-mutton shape, and were also held in place by whalebone strips in the seams, and the sleeve was often slashed open vertically down the front, then partially buttoned across or held by aiguillettes. The high neck-line, slashings, and picadils remained in favour during the whole period, though after 1590 there was a decline in bombast, both on the torso and sleeves, and these returned to a more normal outline (see pp. 126, 129, 131, and 134).

Although the doublet was occasionally worn without another tunic on top, the wearing of a **jerkin** was, in Elizabeth's reign, far more prevalent than previously. It fitted very closely on top of the doublet and therefore followed the same vagaries of fashion during the period 1558–1603. Sometimes, particularly in the latter part of the century, it was worn unbuttoned in front, thus showing the front panel of the doublet. The doublet was also visible through slashes in the jerkin and on the arms, where the jerkin was either sleeveless, with picadils on the shoulders, or had short puff sleeves on the upper arm only. The jerkin either had a high collar, obscuring the doublet collar, or it had a lower, round neck, thus showing the doublet above. Leather or kid were popular materials for the jerkin, or alternatively velvet or satin (see pp. 126, 129, 131, and 134).

Trunk hose and **stockings** had developed by the beginning of the Elizabethan era into the accepted masculine covering from waist to toe. Now that the doublet and jerkin skirt had become so abbreviated, the lower garments assumed greater prominence in the world of fashion. The knickerbocker effect of these trunk hose is familiar to us in all Elizabethan portraits and drawings—they are to our minds as vital a part of the Elizabethan scene as those famous sea-dogs Drake, Raleigh, and Hawkins. As with the upper garments, the extreme modes were prevalent from about 1575 to 1590, the earlier and later types being more moderate. Thus, until about 1570–1575, trunk hose consisted of full breeches, reaching to about mid-thigh and fastened to a waist-band at the top and leg-bands at the lower ends. Vertical strips of material, often of contrasting colour and fabric, and known as *panes*, were attached on the outside, to the upper and lower bands; these panes were usually slashed and embroidered. The leg-bands were then sewn to the stockings which covered the remainder of the leg and foot. **Pockets** were usually inserted in the lining of trunk hose. The **cod-piece** was still apparent, though less prominent than in the earlier Tudor reigns, and after 1570–1575 it was rarely seen. Padding or bombast of rags, bran, hair, or wool was used to keep the shape of the trunk hose and this usage was carried to greater excess as time passed. By 1575 the trunk hose had become shorter and more padded, reaching an extreme style by 1580–1595, when worn in conjunction with the peasecod doublet; the trunk hose then barely covered the hips and were often padded to an excessive width, so much so that it is said that it became necessary to widen the seats in Parliament. Whalebone inserted in the panes or seams helped to give the desired silhouette. The stockings, after 1570–1575, were often worn in two parts: the upper section, known as *upper stocks* or *canions*, were sewn to the trunk hose and ended below the knee; they were often ornately embroidered; the lower section, known as *nether-stocks*, extended from the foot to just above the knee and were fastened on top of the canions by a garter or ribbon-sash below the knee. Stockings were either knitted or tailored. **Clocks,** in gold, silver, or colour, were fashionable at the end of the century (see pp. 126, 129, 131, and 134). A longer style of breeches known as *venetians* became an alternative fashion after about 1575. These varied considerably in cut: some were very full, padded or loose; some were tight-fitting; some were full at the top and tight lower down. All styles were fastened at the knee by a garter or sash, and slashes in different designs were popular. Both trunk hose and venetians were made of rich fabrics similar to the upper garments and were equally lavishly decorated with embroidery, jewels, and slashes.

There were two main types of outer garment, though each of these had many individual styles—the **gown** and the **cloak.** The former, worn either on top of, or as an alternative to, the jerkin, was either very short, hip-length for fashionable younger men, or calf- or ankle-length for older, more serious men. It hung loose and ungirded, often buttoned at the neck only, and usually had a stand-up collar or fur revers as in the previous reigns. Sleeves were various: hanging, puff, fitting, or merely picadils. The cloak, which was perhaps more favoured, and certainly a more typical Elizabethan garment, was seen in many different lengths: anything from waist- to ankle-length was fashionable. Some styles had large or stand-up collars, others had none. Most cloaks were cut in a circular pattern and were worn in different ways: either on both shoulders or slung round one and then draped round the body. As with the other garments, materials were costly and various: satin, velvet, silk, brocade, cloth, and gold or silver fabric were in constant use; trimmings included furs of many types embroidered, jewelled bands or velvet guards, lace and jewels, particularly pearls. Colours were rich and brilliant—they were so for all other items of dress—red, black, green, and yellow being popular. Linings of contrasting colours were also of rich material (see pp. 126, 129, 131, and 134).

Shirts were still made of fine white cambric or lawn and embroidered in coloured, gold, or black silk thread, but were not now visible except through slashes in the doublet, owing to the latter's very high neck-line.

In order to accentuate the contrast between the small waist and the bombasted peasecod-belly and hips, in the period of more extreme styles of about 1570–1595, men often wore whalebone stiffened **stays** or **corsets** as an alternative to whalebone bands inserted in the doublet itself.

There were two types of neckwear for the Elizabethan man: a **collar** or a *ruff*. The collar was fairly small, made of white cambric or holland, lace-edged,

TUDOR, ELIZABETH
1558-1603

SIR CHRISTOPHER HATTON -
c. 1575 - DARK, PATTERNED
CAPE - STRIPED JERKIN - BELT -
RUFFS AT NECK & WRISTS -
CHAIN & MEDALLION -
DARK PATTERNED PANES ON
TRUNK HOSE - BLACK VELVET
HAT - PLUME & JEWELS -
PATTERNED CANIONS -
NETHERSTOCKS -
PANTOUFLES

QUEEN ELIZABETH, c. 1575 -
BLACK VELVET GOWN,
EMBROIDERED ALL OVER IN
GOLD THREAD & PEARLS -
LACE-EDGED RUFFS AT
NECK & WRISTS - BLACK
LACE PARTLET - SLASHES
ON SLEEVES & BODICE -
WHITE UNDERGARMENT
SHOWS THROUGH -
JEWELLED HEAD DRESS -
JEWELLED, GOLD
COLLARS, PEARL
GIRDLE - FEATHER
FAN - GAUZE
VEIL

QUEEN ELIZABETH, c. 1575 - 90 -
DARK VELVET GOWN, BEJEWELLED ON
BODICE, SLEEVES & SKIRT -
RIBBON PUFF UNDERSLEEVES -
JEWELLED BANDS - LACE
EDGED RUFFS - FINE,
TRANSPARENT, GAUZE,
JEWEL-EDGED VEIL & WINGS -
JEWELLED, TURBAN HEAD-
DRESS, FEATHER &
JEWELLED FAN -
JEWELLED, GOLD
GIRDLE & DOUBLE
NECKLACE

MARY, QUEEN OF SCOTS -
1578 - BLACK VELVET GOWN -
WHITE, EMBROIDERED GAUZE
PARTLET - WHITE, LACE-
EDGED CAP, RUFFS &
VEIL - GOLD GIRDLE,
CHAIN, CROSS &
ROSARY - CRUCIFIX ON
BLACK RIBBON

129

embroidered, turned down over the high doublet collar, and tied in front with strings. It was worn throughout the period, though more popular late in the century, and with older men (see p. 131). The ruff, a more typical Elizabethan style of neckwear and perhaps more often worn, began as a small neck frill in the previous reign, sometimes open in front. It gradually increased in size, becoming a complete circle by about 1570, and in the 1580–1595 period it was a large cartwheel shape, about fifteen to sixteen inches across, worn higher at the back and having to be propped up by a wire framework inserted under the collar. It decreased a little in size after 1595. Ruffs were originally made of holland and had to be fairly small, as they could not be stiffened. However, after 1565, with the introduction of starch and its method of use from Holland, ruffs were made of cambric and lawn, starched and then set in the requisite folds or shapes when wet, by heated metal setting sticks. There were many variations of setting and several layers were often worn. The ruff was always white, but was often finely embroidered in gold, silver, or colour, and later edged with lace. It was tied in front with strings. Wrist **ruffles,** to match, on a smaller scale, were worn, or alternatively lace-edged cuffs, but the latter usually accompanied the lace-edged collar. Examples of the ruff can be seen on pp. 126, 129, 131, 134, and 136.

The short masculine **hair-styles** remained in fashion, on the whole, until the end of the century. The top and side hair were worn rather longer and more curled after 1570 and allowed to fall over the forehead a little. Wigs were occasionally worn about 1590–1600. **Beards** and **moustaches** were very popular all through the reign and the former were seen in many styles.

The flat, black **velvet cap** of the previous three Tudor reigns continued in favour until about 1565. However, by this time the style changed considerably: the crown became higher and fuller and was gathered or pleated into the jewelled band, and the hat was then generally worn at an angle, often far back on the head, showing the hair on the forehead. The crown had become very high by 1575, it was stiffened inside with buckram, and this style remained in vogue until the end of the century. Ostrich plumes, spray feathers, a jewelled band, and jewelled brooches were still the usual decoration (see pp. 126, 131, and 136). Alternative **hat** styles were introduced about 1575: made of hard felt or beaver, they were of various shapes, but generally had a high crown, a small brim, and were worn on the side of the head. Ornamentation was similar to that on the velvet hat with perhaps more jewels and brooches (see pp. 129, 131, 134, and 136).

The **shoe** was cut to fit the natural shape of the foot all through Elizabeth's reign. Slashes were still the usual decoration with embroidery and jewels in addition. The majority of shoes were made of leather—though velvet and satin were still in use—in various colours, with no heel or a wedge-shaped sole. Until about 1575 the shoe was cut high on the instep without fastening, but later it was often tied there by a ribbon bow and a small tongue showed above (see pp. 126, 131, and 134). Slippers known as *pantoufles*, with a wedge cork, wood, or leather sole attached to an upper which only covered the front half of the foot, were very fashionable after about 1575 (see pp. 129 and 131). Leather **boots** in black or natural colour were still worn for travelling or riding: they had a turned-down cuff and were calf- or thigh-length. *Boot hose*, consisting

PLATE VI

The bodice cut as a jerkin or doublet.
Surcote worn on top

Queen Elizabeth, c. 1600, *from the
portrait at Corsham Court, Wiltshire*

TUDOR, ELIZABETH
1558-1603

GENTLEMAN. c.1580 -
SILK, EMBROIDERED JERKIN -
PEASCOD- BELLY — GOLD BUTTONS-
WHITE SATIN PADDED DOUBLET
SLEEVES - CARTWHEEL RUFF -
EMBROIDERED PANES ON
TRUNK HOSE - BROCADE CAPE-
VELVET COLLAR -WHITE
HOSE & SHOES -
BLACK FELT HAT-
JEWEL & PLUME
DECORATION

QUEEN ELIZABETH - 1580 -
WHITE GOWN - EMBROIDERED SPRIG -
PATTERN IN GOLD & COLOURS -
GOLD FROG FASTENINGS, CENTRE
FRONT - GREEN & GOLD
EMBROIDERED MANTLE -
WHITE LINING - LACE-EDGED
RUFF AT NECK & WRISTS -
GOLD, JEWELLED COLLAR
& HEAD-DRESS - GLOVES-
FEATHER FAN - PEARL
NECKLACE

QUEEN ELIZABETH. c. 1585-90 -
BLACK VELVET GOWN DECORATED
BY PEARLS & RIBBON BOWS -
LACE COLLAR & CUFFS -
WRIST RUFFLES - PEARL
NECKLACE - WHITE SATIN
UNDERGOWN, GOLD
THREAD & PEARL
EMBROIDERY WITH
OTHER JEWELS -
PEARL & JEWEL
HEAD-DRESS

ROBERT DUDLEY, EARL OF
LEICESTER - 1588 - DARK,
PATTERNED, SHORT GOWN, EDGED
WITH BLACK FUR & JEWELLED,
PADDED SLEEVES - SLASHED
JERKIN - LACE-EDGED WHITE
COLLAR & CUFFS -
JEWELLED COLLAR &
MEDALLION -
PEASCOD- BELLY -
DARK EMBROIDERED
PANES ON LIGHT
TRUNK HOSE -
NETHERSTOCKS-
PANTOUFLES-
BLACK VELVET
JEWELLED CAP-
CANE.

of an extra pair of stockings worn inside to protect the embroidered nether-stocks, were favoured later in the reign.

The feminine figure, and therefore the **gown** styles, were governed by the metal corset and the **farthingale** to an even greater extent in the age of Elizabeth than in the reigns of her three predecessors; indeed, by the end of the sixteenth century it was difficult to trace the shape of the natural figure in the dress at all. The Spanish farthingale remained in vogue throughout the reign of Elizabeth, becoming larger in circumference as time passed, and in the latter years of the century a padded circular roll was tied round the body just below the waist so that the gown material formed a fuller silhouette on the hips than previously. The gown itself, though governed in shape by this farthingale and the metal corset, varied considerably in style as the reign progressed. The mode worn in the time of Queen Mary remained fashionable until about 1570–1575: materials were costly, predominantly velvet, satin, brocade, and silk, plain or patterned, with a lavish use of jewelled embroidery and jewels (see pp. 126 and 129). After about 1575, the farthingale widened at the hem and with the padded tyre worn high round the hips, the skirt silhouette became much wider and rounder; it was also fuller and had more folds of material where it was gathered or pleated at the waist. The waist-line became lower, especially in the pointed front, and narrower. Although the open skirt was seen until about 1585, it tended to go out of fashion after 1580 and the under-skirt was not then visible. Sleeves became wider and of leg-of-mutton shape like the masculine doublet; they were padded at the top or had whalebone bands inserted in the seams. The neck-line was now usually high and hidden under the ruff or, late in the century, very low, exposing part or most of the bosom. Far more jewelled embroidery and jewels were worn on the gown, so that by the end of the century there was hardly a square inch of fabric left unornamented. Long ropes of pearls hung to below the waist, jewelled collars and pendants encircled the neck, ornamental metal, jewelled wrist-bands were worn (see pp. 129 and 131). About 1588–1590 a new type of farthingale became the vogue, although it did not completely oust the Spanish farthingale from fashion in Elizabeth's reign. This new style was called a **wheel** or **hoop farthingale,** because of its shape and construction. It consisted of a canvas petticoat, similar to the Spanish farthingale, but the hoops of whalebone, inserted horizontally, were of equal diameter from waist to ground, the top one being supported by radial spokes of whalebone which were fastened by tapes to a ring round the corseted waist. This ring was not actually placed centrally in the circle, but near the front edge so that the weight of the farthingale was taken on the stomach whilst the widest part of the circular hoop was at the back. The gown, therefore, extended almost horizontally from the waist outwards, dipping slightly towards the front of the farthingale, then fell vertically to the ground in folds at the outer rim of the wheel. In the 1590s, a ruffle or circular frill of the same material as the gown was worn on top of the wheel, giving radiating pleats which accentuated the wheel shape even more. The waist-line of the gown became lower and lower towards 1600, reaching a very low point in front and giving a long, narrow-bodied effect to the gown; a brocaded stomacher, laced across and jewelled, was inserted in the front panel of the bodice. Sleeves were still leg-of-mutton shape, heavily padded at the top and usually had hanging false sleeves which draped behind the arm and hung over the rim of the farthingale to the ground. The neck-line was still often very high and hidden under a large ruff, although the extremely *décolleté* style—popularised by Queen Elizabeth, so it is said, in order to affirm her maidenhood—became increasingly in vogue worn with the wheel farthingale in the last years of the century; the corsage was finished by lace frills, flowers, or jewels. The gown was shorter, often only ankle-length, by 1595–1603, so that the feet were shown for the first time for hundreds of years (see p. 134). Separate bodices, like the masculine jerkin, were commonly worn during the whole reign: they had picadils on the shoulders and tabs at the waist and were usually buttoned centre front from a high neck-line.

A loose open **gown** or **surcote**, which had been introduced in Queen Mary's reign, continued to be worn until about 1575. It was fastened at the neck in front by a jewelled brooch, it had a stand-up collar, surmounted by the ruff, and either small puff sleeves, hanging ones, or merely picadils on the shoulders. The gown hung open in front in an inverted V, and increased in circumference to the ground. Black or dark velvet were the usual materials, with jewelled, embroidered band decoration (see p. 126).

The Plate VI of Queen Elizabeth shows her attired in a gown or **surcote** similar to that just described, edged and lined with ermine, and with hanging sleeves. The **bodice** of the gown itself is separate, like a jerkin, buttoned centre front and ending in a low-pointed waist-line; its **sleeves** are similarly buttoned full-length. The full **skirt** is worn over a Spanish farthingale.

The metal **corset,** covered with leather or velvet and padded, was similar in design to that worn in Henry VIII's reign, until about 1590, when certain modifications became necessary with the introduction of the wheel farthingale. The corset then extended much lower in the centre front, well down the stomach, tapering to a narrow point, and as far down the sides as the pelvis would permit. The corset was then laced up the back, not hinged as previously. This style gave the flat, long-bodied, narrow silhouette as far as the hips.

The feminine **ruff** closely followed the trend of the masculine until about 1580. It began as a small embroidered-edged ruff, open in front and tied with strings; matching **ruffles** were seen at the wrists (see pp. 126, 129, and 136). As time passed, the neck ruff grew larger, reaching about ten to fifteen inches radius by about 1580. More ornate embroideries and lace edges were employed on these large feminine ruffs than on the men's styles. A wire support was necessary under these large ruffs; it was placed underneath at the back, raising the ruff high up the back of the head (see pp. 129 and 131). As an alternative style to these circular cartwheel ruffs, the other type became popular about 1585–1600 with the low *décolletage*, wherein the ruff enclosed the back and sides of the neck only, and was open in front, leaving the bosom exposed (see p. 134). Sometimes when this type of large ruff was worn, a small circular one would be donned inside it, tightly encircling the neck—a style adopted by Queen Elizabeth in her declining years to hide her wrinkled neck (see p. 136). In addition to the ruff, about 1580, a wired **collar** and **veil** were worn behind the ruff. The collar, shaped in two large butterfly wings behind the head, had a wired jewelled edge and was supported on a wire framework attached at the back of the neck and fastened to the bodice on the side fronts. The framework was called a *supportasse*. The collar itself was made of very fine transparent

TUDOR, ELIZABETH
1558-1603

QUEEN ELIZABETH 1592 -
WHITE SATIN GOWN WORN OVER
WHEEL FARTHINGALE -
WHITE SILK & GOLD &
COLOURED, JEWELLED
EMBROIDERY - WIRED,
JEWELLED, GAUZE VEIL -
LACE-EDGED RUFF - PEARL
NECKLACES - JEWELLED
GOLD NECKLACE - FAN
GLOVES -JEWELLED
HEAD DRESS

1602
WHITE SATIN DOUBLET, TRUNK
HOSE & CANIONS - SILVER
EMBROIDERY ON PANES -
BROWN VELVET JERKIN,
EMBROIDERED IN SILVER THREAD
& PEARLS - NATURAL COLOURED
NETHERSTOCKS - WHITE RIBBON
GARTERS - BROWN SHOES -
LEATHER BELT - RUFFS AT
NECK & WRISTS - BLACK
HAT & SPRAY FEATHER

LADY- c. 1600 -
WHITE SATIN GOWN OVER
WHEEL FARTHINGALE -
EMBROIDERED PATTERN IN
COLOURS - RIBBON SASH
WHITE RUFF - COLLAR - SILVER
EDGE - ROSE & LACE
DECORATION TO
SLEEVES, BODICE &
CORSAGE - FLOWERS
IN COIFFURE & ON
GOWN

LADY- c. 1595 -1603 -
SATIN GOWN OVER
WHEEL FARTHINGALE -
JEWELLED, EMBROIDERED
BODICE & PADDED
SLEEVES - METAL
JEWELLED WRIST-BANDS
LACE-EDGED RUFFS -
TRANSPARENT, GAUZE
WINGS, VEIL & HEAD-
DRESS - PEARL EDGE -
PEARL ROPE
NECKLACE &
WRIST-LETS -
FEATHER FAN

134

gauze and the veil portion, made of the same material, often with a pearl, jewel, or lace edge, fell to the ground at the back in soft filmy clouds (see pp. 129 and 134).

Until about 1570 feminine hair-styles were similar to those seen in the previous reign, but after this time the hair was dressed higher off the forehead, later over a pad or wire framework and worn in myriads of curls on top of the head. The coiffure rose higher still late in the century and was assisted by the addition of false hair or a wig if natural hair did not provide the desired effect. Wigs were very popular from 1590 to 1603, and were seen in many different hues, particularly golden or red, in imitation of the Queen. Alternatively, ladies dyed their own hair the requisite colour. Jewels of all kinds, especially pearl ropes, flowers, plumes, and ornaments were arranged in this coiffure for decoration and to give additional height; no other head-covering was then worn at this time, except for riding and travelling (see pp. 129, 131, 134, and 136).

Head-dresses in Elizabethan days were various, in contrast to the earlier Tudor reigns where a definite style of hood had been worn by everyone. The hair was left uncovered a great deal more in the Elizabethan age than hitherto, and one of the most popular head-dresses, particularly until about 1580, was a jewelled, gold network cap worn on the back of the head to enclose the back hair, and showing waves and curls on the top and sides of the head (see pp. 126 and 136). The heart-shaped, wire-fronted head-dress, after the style of Mary Queen of Scots, was also still worn until about 1570; it was white, made of lawn or cambric and edged with jewels and lace (see p. 129). The French hood continued in fashion until about 1575–1580, though worn rather farther back on the head than previously (see p. 136). With the high coiffure of 1580–1603, ornamented by its jewels, plumes, flowers, etc., another head-dress was superfluous, except for riding or travelling when a hard felt tall hat, similar in style to the masculine hats and ornamented by ostrich plumes, sufficed.

Ladies' stockings and shoes were now partially visible by 1590 for the first time for centuries. Silk, wool, or cotton stockings, like the men's, in various bright colours—green, red, white, yellow, etc., and ornamented by clocks, were worn. Silk stockings became more popular as time passed, though they were very expensive. Shoes, made of brocade, velvet, satin, and leather, embroidered, jewelled, and slashed, were similar to the men's styles. Pantoufles were also worn and chopines or clogs were still in use for outdoor wear (see p. 136).

Masculine accessories still included a dagger and/or sword: the former was generally inserted in the waist-belt and the latter was slung from a hanger on the left side. Both sexes carried gloves and handkerchiefs: the former were made of richly embroidered leather or kid, decorated with jewels on the gauntlet and slashed on the fingers to show the finger rings; perfumed gloves were in great demand; handkerchiefs were white, of lawn or cambric, lace-edged and embroidered in gold, silver, or colour; they were also perfumed. Pendant watches, supported from the waist-belt, became in greater demand towards the end of the century: they were exquisitely enamelled and jewelled. Essential items in a lady's ensemble were the small mirror, usually hung from the girdle, and a fan; the latter was made of feathers or plumes set in a jewelled metal holder, though late in the reign, ivory, vellum, and gauze folding fans were introduced.

TUDOR, ELIZABETH
1558-1603

SIR HENRY UNTON -
BLACK FELT HAT -
JEWEL & SPRAY FEATHER
DECORATION -
CARTWHEEL RUFF -
LIGHT JERKIN

SIR EDWARD HOBY - 1578 -
BLACK VELVET HAT -
CRIMSON PLUME -
JEWELLED BAND -
BLACK EMBROIDERED
EDGED WHITE RUFF -
LIGHT JERKIN

QUEEN ELIZABETH. c. 1558 - 70 -
JEWELLED CAP - EMBROIDERED EDGED RUFF -
GAUZE, EMBROIDERED PARTLET - DARK GOWN -
SLASHED & JEWELLED - PENDANT JEWELS

THE ARMADA JEWEL
c. 1588
ENAMELLED GOLD PENDANT SET
WITH DIAMONDS & RUBIES.

c. 1566

WHITE LEATHER GLOVE - GOLD THREAD
& COLOURED
EMBROIDERY

GOLD PENDANT -
ENAMELLED —
AMETHYSTS

GOLD PENDANT -
GARNET & PENDENT
SAPPHIRE

1590 - 1600

GOLD, ENAMELLED
LOCKET IN WHITE, GREEN
& PURPLE - CONTAINING MIRROR - c. 1600

c. 1590
LARGE, LACE-EDGED RUFF - SMALL RUFF
INSIDE - JEWELLED & FEATHER HEAD DRESS -
JEWELLED COLLAR

EMERALD &
GOLD RING

CHOPINE

BLACK VELVET HAT -
RUFF - c. 1580

FRENCH HOOD - c. 1562.

136

Cosmetics, perfume, and **hair dye** were used considerably by women and, to a certain extent, by men also.

It is difficult to describe adequately in words or to show in small-scale illustrations the wealth, splendour, and design of the jewellery worn in profusion on the costumes of both men and women in the age of Elizabeth. Heavy, ornate, jewelled gold **collars** with a **pendant** or pendants, attached either at the pit of the neck or from the collar encircling the shoulders, and hanging to the waist, were worn by both sexes. **Neck-chains** of gold, jewelled, with pendant **medallions, lockets, crosses,** etc., were alternative or additional wear and were so long that they could often be wound two or three times round the neck. Countless jewelled and signet **rings** were worn on all fingers and the thumb; **ear-rings,** or just one ear-ring, usually of drop pearls, were frequently seen; heavily **jewelled ornaments** adorned all hat, cap, and hood styles, the feminine network cap being almost covered with jewels; sleeve ornaments and **aiguillettes** were more intricate and costly in design than ever, and jewels, especially pearls, were lavished all over the costume. Jewellery favoured only by ladies included the heavy jewel-encrusted **girdle** with pendant, **pomander,** mirror, or medallion, and from 1575 to 1603, incredibly long **necklaces** composed of four or five rows of pearl ropes reaching to well below the waist. Examples of the fan, gloves, and various designs in jewellery can be seen on pp. 129, 131, 134, and 136.

Materials, as previously mentioned, were various and costly: velvet, gold or silver cloth, brocade, satin, silk, taffeta, gauze, cloth, and cambric being in chief demand. Unpatterned fabrics covered with jewelled, gold, silver, and coloured embroideries were most popular, though designed velvets, damasks, and brocades were in use throughout the century. **Colours** were rich and vivid. **Trimmings** were of fur, and, with growing popularity, lace and cut-work, especially in the ruff, partlet, collar, and accessories. **Motifs** were chiefly floral and on a smaller scale later in the century.

VI
THE STUARTS AND THE COMMON-WEALTH
THE STUARTS
JAMES I   1603–1625

THE splendour, gorgeous fabrics, jewels, and artificiality of the late Elizabethan era continued until the end of the reign of James I, and with them, except for new developments in detail, the same numbers and styles of garments. In men's dress, the doublet, jerkin, breeches, trunk hose, and cloak were still covered with jewelled embroideries, padded, and decorated by slashings; there was a trend towards wasp-waisted doublets, achieved by corsets or whalebone bands in the doublet seams, padding on the chest, and perhaps in the breeches or trunk hose. Men tended to adopt longer hair-styles; hats were many and varied in shape, with extremely rich, ornate jewelled bands, plumes of different types and jewelled brooches; shoes began to have heels, and large rosettes covered the instep. The ruff had decreased in size considerably and now had competitors for its popularity—the falling ruff and the wired collar or whisk. Lace-edged cuffs also began to usurp the place of wrist ruffles. Lace itself assumed a much greater importance as a trimming on various items of dress, and the collars and ruffs were frequently made entirely of it.

Despite the intricacy and exquisiteness of these white lace and lace-edged cambric undergarments, collars, cuffs, handkerchiefs, etc., worn by both sexes, there was as yet little sign of any reasonable standard of personal hygiene; undergarments were expensive, but only few were possessed: the most infrequent changing of these—perhaps once in three or four weeks—made more unnecessary; cosmetics and perfumes, heavily applied, continued to mask the somewhat unfortunate consequences, at any rate to the satisfaction of persons of that period.

In feminine dress, Anne of Denmark, James I's queen, was perhaps largely to blame for the continued popularity of the wheel farthingale, of even greater circumference, if possible, than that worn at the end of Elizabeth's reign. Queen Anne liked this style and continued to wear it, in conjunction with the circular waist ruffle, low, pointed, narrow stomacher and corset, very low décolletage—often completely baring the bosom—large lace collars or ruffs and the high coiffure of natural or false curls, surmounted by jewels, flowers, plumes, etc., as Elizabeth had done. The ankle-length gowns showed the shoes which had large roses similar to those of the men. Masculine hat styles were adopted for riding and travelling. After the death of Anne of Denmark in 1619, the vogue for the farthingale declined and later in the twenties it ceased to be worn at all by fashionable women.

In masculine attire, both **doublet** and **jerkin**—although the latter was worn far less often in this reign than in that of Elizabeth—were still artificial in shape,

STUART, JAMES I
1603-1625

PRINCE HENRY - PATTERNED JERKIN, DOUBLET & BREECHES - JEWELLED BELT & PENDANT ON RIBBON - LACE EDGED RUFF & CUFFS - RIBBON TIES AT KNEE - SLASHED SHOES WITH ROSES - CLOAK

SMALLER WHEEL FARTHINGALE WITHOUT CIRCULAR FRILL - SILK GOWN - JEWELLED EMBROIDERED BAND DECORATION - BROCADE STOMACHER - LACE EDGED COLLAR, CUFFS & HANDKER- -CHIEF - FOLDING FAN - JEWELLED HEAD-DRESS - PEARL NECK- -LACE & CIRDLE

RIDING COSTUME - DARK SELF-COLOUR PATTERNED GOWN, WORN OVER PADDED ROLL OR SPANISH FARTHINGALE - ELBOW- -LENGTH BUTTONED SLEEVES SHOWING STRIPED, SLASHED UNDER- -SLEEVES - LACE COLLAR & CUFFS - HAT WITH PLUMES & BAND- GLOVES

1614 - LIGHT, SILK, FLOWERED DOUBLET - BRAID TRIMMING - LACE COLLAR & CUFFS - RIBBON & PENDANT - PATTERNED, LOOSE BREECHES - BOOTS, ONE TURNED DOWN GLOVES

but in a rather different manner from that seen in the extreme styles of the eighties. From 1603 until the end of James's reign, the accent was upon achieving a small waist, either by wearing an actual corset or stays, or, perhaps more frequently, by making the doublet into a semblance of a corset by the insertion of vertical bands of whalebone in the seams. Padding was still used by many, but at this time it was concentrated on the chest, not the stomach, as hitherto. The waist-line remained low and narrow at first, but rose towards the end of the reign and became less acutely constricted by about 1625. Sleeves were fairly fitting and long in the early days of the century—padding had almost disappeared from them by about 1606—and after 1610–1612 the newer style, full at the top and paned, fitting on the forearm and buttoned for four to five inches on the outer edge of the forearm, became usual. The sleeve lining, or more commonly, the white shirt, were pulled through the openings between the panes. The small tabs of the skirt became much larger in this reign and were usually known as *tassets*. Shoulder wings were still in vogue, and also rather larger. Leather, velvet, satin, silk, or brocade were popular fabrics for both doublet and jerkin, trimmed with bands of braid, pearls, and other jewelled embroidery and lace (see pp. 139 and 142). The jerkin, when worn, was still almost identical in cut to the doublet, except that it was generally sleeveless, the shoulders being finished by wings (see p. 139).

Both **breeches** after the style of the Elizabethan venetians, and **trunk hose** were worn as alternative modes in this reign: the different versions of these were indeed numerous and varied. Breeches, ending above, at, or below the knee and tied there by a ribbon sash or garter, were worn padded or loose: the padded styles, seen chiefly in the early part of the period, were heavily bombasted, particularly on the hips, and were still commonly ornamented by slashes; the unpadded versions were either very full and baggy to the knee, or full at the top and tight-fitting over the knee itself (see p. 139). Breeches open at the bottom, like shorts, were still occasionally seen and were also knee-length. Trunk hose were very full and worn much longer in this reign: from mid-thigh to nearly knee-length was usual; elaborate slashings on the panes were still in vogue, and though many styles were loose and unpadded, bombast still had a considerable following. As with the upper garments, silk, satin, brocade, and velvet were popular fabrics for all these styles of nether wear, intricately embroidered in colour, gold, silver, and jewels—chiefly pearls—or brocaded or damasked (see pp. 139 and 142). After about 1620, trunk hose ceased to be quite so *à la mode*, and fairly full breeches, ending just above the knee in a lace or silk ruffle, became the leading vogue, as can be seen in the illustration on p. 142. The **points,** still so termed though now in the form of ribbon bows with metal tags on the ends, which attached the breeches to the doublet, could now be seen once more at the doublet waist (see pp. 139 and 142).

Garters were ornate in this reign—the beginning of the long fashion in men's costume in which the knee and lower leg became the chief recipient of the lace fripperies and ruffles—a vogue which lasted till after the Restoration. Silk or ribbon sashes were used as garters, tied in a large bow on the outer side of the leg at, or below, the knee, and hung with fringed ends or in bunches of ribbon loops (see p. 139).

The **stockings**—all knitted now—were by this time separate items from the breeches or trunk hose, and were made of cotton or worsted, and, for those who could afford it, the coveted silk. Stockings were in various colours, decorated by gold, silver, or coloured **clocks** or **quirks** (see p. 142).

Boot hose became an important part of masculine attire at this time. In Elizabeth's reign they had originally been worn to protect the costly silk stockings from the wear occasioned by heavy leather boots; in James's time they ostensibly served the same purpose, but, in fact, were often as costly and ornate as the stockings themselves, and were generally topped by a lace frill or ruffle, just visible inside the top of the boot. Later in the reign they were alternatively worn with shoes. This fashion was carried to greater excesses in later Stuart modes.

In footwear, the **boot** began its rise to popular favour: after about 1612 it was considered modish for most occasions, not just for riding, travelling, etc., as hitherto. Soft leather, in black, light colours, and white was employed, and was cut to fit the leg immaculately, popularly with a turned-down cuff. Sometimes, only one boot was worn turned down (see pp. 139 and 142). **Shoes** developed flat or medium heels for the first time in James's reign, a style which was to last, with sundry variations, and become the modified form of the present day. The Elizabethan bow-tie on the instep had become a large rose or rosette made of ribbon loops of gold, silver, and coloured spangled fabric (see pp. 139, 142, and 144). Shoes for Court and dress wear were often embroidered or painted bright colours, gold, or silver.

The **cloak** remained the most usual outer garment for men; it was worn rather longer in this reign—the abbreviated waist-length styles of the eighties had gone—and had a square-cut collar folded down, or perhaps no collar at all. Linings were rich and brilliantly coloured; embroideries with inset jewels still ornamented the costly outer fabrics. The cloak was either draped round both shoulders or carried over the left arm or shoulder (see pp. 139 and 142).

Alternative types of outer garment to the cloak were the old style of **gown** —ankle-length with long, hanging sleeves, fur edges, fur or velvet guards as ornamentation and chiefly worn by elderly or professional men—and the loose **jacket** of late Elizabethan type, reaching to the hips and usually worn unfastened.

After almost a century of short curly or cropped **hair,** men began to wear rather longer styles once more. By 1625 the hair was generally between ear-level and shoulder-length, and usually curled and waved. The "*love-lock*" was now favoured by early Stuart gallants. It was a longer ringlet, curling down one side of the face to drape on the shoulder and be tied in a ribbon bow. Although short, pointed, curly **beards,** and **moustaches** brushed outwards and upwards were very popular, more clean-shaven men were seen than in the previous century (see p. 144).

Hats were most varied in shape in the first quarter of the seventeenth century. High crowns, like those of late Elizabethan times, were favoured, with narrow brims, or broader ones brooched up on one side. Hard felt or beaver was used for manufacture. Ostrich plumes, spray feathers, brooches, jewels, and very costly jewelled hat-bands decorated these styles (see pp. 142 and 144). Men wore their hats indoors until nearly the end of the seventeenth century when this custom gave way before the advancing desire to show off the enormous curled periwigs.

STUART, JAMES I
1603-1625

1610 - FLOWERED SILK GOWN - BRAID TRIMMING - BUTTONS CENTRE FRONT & SLEEVES - GOWN WORN OVER WHEEL FARTHINGALE - HANGING SLEEVES - PEARL ROPE NECKLACES - LACE COLLAR & CUFFS - FRILL & ROSE AT CORSAGE - BLACK VELVET HAT WITH PLUME & JEWELLED BAND - FEATHER FAN - SHOES WITH ROSES

1616 - SILVER DOUBLET WITH GOLD & BLACK EMBROIDERY - RED & GOLD TRUNK HOSE WITH BLUE & GOLD PANES - BLUE HOSE - GOLD CLOCKS - SILVER SHOES - GOLD ROSETTES - LACE COLLAR & CUFFS

1624 - BRAIDED DOUBLET & BREECHES - LEATHER BELTS - CLOAK - HAT - FALLING RUFF - LEATHER GLOVES - FRINGED EDGES - LEATHER BOOTS - RIBBON & PENDANT JEWEL

QUEEN ANNE - LIGHT SATIN GOWN WITH JEWELLED EMBROIDERY WORN OVER WHEEL FARTHINGALE - PEARL NECKLACE & ROPES - JEWELLED PENDANTS & GIRDLE - LACE-EDGED COLLAR & CUFFS - JEWEL & PLUMES IN HAIR - FEATHER FAN

Shirts were fashioned from fine white cambric, linen, or silk, but were still only visible through slashes on the sleeves and chest of the doublet, owing to the latter's high neck-line.

Neckwear was varied in James's reign, as this period formed the transitional time between the Elizabethan ruffs and the Cavalier Van Dyck collars. Alternative styles included the **ruff**, the **falling ruff,** and the stand-up collar or *whisk*. The ruff was of the same type as the Elizabethan one, but more modest in size (see p. 139). The falling ruff, a derivation from the ordinary ruff, but veering towards a falling collar or band, was composed of several layers of white lace or lace-edged cambric or linen, pleated and falling almost to the shoulder edge (see pp. 142 and 144). The whisk, particularly typical of this reign, though also worn early into the next, was composed of a lace and embroidered white collar wired and starched to stand up at the sides and back, forming a frame or halo round the head. Sometimes the centre portion would be of linen or cambric with a lace edge, but more often the whole collar was composed entirely of exquisite lace of intricate design, perhaps jewelled and decorated with interwoven pearls. A square-fronted shape was popular in the latter years of the reign (see pp. 139, 142, and 144). All these styles of neckwear were tied in front with their white strings, which hung, with minute tassels, on the chest.

Wrist ruffles continued to be worn as a matching set with the ruff, although lace-edged **cuffs,** often in two or three tiers, increasingly accompanied the collar and falling ruff (see pp. 139 and 142).

The even larger **wheel farthingale** provided the basic shape for feminine **gowns** until the 1620s; it was seen with or without the circular waist ruffle, though the latter was still greatly favoured; the waist-line remained low and narrow, achieved by the same type of metal **corset** as previously. The ankle-length or longer skirt was generally open in front to show the costly brocaded or embroidered fabric of the petticoat. A narrow silk sash was often tied round the waist with a small bow in the centre front. Separate **bodices,** like jerkins, with tasset waists, were still seen. The neck-line was round in shape and extremely *décolleté*: often the bosom was completely bare; lace edging, with ribbon bows and flowers, ornamented the corsage. The narrow, long bodice was still often worn over a brocaded stomacher and was occasionally laced across it; the stomacher terminated in the same narrow point in the centre front as previously. **Sleeves** were unaltered in style from those worn in 1600. White became popular, though rich colours were also seen. Silk, satin, velvet, brocade, gold and silver fabric, and cloth were usual materials, with heavy jewelled embroideries, lace, and ribbon trimmings. Numerous layers of petticoats were still necessary to hide the farthingale framework, although only the top one, of very costly fabric, could be seen at the skirt open panel and through slashes on the sleeves (see pp. 139 and 142).

After about 1620 the vogue of the wheel farthingale began to abate: it had no strong adherents after the death of Anne of Denmark, and was either worn on a much smaller scale, or types of Spanish farthingale or padded hip-rolls took its place till the end of the reign. These latter styles were also popular for riding and travelling all through the period (see p. 139).

The high **coiffure** dressed up in front, off the forehead, over a wire framework or pad, remained fashionable until about 1618–1620; **false hair, wigs, and hair**

STUART, JAMES I
1603-1625

Lace collar & neck-edge -
pearl necklace, earrings &
head-dress - jewels on gown & hair

Felt hat - jewelled band -
plume & jewel - lace collar
c.1615

Lace collar - white plume in hair -
pearl earrings - dark gown,
embroidered

Enamelled silver
perfume case

Gold ring
set with
diamonds

Gold ring enamelled -
centre emerald

Lace-edged
falling ruff
c.1620

Pendant with inside miniature -
gold, enamelled in green & white -
set with   diamonds & pearl

Embroidered or painted
shoes with large roses of
ribbon or spangled gold,
silver or colour

James I - hat with plume,
jewel & band - lace-edged collar

Anne of Denmark -
lace collar - necklace -
jewels in hair

Leather glove - embroidered satin
gauntlet

144

dye continued in constant use. The whole coiffure was still decorated by jewels —particularly pearls—flowers, lace, and plumes, and this ornamentation was carried to excess for evening or dress wear. After about 1620, the hair-style became more natural and was lower, without the framework, although it was still dressed in curls in front and the bun at the back (see pp. 139, 142, and 144).

Owing to the high, heavily decorated coiffure, the use of **hats** was still considered superfluous except for riding or travelling, when hats similar to the masculine styles were perched jauntily on top of these high creations (see pp. 139 and 142). Plumes, jewels, expensive bands, and brooches ornamented these hats, which were made of velvet, beaver, or felt.

Feminine styles of **shoe,** made of brocade or satin and visible below the skirt hem, were similar to masculine ones.

As in masculine dress, women assumed several different varieties of neckwear at this time. Despite the *décolleté* neck-line, of a deep, rounded U-shape, the original Elizabethan **ruff,** on a much smaller scale, still had a considerable feminine following; it encircled the neck, and was made of starched cambric with a lace and embroidered edge (or entirely of lace), so that an appreciable expanse of bosom could be seen. The wired **collar** or **whisk** was perhaps the most favoured style of neckwear; it was large, reaching nearly to the top of the head at the back, and was fashioned from exquisite jewelled lace (see pp. 139, 142, and 144). The **combined collar** and **ruff** of the open, late Elizabethan type, composed of several layers of lace and cambric, was still in vogue (see p. 139). Examples of the **falling ruff** were also seen late in the reign. Many variations on all these themes prevailed.

Wrist ruffles were worn in conjunction with the ruff by women as well as men, but lace-edged **cuffs** in two or three tiers were increasingly in demand (see pp. 139 and 142).

The **dagger** ceased to be a fashionable masculine accessory in the early years of the seventeenth century, but the **sword** was still suspended on the left side from a hanger which was attached to the waist-belt. All well-dressed men carried or wore **gloves,** of gauntleted style as previously; jewelled, intricate embroideries and fringed edges ornamented these gauntlets, which were made of silk or thin leather, often in white or cream colour (see pp. 142 and 144). Ladies also carried or wore similar types of glove, and their other essential accessories included a folding or feather **fan** (see pp. 139 and 142), a small fur **muff** in cold weather, and a dainty **hand-mirror,** pendant from the jewelled girdle. **Cosmetics** and **perfume** were lavishly applied, as in later Elizabethan years, and a silk **mask** might be worn when out-of-doors to protect the complexion from cold winds.

A profuse adornment of the person by both sexes with costly jewellery was almost as much the rage in this reign as in the previous one: the most usual examples were numerous jewelled or signet finger or thumb **rings,** worn on each hand; **ear-rings,** particularly drop pearls on one or both ears; jewelled **neck-chains** and **necklaces** with central jewelled **pendants,** and, in addition, for ladies, pearl rope **necklaces,** reaching below the waist, and a **pomander** or perfume case pendent from the girdle. Gold and silver were used in all these examples of the jeweller's art, with coloured or white enamels, filigree work, and a large selection of precious stones set in the metal—pearls especially were used in great profusion. Seed pearls were particularly desired in the jewelled embroideries (see p. 144).

CHARLES I   1625–1649

This Stuart reign—perhaps better known as the time of the Cavalier—is one upon which costume writers agree in their praise of its elegance and picturesqueness. So aptly described by Kelly[1] as the era of "long locks, lace and leather", dress emerges at this time in one of its most attractive forms after the years of extravagant costume characteristic of the Tudors and early Stuarts, under Spanish influence. Cavalier styles have been made familiar to us by the portrait painters of the day, of whom Sir Anthony Van Dyck was perhaps the most famous: his portraits of Charles I, his queen, Henrietta Maria, and other notable Cavaliers and their wives are widely known. Indeed, this painter's influence was such that articles of apparel have been named after him: thus we have "Van Dyck collars" or "Van Dyck edging".

Our knowledge of the costume of Stuart and succeeding periods is of great accuracy because the usual sources of information are supplemented by the most authoritative source of all—actual costumes, still extant in museums and collections.

Spanish domination in the costume of Western Europe diminished after 1620, so that by 1630 the new Cavalier modes were established, lasting at their best until the early 1640s, then deteriorating slightly in taste and discretion until the end of the Civil War. The characteristics of the new styles were principally the looser, less corseted silhouette of both masculine and feminine dress, the higher waist-line, abolition of the farthingale, the replacement of the ruff and whisk by the graceful, lace falling band, long, ringleted hair, sweeping brims, and lace-topped boot hose drooping over wide-cuffed boots. Except for pearls, little jewellery was worn; plain fabrics were preferred to the heavy, formal patterns, and materials were lighter and softer; lace, muslin, silk, and satin replaced brocade, velvet, and damask, and decoration was now provided by ribbon bows and loops, lace frills and ruching instead of the profusion of jewels and jewelled embroideries.

Masculine attire, in particular, was perhaps at its most elegant, befitting, and picturesque. The **doublet** was retained as the chief body garment until nearly 1640, but its rigidity had been somewhat relaxed even by 1625. In the first few years of Charles's reign, the corseted appearance was still visible to a certain extent, provided by whalebone bands in the doublet seams, but after 1627–1630 the garment was worn much looser about the chest and waist, and no longer reinforced. **Tassets** became even larger and deeper, remaining fashionable for as long as the doublet continued to be worn. Long, vertical slashes were made on the chest and back, while sleeves were full, slashed and paned to the elbow, and worn plain and fitting on the forearm. Although the centre V-shaped point in front at the waist was seen until about 1640, it became less acutely pointed, and the waist-line was generally raised to a much higher level than in James's reign. The doublet neck-line remained fairly high and was completely hidden under the large lace collar, which was superimposed on it.

[1] See Chapter IV in *Historic Costume, 1490–1790*, by Francis M. Kelly and Randolph Schwabe.

PLATE VII

Typical "Cavalier" Dress. The lace falling band and boot hose
tops, also the platform sole, should be noted

The Earl of Peterborough, c. 1635, from the portrait by Van Dyck

The ribbon or lace bows, ending in **"points"**, which attached the breeches to the doublet waist, were still visible outside the doublet, although after the early thirties, when the two garments were connected together by hooks, the bows were still apparent, retained for decorative purposes only (see p. 148).

From about 1633 to 1635, the doublet began to change its form entirely, so that by 1640 it had evolved into a **jacket:** the sleeves were worn loose from shoulder to wrist, where they became fitting, and a single slash was made full-length in front; tassets and fitting waist disappeared—the garment was worn loose, only slightly waisted, to the hips—and, although buttons and braid fastenings ornamented the whole centre front of the jacket, from neck to hem, only the first few, on the chest, were fastened, and the garment was left open from there downwards, in an inverted V. Ribbons and bows ornamented this jacket in sundry places, chiefly at the shoulders, sleeves, and neck (see p. 151).

Various colours were used for jacket and doublet, with a preference for pastel shades, in silk or satin, or, occasionally, velvet.

The **jerkin** was worn less and less as time passed; in style it was still like the doublet, though sleeveless or with hanging false sleeves. After about 1632, it was replaced by a loose coat or the **buff-coat:** the latter could either be worn on top of, or instead of, the doublet or jacket. It was made of leather in a natural shade, with or without sleeves, and was tied by a wide silk sash round the waist. It reached about mid-thigh-level, and became very popular during the Civil War; it was of military origin.

Cloaks were still the popular outdoor wear: they were a little longer in this reign—usually mid-thigh to knee-length—and were draped in various ways over one or both shoulders, or carried over the arm. Some styles had a plain neck-line, others a square, turned-down collar; cord fastenings were attached in front, at the neck, and were often tied round one shoulder and the back, permitting the cloak to hang loose behind. Linings were costly, silk and satin being popular for these and the outer fabrics, in pale colours, red, or black. Braid, ribbons, and lace were used for trimming, and the lace collar was frequently arranged on top of the cloak, so that its beauty was not hidden (see p. 151).

The ankle-length **gown** was still sometimes seen, worn by professional or elderly men.

Loose breeches now constituted the universal nether wear for men: trunk hose and padding had gone completely out of fashion by 1625. Actual styles varied throughout Charles's reign: until about 1630–1635 they were usually very full and fastened at the knee by a large ribbon bow or rosette; in the early thirties, some men wore a full type which became tight-fitting over the knee itself; while from 1630 onwards, the popular trend was towards the open breeches, which were looser at the bottom end, over the knee. By 1640, the open style was most often worn, though narrower now, especially at the knee, where it terminated in bunches of ribbon loops, fringes, or braided bands. A vertical band of braid or ribbon usually decorated the outer leg from top to knee. The earlier styles were buttoned at the side, while later versions fastened in front, with a pleat to hide this. As mentioned earlier, the knee was fast becoming a main point of decoration, and as Charles's reign progressed, more and more ribbon loops, lace, and fringes were added above, at, or below

STUART, CHARLES I
1625-1649

c.1629-1633 -
GOLD CLOTH GOWN -
LACE COLLAR - SLEEVE
RUFFLES - LACE CAP -
BLUE BOWS & SASH -
SKIRT OPEN
SHOWING UNDER-
-GOWN OF SAME
MATERIAL - FAN

1631 - GREY-BLUE DOUBLET &
BREECHES - GOLD BRAID TRIMMING -
WHITE SHIRT SHOWS THROUGH
DOUBLET SLASHES - BLUE BALDRIC -
WHITE STOCKINGS - LACE POINTS
AT KNEES & WAIST - BUFF LEATHER
BOOTS & GLOVES - LACE EDGES -
LACE FALLING BAND - DARK
HAIR - BLACK SWORD -
BROWN CANE

c.1628-30 - SILVER
CLOTH DOUBLET & BREECHES -
SLASHED SLEEVES & CHEST -
POINTS AT WAIST - DARK SILK
BALDRIC - BUFF LEATHER BOOTS -
LACE TOPPED BOOT HOSE -
EMBROIDERED, WHITE LEATHER
GLOVES - LACE CUFFS SHOW
ABOVE - LACE-EDGED FALLING
RUFF - LOVE-LOCK - BLACK
HAT WITH JEWEL & PLUME -
SWORD , CANE

c.1638-49 - DARK
SILK GOWN - SKIRT
PINNED UP AT SIDES
SHOWING. PETTICOAT OF PINK
TAFFETA - DOUBLE LACE FALLING
BAND & CUFFS - BLUE SILK
SASH - DARK FUR
MUFF - PEARL NECK-
-LACES - BROOCH

148

the knees (see pp. 148 and 151). Ribbon loops were also attached in front of the breeches at the waist, and on the outer side of either leg, particularly in the latter years of the reign. Breeches were cut to the waist-line until about 1640, when they were made to fit lower down, towards the hips, thus creating a gap between the breeches and centre front of the unfastened jacket, and showing the fullness of the fine white shirt. Silk and satin were usual materials for breeches, or occasionally velvet, in various colours.

Silk **stockings** were in great demand, though still very costly; cotton or worsted provided a second choice. More than one pair would be worn in cold weather.

Boot hose became an essential item of attire for a well-dressed man in Cavalier times, though they were often purely ornamental. Worn inside boots, they were still ostensibly to protect the stocking from the leather boot, but were, in fact, usually of as costly a fabric as the stocking itself, and were decorated by lace tops which hung gracefully over the open top of the boot, just below the knee. Later in the reign, **boot hose tops**—that is, just the lace frill or fall without the actual hose—were worn just below the knee, with either boots or shoes. In the last years of the period, longer boot hose were often attached to the breeches, still with the same decorative lace ruffle at the top. **Garters,** made of a silk sash, were tied at the knee, to contribute yet another large bow to the already adequate knee decoration (see pp. 148, 151, and 153).

Boots were definitely *à la mode* for the Cavalier. They were worn in different styles, reaching extremes in the days of the Civil War, and, despite all criticism, they remained in popular favour until after the Restoration. The tall, fitting boot, with small turned-down cuff, of the latter years of James I's reign remained fashionable until about 1630; after this, shorter styles with wider cuffs, made of softer leather, were worn, and by 1645 the enormous bucket-tops, falling half-way down the calf, were all the rage. Light colours in leather were popular, particularly buff or white. The toe of the boot tapered to a narrow square end after 1640, and this remained the fashionable shape until after the end of the reign. Heels were medium to high, and the **platform sole,** or, alternatively, the **pantoufle** worn over the toe and forming an extra sole, were in great favour. The instep flap of leather grew in size to become the "butterfly" flap of the forties. Expensive silk linings in all colours were visible inside the drooping bucket-tops (see pp. 148, 151, and 153).

Shoes, when worn, were similar to those of James's reign, with enormous rosettes of ribbon or spangled fabric on the instep. Heels were higher than before, often of red leather for dress wear, and the toes tapered to the square narrow end, in the same way as for the boots, in the forties (see p. 153).

The Cavaliers wore their **hair** really long after 1630, and generally curled in ringlets which hung over the shoulders and down the back. Sometimes the ringlets were drawn over the front on to the shoulders, or on one shoulder only; **love-locks,** with ribbon bow-ties, were all the rage. A fringe of hair, often curly, covered the forehead. Some men were clean-shaven, others wore the **moustache** brushed outwards and upwards, as in the portrait of Frans Hals's "Laughing Cavalier", and the small pointed "Van Dyck" **beard.** After 1640–1645, the moustache was sometimes worn without a beard (see pp. 148, 151, and 153).

In **hats,** the Cavalier style is well known to us; that broad sweeping brim, round or square crown, and long curling, white ostrich plume, with the whole **hat** worn at an angle on the head or held in the hand, is indeed familiar from the numerous portraits (see pp. 148, 151, and 153). Sometimes one side of the brim was pinned or brooched up. Felt or beaver were the usual materials, with a jewelled band. Crowns became higher after 1645.

Although the **whisk** and **falling ruff** were still seen until the thirties (see p. 148), the typical neckwear of this reign was the *falling band* or collar. Made of fine white cambric or linen, edged with lace, or fashioned entirely of exquisite, intricate lace, the falling band covered the doublet or jacket from a high neck-line, under the chin, to well over the shoulders, and was fastened in front by tied, tasselled band strings. It was unstiffened and fell gracefully over the shoulders—the *pièce de résistance* of Cavalier attire. It is often known as a "Van Dyck" collar, and was usually arranged outside all garments to show it to advantage (see pp. 148, 151, and 153).

Lace or lace-edged **cuffs,** to match the band, finished the sleeves at the wrists; several layers or tiers were worn.

The beautiful white silk, cambric, or linen **shirt** of the period was now visible in front, where the jacket was unfastened, on chest and back slashes in the doublet, and through the slashed sleeve. It was very full and was draped in graceful folds at these points, thus becoming an important item of attire once more. Expensive shirts, with lace trimming, were desired by all, but as in previous reigns, it was only necessary to possess few shirts, as despite the fineness and costliness of the fabric, they were changed but rarely.

The Plate VII of the Van Dyck portrait of the Earl of Peterborough is a good example of the costume of the typical Cavalier. The red **jacket** with decorative gold fastenings, slit sleeve and decoration, **breeches** with gold side ornamentation, lace falling **band** and cuffs, trailing **cloak** and long curled hair, brushed-up moustache and pointed beard, can all be clearly seen here. The lace-topped **boot hose, boots** with pantoufle sole, **gloves,** and decorative **baldric** or sword-belt, should also be noted.

Feminine **dress** underwent no less transformation in this period than the masculine, and was also no less elegant, though perhaps rather less outstanding and noteworthy. Although the farthingale had vanished from fashionable attire, the narrow, long waist and stomacher were still seen until about 1630. After this time, the waist-line rose considerably and the stomacher had a rounded end instead of a narrow pointed one; the neck-line was still very low and round, partially showing the breasts, the *décolletage* was still trimmed by lace edging, and a narrower wired lace collar continued to ornament the sides and back of the neck. **Tassets** often finished the lower edge of the separate bodice: they were deep and wide and embroidered like the men's. Sleeves were either fitting or, more commonly, full at the top, slashed and paned, then fitting on the forearm like the masculine doublet sleeve. From 1630 onwards, these sleeves tended to shorten and, by 1635, only reached half-way down the forearm, ending in lace ruffles. Skirts hung full and loose, gathered into the waist and falling to ground-level over numerous petticoats. They were sometimes open in front to show the undergown, but were more frequently closed all round in this period. A ribbon **sash,** tied in a bow in front, was worn at the waist (see

STUART, CHARLES I
1625-1649

c. 1635-45 - DARK GREEN
SATIN GOWN - PEARL
EMBROIDERY & GIRDLE -
LACE EDGING TO NECK-LINE -
LACE SLEEVE RUFFLES -
GOLD FAN

CHARLES I c. 1638-40 -
PALE GREY SATIN JACKET -
RED BREECHES - WHITE SILK
GARTERS - BUFF LEATHER
BOOTS & GLOVES - BROWN
LEATHER SWORD BELT -
LACE EDGED COLLAR - DARK
CURLED HAIR - BLACK HAT -
BROWN CANE

CAVALIER STYLE c. 1640-9 -
LACE FALLING BAND - SILK
JACKET - GOLD BRAID BUTTON
FASTENINGS CENTRE FRONT
& ON SLEEVE SLASHINGS -
LACE CUFFS - SILK BREECHES -
RUFFLES AT KNEES -
LACE-TOPPED BOOT
HOSE - LEATHER
BOOTS - SATIN
CLOAK - LEATHER
GLOVES -
EMBROIDERED
GAUNTLETS -
BEAVER HAT - PLUME

QUEEN HENRIETTA MARIA -
LIGHT TAFFETA GOWN
EMBROIDERED ON SLEEVES,
BODICE & TASSETS - SILK
BOWS AT CORSAGE, WAIST &
HAIR - LACE FALLING BAND
& UNDER COLLAR - LACE
RUFFLES AT ELBOWS -
BODICE LACED ACROSS -
PEARL NECKLACE -
PEARLS IN HAIR -
GLOVES

151

pp.148 and 151). After 1635, the stomacher went out of fashion and the waist-line became high and round in shape; sleeves were in one large full puff to the elbow and finished there with lace ruffles,[1] and the neck-line was still low, but was now partially or wholly covered by a large, lace falling band. Ribbon **bows** ornamented sundry parts of the gown, the corsage, the waist, sleeves, and shoulders. Plain **fabrics** were favoured in satin, silk, and taffeta, or, alternatively, dainty sprig patterns. Pearls were used in embroideries, but little other ornamentation was seen (see pp. 148 and 151).

Similarly to the men, ladies wore the wired lace **collar** and/or **ruff** until the early thirties, but from 1630 onwards the lace **falling band** became more popular and was universally worn by the fashionable after 1635. It was cut like the masculine band, in a scalloped lace edge, to drape over the shoulders, and the ladies' version was usually finished by a brooch or ribbon bow on the corsage. Sometimes two or three layers of lace collars were seen covering the gown's low *décolletage* (see pp. 148, 151, and 153).

The lace or lace-edged **cuff** was in use all through the period, but lace frills or **ruffles** at the elbow became more favoured after about 1635.

For outdoor wear, the ladies donned either a cloak or **cape,** made of silk or satin, often fur-lined, with a collar. These either just covered the shoulders or were much longer, reaching to the knees. Alternatively, a short **jacket** was worn loose to the hips, and edged and lined with fur.

By the early thirties, the distinctive feminine **hair-style** of the later Cavalier period had evolved, encouraged by Charles's French queen, Henrietta Maria. The high coiffure of Elizabethan days, which had continued into James I's reign, had been abandoned by 1625 in favour of the hair being drawn back tightly from the forehead to a flat bun, coiled high up the back of the head, with curls framing the sides of the face. By about 1632, the forehead fringe of separate curls—so familiar in Van Dyck's portraits of Henrietta Maria and her contemporaries—had become the vogue and continued to be worn till after the beginning of the Civil War. After 1640, the bun was worn higher up the head, almost at the crown, and the side-curls became longer ringlets. Pearls, gold nets, and ribbon bows ornamented the coiffure, yet it was tasteful in its simplicity in contrast to those of the previous two reigns (see pp. 148, 151, and 153).

Head-covering was still unfashionable for women, even out-of-doors. A gauze or net **veil** might be worn, loosely draped over the head (see p. 153), or a silk scarf; alternatively, particularly in winter, some ladies wore a velvet, silk, or satin **hood,** tied under the chin by a ribbon bow (see p. 153). For travelling or riding some preferred a **hat,** after the Cavalier style, with sweeping brim and plume, and made of felt, beaver, or velvet, and worn at a jaunty angle.

With the longer, ground-length gowns in fashion once more, **shoes** hardly showed, but were of similar style to the men's, with high heels and large ribbon rosettes on the instep.

Among the chief masculine accessories were the waist-**sash** and sword **baldric.** The former was a deep band of silk or satin worn over the buff coat or jerkin, tied round the waist, with the bow at front or side; the latter became increasingly

---

[1] It is interesting to note this first exposure of the forearm in English feminine dress. Despite the complete or partial uncovering of the breasts in earlier ages, it had been considered improper to show the arms at all prior to this time. This seems strange logic to twentieth-century ideas.

STUART, CHARLES I
1625-1649

PEARL NECKLACE & EARRINGS - LACE NECK-EDGING

LACE FALLING BAND

FELT CAVALIER HAT - VAN DYCK COLLAR

GOLD & DIAMOND RING

SILVER GILT, PERFUME CASE

c.1630-40 - RUFFLES END BREECHES - LACE-TOPPED BOOT HOSE - LEATHER BOOTS

SILVER GILT LOCKET

GOLD LOCKET - PORTRAIT INSIDE - ENAMELLED IN BLUE, WHITE, RED & GREEN - SET WITH RUBIES, DIAMONDS, SAPPHIRES, EMERALD & PEARL

GOLD RING SET WITH TURQUOISE

DIAMOND & GOLD NECKLACE WITH PENDENT SAPPHIRE

DARK SILK HOOD TIED WITH RIBBON BOW - BLACK SILK MASK - FUR CAPE - c.1644

RUFFLES AT KNEE - LACE-TOPPED BOOT HOSE - BUTTERFLY FLAPS ON BOOTS

PEARL NECKLACE, EARRINGS & IN HAIR - LACE FALLING BAND

CHARLES I

FELT HAT & WHITE PLUME c.1627-30

NET VEIL 1640

153

popular early in the reign and ousted from fashion the sword-hanger of Tudor times. The baldric or sword-belt was slung over the right shoulder and fastened on the left hip, where it formed a hanger for the sword; it was often rather wide, made of leather, silk, or satin, and beautifully embroidered with intricate designs (see pp. 148 and 151). It was, in reality, a new edition of the medieval baldric, though in Stuart times it had also a utilitarian function, and was not ornamented by silver bells. The **sword** itself was naturally still an essential part of masculine equipment and was long, hanging at the left side. **Gloves** were still worn or carried, with deep gauntlets, embroidered and fringed, or having lace edges. Leather was the usual fabric, popularly in white or natural colour (see pp. 148 and 151). **Canes** were now often carried, ornamented at the gold or silver top by ribbon loops (see pp. 148 and 151). Small **muffs** were sometimes carried by men in winter.

Women also wore **gloves,** as in the last two reigns, but after about 1635–1640, with the advent of the elbow-length sleeves, longer gloves were worn, reaching nearly to the elbow and made of white or light-coloured kid. Lace edging, ribbon bows, or fringing ornamented these gloves, which were now fitting on the arm (see p. 151). Other accessories included black silk **masks** for outdoor wear, a folding **fan,** decorated by colour and lace, a small **mirror** hung from the girdle, and a tiny lace, embroidered **apron.** Fur **muffs** were popular in winter (see pp. 148, 151, and 153).

Only little jewellery was worn in this reign, particularly after 1630, and this was chiefly confined to pearls—in **necklaces, ear-rings,** hair decoration, and **bracelets.** Gold, jewelled **brooches** and **pendants** were seen. Men also wore pearl ear-rings, but little other jewellery of any kind (see p. 153).

Decoration was far more restrained and dignified in Cavalier times, and if not expressed in jewellery and embroidery, was chiefly manifested in lace trimmings, ribbon bows, and loops. **Materials** were usually unpatterned, though dainty floral designs were seen, especially on feminine dress; silk, satin, taffeta, and sometimes velvet were in greatest use, with lace and cambric for bands, cuffs, and trimming. Pastel shades were preferred on the whole, though stronger colours were also seen.

THE COMMONWEALTH
CROMWELL   1649–1660

No new styles of dress came to England under the Protectorate: there existed merely various levels of sobriety or frivolity of attire—according to the political opinions of the wearer—based upon the Cavalier modes established in Charles I's reign, and just described. The cropped hair, plain collar and cuffs, dark, excessively simple garments, and tall black hat, so commonly believed to represent Cromwellian attire, were, in reality, only worn by Puritans holding extreme views; the majority of people were dressed in a restrained version of Royalist attire, while supporters of the late monarchy often flaunted their lace and ribbons to a far greater extent than in Charles's time. Indeed, after 1649, many Cromwellian adherents, and even some of their leaders, bade fair to rival the Royalists in their bright colours and frivolous clothes.

The **jacket** continued to form the basic upper garment of masculine dress. It was almost identical in cut to that seen from 1642 onwards, except that the length varied according to the status of the wearer; Cavaliers wore it very short, to just below the waist, open from the second or third button on the chest, thus showing numerous folds of the exquisite white shirt in front, and on the arm through the slashed full sleeve; Puritans wore a longer version, often completely buttoned, with the skirt slit at intervals, and plain, narrower sleeves (see p. 156).

The **buff-coat** or jerkin was also still popular as an alternative or on top of the jacket. It was usually sleeveless, and tied by a broad sash at the waist.

Cloaks—the usual outdoor covering—also varied according to political opinion; the gallant wore a shorter cloak with a rich lining and large collar, draped over the shoulder or arm, as previously, while the Puritan assumed a longer style with small collar, worn more soberly over one or both shoulders (see p. 156).

Breeches were wider now at the bottom and fairly full; they reached the knee as before, and were either plain or finished by tabs, or, for the Royalist adherents, still ornamented by the frivolous ribbon loops. The vertical band of braid or ribbon on the outer leg was still fashionable. For the gallant, bunches of ribbon loops were attached to the centre front of the top of the breeches, and on the outer side of each knee, where the garter sash added its bow (see p. 156).

Stockings were of silk, cotton, or worsted, and **boot hose** were still worn—lace-edged, drooping in a lace fall over the boot, for Cavaliers (see pp. 156 and 158).

Boots retained their popularity throughout this period: the old Cavalier style in soft leather, often buff or white, with wide bucket-tops descending to mid-calf, were in great vogue, while Puritans wore a simpler version of these, usually in black. Heels were fairly high, and the instep flap was still present, though of more moderate proportions now (see pp. 156 and 158).

Shoes, of leather, in various colours, were almost unchanged in shape, with medium to high heels, instep rosettes of ribbon, and narrow tapering square toes. Ribbon bows tended to replace the rosette later in the period, while a plain bow was worn by the Puritan, whose shoes were of black leather (see p. 156).

It was perhaps in the **shirt** and **falling band** that the greatest difference lay between the dress of the two opposing parties. The Royalist retained his fine silk or cambric white shirt, plainly visible in front at the waist in the gap between jacket and breeches, and in the sleeve opening. His falling band of lace, or lace-edged cambric, was as exquisite as ever, matched by lace-edged cuffs, often in two or three tiers. The extreme Puritan hid his shirt entirely under his jacket, while a small stiff collar and cuffs completed his linen. Many variations between these two styles were seen. In all types of band, the strings with tiny tassels were visible in front (see pp. 156 and 158).

Hats and **hair-styles** also provided a point of difference between the varied opinions: the very short cropped hair, evoking the term Roundhead in the Civil War, was only worn by the zealous Puritan; others adopted styles between this and the long flowing ringleted hair and **love-locks** of the professed Royalist. More men were clean-shaven, although the brushed-up **moustache**, with or

CROMWELL, 1649-1660

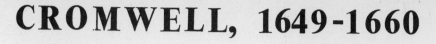

c.1653 - DARK FELT HAT -
PLUME & RIBBON -CLOTH
JACKET - BUTTONS AT SIDES-
PLAIN, WHITE BAND & CUFFS-
CLOTH CLOAK - SILK LINING -
BUTTONS AT EDGE - ATTACHED
BY SHOULDER CORD - LIGHT
BREECHES - RIBBON EDGE &
BAND - STOCKINGS - BOOT HOSE-
BUFF LEATHER BOOTS &
GLOVES - CANE

BLACK FELT HAT - WHITE
RIBBON - WHITE LACE-EDGED
DOUBLE COLLAR & CUFFS —
DARK RED GOWN - CREAM
COLOURED SASH & SATIN
PETTICOAT - DARK FUR MUFF

c 1655-60 - BLUE, SATIN
GOWN - WHITE LACE HEM
EDGING - LACED BODICE -
SILK SASH & RIBBON BOWS-
TIERED LACE-EDGED COLLAR
& CUFFS - CHEMISE RUFFLES
FAN

DARK FELT HAT WITH PLUME -
LACE EDGED BAND & CUFFS -
WHITE SHIRT - GREEN JACKET
& BREECHES - SATIN CLOAK-
RIBBON LOOPS ON
BREECHES & GARTERS -
LEATHER SHOES - SILK BOWS

without the "**Van Dyck**" beard, were still in considerable evidence (see pp. 156 and 158). The typical Puritan hat was of black, hard felt, high-crowned, small or large brimmed, and trimmed only by a ribbon and buckle. Again, many variations were adopted between this and the Cavalier's sweeping felt or beaver hat with its long curling ostrich plumes and/or ribbon loops (see pp. 156 and 158).

In feminine dress, the same manner of representing opinion was seen: the Puritan's wife removed all fripperies from her **gown** and left it plain and unadorned by lace and ribbon bows, but basically the cut of the gown was the same as that of the Royalist supporter. Small alterations in cut became apparent in the fifties: the neck-line was rounder, and almost off the shoulders, while remaining low in front; the waist-line slowly returned to a normal position from the high level it had attained about 1645, and the pointed front, with laced-across bodice also reappeared, though as yet there was no stomacher. The skirt was unchanged, very full and long, gathered in at the waist, and sleeves were also unaltered, worn in one large puff to the elbow or half-way down the forearm, but were narrower and plainer for Puritans. A ribbon sash usually finished the waist-line. Ladies continued the habit of raising the gown skirt at one or both sides to display the petticoat beneath (see p. 156).

The large **falling band** or collar accompanied the *décolleté* neck-line and wholly or partially obscured it. The Puritan lady wore a plain white collar, completely covering her gown neck-line, while the lady of Royalist tendencies adopted a lace-edged collar in two or three tiers, open in an inverted V in front to show the gown corsage which was usually ornamented by a ribbon bow. **Cuffs** appropriately matched these collars (see pp. 156 and 158). White ruffles from the chemise sleeve were often visible below the lace-edged cuffs of the shorter gown sleeve styles.

White **aprons** were fashionable, worn on top of the gown. They were lace-edged and tiny for the less serious-minded, but large, plain, and utilitarian for the Puritan.

Long, full **cloaks** were worn out-of-doors, on top of the gown, cut similarly to those of the men. A hood was often attached.

The feminine **coiffure** had altered little: the hair was still drawn back tightly to the bun worn high up the back of the head, side-ringlets were longer now, and the forehead curls had disappeared. Pearls and ribbon bows were used for ornamentation (see pp. 156 and 158). The more Puritan lady hid her hair under either a lace-edged or plain white **cap**, depending on the strength of her views; this was surmounted out-of-doors by a black or dark felt **hat** of similar type to the men's (see pp. 156 and 158). Dark velvet or silk **hoods,** tied with a ribbon bow under the chin, or a net **veil**, were in use for alternative outdoor head-coverings, as in the previous period.

Ladies' **shoes** were similar to the men's styles, but they were usually hidden from view.

Masculine accessories still included the **sword** and embroidered **sword-belt** or baldric (see p. 158), a **cane,** and **gloves** of leather with plain or embroidered gauntlets, and fringed edges (see p. 156). Ladies also wore or carried long kid **gloves,** usually white and trimmed by a ribbon bow. Large fur **muffs** were carried in winter (see p. 156), and folding **fans** were as popular as ever (see

CROMWELL, 1649-1660

GOLD RING - TURQUOISE SURROUNDED BY GARNETS

WHITE ENAMELLED GOLD RING - CENTRE GARNET

GOLD RING SET WITH CRYSTAL

PEARL NECKLACE & EARRINGS

PURITAN - TALL, BLACK FELT HAT - RIBBON & BUCKLE - PLAIN WHITE COLLAR - DULL GREEN JACKET

POMANDER - GOLD FILIGREE OVER AMBERGRIS

BLACK LEATHER SWORD-BELT OR BALDRIC, EMBROIDERED IN SILVER THREAD - SWORD

CROMWELLIAN ATTIRE

LEATHER BOOT - LACE-EDGED BOOT HOSE - RIBBON TRIMMED BREECHES

BLACK LEATHER MILITARY BOOT

BLACK FELT HAT & YELLOW STRIPED RIBBON & BOW - WHITE LACE-EDGED CAP & DOUBLE COLLAR

NON-PURITAN ATTIRE - LACE EDGED FALLING BAND

DARK FELT HAT - RIBBON LOOPS - PLAIN WHITE COLLAR

p. 156). There was a considerable diminution in the use of **perfume and cosmetics,** although, as apparent later, this was only a temporary phase.

Even less **jewellery** was worn than in the previous period. It was chiefly confined to pearls, in necklaces, bracelets, and hair decoration, or gold, jewelled rings and pendants (see p. 158).

Materials, colours, and **trimmings** varied according to the wearer: the Royalist still used satin, silk, or taffeta for jackets, breeches, cloaks, and gowns, with lace, silk, and ribbon loops, or bows in abundance, and wore pastel shades or bright colours; the Puritan tended to adopt cloth or wool for his or her garments, plain white linen or cambric for collar, cuffs, and undergarments, had little ornamentation, and preferred more sombre hues of brown, grey, dull purple or red, cream colour and black, relieved only by the white collar and cuffs. It must, however, be emphasised that the majority of people assumed a moderate interpretation of the extremes of dress, colour, trimming, and fabrics discussed in this chapter.

THE RESTORATION—HOUSE OF STUART

CHARLES II   1660–1685
JAMES II   1685–1689

With the restoration of the monarchy in 1660 there reappeared all the adjuncts of gay and colourful Stuart dress, but this time in a degenerative version of the Cavalier styles. Those who had retained their ribbons and lace under the Protectorate now gave full vent to their inclinations in this respect, while many others resumed their fripperies; the restraint in colour and decoration which had characterised Puritan attire was now confined to the comparatively few fanatical adherents to the cause. France was the acknowledged leader of European fashions, and Charles II brought back to England all the latest modes from the Court of Louis XIV, where he had spent much of his exile.

Controversial indeed is the question of the introduction of the coat and vest in the 1660s, but whatever view is held of the origins, dates, and styles on this subject, there can be no doubt that these years saw a transformation in masculine attire, from beribboned doublets and jackets to more dignified, though dull, coats and waistcoats, a change so lasting that today men still conform to these latter garments, though in a modified form from those of three hundred years ago.

The introduction of the high, curled periwig was another innovation for men. Again, the origin is debatable: several theories have been advanced, the most popular seems to attribute it to Louis XIV, who, not wishing to lose the admiration occasioned by his long, curled locks when nature saw fit to diminish them, adopted a curled wig. In England, Charles II encouraged the use of the periwig, which was worn in increasing length and height throughout the period, becoming a veritable curtain of curls and ringlets.

Feminine dress had altered less, the changes being chiefly confined to a return to tight-lacing and open skirts showing the petticoat, and added decoration in the form of ribbon bows and lace. A low round *décolletage* was the fashion, exposing to view the neck and shoulders, ornamented solely by a pearl necklace and lace edging.

It was, indeed, an age of ribbon bows and lace ruffles which, carried to such excess, lost that dignity and charm so typical of the dress of Charles I's time, but which, nevertheless, provided a colour and gaiety which in masculine dress, at least, was not to be seen again: it was the last time that mere man emulated that wondrous bird—the peacock.

The short **jacket** of Cavalier and Cromwellian days remained fashionable for a few years after the Restoration: it had become very brief—indeed it did not quite reach the waist—and though there were buttons from neck to hem edge, only the top one or two were fastened. Sleeves were elbow-length, or just a little longer, ending in a fringe of ribbon loops, or later, a cuff; the front slit in the sleeves remained for a few years only. Ribbon bows and loops were worn on the shoulders and sleeves. No under-tunic was adopted, thus the full white shirt billows out on the chest, waist, and forearm, ending at the wrist in deep ruffles (see p. 161).

Popularity for the jacket was soon transferred to the new **coat** and vest, and by 1670 these garments were generally worn. The coat at first was black, about mid-thigh length, and after the Persian cut; it was introduced by Charles II in 1666. By 1670 it had become established in style and was worn in colours, often rich in hue. It was then knee-length and hung loose and unshaped from neck to hem, widening slightly as it descended in a flared skirt. The front edges were turned back three or four inches to display the lining, and showed buttons which could be fastened the full length, though few were used, generally only those of the top section, or those at the waist. Horizontal pocket slits, without flaps, were made on each side in front, just above the hem. The skirt was slit to the hips at the sides and back. Sleeves were elbow-length with broad turned-back cuffs. Embroidery and button trimming was usual at the cuffs, pockets, and skirt slits. The garment had no collar, and the neck-line was completely hidden under the wig and cravat. A sash was sometimes worn round the waist to confine the coat there. Ribbon loops were still worn at the shoulder and/or cuffs (see pp. 161 and 164). Towards 1680, the coat was cut slightly waisted, but by 1689 the waist had become pronouncedly marked; the skirt was now longer and more flared and was often arranged in radiating pleats at the rear of the sides, from the hip. Sleeves were longer, almost to the wrist, and had wider cuffs. Gold or silver braid fastenings for the buttons down the centre front were in vogue, and on pocket and skirt slits, while cuffs were exquisitely embroidered. The turned-back fronts to the coat had disappeared. A lace-edged white handkerchief often dangled from one of the pockets. Ribbon loops on the shoulder were still seen (see p. 164).

The **vest**—or **waistcoat** as it was more commonly called later—was cut similarly to the coat, except that it had longer, narrow sleeves, which either showed below the coat cuffs, or were turned back over them. In the seventies, it hung loose and flared, and in the eighties became more waisted. On the average it was cut a few inches shorter than the coat, though sometimes was seen below, and was either buttoned full-length or at the waist only, where it might be confined by a silk sash. Brocade or embroidered silk or satin were

RESTORATION STUART
1660-1689

GENTLEMAN c.1660-1666 - LIGHT BLUE SILK JACKET & PETTICOAT BREECHES, BOTH DECORATED BY SATIN & VELVET BOWS & LOOPS IN SEVERAL COLOURS - WHITE SHIRT & LACE-EDGED NECKWEAR & WRIST FRILLS, ALSO RUFFLES AT KNEE - GARTER SASHES - SILK STOCKINGS - BLACK LEATHER SHOES - RED HEELS - BLUE BOWS - DARK RED SATIN CLOAK - DARK FELT HAT - RIBBON LOOPS - PLUME - CANE WITH RIBBON BOW - GLOVES

c.1675-80 - GREEN VELVET GOWN - WHITE UNDERSLEEVES - RIBBON BOWS - ERMINE CAPE - DARK SILK HOOD - BLACK SILK MASK - BLACK FUR MUFF & RIBBON BOW - GLOVES

c 1670-80 - SILK COAT & LINING OF DIFFERENT COLOUR - GOLD TRIMMINGS ON CUFFS, POCKETS & SKIRT SLITS - SWORD-BELT - RIBBON LOOPS ON SHOULDER - WHITE SHIRT & CRAVAT - LACE SLEEVE RUFFLES - SILK BREECHES, GARTER SASHES & STOCKINGS - LEATHER SHOES - RED HEELS - RIBBON BOWS - BLACK PERIWIG - FELT HAT - RIBBON LOOPS

GOLD CLOTH GOWN WITH GOLD & BROWN LINE PATTERN - BLUE SLEEVES - WHITE NECK-FRILL & UNDERSLEEVES - PALE PINK PETTICOAT - JEWELLED BROOCHES ON BODICE - PEARL EARRINGS - FAN

161

popular, the pattern contrasting pleasingly with the plain fabric of the coat (see p. 164).

Breeches had perforce to be adapted to suit these new styles. From 1660 to the early seventies they had degenerated from the Cavalier type to effeminate modes known as **petticoat** or *rhinegrave* breeches. These resembled a knee-length full skirt or kilt or, alternatively, very full shorts. Both types were inundated with ribbon loops and bows at the sides, hem, waist, and the centre front panel which they often almost obliterated (see p. 161). With the advent of the coat, these examples of effeminacy were rendered highly unsuitable, and men reverted to fairly full, simple breeches, gartered at the knee with a silk sash (see pp. 161 and 164). This type of breeches continued to be worn throughout the period, but became narrower and more fitting as time passed, so that by 1689 they were very plain and fastened at, or below, the knee by buttons or a strap and buckle. With the longer coat of this time, the breeches were hardly visible (see p. 164).

Knee decoration similarly declined with the advance of simpler styles in breeches. In 1660, in addition to the **garter sash** and **ribbon loops** at the knee, deep white lace **ruffles** or **falls** were also seen, descending below the petticoat breeches like an under-skirt of lace (see p. 161). With the full, plainer breeches of 1670, a garter sash and ribbon loops sufficed, while by 1680, ribbons and bows had vanished.

Silk **stockings** were still sought after, with cotton or worsted worn in lieu. **Boot hose** with lace falls, or **boot hose tops** were seen early in Charles II's reign, but declined in vogue after 1670.

The general use of the **boot,** so characteristic of Cavalier days, began to wane after 1660; **shoes** returned to fashion once more. These shoes were usually made of black leather, and there was a vogue—which promised to be a lasting one—for red heels for dress wear. The shoe had an upstanding tongue, which became very deep in James II's reign. Heels were fairly high; rosettes on the instep had been replaced by ribbon bows, which in turn were replaced, in James II's time, by small, jewelled metal buckles (see pp. 161, 164, and 166). Boots, now relegated to use for riding or travelling, were also of black leather, of a thicker, harder type than in Cavalier times, and were tall, reaching above the knee in a deep cuff; the instep flap was now moderate in size (see p. 166). In the late eighties, *spatterdashes* were introduced: these were a type of gaiters or leggings of soft black leather, worn with shoes in inclement weather, and buttoned up the leg to about mid-calf-level.

Although men continued to wear their own **hair,** curled and waved all over the head, and grown to shoulder-level, the *periwig* became very popular in the sixties. It formed an enormous mass of curls and ringlets over the head, on to the shoulders in front, and reaching well down the back. Black was fashionable, in emulation of Charles II, but later various shades of brown were also seen. The periwig changed its form somewhat during the period: it began by being a curtain of curls and ringlets, but later developed a centre parting on the forehead, where it rose even higher, till in James's time, it formed two high masses of curls on either side of the parting (see pp. 161, 164, and 166). These wigs were very expensive, costing as much as five pounds for one of good quality. Indeed, owing to a temporary shortage of wigs in the early days of their popularity, Pepys tells us of fears that the source of material during the Great Plague of 1665 and 1666 was dubious, rumours being rife that the hair of plague victims was used in their manufacture. The size and weight of the periwig made it so cumbersome that small, full, curled wigs became more popular for travelling or sport, from the late seventies. Most men were clean-shaven, while the hair under the periwig was cut close or shaved.

Hats were still worn indoors by some until the end of this period, though the introduction of the periwig, and the consequent reluctance to obscure its glories, had the effect of curtailing this seventeenth-century custom. The tall-crowned, hard felt hat, with ostrich plume and ribbon decoration, continued to be worn throughout the sixties, but it now had a wide sweeping brim once more (see p. 161). After 1670–1675, lower, round crowns, with fairly wide to wide brims were favoured; ostrich plumes went out of fashion in favour of bunches of ribbon loops and bows (see pp. 161 and 164).

As previously mentioned, the full white **shirt** of silk, linen, or cambric, with very full sleeves, remained an important item of masculine attire in these two reigns; under the short jacket, much of it could be seen on chest, waist, and arms, and although less was visible under the coat, the full sleeve was still apparent on the forearm, terminating in lace **ruffles** over the wrists, and ornamented by ribbon bows. The falling band had become a lace or lace-edged square-folded tucker or bib, falling loosely from under the chin to the end of the sternum. After about 1670–1675, it was replaced by the *cravat*, a band of white silk or linen, tied at the throat, and with hanging ends of fringe or lace, over the chest. The cravat became longer and fuller towards the end of the period (see pp. 161, 164, and 166).

The small-waisted, corseted bodice, which had shown a tendency to return to the feminine **gown** of Protectorate days, became established once more by 1660. The **waist-line** was lower again, shaped round at the back and to a small point in front; the **bodice** was laced up the front or back, or held together by jewelled brooches at intervals, showing the white undergarment in between. The **décolletage** was low and round, almost or partially off the shoulders, and edged with white lace or silk ruffles. **Sleeves** were full, elbow-length and worn in a large puff, gathered in to make a frilled edge, or brooched up in front and hanging freely behind. The white full sleeve of the undergarment showed below in puffs and/or lace or silk ruffles. The **skirt** was very full, gathered or pleated into the small waist, and hung loosely in graceful folds to the ground over numerous petticoats which were worn to make it set well (see p. 161). The fashion for an open skirt returned in the late sixties and seventies: it was caught up at the sides with large ribbon bows, then fell to the ground in folds of drapery, displaying the petticoat of contrasting fabric and colour, with edging of lace or ruffles (see p. 164). Towards the end of the period, the waist became tighter and a row of ribbon bows or jewelled brooches finished the laced-up centre front of the bodice; the neck-line became lower still, and wider; sleeves were narrower and finished with a turned-up cuff; and the skirt was caught up higher and farther back by the ribbon bows. A train was then usual at the back, once more (see p. 164). Ribbon bows and loops ornamented the gown throughout the two reigns, but they were seen in much greater profusion in the eighties, at the corsage, sleeves, bodice front, waist, and skirt. Fabrics

12

RESTORATION STUART
1660-1689

GREEN SATIN GOWN - DARK RED VELVET BOWS - CREAM SILK PETTICOAT - WHITE RUFFLES AT HEM, SLEEVE & NECK - WHITE LACE FRILL AT NECK-EDGE & ELBOW

GENTLEMAN - TEMP. JAMES II - DARK BLUE COAT & BREECHES - GOLD BRAID TRIMMINGS & BUTTONS - EMBROIDERED CUFFS - BROCADE WAISTCOAT - SILK STOCKINGS - BLACK LEATHER SHOES - BUCKLES - RED HEELS - LEATHER GLOVES - CANE - LACE - EDGED CRAVAT & WRIST FRILLS - BROWN PERIWIG - BLACK FELT HAT - RIBBON LOOPS - LACE-EDGED WHITE HANDKERCHIEF

LADY - TEMP. JAMES II - DARK RED BROCADE GOWN - BLUE SILK UNDER - SKIRT - JEWELLED BROOCHES ON BODICE - WHITE NECK & ELBOW FRILLS - VELVET RIBBON BOWS - PEARL EARRINGS AND NECKLACE

c.1670 - DARK COAT - LIGHT LINING - BUTTONS - BROCADE VEST - SILK WAIST SASH - WHITE SHIRT, WRIST RUFFLES & CRAVAT - EMBROIDERED SWORD - BELT - SWORD - BLACK FELT HAT - RIBBON LOOPS SILK BREECHES & STOCKINGS - RIBBON GARTERS - BLACK SHOES RED HEELS - RIBBON TIES - CANE - CLOAK

164

were brightly coloured, generally plain, and of rich material such as satin, silk, velvet, or gold cloth, but brocades and embroidered patterns were also seen. Petticoats were in lighter colours—white, cream, and pastel shades—plain, but of equally rich materials.

Ladies continued to have their **hair** waved and curled throughout the period: the back was still dressed high up the head in a flat bun, and the sides and side-back in curls and ringlets. From 1660 to about 1670–1675 the side-ringlets were fairly short and wired to stand out from the head, then droop vertically, parallel to the sides of the face, but after this the ringlets were worn longer and hung freely, with one or more curling on to the shoulder in front. The centre parting was common, often with wispy curls on the forehead. Ribbon bows and pearls continued to decorate the coiffure; after 1680, lace was also seen on the crown of the head (see pp. 161, 164, and 166).

On the whole, bareheadedness was still preferred, with the adoption of velvet or silk **hoods**—tied under the chin with a ribbon bow—net **veils,** or silk **scarves** for inclement weather; black was usually in vogue for hoods (see p. 161). **Hats,** after masculine styles, with ostrich plume or ribbon trimming, were worn for riding or travelling (see p. 166). Small lace or lace-edged white **caps,** with ribbon bow decoration, became popular in James's reign, for indoor wear, but as these were minute and perched on the back of the head, they hardly obscured the coiffure.

Shoes were again rarely visible under the long, full skirts, but, when seen, appeared to have a high heel, a fairly pointed toe, and the instep decorated by the ribbon bow, or later, the jewelled buckle. Brocade, satin, or silk were used for manufacture.

For outdoor winter wear, ladies continued to don a long, voluminous **cloak,** frequently with hood attached; it was made of silk, velvet, or satin, with perhaps a fur or velvet lining. Short fur shoulder **capes** still enjoyed a considerable vogue (see p. 161).

It was towards the end of this period that the feminine edition of masculine clothing began to be adopted for **riding.** The masculine coat was cut to fit a lady's figure and was worn over a full, long skirt; it had three-quarter sleeves with turned-up cuffs, was fastened full-length up the front, if desired, and had a flared skirt to thigh- or knee-level. The skirt was, as usual, worn over a costly petticoat. To complete the costume, a white lace-edged cravat, white wrist ruffles, periwig, plumed hat, gloves, and cane were adopted.

In masculine accessories, the **sword-belt** or baldric continued to be worn throughout both reigns, broader, and richer in design than ever; it was usually of embroidered velvet, silk, or leather, and the **sword** was rather smaller than previously (see p. 164). The broad silk or satin **sash** was sometimes seen, loosely tied over the new coat—a revival of the style seen over the buff-coat of Cavalier times. Ornate, jewelled or enamelled, gold or silver **snuff-boxes** were carried as indispensable items of a gentleman's attire. Large fur **muffs**—much beribboned—tall malacca **canes,** similarly ornamented, and lace-edged **handkerchiefs** were in great demand by both sexes (see pp. 161 and 164). Ladies also still wore black silk **masks,** long lace-edged, embroidered **aprons,** and carried the inevitable painted or ivory folding **fan** (see p. 161). **Gloves** were carried or worn: the masculine type was still made of leather, and had a fringed

RESTORATION STUART
1660-1689

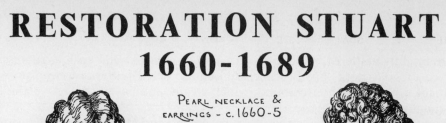

PEARL NECKLACE &
EARRINGS - c. 1660-5

JAMES II
LIGHT BROWN
PERIWIG - LACE CRAVAT

CHARLES II 1684 - LACE-
-EDGED CRAVAT - BLACK
PERIWIG

QUEEN CATHERINE

GOLD RING SET
WITH CRYSTAL

ENAMELLED GOLD.
RING - GREEN STONE

SILVER SCENT
BOTTLE

GOLD ENAMELLED RING
WITH BLUE STONE

c. 1661-2.

c. 1660-70

WHITE OVER-
-STOCKINGS ON
TOP OF DARKER
SILK ONES -
BLACK SHOES -
RIBBON TIE

BLACK
LEATHER
BOOT

BLACK FELT
HAT - WHITE
PLUME

1670-85

DARK BROWN
PERIWIG - LACE CRAVAT -
BLUE SWORD-BELT

BLACK PERIWIG - LACE-
-EDGED CRAVAT - TEMP.
CHARLES II

166

and embroidered gauntlet, while ladies wore an elbow-length kid variety—often perfumed when with full dress—or lace or silk, shorter gloves (see pp. 161 and 164).

A heavy use was made of **cosmetics** and **perfume** by men and women, and the latter especially indulged in the prevailing fashion for black silk face **patches,** usually round or star-shaped, but also of amazing intricacy and ingenuity of design—for example, a coach and horses, executed in minute tracery.

Materials, at this time, were chiefly plain, though rich: velvet, satin, taffeta, silk, brocade, and gold and silver cloth were in constant demand; brocade or embroidered silk was usual for waistcoats, while coats were of a plain, heavier fabric, sometimes even woollen cloth. **Colours** were rich and strong red or blue, with gold trimming being especially favoured; petticoats were of lighter shades. In **trimming,** it was undoubtedly the age of ribbons, in velvet, silk, or satin, but lace, later black as well as white and cream, and gold and silver braid were used in abundance.

More **jewellery** was worn than in the two previous reigns, but its use was still sparing: pearls were in vogue for **necklaces** and **ear-rings,** while gold or silver, jewelled **rings** were also worn (see p. 166). Simple gold chain bracelets were adopted by some ladies, as they could be seen to advantage with the shorter sleeves.

WILLIAM AND MARY   1689–1702
QUEEN ANNE   1702–1714

These short reigns did not witness any notable alterations in costume: with two exceptions, both in feminine attire, there occurred merely the establishment and mellowing of styles introduced in Charles II's time. In masculine dress, the coat was a little more waisted and fuller in the skirt, the huge curled wigs were sometimes powdered towards the end of Queen Anne's reign, and the gentlemen were, on the whole, more soberly attired than previously, otherwise there is little change to note. The ladies strove to add height to their costume in the first of these reigns, and width in the second, both of these aims being achieved by the innovations referred to above. In the time of William and Mary, the height was provided by the head-dress—that erection of some twelve or more inches high, composed of lace, ribbons, and flowers—while about 1711 the farthingale reappeared in its new form as the hoop, and once more ladies had difficulty in negotiating their skirts through a doorway.

France was still the acknowledged leader of European fashion, and she cemented this leadership by exporting her costly fabrics to make up into the styles designed in Paris, and advertised in London and other European capital cities by the fashion dolls of the time—forerunners of the fashion magazines of later periods.

The masculine **coat** was cut more waisted now, and to accentuate this the skirt was arranged on the hips in pleats which radiated from a hip button, thus creating a fuller and wider skirt, which was also rather longer, and still slit up the back to hip-level. Sleeves reached the wrists now, and were narrow on the upper arm, widening towards very large cuffs, which were fastened back by buttons. **Pockets** were still placed horizontally, low on the hips, in front, and towards 1714 were decorated by flaps as well as buttons. The coat was either worn unbuttoned or fastened only at the waist, although buttons were attached from neck to hem as previously. Velvet, silk, and satin were popular fabrics, in strong, bright colours, especially red, mauve, blue, and black (see pp. 169 and 171).

Waistcoats were almost unaltered, being only more waisted to conform to the coat, and cut about six inches shorter. Brocade or embroidered silk were still in vogue.

Breeches were hardly seen under the longer coat skirts; they were plain and fitting, fastening below the knee with a strap and buckle or buttons. Horizontal pockets were inserted in front at the waist. The breeches usually matched the coat or were of darker material.

Silk, worsted, or cotton **stockings** were quite plain now; red and other bright colours were popular.

Shoes were made of black leather, with red heels for dress wear, as in the last reign; they had high upstanding tongues and fairly high heels, with jewelled buckles for ornament on the instep. These buckles became larger in Queen Anne's reign (see pp. 169 and 171). The hard black leather **boot**, described in the last period, was still in use for riding and travelling. **Spatterdashes** were worn with shoes in bad weather.

Cloaks were now only used in winter, out-of-doors. They were long and full to cover the coat adequately.

The **periwig** or full-bottomed wig was in general use; it was still worn in two high peaks above the forehead on either side of the parting, and descended in a mass of formalised curls and ringlets over each shoulder and down the back to cover the shoulder-blades, and sometimes to reach nearly to the waist. The two front masses became exceptionally tall about 1700–1710, diminishing slightly after that. Smaller wigs, tied at the nape with a ribbon bow, were in use for travelling and sport. Although most wigs were dark brown or black until 1714, some grey, powdered ones were introduced after about 1708, as a prelude to the white powdering of Georgian times (see pp. 169, 171, and 173). Men were almost invariably clean-shaven.

That typical eighteenth-century style of hat, the *tricorne*, made its appearance in the first years of William and Mary's reign, and had gained universal favour by the beginning of the new century. It was made of dark, usually black, hard felt in a three-cornered manner, with round crown and upturned brim sides, the edges of which were decorated by fronds of white ostrich plume, gold braid, fringing, or lace (see pp. 169, 171, and 173). It was frequently carried under the arm in order to display the wig to the full. The wearing of hats was by now generally confined to out-of-doors.

The fine white **shirt**, of silk, cambric, or linen, could still be seen in a full puff at the wrist, terminating in lace ruffles. The **cravat** was very long and full, having lace or fringed ends (see pp. 169, 171, and 173).

Feminine dress underwent greater changes than the masculine: this could be seen in the **gown** styles of the period. In the first of the two reigns, the alteration was subtle: the **bodice** was fitting over a linen or soft leather **corset,** which was laced up the back and stiffened with whalebone, or sometimes made in one garment with the bodice itself. The corset, when separate, had shoulder-

STUART, 1689-1714

c. 1690 - PINK TAFFETA GOWN WITH
GOLD STRIPES - RED LINING -
WHITE UNDERGOWN - SILVER
EDGING - GREEN VELVET BOWS -
WHITE LACE NECK-EDGING,
SLEEVE RUFFLES & HEAD-DRESS -
WHITE LACE-EDGED APRON -
WHITE KID GLOVES - IVORY FAN -
PEARL NECKLACE

c. 1690 - 94 - ULTRAMARINE
BLUE SILK GOWN - WHITE LACE
NECK & BODICE FRILLS - WHITE
UNDERSLEEVES - WHITE LACE-
EDGED APRON - JEWELLED
BROOCHES ON BODICE &
SLEEVES - PEARL NECKLACE
& EARRINGS

1695 - SCARLET COAT &
BREECHES - GOLD BRAID &
BUTTONS - BLUE SILK SWORD
BELT - LACE-EDGED CRAVAT,
SHIRT & WRIST RUFFLES - RED
STOCKINGS - BLACK SHOES -
JEWELLED BUCKLES - RED
HEELS - WHITE GLOVES -
BROWN PERIWIG - BLACK
TRICORNE - WHITE
FROND EDGING

TEMP. WILLIAM & MARY -
WHITE SATIN GOWN - WHITE LACE
HEAD-DRESS, BODICE FRONT,
NECK-EDGING, SLEEVE RUFFLES &
BOWS & UNDERSKIRT - BLUE
VELVET RIBBON BOWS - FAN -
PEARL NECKLACE & EARRINGS

169

straps and tabs at the waist, which was cut to a point in front and round at the back (see p. 173). The bodice of the gown was usually open in the centre front over a **stomacher,** and either laced across it or decorated by a vertical row of jewelled brooches or graduated ribbon bows; the lacing and bow trimming were known as the *échelle,* in view of their resemblance to a ladder or steps. The **waist-line** took the same shape as the corset, reaching a point in front and rounded at the back. A low wide **décolletage,** almost off the shoulders, was still in fashion: it was edged with white lace, silk ruffles, or a soft filmy scarf. **Sleeves** were elbow-length or shorter, ending in an upturned, embroidered cuff or caught up in front by a brooch. The white undergarment sleeves showed below in a large puff and deep lace ruffles. The **skirt** was long and full with a train at the back, gathered or pleated into the waist, and was frequently caught up at the sides by large ribbon bows, in one or more loops, then fell gracefully to the ground at the sides and back. The **petticoat,** of lighter but rich fabric, trimmed with ruching fringing or embroidery at the hem, showed in front as in the previous period (see p. 169).

It was in Queen Anne's reign that the padded roll, which had been re-introduced about 1695, and worn under the petticoat to give an extra fullness to the hips, gave place—after the freedom of nearly a century—to the new form of farthingale, known as a *hoop.* This hoop, worn after about 1711, was constructed in a similar manner to the farthingale, from horizontal bands of metal or whalebone fixed into a canvas petticoat, but the silhouette was this time slightly different; it had a circular section at first, and was wider and shaped rounder and fuller at the hips to take the weight of the looped-up over-skirt, consequently it did not have straight sides like the farthingale. The over-skirt, which continued to be caught up at the sides, but farther back than before, showing a considerable area of petticoat, formed a longer train than in William and Mary's time. The bodice and sleeves were almost unaltered (see p. 171). Numerous petticoats were worn to make the skirt set well and to cover the bands of the hoop. Ribbon loops and bows, fringing, embroidery, and ruching were still used in profusion for the decoration of sleeves, corsage, waist, skirt, and hem throughout both reigns. Silk, satin, brocade, and velvet were employed for gowns in plain colours, stripes, or patterns with dainty motifs.

Out-of-doors, in cold weather, ladies wore a **cloak, cape,** or **jacket.** The cloak was ankle- or ground-length and voluminous in order to cover the wide skirts; capes were shoulder- or hip-length, the shorter ones being made usually of fur, and the jacket, fur-edged and lined, was hip-length, fitting to the waist, and had wide sleeves which ended in deep cuffs.

Riding costume was similar to that described previously.

The feminine **coiffure** was still dressed in curls and waves on top of the head and at the sides, with long side and back ringlets, surmounted by the bun at the rear. After 1690, however, the hair on the forehead was worn in two high peaks of curls and waves on either side of the parting, in a similar manner to the masculine periwig; these peaks reached their fullest height about 1700, diminishing after that, so that by 1710–1714 the coiffure was quite low once more and dressed in small forehead curls (see pp. 169, 171, and 173).

The tall head-dress typical of William and Mary's reign was designed to increase the height provided by the coiffure. It was a white silk or linen cap

STUART, 1689-1714

c. 1700-1707 - GREY-BLUE TAFFETA GOWN - CREAM EMBROIDERED SILK CUFFS - CREAM SATIN BOWS - WHITE LACE NECK-EDGING, SLEEVE FRILLS & HEAD-DRESS - WHITE SILK UNDERSKIRT - FAN - CANE - RIBBON BOWS

c. 1711 - BLACK VELVET COAT - GOLD BRAID & BUTTONS - BROCADE WAISTCOAT - WHITE CRAVAT WITH FRINGED ENDS - SLEEVE RUFFLES - BLACK VELVET BREECHES - BLACK LEATHER SHOES - RED HEELS - METAL BUCKLES - CANE & TASSEL - BROWN WIG

TEMP. QUEEN ANNE - MAUVE VELVET COAT - GOLD BUTTONS - GREY PERIWIG - WHITE LACE-EDGED CRAVAT & SLEEVE RUFFLES - BLACK TRICORNE - BRAID, FRINGED EDGE - CANE - GOLD TASSELS - BLACK LEATHER SHOES - RED HEELS - METAL BUCKLES - GREY STOCKINGS

LADY c. 1712 - TEMP. QUEEN ANNE - OLD GOLD COLOURED GOWN WITH SKIRT LOOPED UP AT SIDES TO SHOW WHITE SATIN PETTICOAT, WORN OVER HOOP - WHITE LACE NECK & SLEEVE FRILLS - WHITE SILK SLEEVE PUFFS - DARK TAFFETA BOWS - JEWELLED BROOCHES ON FRONT OF BODICE - LACE HEAD-DRESS - PEARL EARRINGS

which, worn on the back of the head, was decorated in front by layers or tiers of fluted lace and ribbons, wired to keep their shape. Long lappets of lace or white silk descended from the back of the cap over the shoulders in front, and a silk scarf was often tied loosely on top of this erection. The head-dress, known by various names—chiefly *fontange*, or *tower*—grew higher towards 1700, after which time it gradually decreased in size. At the turn of the century, when the fontange was very tall, the high coiffure of that time also had to be supported on a wire framework or pad, sometimes called a *commode*, in order to take the added weight of the head-dress (see pp. 169, 171, and 173). In inclement weather, velvet or silk **hoods** were worn on top of the fontange.

Feminine **shoes,** made of brocade, satin, silk, or leather, had high, curved heels, pointed toes, and were decorated on the instep by jewelled buckles.

The tiny lace or lace-edged, embroidered **aprons,** referred to in the last period, enjoyed an excess of popularity at this time. They were still small, round or rectangular, usually in white or black silk or satin, with lace edging and coloured embroidery, and most elaborate in design (see p. 169).

Masculine accessories included, until the turn of the century, the **sword baldric,** still ornate in design, on rich material (see p. 169), but after this, the **sword** was hung from a more unobtrusive hanger, worn under the waistcoat, and as the sword was shorter, only the hilt was usually visible. Beribboned fur **muffs** were still carried in winter; malacca **canes,** with tassels or ribbons (see p. 171), leather gloves, lace-edged white **handkerchiefs** dangling from hand or pocket, and decorative costly gold or silver, enamelled, and jewelled **snuff-boxes** were still indispensable to the gentleman. The dandy carried a **comb** to adjust his curls, and **cosmetics, patches,** and **perfume** were heavily applied by all who could afford to do so.

The **ladies also carried** large beribboned fur **muffs** in winter, malacca **canes** (see p. 171), or, alternatively, **parasols,** fringed and beribboned, and the essential dainty folding **fan** (see p. 169). They still wore elbow-length white kid **gloves with full dress,** or shorter **mittens** or gloves of lace, silk, or satin for less formal **wear** (see p. 173). Silk or satin embroidered **scarves** in white or rich colours were often draped around the neck and shoulders, out-of-doors. The ladies indulged in the use of **perfume, cosmetics,** and **patches** even more than men.

STUART, 1689-1714

c 1694

LACE & RIBBON
HEAD-DRESS &
LAPPETS

PEARL NECKLACE
& EARRINGS —
BROOCH —
MARY II

WILLIAM III
PERIWIG —
LACE-EDGED
CRAVAT

c. 1713-14 —
WHITE SILK
CRAVAT — GREY WIG

GOLD RING SET
WITH JACINTH

SILVER GILT PERFUME CASE

SOFT LEATHER CORSET —
EMBROIDERED & JEWELLED

ENAMELLED GOLD RING
SET WITH RUBY &
DIAMONDS

QUEEN ANNE
1702

GOLD RING SET
WITH GARNET

GREY WIG —
LACE-EDGED
CRAVAT

c. 1710-12

c. 1690-03

KID GLOVE — EMBROIDERED
GAUNTLET

ENAMELLED GOLD
RING — DEEP RED
STONE

VII
THE HOUSE OF HANOVER
GEORGE I   1714–1727

ENGLISH dress, under the first of the Hanoverians, did not undergo any major alterations: it was, like that of the previous chapter, a short period, and one of little change. George I had already passed his first youth when he came to England on the death of Queen Anne, in 1714, and evinced little exertion or interest in adapting himself to English customs, language, and dress. In consequence, he and his Court made no contributions to the world of fashion, which was still authoritatively led by Paris. Thus it was from France that the chief innovation of the period came—the loose over-gown, from the contouche or morning dress, a gown which subsequently became known as the sack (*sacque*) dress, and worn on all occasions. The wearing of the hoop under the various styles of gown became universal; it was still circular in section at this time, and of a rigid construction, so that dexterity in negotiating it, especially through narrow places, was demanded of the ladies.

Masculine dress had altered little: the **coat** was slightly more wasp-waisted and, in contrast, the skirts were more flared, still arranged in radiating pleats on the hips, slit up the back, knee-length, and now stiffened with buckram or whalebone to make them flare out at the sides and back. Sleeves were long, fairly fitting, and with now truly enormous cuffs, still fastened back by four or five buttons. Pockets on the hips had large flaps, also with buttons. Gold or silver braid and button trimming was still in vogue down the centre front, on pockets, skirt slits, and cuffs. Pastel or stronger shades were popular in red, blue, and green, made in velvet, silk, satin, or wool (see p. 175).

The **waistcoat** was unaltered, except for stiffened flaring skirts to match the coat; it was still made of brocade or embroidered silk or satin (see p. 175).

Overcoats had now begun to replace the cloak for popular winter, outdoor wear. In this reign they were very similar in cut to the coat itself, having long sleeves with large cuffs, flaring skirts, a fitting waist, hip-pockets with flaps, and buttoning down the front. The overcoat, however, was rather longer in the skirt, had a turned-down collar, and was belted at the waist. It was usually made in darker colours than the coat, and of warm materials such as wool or velvet (see p. 177).

Breeches were still fitting, fastened at the knee by buckle or buttons, and made of similar colour and fabric to the coat.

Stockings were of silk, cotton, or worsted, in bright colours or white.

The masculine **shoe** of black leather, with red heel for dress occasions, was still decorated by a square metal buckle, often jewelled, on the instep, and had an upstanding tongue, square tapering toes, and fairly high heels (see pp. 175, 177, and 179). Black leather **boots**, similar to those worn since 1680, were still seen for riding or travelling. **Spatterdashes** of soft black leather were worn with shoes for inclement weather.

HANOVER, GEORGE I
1714-1727

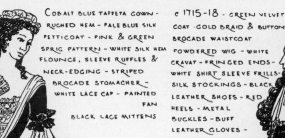

COBALT BLUE TAFFETA GOWN - RUCHED HEM - PALE BLUE SILK PETTICOAT - PINK & GREEN SPRIG PATTERN - WHITE SILK HEM FLOUNCE, SLEEVE RUFFLES & NECK-EDGING - STRIPED BROCADE STOMACHER - WHITE LACE CAP - PAINTED FAN BLACK LACE MITTENS

c 1715-18 - GREEN VELVET COAT - GOLD BRAID & BUTTONS BROCADE WAISTCOAT POWDERED WIG - WHITE CRAVAT - FRINGED ENDS - WHITE SHIRT SLEEVE FRILLS - SILK STOCKINGS - BLACK LEATHER SHOES - RED HEELS - METAL BUCKLES - BUFF LEATHER GLOVES - MALACCA CANE - AMBER TOP

1718-20 - DARK BLUE VELVET COAT - GOLD BRAID & BUTTONS - STIFFENED SKIRT - SILK EMBROIDERED WAISTCOAT - WHITE LACE EDGED CRAVAT & WRIST RUFFLES - DARK BLUE VELVET BREECHES BLUE STOCKINGS - BLACK LEATHER SHOES - METAL BUCKLES - POWDERED WIG - CANE

PALE PINK SATIN GOWN - CUFFS & BODICE PANELS. EMBROIDERED - WHITE LACE CAP, LAPPETS, NECK & SLEEVE FRILLS - WHITE KID GLOVES - EMBROIDERED SILK APRON - WHITE SILK EDGING - BLUE ÉCHELLE PEARL NECKLACE

Thinning hair was still regarded as a stigma, thus the wearing of the **full-bottomed wig** continued throughout George I's reign, although towards the end of it the tendency to tie back the rear portion in a queue became more prevalent—the origin of the various styles so typical of later Georgian times. Powder, in the form of rice-meal or wheat-meal, was used increasingly during this period; at first it was grey, but after 1720–1725 white was more popular. Powder closets were instituted and a bag was held over the face and ears while powdering (see pp. 175, 177, and 179).

The **tricorne** remained the hat of the age: it was made of black felt and its edges were ornamented by white ostrich fronds, gold braid, or fringing (see pp. 177 and 179).

The full white silk or linen **shirt** was unchanged in style; it was visible at the neck, and in the full puff and flounce at the wrists. The **cravat** was still very full and long, edged with lace or fringing, or made entirely of lace (see pp. 175, 177, and 179). Linen was changed infrequently, perfume and powder being used to excess to cover this deficiency.

The feminine **gown** worn over the **hoop,** as described in Chapter VI for Queen Anne's reign, was worn throughout this period, with minor adaptations. The hoop itself was still circular in section, and consisted of the canvas petticoat inset with horizontal, circular whalebone or metal bands. It was tied on at the waist by tapes, and had pocket holes inserted at the hips. As it was not made to fold as yet, it was still necessary to hold it up in front in order to pass through a doorway. Numerous **petticoats,** of fine material, covered the hoop. The actual gown **skirt** was gathered into the waist, and either open in front and looped up at the sides, forming a train at the back, and showing a large area of petticoat in front, or was closed all round. **Pocket** slits were inserted in gown and petticoat skirts. The **bodice** was still tight-fitting, with a narrow waist, pointed in front and rounded at the back; the front was usually open and laced over a patterned **stomacher** or the undergown, then decorated by an **échelle** or brooches. The low **décolletage** was still in vogue, either round or square, with white lace or ruffles as trimming. The elbow-length **sleeves** ended in a cuff, usually embroidered, and the white undergarment sleeves showed below in a puff and lace or silk ruffles (see p. 175).

By the early twenties, the *sack* (*sacque* in France) *gown* was becoming increasingly popular. It had originated from the *contouche*, which was a French style of loose morning dress to be slipped on over the gown proper or an undergown, but the idea became so favoured that ladies wore it as an actual gown, for various occasions, by the end of the reign. In this period it was worn over a dress or under-dress which had the tight bodice and hooped skirt, as just described; the sack gown hung loose at front and back from a gathered neck-line to the ground. It was either sleeveless or had sleeves similar to the average gown. Towards 1727, it sometimes had a semi-fitting bodice, or else was worn open in front in a V-shape to the waist, showing the fitting bodice and *échelle* of the undergown (see p. 177).

All types of gown and petticoat were ornamented by ribbon bows and lace edging, while the hem was flounced or decorated by ruching—a type of ornament which was carried to excess later in the century. **Fabrics** were lighter now: taffeta, silk, satin, brocade, and damask were most popular, either in

HANOVER, GEORGE I
1714-1727

c.1725-7 - PALE GREEN
TAFFETA SACK BACK GOWN
EMBROIDERED IN COLOUR
AT NECK, CUFFS & HEM-
WHITE LACE SLEEVE RUFFLES
& NECK EDGING-
WHITE SILK CAP &
LAPPETS

DARK RED VELVET CLOAK
& HOOD - PALE GREY FUR-
CREAM SATIN BOWS &
GOWN - PALE LAVENDER
STRIPES - LACE SLEEVE
FRILLS - WHITE KID
GLOVES - DARK FUR
MUFF

c.1720-24 - PALE
LAVENDER SILK SACK GOWN
DARK GREEN VELVET BOWS
& PALE GREEN SILK ONES-
LACE SLEEVE RUFFLES & NECK
EDGING - GREEN SATIN
UNDER-BODICE &
ÉCHELLE - CREAM
SATIN PETTICOAT

c.1725-6 - DARK WOOL
OVERCOAT - GOLD BRAID &
BUTTONS - LIGHT BLUE
SATIN COAT & BREECHES-
GOLD BUTTONS & BRAID-
BROCADE WAISTCOAT-
WHITE FRINGED CRAVAT &
WRIST FRILLS - WHITE
POWDERED WIG - BLACK
TRICORNE - PALE GREY
SILK STOCKINGS - BLACK
LEATHER SHOES - RED
HEELS - METAL
BUCKLES -
HANDKERCHIEF

plain, patterned, or striped materials. The **patterns** were chiefly floral, with dainty motifs, arranged in large all-over repeats, or decorating hem and cuffs only. They were printed, painted, or embroidered; appliqué embroidery was in considerable vogue. Pastel **shades** were the rage, in cream, lavender, blue, green, and pink, though stronger colours were also seen, especially in patterned fabrics.

The **corset** was still either made in one with the bodice, or separately. It was laced tightly up the back to produce a small waist, and to assist in achieving this, was reinforced by whalebone or metal strips. The waist was decorated by tabs; shoulder-straps supported the corset at the top, and the material was usually linen, brocade, or soft leather (see p. 179). Corsets were worn with all gowns, and were laced up more tightly for evening wear, in which instance the laces were usually tightened at intervals during the day to produce the desired effect for the party or dance.

For out-of-doors, ladies still wore the shoulder **cape** of fur, or longer **cloaks**, with or without an attached hood. These cloaks were of various lengths, reaching hips, knees, or ankles, and were voluminous in order to cover the hooped skirts. Velvet or satin were popular materials, with fur edges and linings. Most styles of cloak had a square collar, and slits for the hands, in front (see p. 177).

Plate VIII illustrates well the feminine **riding habit.** This costume, modelled on the lines of masculine dress, has been referred to and described in previous chapters, and had not altered greatly from that worn when it was first introduced. The masculine style of coat, buttoning full-length, the large cuffs and the waistcoat worn in conjunction with a long, full skirt can be seen; the latter is worn over a padded roll to resemble the hoop. The lady also adopts the masculine wig, cravat, tricorne, gloves, and cane.

The feminine **coiffure** was still dressed in a bun worn high up the back of the head, but the remainder of the hair was now combed into a simpler style, with curls off the forehead and sides, and an occasional long ringlet descending to the neck and shoulders for evening or formal wear.

Ladies still preferred to be bareheaded except for a tiny white silk, linen, or lace **cap,** with frilled or flounced edges and hanging lappets, which was perched daintily on the crown of the head; this cap was worn indoors and out, though a **hood** was placed on top for outdoor, winter wear (see pp. 175, 177, and 179).

Feminine styles of **shoe** were similar to those described in Chapter VI: they were made of brocade or embroidered silk or satin, with pointed toes, high, curved heels, and jewelled metal buckles ornamenting the instep (see p. 179).

Men wore a small **sword** which was suspended from a hanger under the waistcoat, with only the hilt and tip usually visible. Other accessories included the ever-popular malacca **cane,** with ivory, amber, or silver head, and cord tassel trimming (see pp. 175 and 179), the enamelled or jewelled **snuff-box,** leather **gloves,** lace-edged white **handkerchief,** and a fur **muff,** carried in winter or slung from a waistcoat button.

Feminine accessories comprised a folding **fan** (see p. 175), a fur **muff** in winter (see p. 177), and long white kid **gloves** or short lace or silk gloves or **mittens** (see p. 175). The small embroidered **apron,** made of silk, satin, or lace, with fringed or flounced edges, was still in vogue (see p. 175).

PLATE VIII

A distinctive Riding Habit, based on masculine styles of coat
and waistcoat but worn over a padded skirt

*The Countess of Mar, 1715, from a portrait in the
possession of the Earl of Mar and Kellie, K.T.*

HANOVER, GEORGE I
1714-1727

GREY POWDERED WIG - LACE CRAVAT

GREY POWDERED WIG - WHITE SILK CRAVAT - c.1715

BLACK TRICORNE - WHITE OSTRICH FROND TRIMMING - WHITE POWDERED WIG - c.1720

MALACCA CANES - IVORY, AMBER & SILVER HEADS - TASSELS

FEMININE BROCADE SHOE - JEWELLED METAL BUCKLE

LINEN CORSET - WHALEBONE STIFFENING IN VERTICAL BANDS - BACK LACING

SILVER CRUCIFIX

MAN'S BUFF LEATHER SHOE - JEWELLED METAL BUCKLE

WHITE LACE-EDGED CAP & LAPPETS - PEARL NECKLACE & EARRINGS

ENAMELLED GOLD RING SET WITH DIAMONDS

GOLD RING WITH DIAMONDS

GOLD RING SET WITH DIAMONDS

LACE WHITE CAP - c.1720-27

BLACK TRICORNE - GOLD BRAID TRIMMING

GREY POWDERED WIG - WHITE CRAVAT - c.1725

A moderate amount of jewellery was worn: jewelled rings, pearl necklaces and ear-rings, or chain necklaces with pendants, and jewelled brooches were most popular (see p. 179).

With the new fashion for hair-powder, **cosmetics** were more heavily applied than ever, in order to hide the resultant effect on the complexion; rouge, face-powder, and **patches** were used by men and women; also quantities of perfume to offset the scanty washing activities. **Patch boxes** and **cosmetic cases** were introduced for carrying on the person, and ladies often amended their toilet in public from these, which were made of gold or silver with enamelled or painted miniatures on the lid.

GEORGE II   1727–1760

Eighteenth-century dress, sponsored in England under George II and George III, was primarily noted for its exquisite fabrics in silks and satins, worn in delicate pastel shades, or all-over designs and border patterns in stronger hues, painted, embroidered, or printed on the material. Motifs were dainty, inspired by flora and fauna.

France still led European fashions, and continued to do so until the French Revolution at the end of the century. Styles changed more rapidly now: every few years brought new ideas and fancies, many of which were short-lived; dandies carried these fashions to extremes, and the difference in costume between the various strata of society was marked, particularly in the fabrics and decoration used.

In masculine dress, the wig was the chief item of interest, the rest of the costume remaining similar to that worn in the previous two reigns. But in the coiffure, gentlemen exercised their ingenuity to the full, and various indeed were the styles of peruke to be seen: paramount among these were the tie, ramillie, pig-tail, and bag-wig. Powder was universally adopted; white wigs were thus *à la mode*, particularly until about 1750.

The vogue for decorating the feminine gown and person by ribbon bows and lace, which had lasted since before the Restoration, continued without respite until nearly the end of the century, and to this ornamentation was added—increasingly after 1730–1740—numerous ruffles, ruchings, flounces, and plumes. This idea was carried to such excess that, by 1750–1760, a lady buying a gown, particularly for evening or dress wear, was not considered *au fait* with the fashions unless it had edges and many horizontal rows of ruching and flouncing in addition to the other means of decoration. The hoop was worn throughout the reign of George II, although it altered in shape during this time, becoming flattened at front and back, to give greater width at the sides, later in the period. A folding version of the hoop was invented towards the end of the reign, in order to facilitate the passage of narrow entrances and exits. The sack gown gained a universal appeal, and was moderated and recut after about 1740 to produce the fitting hoop gown with rear "Watteau" pleats.

In addition to the numbers of actual costumes of this period still extant, much useful information can be gained from a study of the work of the painters of the time, foremost among whom must be counted William Hogarth, with his humour and rich knowledge of the dress and mannerisms of people of all walks of life. Early paintings by Sir Joshua Reynolds are also useful.

HANOVER, GEORGE II
1727-1760

c.1730 - DARK BLUE
VELVET EVENING GOWN -
ERMINE EDGING -
JEWELLED BROOCHES
CENTRE FRONT - PEARL
CIRCLE & EARRINGS -
PEARLS IN HAIR -
WHITE SATIN
UNDERSKIRT - GOLD
EMBROIDERY -
POWDERED HAIR -
PAINTED FAN -
WHITE SILK &
LACE NECK &
SLEEVE FRILLS

1735-6 - ROSE - COLOURED
SATIN GOWN - ÉCHELLE
FRONT - CREAM & BLUE
DAMASK UNDERSKIRT -
WHITE SILK & LACE NECK &
SLEEVE FRILLS - PEARL
NECKLACE - POWDERED
HAIR

c.1730 - BLUE - GREY
VELVET COAT - SILK
EMBROIDERED CUFFS &
POCKET FLAPS IN PASTEL
SHADES OF BLUE, GREEN &
YELLOW - WHITE TIE WIG -
WHITE SHIRT FRILLS -
GREY SILK STOCKINGS -
BLACK LEATHER SHOES -
JEWELLED
BUCKLES

c.1745-50 - CREAM -
COLOURED SATIN SACK
GOWN - WATTEAU PLEATS
AT BACK - OPEN IN FRONT
TO WAIST, TO SHOW UNDER
-BODICE WITH BLUE
VELVET ÉCHELLE BOWS
& WHITE LACE NECK
EDGING - WHITE SILK,
LACE-EDGED SLEEVE
FRILLS & CAP WITH
LAPPETS - WHITE
KID GLOVES

As mentioned earlier, only small alterations were apparent in the masculine dress of this time; the **coat** was an example of this. Until about 1750 it remained almost unaltered, typified by the enormous cuffs, the waisted cut, with flared skirt radiating from hip pleats, buttons full-length centre front, though seldom fastened, and hip-pocket flaps. The skirt was still stiffened with whalebone or buckram and flared starkly from the hips. Plain fabrics were chiefly used, silk, satin, wool, or velvet in strong bright colours, while gold braid and frog ornament was seen at the centre front, pocket flaps, and cuffs, though the latter were often embroidered in colour or made of brocade or flowered silk. Gold, silver, or jewelled buttons were used. There was, on the whole, more decoration on the coat than in George I's time (see pp. 181 and 183). After about 1750, the coat was worn a little shorter, less flared, and with slightly smaller cuffs (see p. 185).

The **waistcoat** was also almost unchanged, made of flowered silk or brocade, or, alternatively, embroidered all over in gold, silver, or colours. It remained long until about 1750, when it was cut considerably shorter and was usually buttoned full-length (see pp. 183 and 185).

In inclement weather an **overcoat** would be worn on top of the coat, cut, as in George I's reign, in a similar manner to the coat, though with the addition of a collar and a belt at the waist. Shoulder capes were added after 1750, providing the foundation for the riding coat or redingote of the next reign.

Breeches were unaltered, fitting closely to the knee where they were fastened by buttons or a buckle. **Stockings** were also the same, though an increasing preference for white was shown.

In footwear, high heels had at last been abandoned in favour of a low, flat heel, similar to present-day styles. **Shoe** toes were normal in shape, the square cut having disappeared. Leather was used, generally in black, and the metal buckle, sometimes jewelled, still ornamented the instep (see pp. 181, 183, 185, and 187). Leather **boots** were still seen for travelling and riding, and **spatter-dashes** were worn over shoes in bad weather.

Probably owing to its great weight and cumbersomeness, the curled, formalised **full-bottomed wig** became obsolete by 1740–1750, and most fashionable men discarded it early in the thirties. The trend was then towards tying back the wig to the nape of the neck, and from this idea came the subsequent variations on the theme. There were many of these, most of which remained in vogue until natural hair once more reasserted its predominance over wigs towards the end of the century. The simplest style was the *tie*: in this mode, the hair was fastened back at the nape by a black silk bow and was allowed to fall down the back in loose curls. Two similar styles were the *ramillie* and *pig-tail*: in the former, the back hair was plaited in one queue and secured at the nape and the end by black bows, while in the latter, the same style was adopted, except that the plait was encased in black silk. Another popular type was the *bag-wig*, also tied at the nape by a black bow, but the remaining hair was then placed in a large rectangular black silk bag which was drawn together at the top by the bow. These were the chief modes, although there were sundry variations on these ideas, such as the "major" and "brigadier". The front of the wig was dressed loosely back to the tie at the nape while the sides were arranged in a bushy mass of hair over the ears, known as *pigeon's wings*. After

HANOVER, GEORGE II
1727-1760

c.1735-45 - BLUE SATIN COAT - GOLD FROG & BUTTON FASTENINGS - DARK BLUE VELVET BREECHES - SILK STOCKING'S - BLACK LEATHER SHOES - JEWELLED BUCKLES - WHITE SHIRT FRILLS & STOCK - BLACK SILK TIE - WHITE WIG, BAG WIG STYLE - BLACK TRICORNE - GOLD EDGING CANE

c.1740-50 - MAROON VELVET JACKET - ERMINE EDGE - PALE BLUE TAFFETA GOWN - WHITE, FRILLED EDGED FICHU AT NECK - WHITE SLEEVE FRILLS & CAP - STRAW HAT - BLUE RIBBONS - FAN

c.1745-55 - PALE BLUE SILK GOWN - CREAM SATIN BOWS - WHITE, FRILLED EDGED FICHU, NECK-EDGING, SLEEVE FRILLS & CAP - NATURAL COLOURED STRAW HAT - STRIPED RIBBON - CANE - RIBBON BOW

c.1745-50 - RED VELVET COAT, WAISTCOAT & BREECHES - GOLD BUTTONS & BRAID EMBROIDERY - WHITE LACE-EDGED SHIRT RUFFLES - WHITE PIG-TAIL WIG - BLACK TRICORNE - WHITE OSTRICH FRONDS - WHITE SILK STOCKINGS - BLACK LEATHER SHOES - JEWELLED BUCKLES - SILVER TOPPED CANE - SWORD

about 1740–1745, these masses were dressed in more formalised horizontal curls, usually one or more in rows, one below the other, and by 1750–1760, the front of the wig was dressed higher off the forehead in anticipation of the high coiffures of the George III period. White wigs were all the rage, although powder was used less abundantly after 1750. Most men cut their own hair short or had it shaved, under the wig, although some, with a good head of hair, dressed and powdered it as a wig. All these wigs were highly insanitary, and became breeding-grounds for various types of livestock, and this was accentuated by the wheat-meal or rice-meal used for powdering. The wigs were rarely, if ever, washed, only a fresh application of powder was added to cover the dirt. Illustrations of the different types of wig can be seen on pp. 181, 183, 185, and 187.

The three-cornered **tricorne** remained the distinctive hat of the period: it was made of black or dark felt, and with edges decorated by gold braid, fringing, or ostrich fronds (see pp. 183, 185, and 187).

The fine white **shirt** was still visible on the chest in the waistcoat opening, in frills and ruffles, and at the lace or lace-edged wrist ruffles. The **cravat** became shorter and was replaced by a simple *stock* after about 1735–1740; this was tied round the neck without hanging ends. A black silk ribbon often surmounted the stock, tied in a bow in front, after 1745–1750 (see pp. 183, 185, and 187). Linen was still changed infrequently and was considerably soiled by the use of hair-powder.

The silhouette of feminine dress was governed in George II's reign, as in the Tudor period, by the framework underneath: in this case it was the **hoop** and **corset.** The former consisted, for some years after the accession of George II, of a canvas petticoat similar to that described for the last reign. After 1730–1735, the shape of the hoop slowly changed: the front and back were flattened and the major width was at the sides. This evolution continued until about 1740–1745, when the extension of the hoop was almost entirely at the sides and a flattened oval section had been achieved. By 1750, ladies wore a short rounded hoop covering the waist and hips only, still of a solid construction, covered and padded, and containing pocket holes. It was not until about 1760 when the metal or whalebone folding hoop, in two sections, was established, that ladies could pass through a doorway without lifting the hoop forward or walking sideways. An illustration of the folding hoop can be seen in the next chapter on p. 197. All classes of women wore the hoop, though those adopted by the poorer or servant class were rather smaller versions. Indeed, the popularity and seeming indispensability of this construction was so great that the satirists of the day found ample material for comment; indeed, the fashion reached parallel absurdities with the wheel farthingale of Elizabeth's time. The corset was still either worn separately under the gown or made in one with the bodice. In the former instance, it was laced up the back and stiffened with whalebone to achieve a very small waist in contrast to the wide hoop; it was supported by shoulder-straps and still had waist-tabs. Most corsets were made of soft leather, brocade, or velvet, and were attached to the hoop by means of tapes at the waist.

The **gown** was still frequently cut in three parts, bodice, over-skirt, and petticoat, although in some cases the skirt was not open in front and thus did

HANOVER, GEORGE II
1727-1760

c. 1750-60 - PINK SILK GOWN, BODICE & UNDER-SKIRT - EMBROIDERED IN SPRIG PATTERN IN PINK & GREEN - DULL GOLD VERTICAL BANDS - POWDERED HAIR - PAINTED FAN - WHITE LACE NECK & SLEEVE RUFFLES - WATTEAU PLEATS AT BACK OF GOWN

c. 1755 - CREAM SATIN SACK GOWN - EMBROIDERED IN BROWN, GREEN & RED - WATTEAU PLEATS - SLEEVE RUFFLES - WHITE SILK RUFFLES - WHITE POWDERED HAIR - RIBBON

1750-60 - GREEN WOOL COAT - GOLD BRAID EDGES - GOLD BUTTONS - SATIN EMBROIDERED WAISTCOAT - GREEN WOOL BREECHES - SILK STOCKINGS - BLACK LEATHER SHOES - METAL BUCKLES - BLACK FELT TRICORNE - GOLD BRAID EDGE & TRIMMING - WHITE STOCK & SHIRT FRILLS - LEATHER GLOVES - WHITE BAG - WIG - BLACK BOW - CANE

c. 1755-60 - PALE LAVENDER TAFFETA GOWN WITH PAGODA SLEEVES & RUCHED EDGES IN FLOWER SHAPES - LEMON SILK PETTICOAT WITH ROWS OF RUCHING & FLOUNCING - DARK LAVENDER SATIN BOWS - WHITE KID GLOVES - FAN - BROCADE SHOE - WHITE LACE SLEEVE & NECK RUFFLES - PEARLS IN HAIR

not show the petticoat. The **bodice** was almost unaltered: it was stiffened and fitting on the chest, waist, and back, pointed in front and rounded at the back of the waist. The front was still often laced over a **stomacher,** with jewelled brooches or an échelle as favourite trimmings. The **neck-line** was low and wide throughout the reign, trimmed by lace or silk edging and later finished and partially obscured by a lace or ruched edged *fichu* of soft transparent fabric. **Sleeves** were still elbow-length, finished in a turned-up cuff, which by 1740–1750 was ousted from fashion by flounces and ruching, or the *pagoda* style, ending in a wide flounce or flare. The **skirt** was very full, gathered in at the waist and fitted closely over the hoop to fall in numerous folds to the ground, although after about 1740–1745 shorter gowns were also seen, often disclosing a glimpse of a shoe and stocking to the ankle. Over-skirts were frequently open in front to show the **petticoat,** of the same or contrasting fabric. The edges of both skirts were increasingly ornamented by ruching, while horizontal or wavy bands of flounces were added, chiefly to the petticoat. Pocket slits were made in both skirts, but were not usually visible in the numerous folds and decoration (see pp. 181, 183, and 185).

The **sack gown** became immensely popular in this reign, being worn loose at first, but after about 1740 the bodice was often cut to fit, while the back hung in formalised box pleats, commonly referred to as *"Watteau pleats"*, after the painter, from neck to ground. Sometimes the sack was open in front to the waist, or, alternatively, to the ground, but by 1750 it was usually cut similarly to the ordinary gown, differing only in the Watteau pleats (see pp. 181 and 185).

Materials used for the voluminous gowns were perforce light in weight: taffeta, silk, satin, and damask were most in demand, in pastel shades of plain colours, stripes, or dainty floral patterns. These designs were painted, printed, or embroidered in *appliqué* work. Cream, yellow, blue, lavender, pink, and green were in great favour, with stronger hues in the patterns. White or cream lace, flowers, flounces, ruching, and ribbon bows of velvet, silk, or satin were added, to great excess after 1745–1750.

The feminine **riding habit** still consisted of a masculine type coat, waistcoat, cravat, wig, hat, gloves, and cane, absurdly combined with a full skirt over a hoop.

Out-of-doors, ladies donned a **cloak,** made with or without a hood, similar to that of the last period. Fur edges and linings were still usual. Alternatively, fur **shoulder capes** were still popular, or short hip-length **jackets,** with short sleeves ending in a cuff. Fur edges were popular with these also (see p. 183). Darker colours were used for these outer garments, usually in velvet.

In complete contrast to masculine dress, the feminine **coiffure** was the least ostentatious part of the attire. The lady wore her own hair until the end of the reign, supplemented by false hair from about 1750. Powder was applied throughout the period, particularly for evening and dress wear. In style, the hair was dressed in curls on the top and at the sides of the head, while the back was drawn into the bun high up the head. Ringlets were still seen on the shoulders for evening or formal dress. After 1750, the hair was dressed higher off the forehead in front and over a small velvet pad—a prelude to the immense creations of the seventies and eighties. Pearls, plumes, flowers, and ribbons

HANOVER, GEORGE II
1727-1760

BLACK, GOLD-EDGED TRICORNE –
WHITE WIG – BLACK BOW –
c. 1748-50

WHITE PIG-TAIL WIG –
c. 1740-45

WHITE RAMILLIE WIG – BLACK BOW –
GOLD BRAID EDGED COAT –
1753

WHITE WIG –
BAG-WIG
STYLE – BLACK
TRICORNE –
WHITE FRONT
EDGING

GREEN SATIN LADY'S SHOE
WITH GOLD EMBROIDERY &
SILVER JEWELLED BUCKLE

LEATHER MASCULINE SHOE –
JEWELLED BUCKLE

COIFFURE WITH PLUMES,
PEARLS & RIBBONS –
c. 1755

WHITE TIE WIG –
BLACK BOW

GOLD RING
SET WITH
RUBIES & DIAMONDS –
c. 1759

VELLUM
PAINTED FAN
c. 1750-60

IVORY
STICKS

FILIGREE GOLD
RING – ENAMELLED
STONE

RAMILLIE WIG

PIG-TAIL WIG

ONYX
CAMEO
WITH GOLD RIM

WHITE PLEATED
CAP – VELVET
BOW – LACE
VEIL TIED ON
TOP & UNDER CHIN –
c. 1757-60

WHITE SILK CAP
WITH RIBBONS &
FLOWERS –
c. 1740

BLACK FELT
TRICORNE – GOLD
EDGE – WHITE
CURLED WIG –
c. 1730

were used as hair decoration, more profusely as time passed (see pp. 181, 185, and 187).

Indoors, ladies were often bareheaded still, although the white silk, lace-edged or lace **caps** were again in vogue, with lappets or strings hanging from them. Flowers and ribbon bows were used as ornamentation. Out-of-doors, **hoods** were still worn or, alternatively, from about 1735, straw or silk **hats** were seen, often surmounting the white cap and ornamented by ribbons and flowers, and tied under the chin by a ribbon bow (see pp. 183 and 187).

The feminine **linen** was visible at neck and sleeves. The *décolletage* was still finished by lace-edging and later by the filmy fichu. From about 1740, **lace frills** encircling the throat became increasingly in demand, worn purely for decorative purposes. White lace or silk flounces from the undergarment were still seen below the gown sleeve frills.

White **stockings** also became popular for ladies and were partially visible with the shorter skirts. **Shoes** or slippers still had high, curved heels, pointed toes, and jewelled instep buckles. Brocade or embroidered silk or satin were the usual fabrics for manufacture (see p. 187).

Long or short malacca **canes**, with gold or silver tasselled cords, and amber, ivory, or metal tops were carried by gentlemen. The small **sword** hung from the hanger under the waistcoat, and fur **muffs**, ornate, enamelled, or jewelled, gold **snuff-boxes** and lace-edged white **handkerchiefs** were still common accessories (see pp. 183 and 185).

Ladies still wore small lace-edged **aprons** of silk, satin, or gauze, chiefly in white or black, and long white kid **gloves** or short silk **mittens** or gloves (see pp. 181 and 185). **Canes** or **parasols** were carried, the former had amber or silver knobs and were decorated by ribbon loops, while the latter were silk, gaily coloured with fringed edges, and were small and of the non-folding type (see p. 183). Large beribboned fur **muffs** were carried in winter. All ladies carried small lace-edged **handkerchiefs**, and the inevitable **fan.** It was indeed the age of the fan, which was small and folding, made of ivory, gold, silver, or pearl sticks, with vellum, satin, or silk covering, exquisitely painted in scenes of the period by well-known artists of the day. Many of these fans can still be seen today in museums or private collections (see p. 187). Jewelled or embroidered purses were carried, and small bunches of flowers.

Little **jewellery** was worn, chiefly pearls in necklaces and ear-rings, or jewelled rings or brooches (see p. 187).

The use of **cosmetics,** black silk or paper **patches,** and **perfume,** by both sexes, was at its height, in order to camouflage the damage done to the complexion by hair-powder, and the lack of cleanliness. Perfume, patch, and cosmetic **boxes** were carried; they were beautifully made, of gold or silver, enamelled and jewelled. Enamelled gold or silver **watches** were also carried by men and women.

Several good examples of the dress of about 1745, particularly the masculine, can be seen in the painting by William Hogarth in Plate IX. The pigeon's wings, black silk tie and wig bow, flowered silk cuffs and waistcoat and white stockings of the man seated on the left should be noted, also the lady's gown and cap, and the gold embroidery on the coat of the man seated in the right of the picture.

GEORGE III PART ONE, 1760-1790

In 1760, when George III came to the throne, English costume was still dominated by the French styles: there was, as yet, no definite lead from the royalty in England. The increasing extravagance of garments in vogue at the French Court influenced English fashions to the extent where they became artificial and even fantastic. The peak of these styles was reached during the period 1775-1780, with enormous wigs, wired skirts, bows, ruffles, and ornamentation of every conceivable kind.

From 1780 onwards, the nobility in England began to develop styles of costume which were freer from the French influence. In masculine costume, the English acquired the lead in Europe, and have continued to hold it up to the present day. Nevertheless, in France the Revolution (1789-1794) had a considerable influence on European costume: the movement towards the abolition of class distinction producing far-reaching and often permanent effects. This will be made evident in the succeeding chapter.

During the first years of George III's reign, the style of the masculine **coat** remained unchanged from that of the previous reign. It was nearly knee-length, usually worn unbuttoned, without collar, with fitting sleeves and large cuffs, fastened back with two or three buttons. Commonly the coat edge and cuffs were embroidered in contrasting colours, or gold braid and frog ornamentation. Silk was the favourite material; apple-green or yellow the popular colours. Gradually, in the late sixties, the coat was worn shorter, and less flared, the cuffs decreased in size, a small collar appeared, and wool superseded silk (see pp. 190 and 192).

The slow change of kinds of material for the making of the main garments of men's clothing was beginning at this time. The trend was from the silks, brocades, velvets, satins, and other thinner and more ornate materials towards cloth, wool, corduroy, and stockinet. The transformation was not complete until the end of the reign of William IV in 1837, especially for formal and evening wear, but signs of the movement were evident by 1770, to be popularised for day wear by the economic results of the French Revolution.

A group of young men formed the "Macaroni Club" in the early 1770s. Attracted by costume, they introduced an extreme coat fashion which, though plain in colour, was short, pleated, and flared at the back, with a braid edge. Waistcoats were striped, with plain or striped fitting breeches and stockings. This ensemble was surmounted by an exceedingly high wig (see p. 190).

Within ten years a reversal to longer coats reoccurred, with a deeper collar, higher up the neck. In the early eighties, the *tail coat* appeared, made of cloth, with a very deep, often velvet-faced, turned-down collar, reaching to the ears. The fitting sleeves had small or no cuffs. The skirt portion of the coat was cut away in front to reach tails at the back. Colours were darker and more varied (see p. 194).

The **waistcoat** was, in 1760, about six inches shorter than the coat. Made of silk, often lavishly embroidered, it was sleeveless, and worn partly unbuttoned. Low down on the hips were flap-covered pockets. Later, as the coat became shorter, so did the waistcoat. Within about ten years the pockets disappeared.

HANOVER, GEORGE III
1760-1790

1761 - PALE BLUE SILK
COAT - GOLD EMBROIDERY
& BUTTONS -
FLOWERED SILK WAIST.
-COAT - CADOGAN WIG -
BLUE BREECHES -
WHITE STOCKINGS -
BLACK SHOES

1760's
CREAM SATIN GOWN, PANNIERS
EMBROIDERED IN GREEN, BROWN
GOLD, AND RED SILK, GOLD
FRINGING.
POWDERED WIG.
MALACCA CANE, PINK BOW
PAINTED FAN

1760
WEDDING DRESS
WHITE SATIN LINED WITH
WHITE SILK, WHITE LACE
RUFFLES
PANNIERS
POWDERED HAIR, FLOWERS
APPLIQUE IN SELF-COLOUR
AND MATERIAL IN FRONT

1772
EXAGGERATED
COSTUME OF THE
MACARONIS.

By 1774, white, often embroidered in various colours, became most popular. Spots and stripes also appeared. Then pockets returned again, with cloth as the fashionable material, by the late eighties (see pp. 190, 192, and 194).

Breeches remained almost unchanged in style throughout the period, being fitting to below the knee and buttoned there, or tied with strings. Striped or spotted silk was fashionable in the seventies, and later white buckskin became the vogue. The pockets were beneath the waistcoat, and after 1770 a common ornamentation of dress was a pair of fob watches hung from each pocket, and exposed to view. One of these watches was often a dummy, or what the French called a *fausse montre* (see pp. 190, 192, and 194).

Stockings were commonly white, made of silk or cotton, stripes becoming popular later. For evening, or formal wear, they were adorned with clocks in gold or silver.

The low-heeled **shoes** of black leather had instep metal buckles and leather tongues. Red leather heels were still worn for formal dress until 1789. The Macaronis, in 1772, wore shoes with smaller buckles, often jewelled (see pp. 190, 192, and 194).

Leather **boots** were also fashionable from 1770. They were usually black, but appeared in various styles. In the eighties, two types were popular: one with a turned-down cuff, called the Jack boot, the other plain, and pointed at the top, somewhat like the Hessian boot (see p. 194).

The white cravat or stock was worn throughout the period, full at first, tied twice round the neck, and ending in a flounce in front. Later it was tied in a large bow, but gradually became more discreet with a small bow or frill. White silk embroidery, or white or cream lace edging, was a frequent embellishment.

The **wig** was still an important feature of the period. It was always powdered, and increased in size and popularity until 1780, but subsequently became gradually of smaller dimensions. Various styles were assumed, the most popular in 1760 being the *cadogan* or *club* style (named after Earl Cadogan), and the **pig-tail** wig. The former had its ends looped once or twice at the back, and then tied with black velvet or satin ribbon. The ribbon ends were often brought round to the front of the neck and tied over the white cravat. The latter style of wig had one or two pig-tails at the back which were encased in black silk, and tied top and bottom with a black bow, as in the reign of George II. In both these forms of coiffure, one or two curls were worn on each side of the head, just above the ear. By 1772, wigs were worn high off the forehead, a style especially favoured by the Macaronis with their extreme taste. Still in favour as an alternative fashion at this time was the **bag-wig.** The *hedgehog* or woolly style came from France in the eighties, and achieved a certain popularity. With the decrease in the size of wigs after 1780, natural hair worn in wig styles was also seen (see pp. 190, 192, 194, and 197).

During this period, the most usual wear in hats was still the **tricorne,** made of black or dark felt with a gold or braid edge (see p. 192). The Macaronis assumed a small version of this hat, called a Nivernois, after the French writer. It was worn perched idiotically in front and on top of the enormous wig.

The *bicorne* was also worn about 1775, and later. It had a back and front

HANOVER, GEORGE III
1760-1790

1780
CLOTH COAT
STRIPED WAISTCOAT
TRICORNE
BLACK LEATHER
SHOES
MALACCA CANE
GLOVES

1771
SATIN POLONAISE GOWN
STRIPED TAFFETA
UNDERSKIRT
STRAW HAT WITH
FLOWERS & RIBBONS
POWDERED WIG
CADOGAN STYLE

1773
SATIN DRESS
PANNIER STYLE
POWDERED WIG
WITH OSTRICH PLUMES
AND PEARLS
PAINTED FAN
LACE RUFFLES

1777
CLOAK OR PELISSE
EDGED WITH
ERMINE
FUR MUFF
WITH BOWS
CALASH
POWDERED WIG
TAFFETA GOWN

flap only, with often a fringed edge, and a silk rosette or emblem on one side (see p. 194).

A high-crowned felt hat, alternatively made of beaver, with a rolling brim and ribbon and buckle decorations, appeared in the eighties: this was a forerunner of the top hat. The *Holland* hat with a flatter, round crown was one of the many variations of this fashion. By 1789, they had replaced the tricorne (see p. 197).

The chief of the various types of **overcoat** were the close-fitting *redingote* or *riding coat* of English origin, worn with two or three shoulder capes, and a somewhat shapeless style with large cuffs and a flat collar, to which capes were sometimes added.

Canes, usually of malacca, were still popular. Of various lengths, they were adorned with amber, ivory, or gold tops. Sometimes tassels were attached (see pp. 192 and 194). Other accessories to a gentleman's attire included **snuff-boxes.** These were again very ornate, and regarded as an indispensable item of dress. **Muffs** were still carried at the beginning of the period. Fashionable men assumed lace or lace-edged **handkerchiefs. Jewellery** was rarely seen.

During the greater part of this period, feminine **gowns** were still supported on **hoops.** Ladies still strove after a minute waist which was achieved by tight corsets. These hoops, sometimes known by the French name of *panniers* (French: *le panier*=basket), were made, in the sixties, of metal or whalebone. Constructed in two parts, they were tied by tapes on to the corset at the waist, from which they protruded almost horizontally on both sides. For the first time the framework was made to fold up, to enable the lady to pass easily through a doorway by lifting the sides of the hoop (see p. 197). The gown was still open in front to reveal the **petticoat,** which was usually of a different colour and material. At the back, the large box or Watteau pleats hung straight from the neck to the ground, and frequently a train was worn, especially at evening and formal occasions. Elbow-length **sleeves** ended in bows and lace ruffles. The low neck-line was square and still edged with lace or ruffles (see p. 190). The *"pocket pannier"* gown was an alternative mode. Material or drapery was pulled through the pocket holes to form a festoon on each hip.

France was the leader of feminine fashion until the eighties, especially during the previous decade when Marie Antoinette was a much-emulated example. Numerous changes of style took place at this time, following the whims and fancies of the Court. In the early seventies, the shape of the hoop changed slightly once more, and the skirt became more bell-shaped (see p. 192). The French *polonaise* style was copied at this time with the over-skirt looped up in three festoons, edged with ruffles, and tied with bows. The bodice remained tight and fitting, and boned at the waist. Sleeves were short, ending in the usual rows of lace ruffles or puffs. Shorter skirts, sometimes only ankle-length, were worn. Petticoats were ornamented with bows, ruffles, and ruchings (see p. 192). The six years, 1774–1780, were a peak period for the excessive ornamentation of gowns, slippers, underwear, and wigs by brocades, feathers, flowers, lace ruchings, ruffles, and jewellery, particularly pearls.

Changes began to occur about 1780: the hoop was replaced by a bustle at the back; ornamentation decreased; the waist-line rose, though corsets were still worn, and there was a general trend from extravagance of style and material

HANOVER, GEORGE III
1760-1790

1781 - STRAW-COLOURED
SATIN GOWN - WHITE FICHU
& SLEEVE FRILLS -
CANE - RIBBON BOW-
GAINSBOROUGH
HAT IN VELVET -
WHITE OSTRICH
PLUMES - POWDERED
WIG

1785
DARK GREEN SILK GOWN
APPLE GREEN EDGING
DARK GREEN VELVET HAT
PALE YELLOW RIBBONS
SATIN, WHITE PLUME.
WHITE LAWN
BOUFFANT, AND
WHITE FRILLS AT HEM
AND WRISTS.
WHITE LAWN MOB CAP
APPLE GREEN SATIN RIBBON

WHITE APRON, SPRIG
PATTERN IN PALE GREEN
NATURAL HAIR IN
CURLS AND RINGLETS
SATIN BROCADE SHOES
WITH METAL BUCKLE
GLOVES.

1789
Cloth redingote
Pink gown, ruching
at hem.
Green felt hat
pink ribbons.
Powdered hair
Gloves.

1786
Tail coat
high velvet collar
bicorne hat
fringed edge
leather boots
cadogan wig
malacca cane

PLATE IX

towards simplicity. England led this movement, though the change was completed in Europe by the French Revolution. The *English gown*, called in France *Robe a l'Anglais*, can be seen in the many life-size portraits of the day, painted by Gainsborough and his contemporary artists. It was a simple satin gown with elbow-length sleeves ending in ruffles or a large puff, and a low round neck, finished with a soft fichu (see p. 194). A similar popular style was the *redingote gown*, only worn with a short double-breasted jacket with wide lapels and long sleeves. The jacket was usually dark, contrasting with the pale gown.

Materials during this period included satin, taffeta, silk, velvet, and brocade, and later, in the eighties, cotton and cambric. **Colours** were varied, but pale pink, ivory, lilac, pale blue, and cream were the most popular. **Motifs** were small and dainty, sprig patterns and striped or painted materials being the vogue. **Trimmings** included lace, tulle, bows, ruchings, flounces, fur, and flowers.

In the eighties, **aprons** of purely ornamental function were often worn on top of the gowns, made of lace or cambric. They originated in France with Marie Antoinette's desire to imitate milkmaid costume (see p. 194).

A pouter-pigeon silhouette, produced by the *bouffant*, appeared by 1785. A full fichu covered the neck and breasts, and was tied in a bow in front (see p. 194).

The **wig** was, perhaps, the most fantastic aspect of feminine dress in this very extravagant period. In 1760, the hair was increased in height by the addition of false hair. It was smeared with pomatum and powdered, then ornamented with ribbons, feathers, buckles, and flowers. Until 1782, it grew in dimensions, both in width and height. This was achieved by cotton wool pads placed inside the hair. By 1780, such extraordinary adornments as models of battles, coaches and horses, windmills, butterflies, etc., were worn on the wig. Rivalry was rampant among the ladies to achieve some kind of originality, however ludicrous. Considerable time was needed to erect these elaborate coiffures; in consequence, they were only "opened up" about once in eight or nine weeks to allow air to enter, and livestock to depart. The back hair was dressed in **cadogan** style, or in loose curls or ringlets. In the eighties, simplicity reappeared at last. The coiffure decreased in height, the **hedgehog** style became fashionable, with an alternative in the form of two simple curls worn on each side of the face, with very long ringlets at the back. Examples of these wigs can be seen in the illustrations on pp. 190, 192, 194, and 197.

Headgear had to be adapted to suit these wigs. **Hats** were not fashionable during the period of preposterously high wigs, except small straw or silk hats, perched on the forehead (see pp. 192 and 197). On the other hand, caps, as distinct from hats, such as the *mob, ranelagh,* and *dormeuse*, were worn, and some of these, like the wigs, reached enormous proportions; they had evolved from the white lace or lace-edged caps worn in the reigns of George I and George II, but were now of white silk or lawn, and had numerous frilled edges framing the face, and were tied on top and under the chin by ribbon bows (see p. 197). An extraordinary affair, the *calash*, was fashionable in the seventies, and for several years afterwards, for outdoor wear. A colossal whalebone structure, covered with padding and silk, it could be opened and shut like a perambulator hood, the mechanism being operated by strings or cords in the front. This affair

14

encased the wig, only the face showing when it was fully drawn forwards (see p. 192). As wigs became smaller, more hats and bonnets were worn. A popular feature were the huge picture hats, ornamented with large ostrich plumes and ribbons, known as the "Gainsborough" or "Marlborough" hats, after the painter and his famous sitter. Towards 1790, tall felt or straw hats were worn, decorated with ribbons or plumes; alternatively, a simpler gauze or silk kerchief, ornamented with feathers or a garland of flowers. Hats were also worn on top of the caps (see pp. 194 and 197).

Cloaks, and various styles of *pelisse* were worn, the latter being most fashionable towards the end of the period. These had a broad collar and a hood at the back, and were edged with fur. The favourite materials were velvet or silk in resider green or golden brown, trimmed with ermine (see p. 192).

Coats, being impracticable over the immense wired skirts, were not much seen until the eighties. In the late eighties, the feminine version of the redingote became the mode. Like the masculine variety, it was double-breasted, with a large collar and revers, but had a high, shaped waist, and reached to the ground. It was especially popular for riding and hunting (see p. 194). Various types of loose, short jackets, with short or long sleeves, were worn.

Footwear was of a slipper style, made of satin, silk, or brocade, with an ornate buckle attached on top. The heels were fairly high, and often made of red leather. Less expensive types of slipper, commoner with the middle and lower classes, were made of kid, fabric, or leather. **Stockings** were white, of silk or cotton thread (see p. 197).

Several **petticoats** were worn under the wired skirts, and at least one, of a narrower type, *under* the framework. These were lavishly ornamented, and made of beautiful materials, especially the top one, next to the gown.

The many and varied accessories still included long pale-coloured or white **gloves** of kid or silk (see pp. 192 and 194); lace or silk **mittens**; expensive **fans**, exquisitely painted, embroidered, or carved; long **canes** (see pp. 190 and 194), and **parasols** ornamented with ribbon bows; fur **muffs**, also with ribbon bows; real or artificial flowers as a decoration for the hair or corsage; and a great deal of beautiful and costly **jewellery** in the form of necklaces, lockets, crosses, watches, and pendants or miniatures suspended from a black velvet ribbon worn round the neck. Pearls were very much the mode, either as collars, or in strings wound round the neck, or over the wig. **Perfumes** and **cosmetics**, including face **patches**, were still in great use, this persisting until the French Revolution.

GEORGE III PART TWO, 1790–1820 (REGENCY 1811–1820)
GEORGE IV   1820–1830
WILLIAM IV   1830–1837

The frequent economic, political, and social upheavals in Europe in the era 1790 to 1837 led to many changes in costume. The French Revolution (1789–1794), with its accent on the removal of extreme class distinction, originated and popularised new modes in dress having simple classical lines, and a pseudo-Grecian aspect, especially in the case of feminine wear. In England, simplicity in dress had already been the keynote for some years: the events in France

HANOVER, GEORGE III
1760-1790

POWDERED WIGS DECORATED BY RIBBONS, FLOWERS, PLUMES & PEARLS - CADOGAN STYLE AT REAR - 1775-82

WHALEBONE FOLDING HOOP - TAPE FASTENINGS

WHITE PIG-TAIL WIG - c. 1768

DARK BEAVER HAT WITH RIBBON & BUCKLE - CADOGAN WIG - c. 1787

STRAW HAT WITH FLOWERS & PLUMES OVER WHITE CAP WITH RIBBONS - DARK HAIR

POWDERED HEDGEHOG WIG - WHITE FICHU - c. 1785-7

c.1786 - STRAW HAT WITH RIBBONS & BOWS - LACE EDGING - WHITE FICHU

c. 1760

c. 1780

POWDERED HAIR - WHITE FICHU -

SILK & LACE HAT - c. 1788

SILK HAT WITH PLUMES & RIBBONS - POWDERED HAIR - c. 1777-80

POWDERED WIG - WHITE LACE-EDGED CAP WITH RIBBONS c. 1782

197

merely accelerated and accentuated this state of affairs. In masculine attire, England acquired and held the lead in Europe—an opportunity presented by the disorder rife in France. This ascendancy was particularly aided by the rise to royal favour of George Brummell (commonly nicknamed "Beau Brummell"). Sponsored by the Prince Regent, this remarkable man, an authority on dress, became the leader of the mode during the period 1794–1816. He made noteworthy contributions to English costume, using his great influence to establish a desire for cleanliness, and deplore the unhygienic habits of the eighteenth century. Discarding wigs and powder for the hair, he encouraged the virtue of washing the person, wearing spotlessly clean garments, the laundering of clothes, and starch for the cravat. A slovenly appearance became unfashionable: noblemen vied with one another in their efforts to tie a perfect cravat, or sport immaculate linen.

Perhaps the most important and permanent feature of this changeable period was the replacement of breeches by trousers. Though introduced at the end of the eighteenth century, yet it was not until the accession of George IV that they were universally in favour.

Although the cut-away **tail coat** of 1785 was worn until the turn of the century, the *frock coat* developed about 1790, and by 1797 was the masculine mode. The front was cut away square, slightly above the waist-line, and the tails hung at the back to knee-level. The collar was not so tall as at the end of the previous period, but was still covered with velvet. This coat was double-breasted with large revers, and six buttons in front. The sleeves were full at the top, fitting at the wrists, and worn long without cuffs. It formed the foundation for our present-day evening and morning dress-coats (see p. 199). With the advent of the nineteenth century, revers gradually increased in size, and taller collars were worn, a maximum height being reached about 1810, when they were often half-way up the ears. After 1818, the vogue increased for small waists, achieved and accentuated by corsets or stays, and padding of the shoulders, the tops of sleeves, and the tails at hip-level. This mode attained its maximum about 1830. Soon after 1820, the cut and fit of the coat improved, partly because the tails were made separately, and sewn on to the coat, and partly by the stiffening of the lapels and collar (see p. 201). After 1830, a larger waist—though still corseted—and wider tails appeared, the coat being called a *swallow-tail*. The velvet collar remained throughout the period, with cuffs to match as a later development. Sleeves were very tight, and shoulders gradually became less padded.

With the advent of the frock coat, **materials** used were heavier, cloth, leather, and heavy wool being common. More sombre colours began to appear, dark brown, dark blue, and dull pea-green replacing the light gay colours of 1780, with the addition of grey, buff, and claret from 1820 to 1830. By 1833, a reddish brown and mulberry were the mode, with black or dark blue for formal attire. Beau Brummell indulged one of his fancies by wearing a sky-blue coat for some time, at the height of his power—an idea slavishly copied by a small section of the community, mainly nobility and Court followers. The fashion did not, however, affect the general mode of the day. The black frock coat and the black evening coat had appeared about 1828.

White and piqué continued as the most fashionable colour and material for

HANOVER, 1790-1837

1800
EMPIRE GOWN
GREEK STYLE AND
WHITE AND BLUE
        DESIGNS
CASHMERE SHAWL WITH
GOLD, RED AND
    BLACK DESIGNS
    RETICULE
GRECIAN HAIR
        STYLE

1800
DARK GREEN HEAVY CLOTH
GARRICK OVERCOAT
WHITE BUCKSKIN BREECHES
BLACK LEATHER
        HESSIAN BOOTS
GOLD TASSEL AND
        BRAID TOPS
PEA GREEN CLOTH COAT
WHITE PIQUE
    WAISTCOAT
BLACK AND WHITE
    SILK CRAVAT
GREY FELT HAT —
    SILK CORD

1806
BOTTLE GREEN VELVET
        COAT
BRAID TRIMMING
VELVET HAT —
OSTRICH PLUMES
WHITE LAWN GOWN
    BOA

1806
DARK BROWN CLOTH
        COAT
VELVET COLLAR
WHITE PIQUE
    WAISTCOAT
WHITE COLLAR
BLACK AND WHITE
        CRAVAT
FAWN BEAVER HAT
KNEE BREECHES
BLACK LEATHER BOOTS
    CANE

199

waistcoats until 1835, when stronger hues appeared once more. In 1790, this garment was almost hidden by the coat except for about an inch below the coat at the waist, and a thin line above it on the chest. Sometimes stripes, especially red ones, still adorned the white background. With the new century, double-breasted waistcoats with small lapels, just visible above the coat, became the vogue. Pastel shades of piqué, as well as white, were adopted. Until 1830, only minor variations of this theme occurred: patterns and embroidery were sometimes seen, occasionally stripes appeared, small changes in lapel shapes occurred, pockets alternately appeared and disappeared. The waistcoat, like the coat, developed a small waist about 1817. By 1830, single-breasted garments returned once more, worn with or without lapels, and normally cut lower at the neck for evening wear. Later darker colours reappeared, and a greater variety of materials, such as velvet, corduroy, or fine wool. Often two waistcoats were worn, a dark one under a white, or lighter one. Usually, a gold chain, sometimes with a watch attached, hung from the pocket (see pp. 199 and 205).

During the period 1790–1837, the change-over from **breeches** to **trousers** took place. Incredible as it seemed to the people of 1790, this change was destined to be a permanent one. In 1790, tight-fitting breeches were generally worn either knee-length—as described previously—or ankle-length, buttoned up the outsides to knee- or thigh-level (see pp. 201 and 205). By 1800, light-coloured trousers were seen made of stockinet, cloth, buckskin, or corduroy. They were tight-fitting, and usually fastened by a strap under the instep. Often leather boots, worn on top of the trousers, covered the lower part of the leg. The trousers had a front panel, which could be opened, attached by three buttons to the waistcoat. Until 1820, both breeches and trousers continued in vogue; the former were always worn at Court, and on formal occasions, but the latter gradually gained popularity throughout the country. When George IV came to the throne he gave a definite lead towards the adoption of trousers for all types of dress, and the change-over soon became complete (see pp. 201 and 207). Trousers for evening wear were black, very tight-fitting, ankle-length, and buttoned part-way up the side. *"Peg-top"* trousers came in about 1822, and being very full and padded at the hips, tight-fitting at the ankle, with straps under the instep, they helped to accentuate the small waist of the time (see p. 201). Materials included corduroy—usually white—buckskin, drill, cloth, twill, and stockinet, with cotton for summer wear. Knee-breeches were still sometimes seen, as evening wear, on the older generation. After 1835, trousers widened a little.

The change-over from breeches to trousers brought about an accompanying change from **stockings** to **socks**.

On the whole, and especially until 1830, **boots** were worn rather than **shoes**. These boots were of various styles, the most popular being the *Hessian* boot, the *Wellington*, and the *Jockey* or *Top boot*. The Hessian was made of soft black leather, knee-length, shaped high in front with a tassel, and low at the back (see p. 199). The Wellington was similar, but longer, and without tassels (see pp. 199 and 201). The Jockey was shorter, with a turned-down cuff of buff or yellow leather, or dull-coloured cloth, and particularly popular after 1816. Though the boot was held to be the mode, yet leather shoes were also

HANOVER, 1790-1837

1814
POLISH STYLE OVERCOAT
IN DARK GREY-BLUE
CLOTH
DARK GREY FUR
COLLAR AND CUFFS
WELLINGTON BOOTS
GREY FELT HAT
AND RIBBON

1814
BROWN PELISSE
PALE GREY FUR
GLOVES
PALE GREEN SILK
BONNET WITH BROWN
SILK RIBBON AND BOWS
SLIPPERS LACED ON

1825
WHITE EVENING DRESS
LILAC BOWS &
EMBROIDERY - LACE
PETTICOAT SHOWS AT HEM -
FLOWERS IN HAIR + WHITE
GLOVES & LACE
HANDKERCHIEF

1824
DARK CLOTH COAT
VELVET COLLAR
WHITE CORDUROY TROUSERS
BLACK FELT HAT
WHITE COLLAR UNDER
COLOURED BAND
LEATHER SHOES

worn. These were flat-heeled with round toes, and tied with strings. **Slippers** or **pumps** with flat or no heels were popular for evening wear, or with the ankle-length trousers for day wear (see p. 205). Short **gaiters,** especially for country use, appeared intermittently throughout the period. After 1830, shoes —with a squarer toe—became more the mode again, though a short version of the Wellington boot was still worn, but now under the trousers.

In 1790 the **cravat** or stock was unchanged in style from that of the previous few years, being made of white cambric or silk, tied with a small bow in front, and worn with a frilled shirt-front. A lace edging was seen until the turn of the century, when it was stylish to wear two cravats, a black silk or satin version on top of the white one. Bows were small, ornamented by a discreet jewelled pin. At this time, the **collar** appeared, small at first, stiffened in two points which showed above the stock. As the first few years of the nineteenth century passed, the bow increased in size, and frilled cuffs disappeared altogether. By 1820, the collar was very high, the sides touching the ear-lobes, and was usually made of linen and stiffened. A coloured silk band or scarf worn on top of the collar took the place of the cravat in many cases. Black was worn on formal occasions (see p. 209).

Wigs were completely abandoned by 1800, except for certain professions where, as in the case of law, survivals of this mode persist to the present day. The use of powder also declined, and the new century saw the **natural hair** cut fairly short, especially at the sides and back, with longer curls on the forehead. *Side-whiskers* began their long vogue about 1820, varying considerably in length and position during the ensuing years. By 1830, hair was worn somewhat longer, and gentlemen sought to achieve curls at the sides and on top.

About 1804, the *top hat* became a vogue which lasted for the whole of the nineteenth century. Originally, it was made of beaver or felt, and had a curved silhouette, but later, by 1830, the style became higher and straighter, with polished beaver, straw, and plush as the usual materials. Popular colours were grey, beige, and black (see pp. 199, 201, 207, and 209).

Other hat styles were also seen. The tall **hat,** of French origin, was popular in 1790. This had a large brim, turned up at the sides, and was made of beaver, felt, or straw, whilst grey, fawn, and black colours, with a silk cord trimming were specially favoured. A shorter version of this hat, with a round silhouette, appeared in 1800. Both these styles, with many subtle variations, were seen until about 1830, when the wearing of the top hat became almost universal (see pp. 199, 201, and 209).

Caps, of tam-o'-shanter shape with a leather peak, were common among middle-class people.

Four types of **overcoat** were known during this period. Three of these were of English origin: the *garrick*, the *spencer*, and the **redingote.** The fourth was a Polish style. The first of these was perhaps the most worn, being especially popular for travelling because it was made of heavy cloth, had three or four shoulder capes, a long and voluminous skirt, and was fastened by tabs across the chest. It came into fashion in 1800 (see p. 199). Soon afterwards the Spencer coat was seen. Originated by Lord Spencer—who boasted that he could popularise any style at that time—he merely cut off the tails and shortened the sleeves of his frock coat and wore the somewhat unfortunate result. The familiar redingote was still frequently seen. By 1812, this double-breasted coat had altered in cut, was without capes, and had a fur collar. Single-breasted versions were more popular by 1830 (see p. 207). The Polish type of coat achieved a moderate vogue at the same time as the Spencer coat. It had a long, full skirt, a fur or astrakhan collar, and trimming of cords and braid on back and front (see p. 201).

The cold winter of 1809 gave a stimulus to the reappearance of **cloaks** for masculine attire. These cloaks were made of cloth or silk with fur trimmings in the form of a collar, edging or capes, or were wholly of fur. They remained as an elegant mode for cold weather throughout the period.

A **cane, stick,** or **riding whip** was still a common accessory to masculine costume (see pp. 199 and 207). Large **umbrellas** were carried. Until 1820, large fur **muffs** were fashionable. **Fob watches** were still the mode, but after 1830 began to give place to watches worn on chains dangling from the waistcoat pockets. The **snuff-box** was still assumed by the dandy, but was being ousted by the increasing popularity of smoking. A **purse** in the form of a small bag was affected by elegant young men desiring to preserve the line of their tight trousers from the bulge produced by carrying money in the hip-pockets. **Handkerchiefs** were larger than hitherto, and, being of plain white material, were similar to those of today. **Monocles** were seen later during the period.

After centuries of tight-lacing, corsets, unnatural silhouettes, and layers of garments made of heavy brocades, silks, velvets, etc., the feminine style of dress had changed completely by 1790. The main cause of this *volte-face* has been considered at the beginning of this chapter, but it should be reiterated that the social upheavals in Europe, centred on France in 1789, had a more cataclysmic effect on feminine dress than on masculine, particularly because there was much greater scope for change from the extravagant weight and grandeur of 1770–1785, to the simplicity and dignity of 1790. In other words, and as has so often happened, the feminine modes were more extreme in their interpretations of the periods.

The natural figure, simple, decorative lines of drapery, and soft pastel shades were fashionable for some thirty-five years, and then a gradual return to corsets, heavier decoration, and stronger colours began once more.

In 1793, a high **waist** with the gown falling straight from the waist-line to the feet, became the mode: the use of a whalebone framework under the skirts had vanished. By 1795, **corsets** were out of fashion, and only one thin **petticoat** was worn, the gown being an imitation of Greek drapery and line. The waist-line by this time was under the line of the breasts, and girded by a ribbon or band. Sleeves were short, either in a small puff, or forming a little cap on the shoulder (see p. 199). Between 1795 and 1805, the train became very long: for formal and evening wear it often reached seven or eight yards. In 1798, the *Empire sheath gown* (named after the French Empire) became fashionable in England. The waist was still high; the neck-line was low and wide, and often finished with a soft white fichu fastened on the breast with a brooch; the skirt was long and straight, with a train. Legs were either bare or covered with pale-tinted stockings. Little underwear was worn, and was now washed frequently—an activity greatly sponsored by the Empress Josephine in France (see p. 199).

Materials were all thin and light—muslin, linen, poplin, cottons, tulle, gauze, and taffeta being most popular. Pastel shades of all colours were worn, but white was most frequently seen. **Motifs** were small and dainty, spots being very popular. Designs and decorations were usually confined to the edges and hem of the gown, and were chiefly of Greek origin, the Greek key pattern being an example. Appliqué work and self-colour embroidery ornamented many gowns, as did work with gold and silver thread.

About 1800, a fashion arose for wearing a coloured **tunic,** or shorter garment, over the gown. This was partly due to the inadequacy of the thin materials, and the few garments, in combating the English climate. In this case, the gown, of ground-length, was almost invariably white, and made of muslin or cotton, with a pastel shade tunic of satin or velvet, and about three-quarter length (see p. 205).

Gradually, after 1805, the train disappeared, and gowns became shorter, reaching ankle-length by 1811, though ground-length gowns were worn as an alternative all through the period. Larger puff sleeves were the mode by 1810, with a white lingerie frill at the bottom edge. Long **sleeves** reappeared by 1815, often surmounted by a small puff sleeve at the top. Again, by this time, high-necked gowns were often worn in the day-time, though the low neck-line was still retained for evening wear.

The **corset** had been slowly creeping back into fashion since 1810, and by 1815 the popular version had little whalebone, so fitted the natural figure. By 1821, however, the fully-boned corset proper, accentuating the waist, was worn once more. By 1814, stiffening in the form of buckram reappeared in gowns. By 1820, the classical gown had gone, leaving a dress which was still simple, but belted, and with a normal waist-line (see pp. 201 and 205). At this time, stronger hues returned for day wear—plaids being especially popular, and printed all-over patterns.

Gradual developments took place between 1820 and 1830: skirts became fuller, ankle-length in the day-time, longer for evening wear; petticoats were starched or stiffened; a very small waist at normal level was achieved by corsets; high neck-lines were seen for day wear, low off-the-shoulder gowns for evening; sleeves became larger and larger, culminating in the "ham-shaped", or "leg-of-elephant" sleeve, so-called because it was very wide and full at the top, with a narrow cuff at the wrist for day wear, and lingerie frills at the elbow for evening. The gown hem was still ornamented usually by one of the following: piping, bows, fur, scalloped frills, ruching, or embroidery, and appliqué work. A belt or sash was worn round the waist. Pastel shades were still popular, and materials still light in weight, organdie and taffeta being especially favoured (see p. 207). From 1830 to 1837, the gown neck-line was cut low, and for day wear was covered with two or three deep frilled capes, held in place by the belt at the waist. For evening occasions the shoulders were uncovered. Sleeves were very full and large until 1836, when a gradual decrease in their size took place. Horse-hair, whalebone, small cushions or wicket baskets were worn inside the upper sleeve to maintain its shape. Skirts, which in 1830 were ankle-length for day wear, became longer by 1837. They were worn over two or

HANOVER, 1790-1837

1812
STRAW COLOURED TUNIC
WHITE LINGERIE GOWN
PALE BLUE SPOTTED SCARF
WHITE GLOVES—STEPHANE

1820
SILK SPENCER
FRILLS AT NECK
AND WRISTS
MUSLIN GOWN
SELF-COLOUR
EMBROIDERY
RETICULE
PARASOL
STRAW BONNET
WITH SILK EDGE
AND BOW
GLOVES

1822
COURT ATTIRE
SILK COAT WITH
GOLD EMBROIDERY
WHITE SATIN
WAISTCOAT
AND BREECHES
WHITE SILK
STOCKINGS
BICORNE WITH
FRINGED EDGE
LEATHER SLIPPERS
LACE-EDGED
CRAVAT
GLOVES

1835
EVENING DRESS
TAFFETA GOWN
WITH LACE RUFFLES
AT NECK & SLEEVES
FLOWERS & COMBS
IN THE HAIR

three stiff, starched, and flounced petticoats, which were decorated with ruching and bows. The bodice of the gown was stiffened with whalebone, and the minute waist was achieved by tight corsets. Towards 1837, heavier materials reappeared, especially velvet, brocade, silk, and taffeta, whilst a popular feature was gold embroidery on a black background (see pp. 205 and 207).

A trimming most typical of this era was one which covered and ornamented the neck-line. This was known by various names, and was of various patterns. It originated about 1802—when a low neck-line was the vogue—as a *chemisette* (or camisette), which was made of lace-edged linen, or wholly of lace. Soon afterwards, with the advent of the higher neck-line, the *"betsie"* appeared. This was so-called as a colloquial abbreviation of the name Elizabeth, since this mode was an imitation of the lace-edged ruff of the Elizabethan era. With sundry variations, this style remained till after 1830. By 1829, a lace, and a lace-edged edition of the shoulder cape—which was becoming increasingly popular for day wear—was seen, and remained in fashion till the end of the period. A version of the chemisette, it was known as a *"berthe"*. From 1825 the neck-lines of evening gowns were ornamented with lace ruffles and frills, often in several rows (see pp. 205, 207, and 209).

As in the case of masculine attire, wigs and powder were completely out of fashion by 1795. From 1790 to 1804, the vogue for emulating the Grecian costume extended to the **coiffure.** A chignon was worn at the back of the head; the hair was dressed with ribbon bands, and curls on the forehead (see pp. 199 and 205). With the new century, short hair, worn in various ways, particularly with curls, was the mode for some twenty years. After 1820 a higher coiffure was sought once more; hair was parted in the centre with a knot on top, and curls on each side. For evening, decoration with combs and flowers was an attractive feature. By 1829 the coiffure was partly supported by wire, still surmounted by a knot of hair, feathers and flowers still being used to ornament the side curls. The back hair was now sometimes worn in plaits, held up at the back by combs. By 1835 ringlets replaced the side curls, and the hair was usually covered, when indoors, by a lace cap (see pp. 201, 205, and 209).

The **mob cap** was still being worn in 1790. A small **straw hat,** worn in front and on top of the head, was also common. Both these were embellished by such trimmings as ribbons, bows, tassels, and feathers, with lace veils hanging behind.

In 1800, the *bonnet* became the mode, and remained so for a very long time. It varied in shape, even until 1837. At first the *poke bonnet* was most fashionable. Made of straw or silk, it was trimmed with flowers, feathers, ribbons, and lace veils which fell over the face (see pp. 205, 207, and 209). In winter, fur bonnets were sometimes seen. By 1814 the poke bonnet was smaller, and not of very great depth, but the size increased by 1825, and from 1830 to 1837 it was very large, with a broad brim shading the face, and with even more lavish ornamentation than before. This size and shape then caused it to be known as the *coal-scuttle* bonnet (see pp. 207 and 209).

Silk **turbans** were worn a great deal, especially from 1807 to 1831. They were generally ornamented with plumes or flowers, and ropes of pearls and beads. The later styles were very large, and padded (see pp. 199 and 207).

The gypsy style of **hat,** made of straw, was seen about 1812. This was fastened

1826
SILK TURBAN AND
FEATHER
BETSIE
MULBERRY VELVET
SPENCER
FRILLS AT WRISTS
WHITE GOWN — LACE
RUFFLES

1830
STRIPED TAFFETA
GOWN IN PINK
AND WHITE
PINK SATIN
BONNET WITH
SATIN BOWS
CREAM GLOVES
BLACK SLIPPERS
WHITE FRILL AND
CUFFS

1830
GREY CLOTH REDINGOTE
BLACK FUR COLLAR
GREY BEAVER TOP HAT
BUCKSKIN TROUSERS
LEATHER SHOES
CANE

1835
REDINGOTE WITH
CAPES
DULL PURPLE CLOTH
SILK BONNET AND
BOWS
OSTRICH PLUMES
FUR MUFF

under the chin by a silk kerchief, which extended round the middle of the hat (see p. 209). From 1819 to 1832 large-brimmed **hats,** fashioned from straw or silk, were once more frequently worn. Like the bonnets, they were decorated with bows, ribbons, flowers, or plumes (see p. 209).

The three types of coat worn were the **spencer,** the **pelisse,** and the **redingote.** The first was very popular. Like the masculine version, it was waist-length, and sometimes worn open, sometimes buttoned up the front, but differed in being made of velvet or satin. Its sleeves were long, and later puffed at the top, then fitting to the wrist. Usually a collar was attached, at first a small stand-up style, later becoming larger and flat. Colours were black, purple, or dark green (see p. 205). From 1800 onwards the pelisse was worn. A longer and warmer coat than the spencer, though commonly made of the same materials, it was usually fur-trimmed, straight in cut, belted at a high waist like the gown, with a broad collar and long straight sleeves. Colours included golden brown, peat, and yellow-green. Both these garments were frequently worn with white or very pale-coloured gowns (see p. 201). The redingote was worn more in the latter portion of the period, from 1818 onwards, especially in cold weather in place of a cloak. In 1820 it had a broad collar, a belt at the high waist-line, full, long sleeves, fastenings down the front, and was usually made of heavy cloth in dark colours, sometimes with a fur edging. It was either three-quarter- or full-length. After 1830 this coat became more in keeping with the gown styles of that time: the skirt was fuller and larger; large shoulder capes were worn, and the sleeves were full to cover the large gown sleeves. The waist-line was in the normal position (see p. 207).

Various types of **cloaks,** often fur-edged or entirely of fur, were seen throughout this period. They were more popular than coats for outdoor wear until 1830.

Fashionable features in 1790 were **scarves** and **shawls.** These continued to be worn until 1837, being particularly modish with gowns in the Grecian style. Vivid colours were popular, such as yellow and red on a black background, or designs of plaid, paisley, or stripes. They contrasted effectively with the soft shades of the gowns. Pastel shades and white were also seen. The edges of these scarves and shawls were ornamented with tassels and fringes. A great variety of materials were used, common examples being fine wool, lace, cotton, gauze, and silk. Shapes and sizes also varied considerably from the square to the long and rectangular, from small to excessively large. Again, methods of wearing the garment were numerous: in 1800 it was usually draped over the shoulders, or hung round the arms and across the back; later it was more often wrapped round the figure (see pp. 199 and 205). **Feather boas** were worn in similar ways, especially between 1803 and 1815 (see p. 199). About 1836 black silk *mantillas,* with fringed or ruched edges, appeared.

The heel-less **slipper,** cut low, tied on at the ankle, and laced across the instep, was the principal item of feminine footwear until after 1837. Ribbon, and later elastic, was used for lacing, whilst the slipper itself was made of fabric, or thin kid, of various colours. A tiny bow or rosette was a usual ornament in front (see pp. 201 and 209). Later, ankle boots were worn, also shoes made of fabric, narrow in shape, and sometimes with shiny leather toe-caps. The usual colour was black, with white for evening wear.

Accessories were many and varied. Perhaps the most typical, and seen

HANOVER, 1790-1837

CREAM STRAW HAT WITH FLOWERS, RIBBONS & PLUMES - c.1830

FAWN BEAVER TOP HAT - c.1811

1810 - STRAW BONNET GYPSY STYLE WITH STRIPED RIBBON - BETSIE

c.1830-2 - WHITE COLLAR - STRIPED SCARF - SIDE WHISKERS

PINK STRAW BONNET - PALE BLUE SILK - EDGED FLOWERS & RIBBONS - c.1819

c.1806 MAROON SILK RETICULE EMBROIDERED IN COLOURED SILKS

BLUE FABRIC SLIPPER WITH SILK BOW & TIED WITH RIBBONS

c.1828-30 - STRAW BONNET WITH SILK EDGING & BOWS - OSTRICH PLUMES

BLACK FELT BICORNE - GOLD BRAID EDGE - c.1807

LAVENDER SILK BONNET WITH DARK LILAC RIBBONS & WHITE LACE EDGING WORN ON TOP OF WHITE LACE CAP c.1820

SILK BONNET WITH DARK RIBBON BOWS - c.1835

RED SILK PARASOL - CORD EDGING & TASSELS

FELT, BROWN HAT - CORD TRIMMING - c.1790-95

209

throughout the period, was the **fan:** it was smaller and less ornate after 1800; painted silk, sometimes jewelled, was much used. The **parasol** was greatly in use, especially after 1800. Of small and graceful proportions, usually trimmed with fringing, tassels or lace, it was made of silk, and gaily coloured (see pp. 205, 207, and 209). In 1790, the straight-fitting gowns, ill-suited for pockets, and the small number of garments worn, brought in the use of the **handbag,** either hung over the arm or carried in the hand. Known as the **reticule,** it was made of velvet or silk, painted or embroidered, and decorated with lace edges or tassels (see pp. 199, 205, and 209). **Gloves** were often brightly coloured, contrasting with the pastel-coloured gowns. They were long, and popularly of white kid for evening wear, but short or mitten style in yellow, green, or bright blue for day wear (see pp. 199, 201, 205, and 207). As in men's wear, fob-style **watches** were suspended from the belt. **Muffs,** trimmed with bows, were still carried in winter (see p. 207). In contrast to the period preceding 1790, and especially during the subsequent twenty years, cosmetics were rarely employed.

During the time of pseudo-Grecian vogue, the classical influence also affected **jewellery** designs. A version of the stephane was worn round the forehead (see p. 205). Later, cameos, gold chains, and lockets were seen. Ear-rings were popular.

The two plates in this chapter, numbers I (Frontispiece) and X, reproduced from fashion plates, both illustrate feminine dress. Plate I shows the pseudo-Grecian style of costume, with the white, thin high-waisted gown, short puff sleeves, frilled hem, and coloured girdle. The white fichu, long white gloves, and extravagant turban with plumes and lace veiling can also be seen. The other, plate X, shows the gown of a later period, about 1820. The gown is still white and high-waisted, but the neck-line is higher, and long-sleeves and lace ruffles have reappeared. The frilled lace cap, framing the dark curls, is also typical of the period.

PLATE X

White Morning Dress, with high waist-line still retained.
Lace edging and frills

From Ackermann "Repository of the Arts," c. 1820

VIII
THE VICTORIAN ERA

EARLY VICTORIAN ENGLAND 1837-1860

FROM 1837 onwards the fund of material on which one can draw for information on costume is so extensive and comprehensive that the chief difficulty of the student is to determine the main trends in fashion, instead of searching for information, as hitherto. Added to previous sources, we now have innumerable fashion plates and magazines, adequate collections of actual costumes, and photographs.

The chief centre of masculine tailoring continued to be London, whereas it was Paris for the feminine mode.

Masculine dress was settling into its stereotyped form which, with small variations, has remained until today. Feminine styles underwent the rise and adoption of the crinoline—the newest form of hoop skirt, reaching, this time, greater dimensions than ever before, though, with the invention of a metal frame, it was less burdensome to wear.

There were four principal types of coat for men in this period: the *tail coat*, the *frock coat*, the *cutaway*, and the *jacket*. The first two of these provided the general wear for the whole period and were founded on the style of the thirties. The tail coat was double-breasted and cut away square at the waist in front to hang in square tails at the back (see p. 214), while the frock coat, also double-breasted, was usually worn unbuttoned and hung straight down to nearly knee-level all round (see pp. 218 and 220). The cutaway was also a tail coat: it appeared in the fifties and replaced the tail coat for well-dressed men. It was the foundation of our present-day morning coat, having rounded tails, splaying from the centre button at the waist. Jackets or full suits began to come in from the fifties, for seaside, country, or sports-wear, but were still very much of a novelty at this time (see p. 220). All these coats followed certain general characteristics: in the late thirties, they had high, often velvet, collars, sleeves full at the shoulder and tight at the wrist, a very waisted cut, full on the chest and with flared tails; in the forties, collars were lower, and the sleeve was fairly average in width from top to bottom. The fifties saw less waisted and padded, also looser-fitting coats, small collars and very high, small revers. The tail, frock, and cutaway coats were made of broadcloth or serge, while tweed was more usual for suits. **Colours** were sombre, especially in the fifties, when black, navy, or dark grey were inevitable for formal coats with the addition of brown for suits, replacing the blue, dark green, and wine colours of the early forties. **Braid trimming** to coat edges came in about 1850. **Pockets** were hidden in coat-tails, or were on the hips of tailles coats.

Waistcoats provided the chief spot of colour in an otherwise drab ensemble, especially in the forties when they were still of satin or silk, striped or flowered. After 1850, white or light plain ones were usually worn, or made of the same material as the coat. Styles followed those of the coat in rever shapes and

EARLY VICTORIAN
1837-1860

EARLY 'FORTIES — EVENING GOWN OF WHITE PATTERNED POPLIN IN SELF-COLOUR — CRIMSON BRAID ON SLEEVE — ALSO WHITE LACE FRILLS — FAN — WHITE GLOVES — ROSES IN HAIR

1839 — PLAID WOOLLEN CLOAK & SHOULDER CAPE IN BROWN, RED, & BLUE — BLUE RIBBONS & FRINGING — DARK BLUE SILK DRESS — PALE YELLOW BONNET — ROSES — RIBBONS

1840 — DARK BLUE VELVET CLOAK WITH OPEN SLEEVES — GREY FUR COLLAR, EDGING & MUFF — PALE BLUE SATIN DRESS, BONNET & RIBBONS — SPOTTED VEIL — PINK ROSES — WHITE GLOVES

1840 — PRINTED WOOL DAY DRESS IN RED, GREEN & MAUVE — GREEN BRAID TO COLLAR & SLEEVES — WHITE FRILL AT NECK & WRISTS — WHITE MUSLIN SCARF — MANTELET

length, the straight waist cut being usual before 1850, with the pointed, present-day version predominating after this, while cashmere, piqué, wool, or cloth were popular materials (see pp. 218 and 220).

Trousers were now the accepted nether wear, but varied somewhat in width during this period. Until about 1845 the instep strap was retained with narrow trousers on the lower leg, but it vanished after this when trousers became rather wider. There were no creases or turn-ups. The front flap went out in the early forties in favour of a vertical front buttoning, hidden in the material fold. Grey and fawn were popular early in the period, with white for summer, but after 1845–1850, checks, plaids, and stripes in black, white, and colours began their long vogue; alternatively, the trouser material matched the coat. Black trousers were usual with a frock coat. Braid side-seams came in after 1850 (see pp. 214, 218, and 220).

Overcoats were varied in cut: they were either above the knees or nearly to the ankles, double- or single-breasted, styled with collar and revers or just a collar buttoning up to the neck, with inset or raglan sleeves, and with or without attached shoulder cape. Fur or velvet collars were popular. Belts were optional. Materials varied from heavy to light wools in plain or, after 1850, plaid or check. Large patch pockets were often placed on the hips (see pp. 218 and 220).

Cloaks were common wear until the fifties, with or without shoulder capes. They were usually nearly ankle-length and often fur-trimmed. Black cloaks with shoulder cape and velvet collar were worn with evening dress. **Shawls** of plaid or plain wool were seen.

A white stiff **collar** was retained for most occasions, with turned-out points or of a stand-up variety. Turned-down, softer collars were worn after 1850 for sport or country wear, but were *infra dig* for town. The black silk or satin **stock** was still worn for some years, but was replaced in popularity after 1840–1845 by either striped, checked, or plain silk **neckcloths** or, after 1850, by large bow **ties**. Neckwear became a matter of individual taste at this time, and varied modes were seen. Scarf-pins held the neckcloth in position (see pp. 214, 218, 220, and 222). **Shirts** were still white, with a frilled front at first, giving place to starched or pleated fronts about 1845–1850. Starched shirt-cuffs were often visible in the fifties.

Evening dress was stabilised by 1840–1845, consisting of a black tail coat of broadcloth, with silk-faced revers, cut like the day tail coat, a white or black piqué, velvet, satin, or silk single-breasted waistcoat, and black tight trousers with instep strap. The white shirt and collar was accompanied by a white stock at first, and later by a white or black tie, according to the formality of the occasion. White gloves were essential. The ensemble provided the basis for our present-day "tails".

Men wore their **hair** moderately long, waved and/or curled. It was parted on either side and curled over or round the ears. In the early forties most men were clean-shaven, but by 1850 the Victorian **whiskers** were rapidly becoming a universal feature. Moustaches were generally seen, with side-whiskers which were worn longer as time passed, but left the chin free. By the mid-fifties the use of macassar oil was popular, necessitating those Victorian monstrosities —antimacassars.

EARLY VICTORIAN
1837-1860

c.1842-4 - BLACK SILK TOP HAT - NAVY CLOTH TAIL COAT WITH BLACK VELVET COLLAR - LIGHT GREY TROUSERS - CANE - GLOVES - COLLAR - BLACK SILK NECKCLOTH - BLACK BOOTS

1847-8 - MEDIUM GREEN SILK & COTTON DAY DRESS WITH DARK GREEN PRINTED PATTERN - DEEP LAVENDER SILK MANTELET - FRINGED EDGES - LAVENDER SILK BONNET - WHITE RIBBONS - WHITE SILK PARASOL

1845-50 - EVENING OR PARTY DRESS OF WHITE MUSLIN WITH PALE BLUE SPOT - BODICE & SLEEVES OF COBALT BLUE SILK - WHITE PÉLERINE WITH FRINGE & RUCHED TRIMMING - WHITE GLOVES - FAN - ROSES IN HAIR

1847-9 - AFTERNOON DRESS OF BLUE & WHITE STRIPED SILK - EMBROIDERED CAMBRIC COLLAR & CUFFS

The **top hat** was to the nineteenth century what the tricorne had been to the eighteenth—almost everybody possessed one. Black, fawn, grey, or white in silk or beaver were worn, with the curved shape predominating in the forties, and the stove-pipe, straight style in the fifties. Black silk was reserved then for formal wear (see pp. 214, 218, 220, and 222). After 1850, round felt or straw **hats** with turned-up, floppy brims made their appearance for sea or country wear (see p. 220); alternatively, **caps** with ear-flaps.

Shoes were seldom worn, although black **slippers** with a silk black bow were in use with evening dress. Most men wore **boots** for day wear, under the trousers. The Wellington style was in use until 1860, alternatively, a laced-up boot. Black leather with fairly heavy soles was usual. Light-coloured cloth **spats** or **gaiters** were worn all the period.

The most typical feature of the early Victorian feminine silhouette was the skirt, depending for its shape upon numbers of petticoats, which in turn gave way to the *crinoline*. In 1837 the wider, fuller skirts which had been seen since 1830 were supported by several stiff, flounced petticoats. In the forties the numbers of petticoats increased and the skirt in turn showed a wider silhouette; it was usual to wear at least six or seven under-skirts, comprising one of red flannel, with several white starched calico ones with deep, stiff flounces superimposed—the lady was certainly well protected against the cold, but must have suffered from the weight and warmth in summer. The fifties saw the introduction of the crinoline—the name being derived from the horse-hair fabric from which it was made—into which bands of whalebone were inserted horizontally, as in the prototypes, the farthingale and hoop, although this time the silhouette was rounder and wider at the bottom; petticoats were worn on top as before. By 1857, however, the metal *cage-crinoline* had come to England, providing the requisite shape without the weight and avoiding the necessity for quite so many layers. This latter model was a great success and, being inexpensive, was worn by all, providing wider and wider bell-skirts towards 1860, and requiring more than ten yards of material round the skirt hem to cover it. Both whalebone and metal types were of pliable material to enable ladies to negotiate doorways; nevertheless, the floor-space occupied was considerable.

Bearing in mind the predominant effect of this growth of the crinoline shape between 1837 and 1860, which can be seen on pp. 212, 214, 216, 218, and 220, we can now examine the **day** or **promenade gown** styles. The low **neck-lines** of the thirties continued until the early forties, decorated by large collars or a lace **berthe,** but by 1843–1845 higher necks, indicating the propriety of the period, set in and remained in fashion until after 1860. They were trimmed by a lace collar or the lace-edged **chemisette** showing above. The **corsage** was often decorated by lines of fringing or piping converging to the waist from the shoulders, or was laced across the chemisette in a V-shape in front. A tight bodice was invariable, with a tiny waist provided by the inevitable corset. The rounded back and pointed front to the waist returned to stay by 1840. Shoulders were sloping with off-the-shoulder inset sleeves. In 1837, sleeves were long and wide, gathered in to the wrist, but by the early forties, long, tight-fitting sleeves had replaced them, to give way in turn, in the fifties, to three-quarter length, bell-shaped sleeves which received much decoration in the form of fringing, bows, ruching, etc., and displayed a full under-sleeve ending in a

EARLY VICTORIAN
1837-1860

1850-55 - WHITE NET EVENING DRESS WITH GOLD EDGING & DESIGN - WORN OVER WHITE SATIN WHITE MERINO OPERA CLOAK - FRINGED & DECORATED BY GOLD BRAID - WHITE GLOVES - FLOWERS IN HAIR

1852-4 - DAY DRESS IN RESEDER GREEN SILK WITH WOVEN PATTERN OF BLACK CUT & UN-CUT VELVET - BLACK & GREEN FRINGING - WHITE LACE COLLAR & UNDERSLEEVES - WHITE CAP & BOW

1855 - DARK BOTTLE GREEN SILK DRESS - WHITE LACE UNDERSLEEVES - GREY FELT COAT WITH BLACK VELVET TRIMMING & BUTTONS - STRAW BONNET WITH PINK FLOWERS & BLUE & WHITE RIBBONS

1850 - PROMENADE DRESS OF SHOT SILK - GREEN TO LAVENDER - PINK & BLUE FRINGING - STRAW BONNET - FLOWERS & RIBBONS - PURPLE SILK PARASOL - CREAM TATTING COVERING - WHITE SILK LINING

tight cuff, usually of white lawn or lace. All sleeves were finished by lace cuffs or frills. By 1860, these bell-sleeves were excessively wide (see p. 220). The **skirt** was always very full, gathered in at the waist, and fell in numerous folds to the hem, which became lower again, to reach the ground by about 1845. In the fifties the wide crinolines obliterated many of the folds, which showed only at the waist where the skirt was gathered in. Except in the late thirties, open over-skirts were not fashionable, but knee-length tunic over-skirts and/or several rows of **flounces** became more popular as time passed, so that in the fifties six or seven rows of flounces were common. Skirts and flounces were decorated by velvet, braid, or lace bands, ruching, bows, and flowers.

Except for the *décolletage*, **evening gowns** followed the modes of day wear, though even greater attention was paid to the skirt decoration. A tremendous amount of material was used in over-skirts and under-skirts and in many rows of flounces and tucks. In the fifties, the old pannier style was resurrected with a looped-up over-skirt decorated by roses and other flowers, lace edging and frills, showing a flounced under-skirt. Flowers, lace, ruching, pleating, and flouncing covered most of the skirt. The **neck-line** was always low and wide, partially off the shoulders, and finished by a lace frill or berthe, flowers or ruching. **Sleeves** were short and simple, puff styles being most popular, trimmed with lace. Even more than in the day gowns, the minute waist contrasted markedly with the wide sweep of the crinoline (see pp. 212, 214, 216, and 218).

Fabrics for day gowns included muslin, gauze, satin, silk, brocade, poplin, taffeta, velvet, tarlatan, lawn, damask, moiré, gingham, and serge, while in the fifties soft wools, worsted poplin, merino, and silk were in vogue; a trend towards heavier fabrics was apparent then, especially velvet and wool. For **evening** wear, materials were light in weight to offset the abundance used: lace, tarlatan, tulle, gauze, muslin, silk, and taffeta were favourites. Flowers, especially roses and rosebuds, were ubiquitous **trimmings** all the period, also lace, white and black, embroidery, fringing fur, velvet, or braid bands and appliqué work, while after 1852–1853 the heavy trimmings like chenille fringing, velvet and fur bands, and thick appliqué designs were abundant. White was practically *de rigeur* for evening, but pastel shades were an alternative. Day wear **colours** were tasteful and restrained until the late forties and fifties when the vogue for magenta, purples, royal blue, strong bright greens, crimson, and plum colours was established. These strong colours were often contrasted in a vivid, startling manner in one dress, giving a devastating effect. Checks and plaids were also very popular at this time.

Outer wear was extremely varied in early Victorian England: it ranged from jackets and coats to cloaks, wraps, shawls, and mantles. In consequence of the ever-widening skirts, half- or three-quarter-length outer garments were more prevalent, particularly of a non-fitting variety, thus creating that triangular silhouette so typical of the time, with the tiny bonnet at the apex. In the thirties and forties, three-quarter- or full-length **capes** and **cloaks** were most popular, with or without **shoulder capes,** of wool, velvet, silk, or satin, with fringe or fur trimming (see p. 212). The **mantelet** or **scarf-mantelet**, giving way to the *pélerine*, were also in vogue, with or without upper arm covering, and hanging in two long points in front (see pp. 212 and 214). Shorter capes and cloaks were preferred in the fifties (see p. 218). Three-quarter- or half-length **coats**

EARLY VICTORIAN
1837-1860

c 1845- GREY TOP
HAT -DARK BLUE
CLOTH COAT - BLACK
VELVET COLLAR,
CHECK TROUSERS-
GLOVES - CANE

1857- BLACK STIFF SILK DRESS-
FRENCH BLUE VELVET CLOAK
TRIMMED WITH ERMINE —
ERMINE MUFF LINED WITH
PALE BLUE SILK — PALE
BLUE SILK BONNET — LACE
EDGING - BLUE PLUMES
& RIBBONS - GLOVES

MID 1850's -
BLACK SILK TOP
HAT—BLACK FROCK
COAT- STRIPED SILK
WAISTCOAT - DARK
GREY TROUSERS -BRAID
SIDE SEAMS - GLOVES-
CANE - BOOTS-
BOW TIE - STIFF
COLLAR

1859- BALL DRESS OF WHITE
TARLATAN WITH FLOUNCES &
ROSEBUD TRIMMING - AMBER
TAFFETA BODICE & OVERSKIRT WITH
BANDS OF RUCHING TO EDGE SKIRT
& NECKLINE - WHITE LACE BERTHE,
SLEEVES & OVERSKIRT EDGING-
CRIMSON ROSES & GREEN
LEAVES IN HAIR, CORSAGE
& OVERSKIRT- WHITE
GLOVES -FAN.

were fitting at first, but with the crinoline were loose, with wide bell-sleeves and large cuffs; they were trimmed with velvet bands and bows and were made of cloth or wool (see pp. 216 and 220). **Jackets,** of gown fabrics, of bolero shape or reaching to the waist, with a short frill or basque, were popular for summer and indoors in the fifties; they were open in front and had wide bell-sleeves. **Shawls** and **scarves** were always in demand, especially in summer: paisley, cashmere, lace, net tarlatan, muslin, wool, or silk were usual materials, with fringed edges and embroidered designs (see p. 214). **Evening wraps** were often white and of silk or wool, with gold or coloured fringing and embroidery (see p. 216).

In addition to the numerous petticoats, underwear was also abundant: a high-necked **chemise,** or chemises (low for evening), with short sleeves and ankle-length **drawers** of white material with lace trimmings were an essential minimum. **Stockings** were worn. The **corset** was always stiffly whaleboned to give the tiny waist; it also constricted the lower part of the bosom. Metal was alternatively employed, and front or back laces for tightening. These corsets continued to be worn by everyone, despite the outcry in the medical world.

Heel-less styles prevailed for both indoor **slippers** and outdoor **boots,** until the late fifties, when a small heel reappeared. Slippers were of satin, silk, or kid, in white, black, or bronze, while boots could be of satin, kid, stockinet, or leather, in all colours. Narrow, square toes were apparent in all footwear. Side or front laces or elastic sides were used in boots, with the popular patent leather toes and heels (see p. 222).

Although the exaggerated loops and high curls of the early thirties had gone from the feminine **coiffure** by 1837, the plaited coil was still worn high on the crown. A centre parting was in fashion all the period. Side curls or ringlets, after those of Henrietta Maria, were very fashionable in the forties and lasted into the fifties for evening wear, although by this time the hair was usually drawn down the cheeks and back to a lower bun in a more severe style for the day-time. Waves were introduced in this mode after about 1855 (see pp. 212, 214, 216, 220, and 222). Little **decoration** was seen in the day, but for evening, flowers, especially roses, ribbon bows, pearl ropes, ostrich plumes, and jewelled combs were in use (see pp. 212, 218, and 222). After about 1855, hair-nets of chenille or silk covered the back hair.

In head-dresses the **bonnet** reigned supreme, although it varied somewhat in shape and size. In 1837, the fairly large **poke bonnet** was still predominant, but by 1845 the front had shortened and in the fifties a much shorter, smaller bonnet had come in, worn much farther back on the head, showing the hair. Straw, silk, tulle, gauze, and crêpe were popular materials, with flower **trimming** —especially roses—lace, plumes and velvet, and a large ribbon bow tied under the chin. **Veils** were worn with many bonnets, particularly before 1850 (see pp. 212, 214, 216, 218, 220, and 222).

Large straw **hats** were revived in the fifties, with flower trimming, flat crowns, and loose, hanging ribbons. They were mostly worn by young girls (see p. 222).

Lace or lace-edged muslin white **caps** were worn indoors, a fashion which became more prevalent as time passed, especially with older or married women. The caps were small, worn on the back of the head, and might have ribbon and

EARLY VICTORIAN
1837-1860

EARLY 'FIFTIES -
BLACK SILK TOP HAT
& RIBBON - TWEED
CAPE-OVERCOAT -
BLACK FROCK
COAT - LIGHT WAIST-
COAT & TROUSERS -
STRIPED NECKCLOTH-
BLACK BOOTS -
CANE

1859. CARRIAGE DRESS - DARK
GREEN SILK SKIRT & BODICE-
DECORATED WITH MAGENTA
VELVET, EDGED WITH GREEN
BINDING - BUTTONS - PLAID
TAFFETA OVERSKIRT, SLEEVES &
YOKE IN PINK, GREEN, YELLOW,
BLACK & WHITE - MAGENTA
TASSELS - PINK CRÊPE
BONNET WITH PINK
VELVET RIBBONS &
ROSES - WHITE TULLE
CAP - WHITE LACE
COLLAR & UNDER-
SLEEVES - GLOVES

1859 - PROMENADE DRESS-
BLACK & GREEN SILK - GREY
RIBBED CLOTH COAT
TRIMMED WITH GREEN VELVET-
WITH CAPE & COLLAR - MUSLIN
& LACE UNDERSLEEVES - GREEN
& PINK SILK BONNET &
RIBBONS - BLACK PLUME
& LACE TRIMMING - LACE
& TULLE CAP - GLOVES

1854-60. DARK
BROWN TWEED
SUIT FOR SEA,
COUNTRY OR
SPORTS WEAR -
BROWN FELT HAT-
BLACK BOOTS
& TIE - CANE

220

flower trimming (see pp. 216 and 222). They were frequently worn under bonnets.

With evening gowns, a lace, silk, or wool **scarf** was usually placed lightly over the coiffure.

The fashion plate (Plate XI) illustrates the bonnet and promenade gown of 1854, showing an imitation pannier over-skirt, full, decorated sleeves, and wide bonnet ribbons.

Men wore little jewellery: it was confined to gold **rings** and **cuff-links,** shirt **studs** of gold or pearl, and gold jewelled **scarf-pins.** Their accessories included a large **watch,** with massive gold chain spread across the stomach from one waistcoat pocket to the other, a long **umbrella** or small **cane,** a **monocle** and **snuff-box,** although snuff-taking was on the wane in favour of smoking. **Gloves** were essential to a well-dressed man, and were in light colours for day wear and white for evening.

Feminine accessories were more numerous: the **fan** was a necessary requisite for evening wear: it was small and made of feathers, lace, or silk with ivory, tortoise-shell, or wood sticks; another evening necessity was the small **bouquet** of flowers in a metal holder. **Gloves** were usually short for day wear, in pastel shades of kid or silk, while long or short white ones prevailed for evening. Black lace **mittens** were also popular. Most ladies carried a small **reticule** of velvet or silk with bead or jewelled embroidery. A **parasol** is symbolic of Victorianism: those of this period were small or of a walking type, although very tiny ones prevailed in the fifties. The jointed stick pattern was used in carriages, as it could be held at the appropriate angle to the sun. Fringe, lace, and ribbon bows were used as trimming to the silk or lace covering. Handles were of wood, bone, or metal (see pp. 214, 216, and 222). **Umbrellas,** in contrast to this daintiness, were of black silk or cotton and serviceably large. Fur **muffs** were carried in winter (see pp. 212 and 218). **Handkerchiefs** were white, lace-edged and/or embroidered.

Not a great deal of jewellery was worn, but the existing styles were heavy in design and setting. Large **brooches** for the day-time corsage were usual, also gold **lockets** on a gold chain or black velvet ribbon. **Bracelets** were broad, usually linked. **Rings** were heavy, and wedding-rings especially were very broad. **Ear-rings** were worn; heavy gold **watches** were hung on gold chains from the neck or were pinned at the waist. Cameos were very popular (see p. 222).

MID-VICTORIAN ENGLAND 1860–1880

Masculine dress was now at its most conservative: black and white were the key colours, only enlivened by the growing popularity, in the seventies, of the informal sack coat and check trousers, or tweed suit—forerunner of the modern lounge suit. Black and white or coloured checks and tweeds were employed for suits, alternatively, a dark sack coat combined with trousers of a loud-checked pattern was worn. Although seen occasionally for sport and country wear in the fifties, the sack coat was really an innovation of this period, being cut without the usual waist seam. Informality also crept into hat styles, where the bowler was increasingly apparent.

EARLY VICTORIAN
1837-1860

PINK SILK BONNET & RIBBONS — WHITE LACE & ROSE TRIMMING — 1839

BLACK SILK HAT — WHITE STIFF COLLAR — BLACK SILK NECKCLOTH 1860

BOW TIE — STIFF COLLAR — 1857

EVENING COIFFURE 1837

MAUVE SILK GAUGED BONNET & RIBBONS c.1840

CREAM KID BOOT — BLACK PATENT TOE & HEEL — RED LACES 1860

1840-50 — WHITE & CERISE SATIN LACED-UP BOOT

1830-40 — BLACK FIGURED SATIN

WHITE KID BOOT — ELASTIC SIDES 1860

LONG PARASOL IN BRIGHT GREEN SILK — BRASS STICK & CARVED BONE HANDLE 1840-50

EVENING COIFFURE · 1859 · PEARL, ROSE & PLUME DECORATION

1845 — WHITE SATIN — ROSETTE

1837 — WHITE SATIN

1851 — BROWN STOCKINET & LEATHER BOOT — ELASTIC TOP

BROWN CLOTH & LEATHER 1850

WHITE LACE CAP — RED RIBBONS. 1859

WHITE STRAW HAT WITH FLOWERS & PINK RIBBONS 1860

WHITE CHALCEDONY EARRING MOUNTED IN GILT METAL

c.1845

1855 · GREY TOP HAT — STRIPED NECKCLOTH

OPAL & DIAMOND GOLD RING

EMERALD & DIAMOND GOLD RING

HEAVY GOLD BROOCH WITH AMETHYST CENTRE

WHITE MUSLIN CAP WITH CERISE RIBBONS. 1859

WHITE SILK BONNET — PINK ROSES & RIBBONS — LACE EDGING. 1857

GOLD BRACELET — 10 PLAQUES LINKED TOGETHER

The chief interest in feminine attire was still concentrated on the skirt where the circular crinoline, having reached its climax of width about 1862, then gradually altered in shape, flattening in front and at the sides, and leaving the fullness at the back, until it became a bustle, with draped-up over-skirts and bunched material at the back. After reaching extremes again by 1875, the bustle disappeared and the bunched-up draperies were lowered to the hips, so that a slim figure was visible once more. This proved only a temporary diversion, however, as the bustle returned to favour in the eighties. The rest of the costume was in tune with these changes: in the early sixties the triangular silhouette was maintained with the tiny bonnets and loose cloaks and coats, while in the seventies all the fuss was at the back, with the chignon and back ribbons echoing the bustle draperies.

There were three chief styles of coat for men in this period—the **frock coat,** the **cutaway,** and the *sack coat*; the tail coat had now been replaced for formal wear by the cutaway style. The frock coat and cutaway were the two formal coats, both tail styles (see pp. 226 and 230). They were almost unaltered from the fifties, apart from the smaller, higher revers and looser cut, which were in keeping with the general characteristics of coats of the time. The first of these was the double-breasted formal coat, the second the single-breasted version; the former was usually black and worn by city gentlemen, older men, and for very formal occasions; the latter was black or grey, often had braid edges, and was seen at weddings, the races, or for town wear by younger gentlemen. The sack coat had a very high V-neck with collar and revers, or just a collar. Of the three or four buttons only the top one was fastened. The coat was single-breasted, had rounded or square corners, hip and breast pockets, braid edging, and reached to the hips. It was ill-fitting on the whole, as yet, especially at the collar and armholes. Velvet collars were popular. The sack coat was worn every day by some in the seventies, and most men had one for sport or informal country wear. Dark colours were used, in tweed or homespun (see p. 224).

Single-breasted **waistcoats** to match the coat material were most usual now, although double-breasted ones were worn, also coloured ones of fawn, white, check, striped, or plaid. White or grey was correct in conjunction with a formal coat. Revers were high, as in the coat.

Trousers were rather looser in this period, but still had no creases or turn-ups. Grey- or black-striped ones, or light fawn or grey were worn with formal coats, while large checks, plaids, and stripes, in gayer colours or black and white, were the vogue in conjunction with a dark sack coat. Braid side-seams were seen on all types of trousers (see pp. 224, 226, and 230).

In the seventies, **knickerbockers** were reintroduced for sports-wear. They were fastened under the knee by a garter and were worn with woollen socks and boots, or gaiters with shoes.

Boots were still worn by most men, under the trousers. The laced-up style was still prevalent, but elastic-sided or side-buttoned boots were alternatives. Black or brown leather was used, while black patent leather toes were often added. **Socks** were black. Light-coloured **spats** and **gaiters** were still popular.

Various styles in **overcoats** were seen, both single- and double-breasted, with raglan or inset sleeves, and knee-length to nearly reaching the ankles, in belted or loose styles, of dark or light colours, plain or plaid. Revers were buttoned

MID-VICTORIAN
1860-1880

1860's - DARK BROWN TWEED SACK COAT - BRAID EDGES - BROWN & WHITE CHECK TROUSERS - DARK BROWN WAIST- -COAT - BLACK BOWLER- & BOOTS - BOW TIE - LIGHT GLOVES

1860 - PROMENADE COSTUME - GREEN SILK DRESS OVER CRINOLINE - GREY PALETOT TRIMMED WITH CLARET VELVET BANDS & BUTTONS - SHOULDER CAPE ATTACHED - GREY VELVET BONNET TRIMMED WITH CLARET VELVET & GREY PLUME - GREY RIBBONS - WHITE UNDER- -SLEEVES - GLOVES

1860 - PROMENADE COSTUME - LILAC SILK DRESS OVER CRINOLINE - BLACK SILK MANTILLA WITH MAUVE RUCHED BANDS & BLACK CHANTILLY LACE FLOUNCES - WHITE BONNET & TULLE CAP - MAUVE RIBBONS & VIOLETS - WHITE LACE PARASOL -

1865 - EVENING DRESS - BLACK TAIL COAT - SILK REVERS - BLACK TROUSERS - BRAID SEAMS - BLACK SATIN WAISTCOAT - WHITE COLLAR, SHIRT & TIE - BLACK TOP HAT - BLACK SLIPPERS- WHITE GLOVES

high like the coats. Fur, velvet, and braid were used as trimmings to collar, cuffs, and pockets. Formal overcoats were black or dark (see p. 226). The *Inverness* cape or coat, worn for travelling, was in vogue from the late sixties; it was usually made in plaid or check cloth and reached to mid-calf. A belt encircled the waist and a shoulder cape and round collar were attached on top of the coat. **Evening overcoats** or **capes** were often modelled on the Inverness, though in black cloth, alternatively, a loose black cloak was worn, with or without shoulder cape and with a velvet collar.

The softer, turned-down **collar** was becoming increasingly popular—it was so much more comfortable—although a stiff round, upright style was used for formal wear. Both were white, though stripes appeared on the soft styles in the seventies. Neckwear was varied: **neckcloths,** striped, plain, or check; **bow ties** and **knotted ties** were all equally favoured. Black was usual for formal wear, white for evening, and colours for informal dress (see p. 234). **Scarf-pins** were used with neckcloths. White, starched-fronted **shirts** were still worn with formal attire. Detachable stiff shirt-cuffs were in use, also washable celluloid collars and **cuffs.** Striped or spotted cotton shirts had begun to accompany informal dress.

Evening dress still consisted of a black tail coat, black or white waistcoat, in piqué, cashmere, or satin, white shirt, collar and tie, black trousers, without the instep strap now, and black slippers with a ribbon bow. A black crush hat completed the ensemble which was very similar now to present-day attire (see p. 224).

A centre parting was the average **hair-style** for men in this period, although a side parting was still seen. The hair was worn shorter in the seventies. **Side-whiskers** became excessively long, and the version which left the chin free was most popular—they were known as "*Dundreary whiskers*", or, later, as "*Piccadilly weepers*". A combination of side-whiskers, moustache, and beard, or one or two of these was usual until after 1880.

The **top hat** continued as *the* hat for dress wear, in black, grey, or white, beaver or silk, curved or stove-pipe shape. Some men always wore a top hat, others reserved it for formal dress (see pp. 226, 230, and 234). Partially replacing it for informal wear was the increasingly popular *bowler*, also known as the *derby* or *billycock*. This round felt hat, with rolling brim, in black or brown, had first been worn in the fifties, but it was in this period that it became well known (see pp. 224 and 234). The name bowler was derived from its original hatter, the other names from sponsors. Plaid or check **caps,** with ear-flaps, were in use for sport and travelling.

From 1860 to 1863 the excessively wide, circular **crinoline** dominated the feminine gown styles, but afterwards the shape of the framework began to alter: the front and sides were flattened, while the fullness was retained at the back, a more oval section resulting. Either the metal cage crinoline or the horse-hair type with whalebone bands was worn—only the shape changed (see p. 234). By 1870 the fullness was entirely at the back, the **bustle** silhouette being very pronounced until 1875, afterwards it waned slowly, so that in the last few years of the seventies, the framework was temporarily abandoned and the true line of the hips was apparent once more.

The **bodice** of the **day gowns** continued to be tight-fitting, with a tiny waist:

MID-VICTORIAN
1860-1880

1863 - PURPLE BROCATELLE DAY
DRESS OVER CRINOLINE -
BLACK LEAF DESIGN & BLACK
& WHITE LACE-WORK HEM
TRIMMING - BLACK CASHMERE
JACKET WITH WHITE SILK
EMBROIDERY & BLACK &
WHITE TASSELS - PALE BLUE
CRÊPE BONNET WITH CREAM
LACE & LAVENDER RIBBONS
LAVENDER GLOVES

1870-1 - BLACK
TOP HAT - BLACK
BROADCLOTH
CUTAWAY COAT -
BRAID EDGES - FAWN
WAISTCOAT &
TROUSERS -
BRAID SIDE
SEAMS BLACK
BOOTS -
SILK NECK-
-CLOTH -
GLOVES

1870-4 - BLACK
CLOTH FORMAL
DOUBLE-BREASTED
OVERCOAT - SILK
COLLAR - GREY
STRIPED TROUSERS -
BLACK NECKCLOTH -
GREY TOP HAT
& GLOVES - BLACK
UMBRELLA &
BOOTS .

1862 - BALL DRESS OF PALE
PINK GAUZE WITH WHITE STRIPES
OVER CRINOLINE - WHITE
RIBBON BOWS & TRIMMING
ON FLOUNCES - WHITE LACE
RUFFLES AT SLEEVES & ABOVE
GOWN NECKLINE - BLACK
RIBBON TIE - WHITE GLOVES -
SILVER BRACELET - FAN -
PEARL NECKLACE -
FLOWERS IN HAIR

PLATE XI

A Crinoline Gown: ruching provides jacket and
looped-up pannier skirt effect

From "Les Modes Parisiennes," 1855

it was fashioned either with a square yoke and a high, belted waist-line, or, popularly, with a jacket over-bodice with collar and/or revers, or merely plain and fitting to an unbelted V-shaped waist. This latter style predominated from about 1874, giving place after 1876 to the princess style of gown, with a gored, fitting waist, but no waist seam, the gores continuing over sleekly-fitted hips, to the lower draperies which followed the bustle. The **neck-line** was always high, finishing at the throat in the sixties and higher in the seventies, always trimmed with white lace frills or collar (see pp. 228, 230, and 232). The wide bell-**sleeves** continued to accompany the crinoline, but with the advent of the bustle, narrower sleeves returned, finished at the elbow or wrist by fussy trimmings of lace, ruching, flounces, bows, etc. (see pp. 228, 230, and 232). The **skirt** was indubitably the centre of attraction and the focus was turned more and more to the back as time passed. Several rows of flounces or tunic over-skirts continued in fashion with the wide crinoline, decorated with large, heavy patterns, inset vertical strips of contrasting materials, lace hems, velvet bands, etc., as in the late fifties (see pp. 224 and 226). However, after 1866–1867, the skirt began to be lifted up by cords from the waist, forming bunched-up drapery all round, but particularly at the back, where a train was now seen (see p. 228). By 1868–1870, the over-skirt was open in front and looped back on either side to form the bustle draping, which fell in a complicated array of folds to the train at the back; an apron front (*en tablier*) often accompanied this style (see pp. 228 and 230). From 1870 to 1875, skirts became extremely complicated in draping: the over-skirt was fastened back and up, showing its lining, and the lower parts of the legs were covered by the under-skirt; a full draped bustle formed a shelf at the rear and these draperies fell to a long train, except in the case of walking gowns. Different colours, fabrics, and patterns were used for the over-skirt, lining, and under-skirt, with layers of fringe, lace, accordion pleating, ruching, and flounces decorating all edges. Large ribbon bows ornamented the skirt, particularly the top of the bustle (see pp. 230 and 232). After 1876, with the decline of the bustle, the fitting princess gowns were predominant, with the looped-up draperies in different colours and patterns still worn, but arranged lower at the back and giving a narrow skirt, often tight nearly to the ankles, but ending in a train of accordion pleating and/or lace frills. Cascading lace falls, bows, and draped, bunched material were carefully massed at the back, where all the attention was focused (see pp. 230 and 232).

Evening gowns followed the trend of day dresses, except for the *décolletage* which continued low and wide, partially off the shoulders, in the sixties. It was decorated by a berthe or lace edging, flounces, and flowers. In the seventies, some neck-lines took a deep square shape with lace edging. A train was always a necessary adjunct to an evening gown, and became even longer after 1870. A tremendous amount of decoration was given to the skirt, in lace falls, accordion pleating, bows, and flowers. Puff short sleeves remained in vogue in the sixties, but elbow-length pagoda ones predominated after 1870, with bow and lace trimming (see pp. 226, 230, and 232).

Gown **fabrics** were still heavy from 1860 to 1868, with velvet, cashmere, poplin, merino, silk, satin, and plush predominating, but after this, a stiff taffeta became the favourite material; alternatives were shot silk, corded or moiré silk, poplin, or cashmere. Tarlatan, gauze, tulle, muslin, lace, organdie, silk,

16

1866 - PROMENADE COSTUME - VIOLET SILK DRESS LOOPED UP BY CORDS FROM THE WAIST - UNDER-DRESS OF GREY & WHITE STRIPED FABRIC, DECORATED BY CERISE CASHMERE & BLACK VELVET PIPING & BUTTONS - OVER NEW CRINOLINE SHAPE - BLACK VELVET PALETOT TRIMMED WITH BLACK LACE - YELLOW GLOVES - WHITE VELVET BONNET WITH WHITE PLUME & RIBBONS - WHITE PARASOL WITH GREEN FRINGING

1875-80 - SKATING COSTUME - PALE GREEN SILK HAT & VEIL - FLOWERS - WINE COLOURED JACKET WITH GREY FUR - DARK GREEN DRESS - ACCORDION PLEATING AT HEM IN PALE GREEN - GLOVES

1868-70 - DEEP VIOLET SILK DAY DRESS WITH SELF-COLOUR PIPING & FRINGE TRIMMING, BELT, BOWS & BUTTONS - APRON FRONT - CRINOLINE TO BUSTLE TRANSITIONAL SILHOUETTE - WHITE LACE COLLAR - CREAM STRAW HAT - VIOLET & LILAC RIBBONS - GLOVES

1870 - DELICATE BLUE SILK AFTERNOON DRESS WITH WHITE SPOT SPRIG PATTERN - APRON FRONT - BUSTLE - BLUE & BLACK EDGES TO SLEEVES, APRON, BODICE & BOW - BLUE FRINGING & BUTTONS - WHITE LACE COLLAR & CUFFS - BLUE VELVET BOW IN HAIR

and taffeta were much in demand for **evening gowns.** Velvet and braid bands, chenille and silk fringing and ribbon bows were the principal **trimmings** worn in conjunction with the crinoline, but pleated lace or tulle, accordion-pleated silk or satin, bows, flounces, and fringe were predominant in the seventies. Plaids and stripes were worn all the period, also floral brocades or printed designs and contrasting plain colours in one garment. The strident colours of the fifties were retained in the sixties—magenta, plum, cerise, black, royal blue, emerald green, etc.—with strong contrasts in one dress, but softer shades were seen in the seventies, in greens, paler blues, lilac, turquoise, and rose, with a return to strong blue, bright green, red, and black at the end of the period. White was unsurpassed for evening, with pastel shades as an alternative.

By 1870-1875, more women were beginning to interest themselves in some forms of **sport,** such as golf, skating, and croquet, but their costumes for these, as yet, were little different from their everyday dress, comprising long draperies over a bustle, a hat and veil, long sleeves, high necks, and gloves (see p. 228).

Styles of **outdoor wear** continued to vary between coats, jackets, shawls, and cloaks. The full three-quarter or full-length **cloak-coat** modes were still worn with the crinoline, made of wool or cloth, with fur or velvet band trimming and having wide bell-sleeves and a cape and collar (see p. 224). These *paletots* became more fitting at the waist as the crinoline changed in shape, and were later made to fit over the bustle (see p. 228). Sleeves became longer and more fitting, and ankle-length slimmer **coats** were seen in the late seventies (see p. 232). **Jackets** were always popular with bell-sleeves and slit, fringed skirts in the sixties (see p. 226), but straighter styles with fitting, cuffed sleeves, and fur and tassel trimming, were worn in the seventies (see p. 232). Alpaca, corded silk, cashmere, and velvet were favourite materials for coats, trimmed with astrakhan, fur, velvet, braid, and fringe. Voluminous **cloaks, shawls,** and **mantillas** were much in vogue with the crinoline, of silk, velvet, cashmere, and lace, with ruching, lace, and fringe trimming (see p. 224). **Shoulder capes** were seen all the period.

Many layers of **underwear** were still worn, as in early Victorian days, although perhaps not quite so many **petticoats** with the bustle gowns. However, five or six were still considered usual, of white starched, flounced material, and maybe a coloured taffeta or silk one on top, in the seventies, which showed its rows of ruffles at the hem when the long gown skirt was lifted. **Corsets** were the same as before, providing an even smaller waist in the seventies, to set off the draped hip-line. **Stockings** were usually white, although coloured ones, often striped, were worn after 1870.

Ladies still wore **boots** for out-of-doors, heel-less or with low heels in the sixties, and rather higher ones in the seventies. Buttons, laces, or elastic sides were in use, and leather, kid, satin, or silk in all colours. Patent leather toes and heels were still fashionable. Rounder toes came in about 1875. For indoor or evening wear, **slippers** were heel-less or with a small heel at first, but had a higher, curved heel after 1870. Satin, silk, or kid were used, with a rosette or bow, and an embroidered toe (see p. 234). Short cloth **gaiters** were also worn in winter.

The simple, rather severe **hair-style** with a centre parting, hair waved on the temples and drawn to a bun low in the nape of the neck, was worn until about

MID-VICTORIAN
1860-1880

1873 - PALE BLUE SATIN EVENING GOWN TRIMMED WITH BLUE SILK RIBBON & BOWS, BLUE PLEATED TULLE & BLACK LACE - YOKE & UNDERSLEEVES OF WHITE GAUZE - FLOWERS IN HAIR

1877 - BLACK TOP HAT & FROCK COAT - GREY & BLACK STRIPED TROUSERS - LIGHT GLOVES & SPATS - STRIPED TIE - CANE

1876-7 - PROMENADE DRESS - PRINCESS STYLE IN GREY POPLIN BOWS, ACCORDION PLEATING AT HEM, CUFFS & YOKE IN ULTRAMARINE - CREAM STRAW HAT - WHITE PLUME - GLOVES

1872 - BLACK SILK DAY DRESS WITH BLACK LACE, BUTTONS, FRINGE & BOW TRIMMING - APRON FRONT - BUSTLE - BUTTONED BACK OVERSKIRT - FLOUNCES - JACKET OVER-BODICE - WHITE SLEEVE & NECK FRILLS - BLACK SILK PORK PIE HAT & RIBBONS - CREAM GLOVES

1865, when the chignon styles came in, once more emulating the Grecian modes. A more elaborate coiffure was seen in the seventies, and was most varied in its styles: curls were worn on the forehead; the hair was swept up at the sides—showing the ears once more—to curls on top, and the back hair was dressed in plaits, curls, ringlets, or coils, all cascading down from a high bun or coil, to low in the nape. All the interest was centred at the back, as with the dresses, and for evening, more complicated versions were seen, decorated by bows, pearl ropes, jewelled combs, flowers, and lace. Chenille or silk **hair-nets** were often worn at the back (see pp. 226, 228, 230, 232, and 234).

Bonnets continued to be worn all through the mid-Victorian era, although hats were becoming more popular, and had almost ousted the bonnet from fashion by 1880. The high short-fronted bonnet, worn far back on the head, continued in fashion in the sixties, tied under the chin by a wide ribbon bow, real or imitation, and decorated outside and under the brim by lace, flowers —particularly roses—bows, and plumes (see pp. 224, 228, 232, and 234). In the seventies, bonnets became smaller and smaller and were by 1875 merely a trimming laid on the head and tied under the chin by a bow (see pp. 230 and 234). In contrast to the bonnet which was placed far back on the head, **hats** in the sixties were perched on the forehead like a tiny plate: they were of straw or silk, trimmed with flowers, ribbons, and lace, with veils hanging from the back. There were several styles, all tiny, of which the *pork-pie* is perhaps the best known. Fur, feather, straw, or silk *toques* were also very popular. Although still small, hats were worn farther back on the head in the seventies; they were lavishly trimmed with birds' feathers and wings, ribbon bows, lace, and a small veil (see pp. 228, 230, and 234).

Men still carried small or heavy **canes,** popularly with silver or horn tops. Their **handkerchiefs** were large, white linen squares, like those of the present day. **Gloves** were essential to the gentleman, in leather, suede, or chamois, in grey, brown, or black, with white kid for evening. Jewellery was still confined to a **scarf-pin, studs, cuff-links, signet ring,** and the massive "turnip" **watch** and gold chain.

The **parasol** continued to be a feminine requisite: it was large or very small, of walking length, or perhaps a carriage, tilted pattern; silk was the preferred fabric, plaid, striped, or plain, with lace, fringe, flowers, tassel, and ribbon bow trimming; handles were of carved ivory, wood, or metal (see pp. 224, 228, 232 and 234). **Umbrellas** were still large and of black silk (see p. 232). **Handkerchiefs** were white and dainty, embroidered or lace-edged. Fur **muffs** were carried. Small **reticules** were in use, of velvet or silk, with bead or sequin embroideries. **Gloves** were *de rigeur* at all times: short styles in pastel shades were worn in the day-time, while evening ones were white, reaching to the wrist or forearm, and even longer in the seventies. With ball dresses, the **fan** was still carried, of lace or silk, with wood, tortoise-shell, or ivory sticks (see p. 226); also the small **bouquet** of flowers in a silver holder. **Flowers,** real or artificial, ornamented evening gowns.

Large **ear-rings** were popular in jewellery designs, chiefly of a drop style, also gold **lockets** or **cameos** worn on a gold **neck-chain** or black velvet ribbon; these ribbons were also tied round the wrist for evening wear. The wearing

MID-VICTORIAN
1860-1880

1879-80- BLUE-
-GREY COAT WITH
SHOULDER CAPES-
DARK BLUE
VELVET BONNET
WITH PLUMES -
DARK BLUE GLOVES-
BLACK UMBRELLA

1875- DARK BROWN SILK AFTERNOON DRESS WITH BUSTLE-
SKIRT DRAPED UP TO SHOW LINING OF APPLE GREEN,
BROWN & COPPER FLORAL PATTERN - UNDERSKIRT OF
PALE COPPER SILK WITH SELF-COLOUR FRINGED &
ACCORDION PLEATED EDGES - WHITE LACE TRIMMING AT
NECK, SLEEVES & HEM, THE LATTER PLEATED - DARK
BROWN BOW & BUTTONS - APPLE GREEN BOW
IN HAIR

1877-8- DRESS
OF LIGHT COLOURED
& PLAID WOOL -
BOX PLEATED HEM-
DRAPERY BUNCHED UP
LOW ON HIPS AT BACK-
PLUM COLOURED
VELVET JACKET
WITH GREY FUR &
TASSEL TRIMMING-
SILK BONNET WITH
RIBBON, PLUMES
& FLOWERS -PLUM
COLOURED GLOVES-
PARASOL

1878- DINNER DRESS IN
MAROON SATIN & GREY RIBBED
SILK - PRINCESS STYLE- MAROON
BOWS & ACCORDION PLEATING -
WHITE LACE RUFFLES AT HEM, NECK
& SLEEVES - BLACK VELVET NECK
& WRISTBAND - CAMEO -
FLOWERS IN HAIR - FAN

of **neck-laces** was confined to ball dresses, owing to the high neck-lines of day gowns; pearls were especially worn. **Rings** and **bracelets** were still massive in design, in complicated settings (see p. 234).

LATE VICTORIAN ENGLAND 1880–1901

In the masculine attire of the late Victorian era can be seen the prototypes of modern dress: the extreme formality of the top hat and frock coat, depicted in a scheme of black and white, were being relegated more and more to dress wear, while the demands of sport, country attire, and comfort emerged more strongly towards the end of the century. The sack coat and trousers, and the early lounge suits were becoming everyday costume, accompanied by a bowler or straw boater, according to the season, while the Norfolk jacket, knicker-bockers, cap, and stockings provided a comfortable, sensible ensemble for active enjoyment.

In feminine costume, although emancipation was yet to come, indications of the twentieth-century woman were apparent in the effect on dress of the increased desire for participation in sport: by the nineties, special costumes for various sports were designed, and were worn by enthusiastic, though still daring, women; tennis, bathing, cricket, and cycling costumes were seen, and the skirt or, most daring of all, the knickerbockers, were raised above the ankle. This practice was still condemned by the majority of the feminine sex, despite the fact that the "exposed" ankle was warmly clad in stockings, gaiters, and boots. Hats and gloves, with high-necked shirt blouses, completed these outfits, so it can hardly be said that comfort and practicability had yet arrived. In day and evening attire, there was still no indication of emancipation: long trains, coyly held up to display frilled, lace-edged petticoats, enormous leg-of-mutton sleeves, large veiled hats, with superimposed plumage, and, in the eighties, the return of the bustle, were all elegant modes. Clothes suitable for women to work in were still not required—the activities of the ladies had not yet spread to professional spheres.

The **lounge suit** or **sack coat** and checked, striped, or plain trousers provided now the everyday attire of the majority of men. The former had a coat, waist-coat, and trousers of matching material, usually in tweed of some kind, often in a check or plaid design. The cut of the jacket was still, however, rather different from that of the present day: the lapels and collar were small and buttoned high; the coat was single-breasted with three or four buttons, and reached the hips with rounded front edges; sleeves were, as now, even in width from shoulder to cuff; braid edging was still in vogue and the coat had hip- and breast-pockets (see p. 236). In the late nineties, the lapels became longer, so also did the coat which had square corners once more. A **dress sack coat** of black or dark serge or broadcloth was then worn for semi-formal dress, with black waistcoat and grey-striped trousers; this partially replaced the frock coat and cutaway styles in this respect (see p. 240). For formal occasions, however, and older men, the **frock** and **cutaway coats** held their own, having changed little in cut from mid-Victorian times; they were accompanied by grey, fawn, white, or black waistcoats and grey-striped trousers (see p. 244). The *Norfolk*

MID-VICTORIAN
1860-1880

PURPLE VELVET BONNET WITH CREAM LACE & VIOLET TRIMMING - c.1863

BROWN VELVET BONNET - BROWN PLUMES & RIBBONS - HAIR NET - 1879

CREAM LEGHORN HAT - BLUE VELVET EDGING & RIBBONS - VEIL - 1868

BLACK TOP HAT - DUNDREARY WHISKERS - BOW TIE - 1863

PUFFED HORSE-HAIR CRINOLINE 1862

2 ft

WHITE WATERED SILK PARASOL - IVORY HANDLE - PINK & WHITE FRINGING c.1860

BLACK BOWLER - WHITE COLLAR - SILK NECKCLOTH - SCARF PIN c.1870

BUSTLE SHAPE - c.1872-5

GREEN SILK CIRCULAR FOLDING FAN - WOOD HANDLE 1870-80

WHITE QUILTED LINEN CAP - WHITE ROSETTES - BLUE RIBBON - c.1867

WHITE WATERED SILK BOOT & ROSETTE SIDE LACING - 1860's

CHANTILLY LACE FAN - TORTOISE-SHELL STICKS - 1860-70

WHITE CHIP BONNET WITH PINK ROSES & BLACK LACE TRIMMING - WHITE TULLE CAP - PINK STRINGS - 1863

BRONZE KID SHOE 1860-70

BLACK KID & WHITE SILK SHOE - 1868-70

CREAM SATIN SHOE & BOW - AMBER-COLOURED GLASS BEADS - 1877

YELLOW SATIN SHOE & BOW 1865

WHITE KID LACED BOOT 1860

GREEN LEATHER & BLACK PATENT LEATHER BOOT. 1860

GREY SILK HAT - PINK RIBBONS & PLUMES. 1872

CREAM STRAW HAT - BLACK VELVET RIBBONS - WHITE BIRDS' WINGS 1875

GOLD EARRING WITH GOLD FILIGREE CORDS - c.1875

COIFFURE c.1874-5. RIBBON BOW & JEWELLED COMB

WHITE BEAVER TOP HAT - WHITE RIBBON - METAL BUCKLE - 1873

BROWN STRAW TOQUE HAT - PLAID BAND - WHITE, RED & BLACK PLUMES - 1864

GOLD RING SET WITH DIAMONDS & RUBIES

234

jacket was an innovation of this period, and was intended primarily for sports-wear. It was cut similarly to the sack coat, but was distinguished by a waist-belt and vertical pleats back and front. It had large hip-pockets and was usually made of check or plaid tweed. It reached a height of popularity in the nineties, with the new enthusiasm for cycling (see p. 246). At this time, other jackets were affected by its style, and also appeared with pleated backs.

Waistcoats usually matched the coat now, except with formal coats, when white, fawn, or grey were most usual. Single-breasted styles were predominant.

Trousers remained fairly narrow until the end of Queen Victoria's reign, although, with the appearance of trouser-presses in the late nineties, some men began to assume a vertical crease in the slightly wider trousers of the lounge suit; turn-ups were also seen in these suits, but for formal wear the uncuffed, uncreased style was retained (see pp. 236, 238, 240, and 244).

Knickerbockers accompanied the Norfolk jacket for sports- or country-wear, usually matching its material. They were worn in conjunction with woollen socks, gaiters, and boots or shoes (see p. 246). White knickerbockers or trousers were worn for tennis.

Neckwear was varied in this period. The deep turned-down softer **collar** was most popular with lounge suits and sports attire, although a round, up-standing, stiff white collar, or a winged one, were worn by well-dressed men. The higher, upstanding or winged, white stiff collar remained *de rigeur* for formal wear, with the frock or cutaway coat. Silk, striped, or plain **neckcloths, knotted** or **bow ties** were all equally in favour; black was usual with formal dress (see p. 248). White **shirts** with stiff or pleated fronts were still predominant, and detachable stiff **cuffs** were still in use.

Evening dress was virtually unchanged from that described in the mid-Victorian period (see p. 224). The prototype of the dinner-jacket appeared in the nineties, cut like a dress sack coat.

Shoes were as yet rarely worn except for a soft leather or canvas type, with rubber sole, for tennis and other sports. The **boots** for everyday wear were still of a laced or buttoned style, worn under the trousers. Black or brown leather was used, with black patent leather for dress wear. Light-coloured cloth tops came in and were popular and informal. **Spats** and **gaiters** continued in favour. **Socks** were still black. Woollen or leather **slippers** were worn indoors, while black patent leather slippers or boots accompanied evening dress (see p. 248).

There was a varied selection of **overcoats** from which men could make their choice, although certain of these were reserved for more or less specific occasions. For instance, a single-breasted black overcoat—commonly called the *Chesterfield*—was considered a dress coat to be worn with evening or formal attire; it had high revers, a black velvet or silk collar, reached to the knees, and had hidden buttons down the front (see p. 242). It has survived till today as a dress style. The extremely short, barely hip-length, light-coloured loose overcoat with large pockets was generally worn by younger men (see p. 238). The **Inverness coat** was very popular for travelling, and in cold weather. It was made of check or plaid material, and has been immortalised as the habitual outdoor wear of Sherlock Holmes (see p. 240). Another type of dress overcoat was provided by the double-breasted, long, mid-calf style, with wide revers. Many variations of these coats were worn in light or dark, plain or plaid

LATE VICTORIAN
1880-1901

1885-6 - TWEED SUIT - BRAID EDGES TO COAT - BLACK BOWLER - GREY RIBBON - TURNED DOWN COLLAR - STRIPED TIE - GLOVES - CANE

1883 - WEDDING DRESS OF PALE GOLD SILK DAMASK - UNDERGOWN OF WHITE SATIN - PLEATED SKIRT & BODICE - WHITE RIBBON BOW - WHITE LACE AT NECK & SLEEVES, ALSO CAP

1884-5 - AFTERNOON GOWN IN GREEN-BLUE SATIN WITH INSET PIECES ON SKIRT, SLEEVES & COLLAR OF PATTERNED MATERIAL WITH BLUE PREDOMINATING - GREEN-BLUE SILK BOWS & RIBBON - WHITE SILK BOW AT NECK & WHITE SILK FRONT TO BODICE & SKIRT - WHITE LACE PLEATED EDGING & APRON FRONT - BLUE VELVET BONNET - WHITE PLUMES & RUCHED EDGE - WHITE PARASOL - IVORY HANDLE - GLOVES

1885 - BLACK SILK COAT WITH BLACK VELVET COLLAR & CUFFS - WORN OVER BUSTLE - BLACK WATERED SILK RIBBON - BLACK VELVET, STRAW & LACE HAT - SCARLET RIBBONS - DARK FUR MUFF

236

materials, and varying from hip- to nearly ankle-length. Velvet or plaid collars and fur trimmings were in vogue. A black version of the Inverness was also still seen with evening dress.

Woollies in the form of knitted cardigans and waistcoats began to make their appearance in the nineties, especially for sports-wear.

Men wore their **hair** rather shorter now, although still longer than styles of today. The centre parting was still seen, with side partings or the hair combed straight back as equally favoured alternatives. **Side-whiskers** became less fashionable, and by the nineties were seen only on older men. **Moustaches** were retained by most men, of handle-bar variety for preference, and worn with or without a **beard,** until 1890, when the latter declined in vogue.

The **top hat** was as yet by no means out-moded; it was seen everywhere as a mark of distinction and was *de rigeur* with formal dress. Grey or black were worn (see pp. 242, 244, and 248). Other hats were, however, taking its place for everyday wear by the majority of men: the **bowler** was the foremost of these, worn in brown, black, or grey felt, with a higher crown at the end of the century (see pp. 236, 238, and 248). Another hat, a typical innovation of the period, was the straw *boater*. By 1880–1885, its use was not confined to boating, but extended to summer wear, for holidays, sea and country, and for all sports. It had a flat circular crown and brim, and a ribbon, usually striped. An elastic cord often attached the brim to the coat lapel as a defence against the wind (see p. 248). At the end of the century, the prototype of the felt *trilby hat* appeared, worn in shades of fawn or grey (see p. 248). **Caps** of different shapes were worn, especially for sports- and country-wear. These were chiefly in tweed or check material, commonly with a peak fore and aft and ear-flaps (see pp. 240, 246, and 248).

A small waist was a feature of the late Victorian period in **feminine dress,** maintained as hitherto by the indefatigable corset, which provided the famous wasp-waist of the nineties. Apart from this common factor, the eighties and the nineties differed considerably in styles of gown: the dresses of the early eighties were characterised by the return of the **bustle,** which reached an extreme of fashion by 1885, while it declined slowly towards 1890, and the gowns of the following decade began to assume the hour-glass silhouette, with wasp waist and a bell-shaped skirt, fairly fitting to the knees, but flaring out at the hem with the assistance of frilled petticoats.

The **bodice** of **day gowns** still fitted closely over the corseted figure, in fact it was often boned also. Princess styles were frequently seen in the early eighties, sleekly fitting over the upper hips, as in the late seventies, but with the return of the bustle the jacket bodices with flaring peplum were fashionable again, frequently buttoned centre front from neck to waist. Alternatively, the front was left open in a vertical band to show the lace, frilled chemisette, or undergown (see p. 236). These styles were carried into the nineties when a pointed front or jacket bodice was popular, with tab peplum; bolero jacket over-bodices were often seen: numerous lace frills, jabots, and ruffles decorated the centre front. By the late nineties the front was fuller, usually with open jacket showing the full lace blouse underneath (see pp. 242 and 244). The **neck-line** was very high all the period, forming an upright collar surmounted by a lace ruffle. In the nineties, it rose even higher, and the lace ruffle was

LATE VICTORIAN
1880-1901

1886. DARK GREEN
VELVET JACKET OR
MANTEAU DE VISITE -
GREY FUR TRIMMING &
MUFF - GREEN RIBBONS -
SCARLET SATEEN DRESS
WITH WHITE SPOT PATTERN
& CREAM LACE TRIMMING
AT HEM & BUSTLE
DRAPERY - CRIMSON
SATIN RIBBON -
GREEN VELVET -
TURBAN WITH
VIOLETS - ALSO
ON MUFF -
GREY GLOVES

1888 - DOLMAN COAT OF
WOVEN PAISLEY DESIGN IN
REDS, DARK GREEN, PALE BLUE,
YELLOW & BLACK - PADDED
& QUILTED SILK LINING -
BLACK FUR COLLAR & CUFFS -
PLAIN RED INSET PANEL -
RED VELVET BONNET &
RIBBONS - BLACK PLUME -
GLOVES - PARASOL -
CREAM SATIN DRESS

1886 - EVENING GOWN OF ELECTRIC
BLUE SATIN - ACCORDION PLEATED
UNDERSKIRT HEM & FLOUNCED OUTER
HEM - DEEP BLUE VELVET FRONT TO
BODICE & OVERSKIRT - LACE COVERED
VELVET COLLAR - LACE AT NECK &
SLEEVES - FAN - FLOWERS IN HAIR -
WHITE GLOVES

1885 - 90 - FAWN
OVERCOAT - GREY
BOWLER - DARK
GREY RIBBON -
MONOCLE - CANE -
CHECK GREY-GREEN
TROUSERS - BLACK
BOOTS

238

under the ears and chin, supported by vertical strips of whalebone at the sides. Until 1891–1892 **sleeves** were simple and fitting, as in the late seventies, ending at the elbow or forearm and finished by lace ruffles and cuff. After this time, however, a reintroduction of that style so typical of the thirties took place: the **leg-of-mutton** and **balloon** sleeves dominated feminine modes once more. The sleeve was fitting on the forearm and reached the wrist, but ballooned on the upper arm from the shoulder, where it was gathered or pleated into the armhole. By 1895–1896, extremes were reached again and sleeve bustles, whalebone and stuffing were used to keep the requisite shape. A decline in size began in 1897, and by 1900 very long, tight-fitting sleeves had returned (see pp. 236, 238, 242, 244, and 246). Until 1890 the **skirt** remained the centre of attraction in the gown: princess styles predominated until 1882, with low draped-up overskirts, but with the return of the **bustle** in 1882–1883, the material was festooned up higher again, so that by 1885 an echo of 1875 was seen in a shelf-like formation at the rear and cascading falls of lace, bows, and skirt draperies descending from it to a train on the ground. This second appearance of the bustle was not quite identical with the first: the shape was different. The new bustle was a wire-braided or metal-banded basket tied on at the waist and just forming a rounded shape at the back; it was not connected to any whaleboned petticoat or metal cage as opposed to its predecessor. It formed, therefore, an acute fullness at the rear of the hips, but the skirt material then fell vertically, where it was now draped upwards, instead of flaring outwards as in the seventies. There was a gradual increase in the size of the bustle from 1881 to 1885 and an equal diminution from 1885 to 1890, by the end of which period it had completely disappeared. Trains became longer in the mid-eighties, even on walking gowns, and dresses were still decorated by an abundant distribution of bows, ribbons, lace falls, accordion pleating, and ruffles (see pp. 236 and 238). In the early nineties, although the bustle had gone, the main fullness in the skirt was still concentrated at the back and trains swept the floor (see pp. 242 and 244). By 1893–1894, the hour-glass silhouette had come in; a wasp-waist was essential for this, and the gown was slimmer on the hips, and even fairly narrow to the knees, below which it flared out fully to the ground. It was very long and was usually gracefully held up at one side, displaying the innumerable lace frills of the petticoats. Pleated skirts became the vogue, with vertical organ or box pleats, widening steadily from waist to hem and held in position by horizontal tapes sewn inside as far as the knee. Skirts had taffeta linings for preference, to produce the coveted rustle when walking. Towards 1901, the narrowness at the knee became accentuated, simultaneously with an even wider hem sweeping the ground, so the bell-shaped skirt resulted (see p. 244). Lace insertions and appliqué work were seen everywhere: the turn of the century became an age for lace once more.

Evening gowns were modelled on those for day wear, but had longer trains all the period, sweeping the floor or being attractively lifted for dancing. The **bustle** remained in vogue rather longer for evening wear, with the accompanying festooned draperies. The square and heart-shaped **neck-lines** were generally worn in the eighties, but a lower *décolletage* was more prevalent after 1890, in a V, round, or square shape decorated by a lace frill or velvet ruffle. Very low V-shapes were seen by the end of the century, with lace insertions in front.

LATE VICTORIAN
1880-1901

1893 - BROWN
TWEED COSTUME -
JACKET, BLOUSE OR
WAISTCOAT & SKIRT
OF SAME MATERIAL
BROWN FELT HAT -
RIBBONS - GLOVES

PLAID INVERNESS
COAT & WOOLLEN
CAP - LIGHT
TROUSERS - SPATS -
GLOVES CANE

1892-5 - BLACK
DRESS SACK COAT -
& WAISTCOAT -
GREY STRIPED
TROUSERS - GREY
SPATS - BLACK
PATENT
LEATHER
BOOTS -
STRIPED
NECK -
- CLOTH -
- WATCH -
- CHAIN

1894-6 - EVENING DRESS OF
CREAM SATIN WITH TINTED FLORAL
PATTERN - DEEP CRIMSON VELVET
SLEEVES & NECK, HEM & WAIST
TRIMMING - WHITE GLOVES - FAN -
AIGRETTE & FLOWERS IN HAIR

The short, straight elbow-length **sleeves,** ending in a cuff and lace ruffles, were most popular in the eighties, while large puffs echoed the leg-of-mutton styles of the nineties; by 1898, small puffs or cap sleeves were usual (see pp. 238, 240, and 242).

An innovation of this period for ladies was the **costume** or **tailor-made:** this became established by the early nineties and increased in popularity for walking and sports-wear as time passed. The cut followed the vagaries of dress styles, but basically it was composed of a **jacket, skirt,** and **blouse,** and/or **waistcoat.** Blouses varied tremendously according to individual taste and the occasion, from a masculine shirt blouse, collar, and tie, to a frilly feminine lace creation, boned up to the ears, and having leg-of-mutton sleeves. Jackets were waist- or hip-length and usually had wide revers, and leg-of-mutton sleeves when in fashion. Tweeds, serge, and wool were popular fabrics in winter, and linen in summer. Trimmings were in velvet, fur, braid, and cord (see pp. 240 and 244).

It is becoming increasingly difficult to chronicle the **fabrics** and colours in use; they become more numerous and varied as time passes; one can only mention the most popular. For day wear, silk, velveteen, plush, cashmere, wool poplin, satin, lace, muslin, and tulle predominated, with the addition of taffeta, crêpe, gingham, organdie, and linen in the nineties. For evening wear, lace, gauze, satin, crêpe, taffeta, velvet, or silk were preferred, with an increasing predominance of lace towards 1901. Velvet and fur were popular **trimmings,** also lace, flowers, bows, and embroidery, with bead, lace, and sequin insertion. Plaid, stripes, and spots were in vogue all the period, but plain materials, contrasting against one another, were greatly favoured. White and pastel shades were retained for evening, while day **colours** still tended to be vivid in the eighties, particularly electric blue, scarlet, plum, bright green, magenta, and black. Softer colours were more prevalent after 1890, with navy, brown and black and white for suits.

By the early nineties, several specific **costumes** were evolving for different forms of sport—**tennis, cycling, bathing, cricket,** and **hockey** in particular. None of these costumes was what a modern girl would call practicable, but they were at least a step in the right direction towards that end and a step away from the mid-Victorian attire and everyday clothes of this period. A navy serge skirt to the ground, a high-necked shirt blouse and tie, jacket, straw or felt hat, and canvas shoes or leather boots were used for most sports (see p. 246), while for **cycling** the attire varied from ordinary day dresses to the special costume for the enthusiast, which can be seen on p. 246. Mid-calf or ankle-length skirts were often substituted for knickerbockers, and a felt hat for the straw one. Many types of **bathing costume** existed, but short sleeves were general, also knee-length or longer trousers with a skirt on top. Dark colours were usual, with braid and lace decoration (see p. 246). These concessions to sport and comfort do not sound great contributions to us today, but when it is remembered that a few years earlier bustles, trains, and veils had been worn for skating, tennis, and hockey, and that the pioneer sportswomen had been subjected to fierce opposition and ridicule, they were indeed achievements.

Waist- and hip-length **jackets** or long and three-quarter-length fitting **coats,** were the most popular form of outer wear in this period. In the eighties, they

LATE VICTORIAN
1880-1901

1897- EVENING DRESS OF APPLE GREEN SILK REP WITH PALER GREEN CRÊPE BODICE FRONT & DARK GREEN VELVET TRIMMING - CREAM SATIN CAPE WITH SABLE EDGING & WHITE SILK FLOUNCING - WHITE LACE & CHIFFON FRILLS AT NECK- FAN - PEARL NECKLACE- FLOWERS & PEARLS IN HAIR

1888 -90 - BLACK FORMAL OVERCOAT- SILK COLLAR- EVENING DRESS COAT & TROUSERS- WHITE COLLAR & TIE- BLACK SILK HAT- WHITE GLOVES

1893-4- SEALSKIN COAT TRIMMED WITH CONTRASTING FUR - VELVET HAT WITH RIBBONS & PLUMES - FACE VEIL - GLOVES- UMBRELLA

1893-4 - PROMENADE GOWN OF DULL PINK SILK - WHITE LACE AT NECK, CUFFS, WRIST FRILLS & WAIST & SLEEVE INSERTIONS, ALSO BAND AT HEM - NAVY STRAW HAT & VEIL- BLACK RIBBONS - FLOWERS & WHITE PLUMES - GLOVES

were made to fit over the bustle, often with a large bow upon it, while after 1890 paletots cut on princess lines were more prevalent. The jackets had tab skirts at the back to rest on the bustle, and hung lower in front in pleats and tabs. Sleeves and collars followed the styles of dresses. Various materials were used, chiefly velvet, satin, silk, cloth, and brocade, with velvet, braid, and bow trimming. A tremendous increase in the use of fur trimming was apparent in this period: it was used on cuffs, collars, hem, and in decorative bands, also for lining purposes (see pp. 236 and 238). Sealskin and other furs were even used to make jackets and coats in the nineties (see p. 242). *Dolman mantles* and *coats* were frequently worn over the bustle gowns; they were cut to fit over the bustle, had part-sleeves, and hung loose all round. Heavy fabrics such as velvet, plush, and cashmere were used, in decorative patterns, especially paisley. Trimmings were in velvet and fur, while padded, quilted silk linings made the coat a warm one for winter (see p. 238). **Cloaks** and **capes** returned to favour once more in the nineties, as they were more comfortable over the large sleeves. Lengths varied from ankle to three-quarter, while **shoulder capes** were especially popular. All styles had high upstanding collars. Cashmere, plush, velvet, plaid or plain cloth, and fur were used, with fur and velvet trimming (see p. 244). **Evening capes** were of satin, silk, taffeta, and chiffon, with elaborate decoration (see p. 242).

Underwear was almost unaltered in the eighties from that worn in earlier Victorian times. Numbers of white starched flounced **petticoats** covered the white **drawers, chemises,** and corset. By 1890–1892, however, rather fewer petticoats were worn, and some of these, particularly the outer one, were of silk or taffeta for preference and had numerous flounces at the hem to make the gown skirt stand out; from waist to knees they were more fitting than earlier. Under petticoats were still of white starched material, while the inside one of flannel was still considered to be a necessity. The **corset** continued to be heavily boned, and a tiny waist was the aim of the ladies, who strived for a maximum of fifteen to eighteen inches circumference in the nineties. The corset was made deeper after 1890, covering part of the bosom and the hips. A full bosom was then desired, and false ones were added where necessary. Suspenders attached to the corset began to come in at this time also, although the wearing of garters was still usual. Lace edging, silk flounces, and ribbons decorated all underwear which by 1900 was much more delicate and of finer materials than hitherto. The white **stockings** began to give way to black or coloured ones in this period; they were made of cotton or lisle, or silk as a luxury.

Boots were still usual for outdoor wear, with buttoned, laced, or elastic sides. Heels grew higher and more curved in the nineties, and toes more pointed (see p. 248). Leather, kid, or patent leather were used, often with cloth or silk tops, or with cloth **gaiters** worn on top and buttoned up the outside of the leg. These, reaching high up the calf, usually accompanied cycling costumes (see p. 246). **Shoes** and **slippers** for indoor and evening wear and, towards 1900, for outdoors also, were generally low-fronted, without fastening, and had pointed toes and high, curved heels. White, black, or bronze satin or silk was used for evening, with rosette or bow trimming and bead-embroidered toes (see p. 248).

17

LATE VICTORIAN
1880-1901

1896 - DAY DRESS IN DAMASKED SATIN IN GREEN-BLUE & GOLD - BOLERO JACKET - LEG-OF-MUTTON SLEEVES - GREEN-BLUE VELVET ON REVERS & LOWER SLEEVES - GOLD EMBROIDERED BANDS AT NECK, BOLERO & HEM EDGES - WHITE FRILLS AT NECK & WRISTS - WHITE SILK & LACE PARASOL - GLOVES - STRAW HAT WITH LACE & PLUME TRIMMING - VEIL.

1895 - TAILORED COSTUME FOR WALKING OR SPORT, IN NAVY LINEN WITH WHITE BRAID TRIMMING - WHITE WAISTCOAT & SHIRT-BLOUSE - TIE - GLOVES - BLUE STRAW HAT - RIBBONS & PLUME

1898 - 1901 - BLACK CUTAWAY TAIL COAT FOR FORMAL DRESS - GREY TOP HAT - GREY STRIPED TROUSERS - GREY SPATS - BLACK BOOTS & UMBRELLA. CHAMOIS GLOVES

1900 - DARK GREEN WOOL SHOULDER CAPE IN THREE TIERS - WHITE SATIN PIPED EDGES - GOLDEN BROWN WOOL PROMENADE DRESS - PLEATED SKIRT - FUR MUFF - VELVET HAT & RIBBONS - PLUMES - GLOVES

The prevalent style of **coiffure** in the eighties was a curly fringe ending in tiny curls on the forehead, with the side and back hair swept up to a fairly high coil of plaits or a bun. The ears were visible and tendrils of curls curved behind them at the nape. By 1892–1895, the looser pompadour styles became more popular; curls were still retained by many, but towards 1901 they gave way to a soft, loose pompadour mode, supported over a small pad on the crown. The back and side hair was still swept up, but more loosely, and it partially obscured the ears. Ringlets remained fashionable for evening in the eighties, but began to decline after 1890. False hair in the form of curls was often added to the coiffure. Flowers, bows, and aigrettes ornamented evening coiffures (see pp. 238, 240, 242, 244, and 248).

Small fussy **bonnets** were still seen until the late nineties, getting smaller and fussier as time passed; they were always tied under the chin by a bow and perched far back on the head. Many styles consisted only of lace, bows, plumes, and flowers; others had a straw, satin, silk, or velvet foundation. They were particularly fashionable with the bustle gowns (see pp. 236, 238, and 248). **Hats** varied greatly throughout the period, with several styles popular contemporaneously. On the whole, it can be said that they were fairly small and high in the eighties, in **toque, turban,** and **flower-pot** shapes, while **larger hats** were predominant in the nineties. Profuse trimming was present all the time, consisting of ribbons, bows, plumes, birds' wings, fur, velvet, flowers, and a veil. Veils were either short to the end of the nose, or covering the whole face and tied back to behind the head, the latter type being prevalent in the nineties, when trimming was also at its most profuse. **Straw boater hats** with or without trimming were worn for sport and by many young ladies for everyday wear. Toques of fur, felt, feathers, or velvet were popular all the period. Flower trimming abounded; bunches of violets were predominant in the eighties (see pp. 236, 238, 240, 242, 244, 246, and 248). White lace and muslin **caps** were still often donned indoors.

Masculine accessories remained the same as in the last period, comprising chiefly a large **watch** and **chain,** a **monocle, cane** or **umbrella** (see p. 244), and **gloves. Pyjamas** were beginning to replace the Victorian nightshirt for sleeping attire.

Feminine accessories were, as usual, more numerous, and were also similar to those of mid-Victorian times. Considered most necessary among these were **gloves;** evening styles were very long, to above the elbow. Suède, kid, and chamois were in constant use for day wear, in pastel shades or black. Bead or fabric **handbags,** small fur **muffs** with flower decoration (see pp. 236, 238, and 244), **umbrellas** (see p. 242), and **parasols** were carried. The latter were still made in various designs, fairly small in the eighties, and long walking types in the nineties. All colours were seen, preferably in pastel shades, with fringe, lace, tassel, and ribbon bow trimming. Silk, taffeta, chiffon, and satin were the principal fabrics, with wood or ivory handles (see pp. 236, 238, 244, and 248). Fur or ostrich-feather **boas** were worn in the nineties. **Fans** were still carried with evening dress, and flowers were affixed to the corsage. **Lorgnettes** as a purely decorative feature became fashionable after 1890. **Cosmetics,** having been "taboo" for almost the whole of the nineteenth century, were now occasionally used in strict moderation and privacy.

LATE VICTORIAN
1880-1901

1890's - SPORTS COSTUME FOR CYCLING, SKATING ETC. - TWEED NORFOLK JACKET & KNICKERBOCKERS, ALSO PEAKED CAP - WOOLLEN SOCKS. LIGHT COLOURED GAITERS

1898 - CYCLING COSTUME FOR THE ENTHUSIAST - GREY TWEED COAT & KNICKERBOCKERS - WHITE BLOUSE - FAWN GAITERS & GLOVES. BLACK BOOTS - STRAW HAT WITH RIBBONS & PLUME

1890s - TENNIS COSTUME - STRIPED SHIRT- BLOUSE - NAVY SERGE SKIRT - BLACK BELT & TIE - BLACK CANVAS SHOES - STRAW HAT - STRIPED RIBBON

1885-90 - BLUE SERGE BATHING COSTUME WITH WHITE LACE & BRAID TRIMMING - WHITE SASH - WHITE CAP - BLACK SHOES & RIBBONS

Little **jewellery** was worn in the day-time except **rings**—which were narrower and daintier in setting now—**fob watches,** and **hat-pins** in the larger hats. However, for evening wear, **necklaces** were indispensable, of pearls, or black velvet ribbon or gold chain with **locket** or **cameo,** or jewelled styles. Deep-collar versions were in demand, with several rows of pearls. **Bracelets** were also seen, of chain or band type. **Brooches** ornamented the evening corsage and were now smaller and more delicate in design.

LATE VICTORIAN
1880-1901

BLACK SILK TOP HAT - WHITE COLLAR - KNOTTED TIE - 1890-5

COARSE CREAM STRAW HAT WITH GOLD VELVET RIBBON - 1887

GREY CHIP STRAW BONNET - GREY STRIPED RIBBON - GREY LACE & PLUMES c. 1883

BLACK & CREAM LACE BONNET - PALE BLUE & BLACK VELVET RIBBONS - BLACK PLUME - 1896

BLACK SILK SLIPPER - RIBBON EDGE & BOW - BLACK BEAD DECORATION - 1890

BLACK LEATHER BOOT 1880's

c.1880

CARRIAGE PARASOL IN PALE BLUE SILK WITH WHITE EMBROIDERY - WHITE PAINTED WOOD HANDLE -

GREEN SILK c.1890 PARASOL - WALKING LENGTH - GREEN FRINGING

GREY FELT HAT - TRILBY SHAPE - BLACK BAND - c.1900

RED & BLACK LEATHER SHOE - 1897

PALE GREEN SILK DAMASK SLIPPER 1890's

WHITE SATIN EVENING SLIPPER - SATIN ROSETTE - 1890's

MASCULINE SLIPPER - SNAKESKIN & BLACK LEATHER

STRAW BOATER

1890

EVENING COIFFURE WITH WHITE PLUMES, ROSES, BLACK VELVET RIBBON & CAMEO

BLUE VELVET HAT - BLACK VEIL - BLUE RIBBONS - PINK ROSES - c.1891

WHITE LACE & TULLE HAT - RED RIBBON & WHITE PLUME TRIMMING - 1897

COIFFURE - 1901

1890 BLACK VELVET HAT & VEIL - LACE & PLUME TRIMMING

TWEED CAP WITH EAR-FLAPS & PEAKS - 1885

GREY BOWLER - BLACK RIBBON - BOW TIE

BONED CORSET - SUSPENDERS - 1890-5

EVENING COIFFURE 1889

STRAW HAT - BIRD'S WING, RIBBON & FLOWER TRIMMING - VEIL

IX
THE TWENTIETH CENTURY
EDWARDIAN AND WARTIME ENGLAND 1901–1918

EDWARD VII   1901–1910
GEORGE V PART ONE   1910–1918

MASCULINE dress in the twentieth century reveals, up to the present day at least, no major alterations in style. Standardisation has set in, accelerated by mass-production tailoring, and although there are, especially prior to 1939, specific rules for correct attire on certain occasions, informality became more and more the keynote with the approach of the year 1950. Changes are seen chiefly in lapel shapes, numbers of buttons, length and width of trousers. The lead in styling for the well-dressed man is still given by London tailors.

So the predominant interest in this period, as in the remainder of the twentieth century to date, is in feminine dress. The first two decades of this century show three distinct basic styles: the Edwardian, the 1910–1914 pre-war period, and styles worn during World War I. Edwardian dress is synonymous with grace, carried out in flimsy fabrics with fussy trimming at neck and hem, on a tall full-bosomed but wasp-waisted figure. Femininity, gracious manners and behaviour indicate the Edwardian lady: the ankles are not to be seen; gloves must always be worn; the pompadour coiffure is surmounted by a sweeping hat and a garden of ornament; in short, this period represents the final appearance of the lady of leisure, with her feminine charm, graceful mien, and knowledge of her "correct" place in the world of men. By 1910, however, a few women had begun to challenge the accepted view of their status: suffragettism was under way; more women had begun to work for a living and earn independence from their men-folk; some professions were attacked and successfully entered. A reflection of this is seen in their dress: the frills and lace had gone, so also had the wasp-waisted corset, trailing gowns, and flower-garden hats. But not yet was the time of sensible yet feminine attire for working women. The years 1910–1914 show a period of transition, of a desire to throw off feminine but unsuitable clothing, but with no real knowledge of how to replace it with something better. The result is seen in the absurdities of the hobble skirt, the peg-top and lampshade skirts, and the wide-brimmed hats, whose diameter exceeded the width of the shoulders. It was finally, however, the war which established the fact that women were capable of skilled work in addition to, or instead of, domesticity, and in the same way it was the war which necessitated more practical clothing for the job. Some women wore uniform, but these were a minority, and the chief effect of the war was on civilian dress, producing a skirt above the ankle for the first time—and one of sensible width for movement—small hats, and more comfortable underwear. The girl of World War II would judge these clothes to be dowdy and frumpy,

EDWARDIAN, 1901-1910

1905 - Oyster coloured chiffon & lace blouse - blue velvet bows - grey serge gored skirt - black leather belt & buckle

1901-2 - Grey woollen coat with squirrel fur trimming - black belt - lace blouse - black umbrella - black velvet toque - scarlet ribbons - veil - gloves

1903-5 - Evening dress of cream satin, decorated by coloured ribbon embroidery & lacework on bodice & skirt, over pink slip - lace neck-edge - white, pleated chiffon sleeves with coloured ribbon edges - flowers & aigrette in hair

1907 - Evening dress - black tail coat & trousers - black silk lapels & braid side sleeves - white satin waistcoat - white shirt collar & tie - black patent leather slippers & ribbon - black socks - black silk top hat - white gloves

but they were the beginning of the revolution in dress, which accompanied the social and economic emancipation.

The **lounge suit** was now established for everyday masculine wear. It was cut rather looser than in the nineties, single- or double-breasted, and turn-ups and creases were more common, although **trousers** were still narrow. Plain, striped, and herring-bone materials were worn in tweed or worsted. Colours were more varied, although still conservative; shades of brown, grey, and navy were usual (see p. 257). The **Norfolk jacket** of tweed, worn with **knickerbockers** or trousers, retained its popularity for sports- and country-wear.

Formal day dress was provided by the **cutaway coat** of black broadcloth or worsted, with grey-striped, uncuffed **trousers,** grey **waistcoat,** black socks and boots, and black silk **top hat.** It had now evolved into almost a duplicate of our present-day morning dress. Grey **gloves** and **spats** completed the outfit. An alternative formal coat for older and professional men was the **frock coat,** which remained in favour, worn with the same accessories. The lapels were usually silk-faced (see p. 254). Formal **evening dress** was unaltered except for the white waistcoat which now accompanied "tails" (see p. 250).

The short, abbreviated **overcoats** of the nineties were out of fashion now, otherwise styles were almost unchanged. The **Chesterfield** was kept for dress wear, while tweed-patterned and plain coats were worn for every day. The loose, single-breasted style, reaching to mid-calf and having large hip-pockets, was favoured (see p. 252). Velvet and fur collars were seen on heavy winter styles, and the **Inverness** was still in use for travelling. Raglan or inset sleeves were seen on all coats.

Boots were still worn by most men in preference to shoes, in brown or black leather, buttoned or laced (see p. 261). **Spats** in fawn, white, and grey were still used. **Socks** were black, although young men had begun to adopt coloured-patterned ones.

By 1914–1915, knitted V-necked **pullovers** and cardigans had begun to replace the waistcoat for informal wear; their popularity was increasing steadily.

The masculine **coiffure** was, by 1910, almost as it is today, with the parting and length dependent upon individual choice. **Moustaches** were still in vogue, especially the large bushy variety.

The **bowler hat** and felt hats of **trilby** shape were the most popular form of headgear (see pp. 252, 257, and 261), while **straw boater** styles were still fashionable in summer (see p. 261). Peaked **caps** of tweed were worn by many (see (p. 261). The black silk or grey beaver **top hat** was now reserved for formal dress wear (see pp. 250 and 254).

Collars were high until the war, when lower styles returned. White stiff ones accompanied formal attire in wing or upright shapes, but the turned-down softer one was more favoured with informal dress. White soft cotton **shirts,** with stiff collar and cuffs, were most usual still, although the coloured striped shirts, with collar to match, were seen more often now. Stiff-fronted white shirts accompanied evening dress. Knotted or bow **ties** were equally popular, in all colours for informal wear and black with formal dress. A white bow tie was correct with evening "tails", and black with a dinner jacket.

It will be remembered that in the descriptions, in Chapter VIII, of the gowns of the nineties, a narrow corset, chiefly confining the waist, produced the

EDWARDIAN, 1901-1910

1908-9. BROWN HERRINGBONE TWEED INFORMAL OVERCOAT - DARK BROWN STRIPED WORSTED TROUSERS - BROWN LEATHER BOOTS - BROWN FELT BOWLER & RIBBON - LIGHT COLOURED GLOVES - CANE - SPOTTED SILK TIE

1907-8. TENNIS COSTUME - WHITE SILK BLOUSE - BLACK TIE - WHITE BELT - METAL BUCKLE - WHITE LINEN SKIRT & CANVAS SHOES

1906-7. GREY-GREEN COSTUME WITH GREEN BRAID & BUTTON TRIMMING. WHITE COLLAR & CUFFS. FAWN FELT HAT - DARK BROWN OSTRICH PLUMES & HANDBAG - FAWN GLOVES - LACE BLOUSE

1905. MAUVE POPLIN AFTERNOON DRESS, COMPRISING BOLERO JACKET & SKIRT, TRIMMED WITH CREAM LACE APPLIQUE WORK & EDGING - TUCKING & PLEATING - WHITE LACE BLOUSE, CUFFS & RUFFLES. NATURAL STRAW HAT WITH MAUVE RIBBONS & FLOWERS. CREAM PARASOL & GLOVES

wasp-waist and hour-glass silhouette of the gown. Edwardian dress was equally noted for its wasp-waistedness, but owing to the introduction of a new **corset** in 1901–1902, the silhouette became rather different from that of the nineties. The new corset confined the waist even more than before, if possible, but, in addition, it flattened the abdomen, left the breasts free, and gave that S-bend silhouette so typical of the time. To carry this figure well, a woman required a good carriage, and ample bosom and hips; the corset did the rest. It had two vertical centre strips of whalebone in front, which tilted the body back at the hips; suspenders were attached to the bottom edge, and hip and bosom pads were added where nature defaulted (see p. 261). By 1907–1908, the wasp-waist was less acute; corsets were straighter and the S-bend had gone. By the end of Edward VII's reign, the extremely long corsets had come in, reaching from just below the breasts nearly to the knees, in a straight pencil silhouette, flattening hips and waist alike. This soon shortened—it was so impracticable for sitting down—and by 1914 the corset reached to the hips only. A straight outline was then preferred and an endeavour was made to slim the hips—an innovation indeed! No attempt was made at this time to accentuate the breasts —the full-bosomed Edwardian lady had vanished—a band type of **brassière** was worn, chiefly to hold and flatten the breasts, with a resultant fairly straight figure. Corsets were still boned, although much less heavily than Edwardian or Victorian ones (see p. 261); they were made of satin and/or tricot elastic. A factor which was effective in the movement towards the abandonment of heavily-boned corsets, at least by young girls, was the impossibility of performing the hectic dances of the time while so attired.

The **day gown** styles were inherently dependent on these variations in corsetry, as can be seen in the illustrations. The **Edwardian gown** was confined at its wasp-waist by a sash or belt. The **skirt** then fitted fairly closely on the padded hips, but flared out fully below the knees. Pleats and gores were still very fashionable, held in place by horizontal tapes, sewn to the inside as far as the knees. Gown skirts were extremely long, with a train at the rear; even walking gowns swept the ground. Much ornamentation was added to the hem edge— ruffles, fur, velvet or braid bands, lace, pleating, and tucks. The gown hung straight in front, vertically from the waist; the chief fullness was always at the back. Knowledge of the art of holding up the skirt gracefully to display just the correct amount of ruffled petticoat was necessary. Skirts were lined, preferably with taffeta to give the rustle, and rows of ruffles were sewn inside the hem to produce the required sweep to the hem. The **neck-line** was always very high, finished by a lace ruffle under the ears and chin, and supported at the sides by inserted vertical whalebone strips. The **corsage** was fussily trimmed by a jabot and/or bows and lace ruffles. The front of the **bodice** was loose, draped over the sash to accentuate the contrast between full bosom and tiny waist. Many gowns were made with a long-sleeved bolero or **jacket** to the waist, worn over a lace **blouse. Sleeves** were either long and fitting or of fuller, bishop style. Three-quarter sleeves were popular after 1904–1905, showing a full under-sleeve with tight cuff (see pp. 250 and 252).

By 1910, the **day gowns** had altered completely. The **neck-line** was descending, to uncover the throat by 1912, and becoming low V- or U-shapes by 1914. Roll or wide collars were worn, or merely a frilled edge. The **waist-line,** which

1901-1918

1910-11 - FORMAL DAY
DRESS - BLACK FROCK COAT-
SILK FACED LAPELS - GREY
& BLACK STRIPED
TROUSERS - WHITE PIQUÉ
WAISTCOAT - WHITE COLLAR-
BLACK TIE - PIN - GREY
SPATS WHITE GLOVES-
CANE - BLACK SILK
TOP HAT

1913- ROYAL BLUE SILK TUNIC
DRESS, WITH LOOSE KIMONO
BODICE & PEG-TOP SKIRT-
PINK LACE BLOUSE - CERISE
BELT & HAT RIBBON - PINK FELT
HAT - NAVY POM-POM - GLOVES-
SILK HANDBAG - BLACK
VELVET LACED BOOTS

1910-11- CRUSHED
STRAWBERRY COLOURED
SATIN EVENING GOWN -
PINK SATIN BOW ROSETTE-
SILVER & MAUVE
EMBROIDERED BANDS-
WHITE KID GLOVES -
PEARL & JEWELLED
NECKLACE -
BRACELETS - AIGRETTE
IN HAIR

EDWARDIAN BATHING
COSTUME OF CREAM
COLOURED COTTON WITH
GREEN & RED CHECKS -
BLACK BRAID EDGING & GIRDLE-
WHITE STOCKINGS & SHOES -
BLACK ROSETTES &
LACES - GREEN CAP
WITH WHITE BOW

had become more natural in size, began to rise, and from 1909 to 1911 was almost up to the breasts in imitation of Grecian and Empire modes. It descended again after this, but not to the natural waist-line until after 1914. Full kimono types of **sleeve** were in vogue from 1910, cut in one with the bodice, and giving a full draped waist. The length of sleeve varied from very short to wrist-length. During the war a full three-quarter- or full-length sleeve was predominant. The most striking and frequent changes were seen in the **skirt:** trains had begun to disappear by 1908–1909, and the skirt just cleared the ground, becoming shorter by 1910, so that the toes were displayed. As skirts became shorter they also became narrower: by 1910 they were very slender, especially at the ankles, with the appearance in 1910–1912 of the *hobble skirt*—a suitable term for the action achieved when walking was attempted since the circumference at the ankles, where a ribbon bow was often tied, was barely a yard. This impracticable style soon gave way to others, the *peg-top skirt* being the chief of these. In this model the material was draped fully at the hips, falling to a tighter skirt at the ankles, where it was usually slit in front to permit a reasonable stride. *Tunic skirts* were also popular, with one or more tunic layers, often in conjunction with a peg-top under-skirt. Many absurd variations were worn, in several puffs or layers, sometimes wired to stand out from the body (see pp. 254 and 257). More practical skirts came in with the war. Until 1916 they remained fairly narrow in tunic styles, but with much simpler and straighter cut (see p. 259). In 1916, very full, flared, but rather shorter skirts were worn; they were some eight to ten inches from the ground. In 1917 and 1918 somewhat narrower styles returned, and the tunic patterns began to fall out of favour.

Evening dresses adhered faithfully to day gown styles, but were carried to greater excesses in the pre-war period. The Edwardian **neck-line** was *décolleté*, round, or square, often off the shoulders, and edged with lace ruffles (see p. 250). Higher square or round neck-lines were fashionable by 1908, and lasted until the war (see p. 254) when a lower *décolletage* reappeared with a round shape or in almost a horizontal line, and with shoulder-strap supports. Elbow-length puff **sleeves,** or a shoulder frill, were usual with Edwardian styles (see p. 250), and small puff sleeves in the pseudo-Greek period (see p. 254). During the war, sleeves were very small, or non-existent. In the Edwardian evening gown the S-bend was apparent, with a tiny waist encircled by a sash, and a full **skirt** with flaring wide hem and train. A great deal of ornamentation was added in the form of lace or silk ruffles, pleating and bows (see p. 250). After 1909, the train became farcical, being merely a narrow tail, often false, hanging as a separate panel from the waist at the back. From 1910 to 1914, skirts included the whole gamut of peg-top, pseudo-Grecian tunic, lampshade, and hobble styles, each carried to even greater absurdities than in the day wear (see p. 254). Simpler modes prevailed during the war, ankle-length and fairly full, flaring out to the hem.

As in the nineties, lace was *the* **material** of Edwardian days with the addition, for day wear, of velveteen, velvet, silk, organdie, gauze, muslin, linen, gingham, net, serge, alpaca, cashmere, and satin. By 1909–1910, crêpe-de-chine, chiffon, and georgette were added, with taffeta later. During the war, stockinet and gabardine were also popular. For evening wear, lace was predominant until 1907, but taffeta, silk, satin, velvet, and crêpe-de-chine were favoured during the whole period. Tasteful, quiet **colours** represented Edwardianism, in greys, browns, black, navy, and white, with brighter colours for decoration. White and pastel shades remained in vogue for evening. In conjunction with the absurd skirts of the pre-war period, gay colours came in fashion, particularly cerise, orange, yellow, bright blue, and green, but more subdued shades returned with the sobering influence of the war with its perpetual khaki. Lace was the primary **trimming** until 1911–1912, also braid, tucking, fur, and velvet. Coloured embroideries were in vogue after this in borders and all-over patterns, also coloured ribbons and buttons. Fur was the chief war-time trimming in bands and on accessories.

Suits and costumes, or a **blouse** worn with a separate **skirt** were common wear in this period; their popularity was increasing. The Edwardian suit was severely tailored, had a long three-quarter-length coat, very waisted, and a full, long skirt sweeping the ground. The coat had collar, revers, cuffs, and pockets, usually braid and button trimmed (see p. 252). Short-waisted suits were prevalent 1910–1915, with short jackets and tight or peg-top skirts. During the war, the short jackets prevailed, but the skirts followed the lines of the gowns (see p. 257). The Edwardian blouse was of lace or lace-trimmed silk or chiffon, with very high neck, full long sleeves, a yoke, and fussy corsage (see pp. 250 and 252). Simpler V-necked blouses, with or without collar, followed these (see pp. 254 and 257). More severe shirt blouses, with collar and tie, were worn all the period for sport or business (see pp. 252 and 259).

Outdoor **coats** were fitting in Edwardian times, with long revers to the belted waist. Sleeves were long and wide. The length of the coat varied from three-quarter to the ground (see p. 250). Looser, high-collared styles to cover the dress were popular during the war (see p. 257). Short **jackets** were in favour all the period, also three-quarter- or waist-length **capes** and coats (see p. 259). Cloth, serge, wool, and tweed with fur trimming were used for winter coats. Fur coats, jackets, and capes were more in demand, also fur linings to cloth coats. Most popular furs were squirrel, seal, astrakhan, beaver, chinchilla, and sable, but some of these were highly expensive, even in those days. **Evening cloaks** and **coats** were of velvet or brocade with fur trimming.

Sports-wear was becoming more practical: the skirt was a little shorter in Edwardian days, whilst later the hem rose to accord with that of the day skirt; the peg-top and other varieties were ignored as impracticable for active exercise. For **tennis,** hats were abandoned by 1908, and the costume was all white from then onwards, although stockings continued to be worn (see p. 252). A calf-length navy skirt was usual for other **games,** and a knee-length style with knickerbockers for **gymnastics. Bathing costumes** were still highly unsuitable: they included stockings and a knee-length dress with short sleeves, worn over knee-length full knickerbockers. Various colours and materials had been introduced by now, either plain or in checks, stripes and floral designs. Shoes, laced up the leg, and a cap completed the outfit (see p. 254). Sports costumes were becoming so much a part of a lady's wardrobe that they were included in fashion journals from Edwardian times.

Several layers of **underwear** were still worn in Edward VII's reign: a vest or **chemise,** the **corset,** a white, stiff **corset cover,** white **drawers, flannel petticoat,** and then one or two white muslin **petticoats** with flounces at the hem were

1914-1918

1916 - COSTUME OF BROWN SERGE - BLACK VELVET & STITCHED TRIMMING - FELT HAT IN BROWN & RED - FEATHER - GLOVES - FUR MUFF - WHITE BLOUSE - GAITERS - BLACK SHOES

1914 - GREY STRIPED MIXTURE LOUNGE SUIT - GREY TRILBY HAT - BLACK RIBBON - STRIPED TIE - WHITE COLLAR - BLACK PATENT LEATHER BOOTS - CLOTH TOPS - LEATHER GLOVES - CANE

1917 - BEIGE WOOLLEN WINTER COAT WITH COLLAR, CUFFS & HEM EDGING OF SKUNK - BLACK FUR & BEIGE FELT HAT - BLACK UMBRELLA - GLOVES - FAWN GABARDINE TOPPED BLACK LACED BOOTS

1914 - CERISE & WHITE STRIPED AFTERNOON GOWN WITH BLUE VELVET JACKET LINED WITH THE STRIPED MATERIAL - DOUBLE TIERED TUNIC SKIRT & PEG-TOP UNDERSKIRT - WHITE SILK BLOUSE - STRIPED COLLAR - CERISE BOW - WHITE STOCKINGS - BLACK PATENT LEATHER SHOES - BLACK UMBRELLA - LEATHER HANDBAG - BLUE VELVET HAT - BLACK & WHITE PLUME - GLOVES

usual, and finally a coloured taffeta petticoat with rows of flounces from knee to hem to give the desired rustle, and to hold out the hem of the gown. With the narrow skirts, the number of petticoats decreased and the hem ruffles vanished. By the end of the period, underwear was in pastel shades of silk or satin with lace edging; the drawers had become shorter knickers, and the petticoats were reduced to one or two straight slips.

The loose, swept-up, pompadour style was the prevailing type of **coiffure** until 1910, worn over a pad in front, and fastened in a coil of plaits on the crown. Combs were worn at the back. False curls were still used where necessary (see pp. 250, 252, and 261). A more complicated style was typical of 1910–1913; it was not as high, but was more varied in its method of dressing the waves, curls, and plaits (see pp. 254 and 261). After 1913, the coiffure was simple, with a centre or high side parting, and the hair waved loosely back, covering the ears, to a bun at the nape (see p. 261). Bobbed hair began to appear by 1918, but had a limited following as yet. Before the war **evening coiffures** were more elaborate than those of the day-time, being ornamented by aigrettes, flowers, jewelled combs, and ribbon bows (see pp. 250 and 254). During the war, combs were usually the sole decoration.

Considerable variety existed in the **hats** of this period. Until about 1907–1908, the majority of styles had fairly wide, sweeping brims, often partially turned up, and shallow crowns. From about 1903 to 1906, the hat with a brim which projected some distance in front, but which was turned up at the back, was in vogue. Straw was in great demand, also felt, velvet, and silk, with trimmings of flowers, ribbons, and ostrich plumes. Face veils were considered *à la mode*. Alternative styles were also worn, in particular sailor straw hats and toques of feathers, velvet, fur, or beaver (see pp. 250, 252, and 261). By 1907, the crown rose higher and the brim was still large, though now turned down all round. Trimming was profuse—a veritable garden surmounted the crown (see p. 261). After 1909 the brim diameter grew steadily until 1911, when it was greater than the shoulder width. Worn in conjunction with the narrow skirts, these hats gave the wearer a top-heavy appearance. To add to this illusion, abundant trimming, especially large ostrich plumes, decorated the hat (see p. 261). Very large, dangerous hat-pins secured these creations, often creating a menace in a bus or to passing crowds. By 1912 smaller hats returned, whilst during the war they were chiefly of a turban or fitting style, worn on the forehead, or fitting well down over the ears. Trimming was sparse, mainly confined to a single tall plume. Various materials were used, principally velvet, beaver, and fur. Veils had almost gone out of fashion (see pp. 254, 257, 259, and 261).

Boots were still preferred to shoes for outdoor wear by most ladies. Styles were higher than hitherto, often reaching to mid-calf by 1910; buttons or laces were employed, on leather, suède, or velvet. Gabardine, kid, or suède tops, in light colours, were very popular, especially during the war. Heels were fairly high and curved, and toes were pointed (see pp. 254, 257, 259, and 261). The fashion for wearing light-coloured cloth **gaiters,** buttoned down the outside, over the leather shoes, was becoming more popular (see p. 257). **Shoes** were fastened by an instep strap and had fairly low fronts; court styles were also seen (see pp. 257 and 261). **Dress** and **evening shoes** and slippers were in bronze, black and white kid, or satin, to match the gown. **Stockings** either matched

1914-1918

A MEMBER OF THE W.R.A.F.
(WOMEN'S ROYAL AIR
FORCE) · 1918

SERGEANT OF THE
BRITISH ARMY IN
UNIFORM OF WORLD
WAR I · KHAKI
UNIFORM · BLACK
BOOTS

POSTWOMAN OF WORLD
WAR I · NAVY BLUE
TO BLACK UNIFORM ·
WHITE SHIRT BLOUSE ·
BLACK TIE · BLACK
LEATHER BOOTS &
BLACK STOCKINGS ·
DARK WOOLLEN
GLOVES

1915 · FUR CAPE WITH
SLEEVES · LINED WITH
LIGHTER FUR · GOLDEN
BROWN VELVET TUNIC
DRESS · BLACK FUR EDGING ·
PLAID & VELVET HAT &
FEATHER · GLOVES ·
BLACK PATENT LEATHER
BOOTS WITH GABARDINE
TOPS · LACES

259

the dress or were black, grey, or white, in lisle or cotton. Silk was still a luxury.

Woollen **pullovers** and **cardigans** were worn for sport, in gay colours.

Nightdresses were still decorous in Edwardian times, of white material decorated by lace and embroidery, with long sleeves and high neck. After this, however, short sleeves came in and, during the war, lower, square or round necks.

Masculine **accessories** constituted chiefly a **cane** or **umbrella,** a **monocle,** and for smokers, a **pipe** or **cigarette case.** **Gloves** were essential to the well-dressed man: both these and **handkerchiefs** were virtually of the same type as those of today. Ladies still carried a **parasol** or **umbrella,** according to the season: the former was most popular in the Edwardian era, of walking length and trimmed with bows and lace (see p. 252); the latter was walking length all the period, with a dark silk cover (see p. 250); by 1914, thin pencil styles were in vogue, though still of the same length (see p. 257). **Handbags** were becoming more essential, particularly after 1912–1914, when a lady required to carry a comb, mirror, purse, etc. Designs varied considerably, but, broadly speaking, small bead, chain, or velvet types with metal mounts were usual in Edwardian days, and much larger ones later, of leather, tapestry, or suède, in gay colours and embroidered in coloured wool or silk (see pp. 252, 254, and 257). Day **gloves** were wrist-length, except after 1912–1913, when elbow-length styles often accompanied short-sleeved dresses. Kid, leather, or silk were used, in light colours. Long white kid gloves continued to be worn for evening, when a **fan** was still carried, at least until the war, and **flowers** were worn in the corsage. In the pseudo-Greek revival period an accompaniment to evening dress was a gaily-coloured chiffon, wool, or lace **scarf,** with fringe or bead edging, lightly tossed round the head or shoulders. For winter day wear, fur accessories were popular—**muffs, boas, scarves,** and **stoles** (see p. 257). **Feather boas** of ostrich plumes were revived in Edwardian days.

Cosmetics were still used sparingly and in private: they were usually limited to powder, preferably in leaflet form, and, during the war, a touch of rouge.

Men wore little **jewellery:** it took the form of jewelled, gold **tie-pins,** signet **rings,** and **watches,** either fob or on a gold chain: wrist-watches appeared during the war. Ladies also wore fob **watches,** pinned to the lapel or waist-belt, followed later by wrist-watches. Their other forms of jewellery were **bracelets, rings, ear-rings,** and **necklaces;** the latter were of dog-collar type, especially of pearls until 1910, when long bead necklaces became more popular. Jewelled combs were worn in Edwardian hair-styles.

BETWEEN THE WARS 1918–1939

GEORGE V PART TWO	1918–1936
EDWARD VIII	1936
GEORGE VI PART ONE	1936–1939

The trend in masculine clothing during this period was still towards greater informality, comfort, and standardisation. The **lounge suit,** single- or double-breasted, remained as it is today, the most usual wear; it altered only in the

1901-1918

1904 STRAW HAT TRIMMED WITH VELVET RIBBONS & DARK OSTRICH PLUMES

1915 BLACK BOW TIE - WHITE COLLAR

1903 - CREAM STRAW HAT WITH FLOWERS & RIBBONS

1917

1909 - DARK STRAW HAT TRIMMED WITH WHITE ROSES & RIBBONS

FAWN FELT HAT - BLACK BAND - BLACK TIE -

BLACK VELVET BOOT WITH BLACK BRAID STRAP EDGING & BUTTONS 1910

1912

LIGHT BROWN LEATHER SHOE

BLACK LEATHER BOOT 1909

1916

1916

FAWN SUÈDE LACED BOOT - BLACK LEATHER TOE & HEEL

CREAM STRAW HAT - 1916 - WHITE OSTRICH FEATHERS - BLACK RIBBON EDGE - SPOTTED VEIL 1912

CORSET 1903-4

1911

BLACK FELT BOWLER - WHITE STIFF COLLAR - BLACK TIE 1915-16

TWEED CAP - 1910

STRAW HAT 1914-16

BRITISH ARMY OFFICER 1918

VELVET HAT & PLUME 1915

1905 - CERISE FELT HAT - WHITE FEATHERS

STRAW BOATER WITH VEIL, RIBBON & FEATHER - 1902

increased width of trousers, addition of waist tucks and side buttonings when it was desired to avoid braces, a longer coat and lapels, and handstitched edges (see p. 263). The suit was generally of one material, although a black or dark jacket worn with grey-striped trousers and black waistcoat was retained for more formal wear. By 1925 the appearance of "*Oxford bags*" set the fashion for wider trousers, also **flannel trousers**, to be worn with a **sports jacket,** for informal occasions. Towards 1939, other types of material and colours were used for trousers, still worn with a sports jacket of contrasting fabric. **Pullovers** became the usual wear with informal dress, replacing the waistcoat; various patterns in gay colours, originally based on Fair Isle designs, became the vogue. *Plus fours* with jacket to match evolved from the Norfolk jacket and knicker-bockers, and were the rage of the twenties; a tweed cap, woollen socks, and shoes completed the outfit (see p. 265).

Formal wear was unaltered except for lapel shapes and width of trousers. The black **morning coat** and waistcoat, grey-striped trousers, black top hat, black socks and shoes, grey spats and gloves, black tie, white shirt and collar, and black rolled umbrella still represented formal day dress, and can be seen illustrated on p. 278. **Evening dress "tails"** and **dinner jacket** can be seen in this chapter on pp. 267, 271, and 275.

Raincoats, mackintoshes, and **overcoats** existed in many styles as they are today: they were single- or double-breasted, belted or loose, with side-slit and patch pockets, revers or just a collar, raglan or inset sleeves, and with or without a yoke. Most styles were worn rather shorter than those of today (see p. 271).

For holiday and informal wear, the coloured sports **shirt** with attached soft collar was becoming more prevalent. Aertex, silk, rayon, and other fabrics were in use, as well as cotton. **Ties** were now becoming louder and gayer, although more sober versions could still be bought in England.

Far fewer men wore a **hat** in the thirties, but the **bowler, felt trilby,** and **homburg** styles were still the vogue for those who did, while the **top hat** was reserved for evening or morning dress (see pp. 263, 271, and 273).

Socks were also in gayer colours and patterns. **Shoes** had largely replaced boots, especially by the thirties; crêpe and rubber soles appeared before the war. Black patent leather shoes were worn with evening dress.

Bathing costumes became scantier: the sides were cut out and finally, before the war, trunks became the favourite style. Accessories were more or less unaltered.

Masculine underwear was also becoming briefer, especially for younger men. Short elastic-topped pants and sleeveless vests or singlets in interlock or rayon were adopted by the end of the period.

In writing this book, the author has made every endeavour to present the succeeding fashions through the ages as dispassionately and in as unbiased a manner as possible, without undue personal comment. However, it is impossible for a woman to describe the feminine modes of this period, especially those of the twenties, without expressing some vestige of horror at the supreme ugliness to which women submitted themselves at this time. Although the writer does not believe that the feminine sex is alone in its slavish following of fashion changes, the fact cannot be denied that women of all figures and

1918-1939

1922 - SUMMER DRESS OF PINK VOILE WITH EMBROIDERED APPLE DESIGN IN RED, YELLOW & GREEN - PEARL BUTTONS & HEM-STITCHED DECORATION - LOW WAIST-LINE - WHITE MUSLIN PETTICOAT - WHITE SUÈDE GLOVES. WHITE STOCKINGS - BROWN SUÈDE SHOES -BUCKLES- EMBROIDERED HANDBAG - PINK SILK HAT WITH BROWN VELVET RIBBONS & RUCHING

1920-1 - GREY-BLUE GABARDINE SUIT - PALE SILK STRIPED BLOUSE - NAVY STRAW HAT & RIBBONS - FLOWERS - GLOVES - LEATHER HANDBAG - BLACK UMBRELLA & STOCKINGS - BLACK PATENT LEATHER SHOES - METAL BUCKLES.

1926 - NAVY STRIPED, WORSTED, DOUBLE-BREASTED LOUNGE SUIT - WHITE SHIRT & COLLAR - STRIPED TIE - BLACK BOWLER - BLACK LEATHER SHOES - CANE - FAWN GLOVES

1925 - BLACK WOOL COAT WITH GREY FUR TRIMMING - CERISE FELT HAT - BLACK SATIN BOW - BLACK PATENT LEATHER SHOES - FLESH -COLOURED STOCKINGS - GLOVES - UMBRELLA.

ages entered into the anti-femininity campaign of 1920 onwards with zest and interest, as those now over thirty-five can clearly remember. In retrospect, it is now plain to us that these styles were a reaction from Victorianism and Edwardianism, in the same way as was the social behaviour of the twenties; with that reaction was inextricably bound up the new-found freedom of women in the economic field. The desire to throw off unsuitable hampering clothes was paramount, and with this came an equal wish to hide those attributes of femininity—the breasts, sloping shoulders, tiny waist, ample hips, and abundant flowing locks of Victorianism. For nearly ten years women hid these assets to their sex in an endeavour to emulate masculinity and, to assert their new so-called sex freedom, exposed their legs instead. The result of this in dress was seen in a combination of styles which was new in costume, and, the writer fervently hopes, will never be seen again. The chief attributes were an absence of waist, a tubular silhouette, a mock waist on the hips, skirts rising to the knees, short straight hair, cloche hats, and pointed patent leather shoes. The fox fur came into its own to relieve the severity of the tubular suit; the evening dress became a mockery in its emulation of those of the day-time; silk, flesh-coloured stockings became the vogue to enhance the now visible legs. The corset was abandoned; the breasts were flattened.

The thirties were an improvement, with a return to the normal waist-line and a lowering of the hem, longer, curlier hair, and more attractive hats, but the straight silhouette remained with no accentuation of the breasts, waist, or hips. Femininity was slowly returning, in company with practical clothes, but not until after World War II did it receive any notable impetus.

The wardrobe of the average woman was now so specialised, with clothes for different occasions, that space does not permit a full description of all of them, so an attempt will be made to depict the principal features of each successive change. The **hem-line** was perhaps the subject of most variation: in 1918 the **skirt** was some six to eight inches from the ground, often with an uneven hem-line caused by floating top panels attached from the waist; the skirt was still fairly full. By 1921 ankle-length styles had returned, but after 1922 the hem-line steadily rose, reaching a climax with the knee-length, or even shorter, skirts of 1927. As the skirt was shortened it was also made narrower and straighter, so that it was like a tube by 1925. Efforts were made by designers after 1927 to lower the hem-line by reintroducing longer panels of drapery on top of the skirt, but no permanent effect was seen until after 1929, when the actual hem-line began to descend once more. Once the idea of a lower hem had begun, it gained impetus, so by 1931 skirts were quite long again, and, with small fluctuations, remained covering mid-calf until 1938–1939, when they began to rise once more. With the skirts of the thirties came an endeavour to slim the hips as much as possible, and the material was cut on the cross and in panels to ensure a fit over the hips, with pleats or gores from the knee. Fuller skirts, usually gored, were in fashion by 1939, but were still fitting on the hips.

The natural **waist-line** had vanished by 1921–1922 and did not reappear until 1930. The bodice was loose and tubular, ignoring the waist and ending in a band or belt low on the hips by 1923–1924, and remaining there until 1929–1930, when it began to rise to the normal position. From 1930 to 1931 onwards, the waist was normal in size and position, and usually marked by a belt or sash.

1918-1939

1926 - PRINTED CHIFFON
AFTERNOON DRESS IN SHADES
OF PINK - BLACK SATIN
BOW, COLLAR, CUFFS &
HEM - BLACK SILK HAT -
RED VELVET RIBBON -
EMBROIDERED HANDBAG.
FLESH-COLOURED
STOCKINGS - BLACK
PATENT LEATHER
SHOES

1926 - MUSTARD YELLOW
WOOLLEN SUIT WITH
YELLOW-GREEN COLLAR,
CUFFS & BELT - PLEATED
SKIRT - YELLOW-GREEN
FELT CLOCHE HAT -
BLACK FUR - FLESH
-COLOURED STOCKINGS -
BLACK SHOES -
GLOVES

1928-9 - BLACK LACE
DINNER GOWN WITH
BLACK CRÊPE DE CHINE
LINING - FLESH-COLOURED
GEORGETTE TOP &
STOCKINGS - SILVER
SHOES - PEARL NECK-
-LACE - SILVER
BRACELETS

1930 - BROWN
HERRINGBONE
TWEED PLUS FOURS
& JACKET - DARK
GREEN WOOLLEN
PULLOVER & SOCKS -
COLOURED TOPS -
BROWN TWEED
CAP - BROWN
LEATHER SHOES -
BROWN STRIPED
SHIRT - DARK
TIE

Neck-lines were plain and unadorned in the twenties, very low in V or round shapes or with an alternative round, nearly off-the-shoulder type. Higher necks returned in the thirties in varied but fussy styles. The cowl version was predominant, also V-necks with revers and collar, and square or round shapes.

Sleeveless dresses were popular in the mid-twenties, alternatively short or long inset-fitting sleeves or magyar ones. Fussy **sleeves** were typical of the thirties in bishop or leg-of-mutton designs with inset gatherings and puffs. Straighter, simple styles prevailed by 1939. Padded shoulders to tailored dresses were increasingly prevalent from 1935. Examples of day dresses can be seen in the illustrations on pp. 263, 265, 267, and 271.

Until 1930 **evening gowns** closely resembled those of the day: the hem-line was the same, and a marked preference was shown for the longer side and back panels of 1928 and 1929; low, round, or V neck-lines were worn, plain and unornamented; most gowns were sleeveless (see p. 265). By 1930 the new idea of a different hem-line for evening wear was established, and ground or ankle-length evening gowns were worn. Skirts were cut on the cross as in day clothes, often flaring out in inset gores from below the knee. Alternative styles in the later thirties were a full-flared skirt from the waist or one with a draped classical line. Another innovation of the thirties was the **backless evening gown,** beginning with a modest V-shape at the back, but expanding into various designs of straps and panels by 1934. Strapless styles followed with boned bodices to defy the force of gravity, and off-the-shoulder modes with draped *décolletage* were typical of 1938–1939. Backless gowns were perforce sleeveless, but puff or small sleeves were retained in less sophisticated gowns for younger ladies (see pp. 267 and 271).

The ideal figure of the twenties was a slim, flat one. To achieve this aim, slimming became a fashion: exercise, diet, and patent medicines were the resort of the amply built. The **corset**—that controller of the fashionable figure of the past—had gone, and most women wore an elastic or satin belt which covered the hips only, or, if the wearer had too large a bosom for the dictates of fashion, covered and flattened the body from above the breasts to the hips, and was supported by shoulder-straps. Bones were rarely used now. The belt was frequently worn next to the skin now, for the first time (see p. 273). By 1930 the separate hip **girdle** and **brassière** were more popular, although the latter was still designed to flatten the breasts instead of accentuating them. It was not until the late thirties that the "uplift brassière" became the vogue, and for the first time the idea of enhancing the individual shape of the breast was established. At this time also came the new elastic belts with a "two-way stretch", and alternative new styles of brassière and belt in one, as a **corselette.**

Underwear was scanty in the twenties in contrast to the preceding decades. Knickers, pantees, or cami-knickers and a short petticoat or slip, in pastel shades of satin or silk, were usual. Crêpe-de-chine was used later, also artificial silk.

The costume or **suit** was a useful item in the wardrobe, worn with a blouse, or, by the mid-twenties, with a jumper. **Skirts** followed the line of dresses, while the **coat** in the twenties was medium length, had long revers, and buttoned on the hip (see pp. 263 and 265). Coats were shorter in the thirties, with shorter, broader lapels, were more waisted and sometimes belted. Shoulders

1918-1939

1939 - EVENING DRESS - DINNER JACKET & TROUSERS OF BLACK WORSTED - BLACK CORDED SILK LAPELS - BRAID SIDE SEAMS - BLACK SILK TIE - WHITE WING COLLAR & PLEATED SHIRT - BLACK PATENT LEATHER SHOES

1934 - TURQUOISE GREEN CRÊPE EVENING DRESS - SILVER LAMÉ HANDBAG SILVER KID SHOES

1936 - PRINTED GEORGETTE DRESS IN BROWN, ORANGE & YELLOW - BROWN SASH - PALE GREY GLOVES & FUR - BROWN HAT - VEIL - BROWN SUÈDE HANDBAG - BROWN LEATHER SHOES - LIGHT SILK STOCKINGS

1933-5 - RUST COLOURED CLOTH COAT - GREY FUR COLLAR - HAT TO MATCH COAT - BLACK SUÈDE SHOES & HANDBAG - FAWN GLOVES

were padded to a square outline in the late thirties. Jackets and skirts of contrasting colours and materials became popular at that time. **Blouses,** till 1930, were loose and long, worn outside the skirt and pulled down to the hips; they had low V-necks, with or without a collar, and often a large bow at the corsage. In the thirties, various neck-lines were seen, usually much higher, and the blouse was much shorter and worn inside the skirt or finished with elastic at the waist. **Jumpers** and cardigans followed similar lines and increased in popularity towards 1939, when a jumper, often home-knitted, and skirt became the favourite attire for many women.

The typical outdoor **coat** of the twenties was the wrap-round style, either held in place by the hand or buttoned low on the left hip. No belt was worn on most styles and the revers were long and narrow. Large fur collars and cuffs were in vogue (see p. 263). In the thirties, sleeves followed the fussy lines of dresses, and belts reappeared; shoulders were padded later. Fur collars remained popular with dress styles, but more sporting coats with wide revers and collar provided an alternative. The coat was now much more waisted (see p. 267). **Fur coats** were in demand for those who could afford them, though with the improved means of making up cheaper furs to imitate the costly varieties, a fur coat no longer symbolised wealth, as hitherto. **Fox fur** was typical of the twenties, especially the coveted silver fox; complete furs were in the height of fashion, worn with suits and coats. By the thirties popular furs had become too numerous to chronicle. Silk and cotton **rainwear** in all colours was fashionable from the twenties.

Materials in use were by now far too numerous and varied to list adequately; only the most predominant are noted. Silk, wool, stockinet, gabardine, crêpe, velvet, cashmere, satin, chiffon and georgette were typical of day wear in the twenties, with lace, crêpe-de-chine, chiffon, and lamé for evening. Artificial silk began to assume prominence by 1929. In the thirties, cotton and piqué were revived for summer dresses, in addition to georgette, artificial silk, and crêpe-de-chine. By 1939, it was difficult to detect artificial silk or rayon from the genuine fabrics. Printed, flowered patterns were in vogue all the period, and geometrical designs returned to favour in the late thirties. Stripes, checks, and plain or self-coloured patterned fabrics retained their popularity. **Colours** were indeed varied: quiet tones followed the war, but an outbreak of cyclamen, cerise, pinks, and mauves, red, black, and soft blue reoccurred by the mid-twenties. Orange, yellow, greens, and red were preferred by 1935. Black and navy were considered smart for dresses and suits for town wear, while for evening, white, gold or silver, and black were always in fashion, in addition to other colours. Notable **trimmings** of the twenties were sequins, artificial flowers, tassels, bead embroidery, and fur.

Shorts and **slacks** had come in by 1930 for sport, cycling, hiking, and beach wear. The early shorts were narrow and masculine, but pleated, fuller styles appeared by the mid-thirties (see p. 269). Sunbathing was all the rage by that time, and **sun-suits** of brassière tops, shorts and/or button-through, **wrap-over skirts** or **divided skirts** were in vogue by 1939, made of gaily-coloured printed cotton and artificial silk (see p. 269). **Bathing costumes** gradually became more daring, from the high-necked, skirted types of the twenties to the backless styles of the thirties, which in their turn gave way, by 1939, to the two-part

1918-1939

1938 - Printed cotton sun suit with wrap-over skirt to match, hung over arm - floral pattern in reds & greens - pale green linen hat - striped ribbon - coloured canvas sandals - cork soles

1929 - White & black cotton bathing costume - green braid edging - white belt - white rubber cap

Hiking costume 1931-2 - Orange woollen jumper - dark green linen shorts - fawn woollen socks - leather shoes - black beret - stick

1927 - White tennis dress - white stockings, socks & canvas shoes - white bandeau

269

costumes of brassière top and panties. Cotton gave place to knitted wool and colours became brighter (see p. 269). The white sleeveless, shapeless **tennis dress** of the twenties was still worn with white stockings and socks (see p. 269), but bare legs and white blouse and shorts replaced them in the thirties.

The main features of **footwear** in the twenties were the pointed toes and high curved heels. Court shoes were worn for dress wear, and strap styles or laced shoes for walking. Lower-heeled walking shoes appeared by the mid-twenties. Black patent leather was in vogue, also leather or kid in brown or black, lizard-skin and suède; white buckskin was worn in summer with brown leather. In the thirties, toes were rounder and had shorter fronts, and high heels were straight. Flat and Cuban heels were worn for walking; rubber and crêpe soles appeared. Leather dyed blue, red, and green became popular. **Sandals** for summer wear became the rage by the late thirties; they were seen in many styles—backless, toe-less, and sometimes heel-less. Canvas, leather, and suède were used. **Evening slippers** and sandals were in gold, silver, or bronze kid, black silk, or brocade (see pp. 263, 265, 267, 269, 271, and 273).

With the advent of short skirts, flesh-coloured **stockings** became the fashion: more attention was paid to these items of dress than formerly, and silk and artificial silk were *à la mode*. Lisle and wool were still worn by the less fashionable. Light-coloured stockings in fawns and beige lasted throughout the period, but with the increased popularity of sunbathing, and the new styles of sandals, many girls went stockingless in summer by 1935.

Throughout the ages, long **hair** had been considered a symbol of feminine beauty: in some periods it had been covered, or even cut shorter, but it was not until the 1920s that *bobbed* hair was so universally accepted by women. Femininity had to be suppressed and independence asserted—perforce the hair must be cut. Having adopted bobbed styles and discovered the ease and comfort of maintaining them, the ladies carried the idea even further; by 1924 *shingled* hair was popular and, following this a few years later, many brave spirits indulged in an *Eton crop*. The very short styles lasted until 1929–1930, but women varied in the wholeheartedness of their support to the new idea— only the most fashionable went to extremes. These hair-styles were comfortable and easy to maintain, but were not pretty or attractive except on women who possessed beautiful features. The hair was often straight or iron waved, so the effect was masculine and severe. After 1930, a slightly longer coiffure was worn, dressed in waves on top and curls at the nape. Later in the thirties, much longer styles, dressed in various ways, were fashionable—the page-boy type, a side or centre parting, curls on the forehead or waved to curls at the nape. Permanent waving brought the up-to-date coiffures within reach of all women, who could now maintain them with a minimum of effort (see pp. 265, 267, 271, and 273).

Hats in the twenties were designed to cover the hair completely; they were pulled down over the ears to eyebrow-level until 1924–1925. The small brims of 1918 gave way in 1922–1924 to large ones again, with heavy trimming of velvet or silk bows, plumes, and flowers (see pp. 263 and 273), but by 1924–1925 the *cloche hat* in all its ugliness had come to stay until 1930. The chief feature of the cloche style was in its resemblance to a saucepan or helmet, pulled down to eye-level in front, and the nape at the back. Little decoration was added to

1918-1939

1931 - WHITE GEORGETTE EVENING DRESS WITH WINE-COLOURED LACE TRIMMING & VELVET SASH- SOFT PINK SUÈDE EVENING GLOVES - WHITE SILK HANDBAG

1937 - EVENING DRESS BLACK WORSTED TAIL COAT & TROUSERS - BRAID SIDE SEAMS - WHITE COLLAR - BLACK PATENT LEATHER SHOES

1933 DARK FAWN WATERPROOF TRENCH COAT - LEATHER BUTTONS - BROWN WORSTED STRIPED TROUSERS - BROWN FELT HAT - BROWN STRIPED SHIRT - COLOURED TIE - BROWN LEATHER SHOES

1938 - CREAM LINEN SUMMER DRESS - STRIPED BOLERO JACKET & SASH - WHITE LINEN HANDBAG - NO STOCKINGS - WHITE CANVAS SANDALS RED & BLACK HAT

relieve its severity, and these hats were made of felt, velour, or straw, with the addition of merely a ribbon, brooch, or feather. Most styles had no brim or only a small one, although large-brimmed hats were seen in summer, worn in the same way (see pp. 263, 265, and 273). Styles of the thirties were so varied that only the most notable can be listed. Most hats were flat, like a plate, with medium, large, or no brim, and worn on one side of the forehead, almost obliterating the vision of one eye. Ribbon or elastic secured the hat at the back and small veils—which had been out of fashion for a decade—returned. **Pill-box** shapes, **sailor hats,** a *Tyrolean* style, the *halo hat*, **berets,** and *Juliet caps* were all fashionable. **Chenille nets** or snoods were worn alone or attached to a hat. **Scarves** began to usurp the function of a hat by 1939, and many women went hatless except for town wear (see pp. 267, 269, 271, and 273). An increase in the use of **cosmetics** was seen after 1918. In the mid-twenties, powder, lipstick, rouge, and eye make-up were heavily employed by many women, with less artistry than abundance. Making-up in public became a vogue and the handbag contained a compact, lipstick, and comb. By the late thirties, make-up was less heavily and more accurately applied: correct shades of cosmetics were used; more attention was paid to achieving a natural effect. Public making-up was considered unladylike. Coloured nail-varnish became fashionable.

Feminine accessories were now fewer in number: the **handbag** was the most essential of these, and most designs were fairly large in order to carry cosmetics, keys, money, nail-varnish, etc. Leather and suède were the commonest materials in many patterns, of which the envelope type predominated in the twenties, and the design with an attached handle, which could be hung over the arm, in the thirties. Brocade, silk, or bead small bags accompanied evening dress, in white, black, gold, or silver (see pp. 263, 265, 267, 271, and 273). **Gloves** were still worn, of a slip-on style, with or without a gauntlet. Winter gloves were of fur, leather, suède, kid, or wool, while summer ones were made in net, lace, fabric, or silk. Short stubby **umbrellas** replaced the war-time pencil styles, and gay colours were seen as well as the old-fashioned black (see p. 273). *Zip fasteners* were in great demand by the thirties. *Sun-glasses* were worn at the sea in summer. **Jewellery** was now often artificial and of little intrinsic value, but became more varied in design, Materials such as glass, wood, and plastic made their appearance in various guises. **Rings** were narrow and dainty, in small settings. Platinum and silver **wedding-rings** were popular, as well as gold, and many had engraved designs on them. **Diamanté clips** and **brooches** were worn, especially for evening. **Bracelets** were often heavy, of the slave bangle type. Long drop **ear-rings** were typical of the twenties, but clip-on and screw-on styles, often composed of one large pearl, were more usual in the thirties. **Necklaces** were long with the short dresses, often reaching to below the waist, and knotted there; short choker styles were the reaction by 1936. By 1925 many women possessed **cigarette cases** and long cigarette holders, but the latter were rarely seen in the thirties.

1918-1939

Red woven fibre cloche hat - red plumes - 1928

Brown felt hat & ribbons - 1937

White woven fibre hat - navy ribbon & elastic - 1935

Black patent leather & lizard skin shoe - 1927

Black bowler 1933

An elastic, rubber & satin suspender belt - 1925

Embroidered & beaded silk handbag - metal mount - 1927

Leather shoe 1924

Gold kid evening shoe - 1925

Brown leather & suede shoe - 1931

Striped silk umbrella in blue, pink & white - cream handle

Blue leather walking shoe - natural leather heel - 1935

Light fawn felt hat - brown ribbon - 1934

Felt & fur cloche hat - 1927

1928

Red, tyrolean style of hat - 1936

Cream straw hat - navy ribbon & feather - cowl neckline - 1935

Felt hat - velvet bows - plumes - 1923

1922

Grey felt hat 1929

Navy velour hat - red feather - 1928

1931

Turquoise felt hat - coloured plume - ribbon edge - 1936

273

CONTEMPORARY DRESS

GEORGE VI   PART TWO   1939–1952
QUEEN ELIZABETH II   1952–

It is not proposed to describe in detail the costume of this period. For some years to come, the clothes will be sufficiently familiar to render full description superfluous; again, it is not possible to gain a true perspective of contemporary events; finally, the variety of garments for different occasions is so great that space in this book is inadequate for a full description. Summary remarks on the general trend of fashion in conjunction with the detailed illustrations are considered to present a sufficient picture.

Although the alterations in masculine attire in England are less fundamental and numerous than those in feminine dress, nevertheless, the changes which have taken place between 1939 and 1960 illustrate a definable trend. This movement is towards a greater variety in clothes for men to be worn on different occasions, employment of the newer materials and a less conservative approach to colour. Naturally, the more modern, catholic taste is shown primarily by younger men as well as by those whose income will support a larger wardrobe, which includes "desirables" as well as "essentials". Naturally also, wives and girl-friends exercise considerable background influence in this respect.

During World War II a number of innovations were introduced into **service uniforms** as compared with those worn by the earlier generation in World War I. These included the battle-dress design with, later, a collar and tie for all ranks, the forage cap and, at the end of the war, plastic buttons to replace brass ones on many uniforms (see pp. 275 and 287).

With the reversion to civilian clothes once more in 1945–6 small changes became apparent. During the fifteen years up to 1960 these are manifested in line, colour, materials and in new items of clothing. Changes in line have been very gradual but definite. **Trousers** have become narrower, especially towards the cuff; **lapels** are now cut lower and **jackets** much looser and longer. In clothes for informal occasions these points are accentuated. With regard to colour, charcoal grey, and other greys with small flecks of colour are in general use for business and professional wear, but with informal clothes, a far greater range of colour and materials are employed, especially for trousers. Here, **terylene** has made its appearance, while gabardine and cavalry twill designs have ousted the flannel trousers. **Lightweight summer suits** of linen, terylene and rayon are being bought by an increasing number of men. This is probably in direct proportion to the increase in Continental tourist travel, since the English climate does not appear to have altered. Among the newer range of designs are the **short overcoat,** the reintroduction of the **smoking jacket** (now generally referred to as a host coat), the wide variety of **woollen cardigans, pullovers** and **coats,** and the **suède, sheepskin-lined jackets. Long, heavy overcoats** are now in much smaller demand; this is thought to be largely due to the increased prevalence of the automobile. More extensive travel by this means—generally with interior heater—has largely obviated the need for the long overcoat which is cumbersome and awkward for the driver (see pp. 275, 278, 280, 282, 283, and 284).

1939-1960

SUB-LIEUTENANT ROYAL NAVY 1939-45. MIDNIGHT BLUE REEFER DOUBLE-BREASTED JACKET WITH HACKING VENTS, & TROUSERS - BRASS BUTTONS. CAP TO MATCH UNIFORM WITH BLACK PATENT PEAK & R N BADGE - WHITE SHIRT & COLLAR - BLACK TIE - GOLD HALF-RINGS - BLACK SOCKS & SHOES

FLIGHT OFFICER W.A.A.F. 1941 - AIR FORCE BLUE BARATHEA UNIFORM - BRASS BUTTONS, A's & BUCKLE - BLUE SHIRT & COLLAR - BLACK TIE - BROWN BUTTONED LEATHER GLOVES - GREY LISLE STOCKINGS - BLACK LEATHER SHOES RAF CAP BADGE, EMBROIDERED & WITH METAL WINGS

FORMAL EVENING DRESS - 1941 - BLACK TAIL COAT & TROUSERS. BLACK CORDED SILK LAPELS - BRAID SIDE SEAMS. SEMI-STIFF WHITE SHIRT PEARL & GOLD STUDS - WHITE STIFF WING COLLAR - WHITE PIQUÉ TIE & WAISTCOAT - BLACK PATENT LEATHER SHOES - BLACK SOCKS

1943 - PALE BLUE RAYON DRESS WITH WHITE SPOT PATTERN - NAVY SUEDE HANDBAG, GLOVES & SHOES - NAVY HAT OF VELVET LEAVES WITH VEIL

275

1939-1960

1943 - Grey suit with chalk stripe - maroon felt hat - black suede handbag - maroon gloves - black leather shoes - green wool jumper

1946 - Emerald green wool coat - & sash - red leather shoes & handbag - gloves

1944 - Brick red crêpe dinner gown - silver kid evening bag & sandals - silver bracelet - flower in hair

1945 - Tan mohair coat - nigger brown felt halo hat - brown leather gloves & handbag - tan leather wedge soled shoes

Until 1946 feminine dress remained fairly static, due in no small measure to the war. **Skirts** were short, just covering the knee; **shoulders** of tailored garments were excessively padded, giving that square-box silhouette so typical of the time; there was no accentuation of the breasts, waist, or hips, although a belt usually confined the waist at the normal level, and a somewhat masculine, efficient and practical ensemble was seen with **suits** and **coats.** In summer and afternoon **dresses,** the "little girl" effect was provided in the fuller but still abbreviated skirts, and accentuated by long, flowing hair-styles in curls or page-boy coiffures. Yokes were popular on all garments; **suits** were of tweed or pin-stripe worsted, with long jackets and box-pleated skirts; they had little fuss or decoration and were severely simple; **jumpers** and **skirts** and/or suits were the most popular attire. **Hats** were in various styles—halo, beret, petal decoration, etc.—often with short frilly veils, but more women were going hatless or wearing a square or **scarf** tied under the chin; these scarves became a fashion in their own right and were made of expensive materials, printed, woven, or embroidered in a variety of designs. Clothes rationing induced many women to abandon **stockings** for much of the year, and in winter some took to **slacks** instead. Low **heels** were fashionable and were even worn with dress clothes, for the first time for many years. Laced styles in flat or Cuban heels were frequently seen, but **wedge** and **platform soles,** with **sling-back** and **ankle-strap** fastenings began their ascendancy in popular favour by the end of the period. **Handbags** were large and capacious in handle or envelope styles, but sling handbags were in fashion before the end of the war. **Underwear** had changed little since 1938: most girls wore a two-way stretch roll-on belt or pantees, with an uplift brassière; ampler women wore corselettes or corsets. Knickers, cami-knickers, or French knickers and a petticoat and vest completed the set. **Backless evening gowns** were still fashionable and all gowns reached the ground. An evening blouse and dark or black skirt had become a popular alternative by 1943. Other styles of evening gown had short or no sleeves, and most skirts were narrow or draped. Crêpe, silk, or satin were favourite materials (see pp. 275, 276, 278, and 287).

The **uniforms** of the Women's Services during World War II were neat, smart, and practical; the dowdy attempt at serviceability in the previous war had vanished (see p. 275).

The years 1946–1947 provide a period of transition between the styles just described and the "*New Look*", which began to affect London fashions in 1947. Early signs of the new modes were seen in the batswing **sleeves,** swept-up pseudo-Edwardian **hair-styles, hoods** attached to rainwear and coats, a slightly lower **hem-line,** the appearance of **slack back coats,** and the increased accent on hip decoration (see p. 278). It was by 1947, however, that femininity returned to ladies' fashions, with a grace and attraction which had been absent since 1908. For the first time practicability had been combined with femininity —Dior had given us the "New Look". However, comparatively few women in Britain could afford to re-stock their wardrobe completely—for that was what these innovations necessitated—so that it was not until 1948 that the new vogue was thoroughly established here. By then it was seen everywhere, typified by the long **skirts**—eleven to thirteen inches from the ground—in their sweeping full line given by gathers, pleats, panniers, peg-top, or washerwoman

1939 - 1960

1946 - ICE BLUE SATIN
EVENING GOWN WITH
BLACK SATIN CUFFED
DÉCOLLETAGE &
BLACK SUÈDE GLOVES -
SILVER SANDALS

MORNING DRESS 1946.
BLACK TAIL COAT & WAIST-
-COAT - GREY & BLACK
STRIPED TROUSERS -
WHITE WING COLLAR &
SHIRT - BLACK TIE - GREY
SPATS - CHAMOIS GLOVES -
BLACK LEATHER SHOES -
BLACK UMBRELLA -
BLACK TOP HAT - FELT
BAND - SILK LINING

1947 - BLUE-GREY WOOL
DRESS WITH SWATHING
HIP DRAPERIES - DARKER
SHADE OF FELT HAT - NAVY
LEATHER SHOES & BAG -
NAVY HAT RIBBON &
GLOVES

1946 - GREEN
PLASTIC MACKINTOSH
WITH HOOD, PATCH,
POCKETS, & RAGLAN
SLEEVES - BROWN SUÈDE
BOOTS WITH CRÊPE
SOLES & LAMB'S
WOOL LININGS

design: tiny **waist** accentuated by corset and sash or belt; dainty, curved breasts, uplifted by a good brassière; taffeta, rustling **petticoat,** edged with lace and coyly just visible below the skirt hem, and three-quarter cuffed kimono **sleeves.** The interest centred on the skirt and hip-line: it was provided by panniers or pockets, frills or draperies to contrast with the slender waist. **Coats** were either waisted and very full, or tent, full-backed styles; **collars** were large and high. **Hair** was short again, though not stark, as in the twenties, but feminine and gay, curling slightly to frame the face. **Hats** were small, to suit the large collars, but **boaters** with **face veils** re-echoed Edwardianism. In **evening dress** there were two lengths, the new ballet length to the ankles, or a skirt to sweep the floor. Yards of material went to make an evening dress again, billowing from the tiny waist in myriads of gathers or pleats. **Blouses** and **skirts** were very popular for evening. The back-dipping hem-line came in with uneven edging. Pseudo-crinolines and bustles appeared for evening wear. Even the suit became feminine: jackets were short with flared peplum or skirt, worn with a full gathered or pleated back to the skirt. **High heels** returned to set off the long skirts, and **ankle-straps** or **sling-backs** were the rage, with peep-toe styles. In lower-heeled shoes, **wedge soles** were ubiquitous, combining both comfort and daintiness for the first time. **Nylon** became the most sought-after fabric for stockings, blouses, underwear, etc., and corduroy, wool, chiffon, and tulle were in great demand. **Colours** were delicate, with an especial vogue for pinks, duck-egg and other blues, navy, black, and grey. **Pencil umbrellas** returned, particularly in tartan, and **handbags** were box or drum shapes for preference, and hung over the arm (see pp. 278, 282, and 287).

The year 1949 saw the crystallisation of these modes (see pp. 278 and 282), but in 1950 the fashions began to change once more. At first there was no perceptible trend but soon it became apparent that straighter, shorter clothes were being introduced once more. The feminine line was retained in that shoulders still sloped, and the square-cut silhouette of the war years did not return. In 1951 and 1952 French designs showed strong leanings towards fashions of the 1920's; much shorter **skirts,** low or non-existent **waistlines,** plain, décolleté **necklines** and a draped **bodice** to hide the breasts. In England, however, this did not appeal to the majority of women and the line which finally emerged and was accepted in the mass-production stores of the big cities was a greatly watered-down version of the Paris designs (see p. 283).

From 1952–1960 the trend has been towards very simple clothes and shorter **skirts** of two styles, one with a straight, slim line and the other a very full, bouffant pattern which is often puffed out by a frilled, nylon **waist petticoat.** The former are more practical, and are in general use for suits, day dresses and for business and professional wear, while the latter are generally reserved for parties, summer dresses and evening attire.

Evening dresses are in two lengths: to the ground or day length. They are pencil slim or draped, or very bouffant. Ballet length was popular for a time in the early 1950's (see pp. 282 and 285).

In 1960 the general accent is on simple line, a fuller top and plainer **skirt,** sloping shoulders, short, straight **jackets** and **waistlines** are either accentuated or obscured. **Summer wear,** especially for holidays, is more colourful every year. The Italian and Spanish influence is marked in this range and, as with men, the

1939 - 1960

1949 - NIGGER BROWN
WAISTED FULL COAT -
ASTRAKHAN COLLAR -
RED FELT HAT - BROWN
POM-POMS - RED
LEATHER SHOES &
GLOVES

1952 - GREY GABARDINE
RAINCOAT - GREY PIN-STRIPE
SUIT - DARK GREEN FELT HAT -
WHITE SHIRT & COLLAR -
STRIPED TIE - PIG-SKIN
GLOVES - CANE -
BROWN LEATHER SHOES

1951 - BROWN CHECK
TWEED SPORTS JACKET -
NIGGER BROWN WOOL
TROUSERS - LIGHT GREEN
LINEN SPORTS SHIRT -
TAN LEATHER,
CRÊPE-SOLED SHOES

1949 - BLACK SUIT WITH
BLACK VELVET COLLAR -
PLEATED PEPLUM & SKIRT -
BLACK CORDUROY HAT - RED
PLUME - BLACK SUÈDE SHOES
& HANDBAG - BLACK NYLON
UMBRELLA - GREY LIZARD
HANDLE - RED SUÈDE
GLOVES

280

increased popularity of Continental holidays has inspired a desire for gay **colours** which are so attractive in hot sunshine. For wear in England, grey and black are always in fashion; in 1958–1959 shades of nasturtium and apple green were very fashionable; in 1960 all shades of mauve, from pale lilac to deep purple, are immensely popular. **White** is worn more than ever before in summer and the use of this is encouraged by the perfection of techniques for **permanent pleating** in terylene, tricel and banlon. Pleated skirts, blouses and dresses are made in these materials which can be washed easily and do not need ironing. Indeed, the whole range of **nylon** and its associated materials has revolutionised dress design and these fabrics make packing, especially for air travel, a much easier task (see pp. 284 and 285).

Although short **hair styles** have remained in fashion throughout this period, straighter or much more softly curling hair is usual towards 1960. At the same time, long or **longer hair** has been worn by many women since 1954–1955. This was then dressed in knot, chignon or plait at the nape, higher, on the crown, or coiled round the head. **Pony tails** became the teen-age trademark. By 1959 the high, bouffant (beehive) look was in fashion, with the hair dressed loosely high above the forehead but descending low at the sides and over the ears. The mid-Victorian style of centre parting and straight side sweeps was much in vogue but was generally dressed more softly than in the nineteenth century. By the end of 1960 the very tall coiffure has faded from fashion but long hair, straighter hair and coiffures over the forehead and ears remain (see p. 287).

Hats were small in the early 1950's. **Crowns** then gradually became higher and the hat was worn further forward. **Materials** were varied and most attractive: velvet and silk in toque and turban modes, and fluffy nylon furs and felts with velvet ribbons on the tallest hats (see p. 287).

Over the last decade the **stiletto heel** has developed in feminine **footwear**—a range in which Italy has been and still is predominant. This does not mean that everyone wears four-inch heels with tips of three-eighths of an inch in diameter but many people do, especially younger girls, to the great detriment of their feet, as is apparent in summer sandals. However, the thinner, more elegant, curved **heel**—of varying heights from one inch to four inches—appears to have come to stay. With it, the court styles, also the dainty T-strap, are far and away the most general designs for footwear in all seasons. These are low cut at the sides and front and have pointed toes, sometimes in a very extreme manner. Unless worn with a very high heel, the style is comfortable and elegant, also is suited to all ages of women. **Colours** and **materials** are diverse. Black, navy and white are most common, but leathers and suèdes can be obtained to match almost any garment. In summer, **sandals** with a minimum of strap are most popular, while in town white and pastel shade court shoes are worn more often than the sandal and are more suitable with town dresses and suits (see p. 287).

For the manufacture of **stockings, nylon** now holds the field entirely and is produced in a very wide range of textures, colours and weight. Flesh tones vary greatly in colour also in denier from the party version—9 denier—to the heavier, general-purpose line—30 denier. Brightly coloured or black stockings in fine nylon also in a very heavy version, with coloured clocks, are also fashionable; the latter especially so with students and other young people.

The most notable **accessories** of the 1955–1960 period are large **handbags,**

1939 - 1960

1948 - GREY BIRD'S EYE SINGLE-BREASTED LOUNGE SUIT - BLACK LEATHER SHOES - BLUE SHIRT & COLLAR - PATTERNED TIE

1948 - DULL RED & BLACK HERRINGBONE TWEED COAT - BLACK VELVET COLLAR & CUFFS - RED HAT WITH BLACK FEATHERS - RED GLOVES - BLACK SUÈDE ANKLE-STRAP SHOES

1948 - SAPPHIRE BLUE TAFFETA DINNER GOWN - VELVET HAIR RIBBON & BLACK VELVET NECK-BAND WITH CAMEO CENTRE - FAN

1948 - LAVENDER CRÊPE DRESS WITH DOLMAN SLEEVES - PLEATED SKIRT TOP - NAVY SUÈDE ANKLE-STRAP SHOES

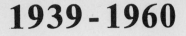

1950. RED, WHITE & BLACK WOOL, LOOSE FULL JACKET - LINED WITH RED WOOL, TURNED BACK ON REVERS & CUFFS - BLACK WORSTED SUIT - BLACK SUEDE HANDBAG & SHOES - RED FELT HAT & RED FABRIC GLOVES

1950 - BROWN TWEED HERRINGBONE OVERCOAT - RAGLAN SLEEVE - FAWN GABARDINE TROUSERS - BROWN LEATHER CRÊPE - -SOLED SHOES - BROWN FELT HAT - BROWN STRIPED SHIRT & COLLAR - DARK RED TIE

1952 - BROWN & WHITE CHECK WORSTED SUIT - HIGH POCKETS - BROWN BUTTONS & COLLAR - BISCUIT SILK HAT - BROWN SUEDE SHOES, GLOVES & EMBROIDERED BAG - UMBRELLA

1950 - TARTAN TAFFETA DRESS IN SHADES OF TURQUOISE GREEN & VERMILION - GREEN CUFFS & BELT - RED LEATHER SHOES

1939 - 1960

1958-9 EVENING GOWN OF SILVER GREY NYLON NET - GOLD KID SANDALS

1956-7 BLACK JERSEY AND DULL YELLOW TWEED SKIRT - LEATHER SHOES

1955 RED SATIN EVENING GOWN DARK RED GLOVES

1953-4 PATTERNED BRIGHTLY-COLOURED COTTON SUN-DRESS WITH MATCHING JACKET - WHITE KID SANDALS

1939-1960

1960 LILAC
WOOL DAY DRESS -
BLACK TRIMMING

1960 SHORT, SOFT
TWEED OVERCOAT WITH
FLEECE LINING —
WORSTED TROUSERS.
BLACK LEATHER
SHOES - FELT HAT

1960 DEEP GREEN
WINTER COAT—
NYLON FUR MAUVE
HAT

1960 JERSEY WOOL
AUTUMN SUIT IN
SOFT, LIGHT GREEN -
BLACK PATENT
LEATHER HANDBAG-
FELT HAT - PATENT.
LEATHER SHOES

285

frequently of Italian origin, in leather, raffia, wool, beads and wood. There is also a tremendous diversity of design in inexpensive **necklaces** and **ear-rings**. The former are often in three- or four-string choker form or are very long—below waist length—as was fashionable in the 1920's.

And what of the future? It would be brave and yet foolhardy to indulge in speculation since the mode is largely controlled by the commercial and artistic interests of designers and the fashion-houses. In Britain and on the Continent, the rising cost of living will no doubt play some part in restricting frequent changes of wardrobe styles for the majority of women; such has plainly been the case to a certain extent since the war. One fact is sure, that though the future may bring new synthetic materials, and new methods of manufacturing clothes, yet there can now be nothing new in design, but only various permutations and combinations of past creations.

1939 - 1960

Silk pill-box hat 1943

1944

A 'WREN' 1941-5

White felt hat & ribbon 1942-3

Red leather handbag - zip-fastening - 1950

1960

Flight Lieutenant R.A.F. 1939-45

Brown leather 1945

White leather 'Cossack' boot

Private. A.T.S. 1945

Blue suède & leather shoe 1944

Leather soled boot - leather guard - suède top - 1950

Navy straw hat & veil - flowers & snood - 1945

Man's brown leather shoe 1948

Man's leather sandal - crêpe sole 1949

Pale blue satin & elastic corselette 1950

Apple green suède shoe 1958

Tan leather & white buckskin 1946

Blue leather & white buckskin - 1946

Deep purple wool handbag 1960

1948.

Copper coloured kid shoe 1960

1960

1960

White felt hat 1960

Black patent leather shoe 1960

Powder blue felt hat & ribbons - 1949

1949

Lilac nylon fur hat 1959

Crimson suède sling-back shoe 1950

Grey felt hat - pink ribbon - 1948

Black suède ankle-strap & platform sole shoe - 1950

Buff leather - 1950

287

INDEX

GLOSSARY

SOME EQUIVALENT TERMS IN ENGLISH AND AMERICAN COSTUME

English	American Equivalent
Bespoke tailoring, i.e. clothes made to measure	Custom clothes
Bowler hat	Derby hat
Braces	Suspenders
Calico	Muslin
Collar stud	Collar button
Cuff links	Cuff buttons
Dinner jacket	Tuxedo
Dressing gown	Bath-robe, slumber-robe etc.
Felt and Trilby hats	Fedora and Homburg hats
Frock coat	Prince Albert coat
Jumper	Sweater
Knotted tie or scarf	Four-in-hand
Lounge suit	Business suit
Nail varnish	Nail enamel
Nightclothes	Night robes
Overshoes	Rubbers
Permanent wave or "perm"	A permanent
Poplin	Broadcloth (particularised i.e. cotton broad cloth)
Ready-made or reach-me-down suit	Hand-me-down suit
Scarf–male neckwear	Ascot
Shirt front	Shirt bosom
Shoes (certain styles in leather)	Oxfords
Slippers or men's evening slippers	Pumps
Tailored blouse	Shirtwaist
Trouser turn-ups	Cuffs
Waistcoat	Vest
Vest	Undershirt